NOTORIOUS
New Jersey

NOTORIOUS
New Jersey

100 TRUE TALES

of

MURDERS AND MOBSTERS, SCANDALS AND SCOUNDRELS

Jon Blackwell

Rivergate Books

AN IMPRINT OF RUTGERS UNIVERSITY PRESS
NEW BRUNSWICK, NEW JERSEY, AND LONDON

Fourth paperback printing, 2009

Library of Congress Cataloging-in-Publication Data

Blackwell, Jon, 1970–
    Notorious New Jersey : 100 true tales of murders and mobsters, scandals and
scoundrels / Jon Blackwell.
        p. cm.
    Includes bibliographical references and index.
    ISBN 978-0-8135-4177-8 (pbk. : alk. paper)
    1. Crime—New Jersey. I. Title.
    HV6795.N35B53   2007
    364.109749—dc22

                                                                    2007000038

A British Cataloging-in-Publication record for this book is available from the
British Library.

Visit our Web site: http://rutgerspress.rutgers.edu

Manufactured in the United States of America

❧ CONTENTS ❧

❖ ACKNOWLEDGMENTS ❖

Although this book is about the worst of New Jersey, it would not have been possible without the generosity and assistance of many people in that state. I owe a special debt to Marlie Wasserman, director of the Rutgers University Press, who suggested two years ago that I write a work on New Jersey history. Thanks to her assistant, Christina Brianik, the press's senior production coordinator, Anne Hegeman, and copy editor Derik Shelor. My former editor at *The Trentonian*, Paul Mickle, fired up my interest in Jersey crime back when I worked for him in the late 1990s, and was of great help this time around, too.

Thanks also to Caren Lissner, who suggested the title; Brad Small and the researchers at the Newark Public Library; the staff of the New York Public Library, the New Jersey Historical Society, and the Rutgers University Libraries; Marc Mappen, who provided helpful insight on colonial and nineteenth-century history; Patterson Smith, who helped me dig up old crime magazine stories; Deirdre Fedkenheuer of the New Jersey Department of Corrections, who provided me with priceless mug shots; and Helen-Chantal Pike, Art Scott, and the late Karen Plunkett-Powell.

My friends and coworkers at the *New York Post* were invaluable in my research, writing, and rewriting. They include Deb Pines, who brought a great mystery writer's touch to smoothing out the copy; librarian Bruce Furman, who dug up countless nuggets from the *Post*'s morgue; photo editor David Boyle and his staff, who helped me find illustrations; Milton

Goldstein, who helped me scan the photos; and my boss, Barry Gross. Also helping were Joe Cunningham, Dawn Eden, Hasani Gittens, Joe Illuzzi, Michael Kane, Clemente Lisi, Joshua Tanzer, Todd Venezia, Robert Walsh, and Ion Zupcu.

≫ ≪

My agent and friend, Janet Rosen, has been a valued literary coach. Thanks to my friends, Paolo Frassanito, Tony Hightower, Michael Malice, Mark Willey, and Dom Yanchunas, and to my brother- and sister-in-laws, Matt and Jennifer Goodman. Most of all, thanks to my parents and my wife, Valerie.

✤ INTRODUCTION ✦

New Jersey has an image problem. Suburban sprawl, toxic waste dumps, the Mafia, jammed highways—to outsiders, these are all more recognizable as state symbols than, say, the New Jersey state bird or state seal. On each end, New Jersey is overshadowed by the metropolises of New York and Philadelphia. The Jersey joke is a crutch to every bad New York comedian, and even a few good ones. ("An intelligence governs our universe, except in certain parts of New Jersey," Woody Allen once said.) The sport of Jersey-bashing has even spread to Jerseyans themselves, as evidenced by the contest held in 2005 by Governor Richard Codey to give the state a new tourist slogan. All the positive mottoes were forgettable; the best ones included "New Jersey: Most of Our Elected Officials Have Not Been Indicted."

Civic-minded writers have striven to set the record straight. They have told the world that New Jersey is also a state of beautiful beaches, quaint towns, unspoiled Pine Barrens, strong earning power (it has the second highest per-household income of any state, after New Hampshire), and cultural greatness (it is the home of Sinatra, Springsteen, and Einstein). Their work to rehabilitate the state's image has been admirable. This book will make no such effort. *Notorious New Jersey* instead tells the tales of one hundred criminals, rogues, and controversial figures who shaped the Garden State for worse, not for better.

In the popular imagination, New Jersey is home of "The Sopranos."

But the state has so much more to offer than fictional mobsters. For one thing, it has real mobsters. It also has corrupt politicians, industrial polluters, serial killers, rampage shooters, terrorists, and the Lindbergh baby. Of the fifty states, maybe New York, California, Texas, and Illinois can match New Jersey for sheer sensational crime, but no place surpasses its blatant rascality. Nothing to be proud of, maybe, but certainly worthy of historic interest.

New Jersey's reputation as a land of rogues is nothing new. The first chapter of *Notorious New Jersey* describes the unsavory characters who populate the state's history before the twentieth century. There were rotten governors galore, among them a corrupt businessman who stole from his own mother and Benjamin Franklin's illegitimate son, who turned traitor against his country during the Revolutionary War. There was the grisly case of Antoine LeBlanc, who butchered a farm family in an 1800s version of *In Cold Blood*—only instead of his story being made into a bestseller, his corpse was made into book covers. And no book about New Jersey notoriety would be complete without the Aaron Burr-Alexander Hamilton duel.

New Jersey is hardly the murder capital of America—its homicide rate in 2005 ranked below the national average—yet its murders are often a big national story, especially when they shatter the supposed serenity of the suburbs. Chapter 2 recounts the worst murderers from the last hundred years. Among them are outwardly respectable professionals exposed as men who hired contract killers (insurance salesman Robert Marshall and rabbi Fred Neulander), psychopaths who exploded in an instant of rage (Howard Unruh, whose 1949 massacre of his neighbors is often cited as the first gun rampage), serial killers (Robert Zarinsky and Charles Cullen), and stealthy poisoners (Carl Coppolino and Frances Creighton). The evil deed of one New Jersey murderer—Jesse Timmendequas, who killed a seven-year-old neighbor—might have gone unremembered had it not led to Megan's Law, the national statute for tracking pedophiles.

Chapter 3 is reserved for that species of criminal most closely identified with New Jersey—the gangster. Spectacular rubouts occurred here

(Dutch Schultz in 1935, Willie Moretti in 1951), and two of the most ruthless crime lords ever to reign over New York's Five Families (Albert Anastasia and Vito Genovese) lived not in Gotham but in the Jersey suburbs. Homegrown mobsters achieved their own success—Simone "Sam the Plumber" DeCavalcante, a boss who earned independence from New York, is the most likely real-life inspiration for Tony Soprano. And while it is probably not true that Jimmy Hoffa is buried at Giants Stadium, his murder was ordered by a Jersey Teamsters boss, which is good enough.

Why has New Jersey been so hospitable to the mob? The answer lies in chapter 4: the corrupt official. With 566 municipalities—not to mention a state government not always notable for its honesty—New Jersey offers many nooks and crannies where bribery can flourish. Here is bipartisanship in action. The Democrats provided Jersey City boss Frank Hague, who lived like a millionaire on a $7,500 salary, and from the Republicans came "Nucky" Johnson, who turned Atlantic City into an open city for organized crime. The chapter on corruption also covers corporate outrages, such as Johns-Manville, a company that literally worked its employees to death while lying to them about the dangers of asbestos exposure.

Chapter 5 details New Jersey's history of political, religious, and racial hatred—and outright enemy attack. Terrorism in the last decade has been widely reported, from a mail bombing carried out by the Unabomber against a Jersey ad executive in 1994 to the anthrax attacks of 2001 that were apparently carried out in the Princeton area. Less well known is an act of German sabotage during World War I against a Jersey City ammunition dump known as Black Tom, which shattered windows all over the New York area, or the chillingly open activities of the Ku Klux Klan and the Nazis in the 1920s and 1930s.

Some of New Jersey's most celebrated cases were settled in courts of law but remain contentious in the court of public opinion. Chapter 6 features a few of these. They include two classic murder mysteries (the Lindbergh baby case, the Hall-Mills trial) that armchair detectives are still having a go at after more than sixty years. There are defendants who may well have been guilty (Hurricane Carter, Mario Jascalevich) but went free amid accusations of prosecutorial bias. There are civil court cases that illuminated great questions of the day (Baby M and surrogate motherhood, Karen Ann Quinlan and the right to die.) And there are blatant injustices—criminal defendants who were innocent but went to prison anyway (Margaret Kelly Michaels, Clarence Hill).

The number of "Notorious New Jersey" cases was arbitrarily placed at one hundred, not nearly enough to accommodate all the killers, gangsters, or thieves of historical note. I apologize in advance to true crime aficionados who might complain about my omission of mobsters John DiGilio and Corky Vastola; penny-stock swindler Robert Brennan; corrupt pols Cornelius Gallagher, Michael Matthews, and Jim Treffinger; and killers Michael Fekecs, Edwin Grace, and Leslie Nelson (the only transsexual ever to have been on New Jersey's death row).

Notorious New Jersey is certainly no paean to the great state of New Jersey. But rest assured it is also no slur. Consider it, instead, to be proof of the slogan worn on so many T-shirts: "New Jersey: Only the Strong Survive."

NOTORIOUS
New Jersey

Old Rascals

CRIME AND VILLAINY
BEFORE 1900

❧ ORIGINAL SIN ❧

WILLEM KIEFT, COLONIST
1597–1647

JUST HOW DEEPLY EMBEDDED is the culture of corruption and racketeering in New Jersey's history? Consider the career of the region's first governor, a tyrannical seventeenth-century Dutch overlord named Willem Kieft. As director-general of the West India Company, Kieft ordered the Indian tribes on both sides of the Hudson River to pay a "tax" for protection. Then he had them chopped to pieces in New Jersey's first recorded mass murder.

Before there was an English colony of New Jersey, there was the Dutch territory of New Netherland, encompassing all the land between Delaware Bay and modern-day Connecticut. The white settlers lived peacefully with the natives, paying them handsomely with tools and weapons in exchange for highly desired beaver pelts.

This tolerant attitude changed practically overnight in 1638 with the arrival of Kieft as governor, with headquarters in New Amsterdam (modern-day New York City). Originally from old Amsterdam, the ill-tempered martinet had involved himself in business schemes from France to the Ottoman Empire. All of them failed. But the West India Company, which was responsible for the Netherlands' overseas trade, saw toughness

I

in his character. The Dutch outpost in America was having some financial difficulties, and Kieft was picked to straighten things out.

In governance, Kieft combined the charm of a drill instructor with the ethics of an embezzler. Among his first acts was to ban the settlers from "carnal relations with Negroes or heathens." Shortly afterward, he announced his new policy of forcing native tribes to pay tribute, in the form of pelts, maize, and the bead currency known as wampum, for their own protection. This took a certain nerve, since the tens of thousands of Indians vastly outnumbered the four hundred white settlers.

Kieft "must be a very mean fellow," protested the Tappan Indian tribe of New Jersey, "to come to live in this country without being invited by them, and now wish to compel them to give him their corn for nothing." But the Tappan paid.

The money Kieft collected may well have helped build the defenses for New Netherland. But colonists soon were accusing him of fattening his own purse with it. It was reported that he was drunk on the job and amassing a fortune through extortion. The amount was said to total 400,000 guilders—a tidy sum, considering that Manhattan's famous $24 purchase price from the Indians was the equivalent of sixty guilders.

Trouble surfaced in 1640 when the Raritan tribe refused to pay Kieft's tribute, raided a farm on Staten Island, and killed some of the colonists' pigs. Kieft dispatched a troop of soldiers to hunt those Indians down near the banks of the New Jersey river that now bears the Raritan name. The Dutch force killed four Indians and used splinters to torture their chief in his "private parts." Then Kieft issued a proclamation calling on other Indians to hunt down and kill Raritan tribesmen. For each severed head brought to him, Kieft said, he would pay a bounty of twenty strings of wampum.

Through sheer ruthlessness, Kieft seemed to have tamed the Indians. But a few years later came the revenge murder of a Dutch colonist in New Amsterdam, by a man of the Wickquasgeck tribe. This provided an excuse to utterly destroy Indian power. Kieft sent a message to the Wickquasgecks, encamped in the plantation of Pavonia in what is now Jersey City, demanding that the killer be turned over. The tribe insisted no such man lived there. Kieft declared he "had a mind to wipe the mouths of the savages" and assembled a party of troops armed with muskets and axes.

On the frigid night of February 25, 1643, this expedition crossed the Hudson and fell silently on the Wickquasgeck camp of Pavonia. It was a soft target. The tribe was asleep. Their grounds were also overcrowded with refugees from the nonhostile Tappan tribe, including many women and children. When these Indians found themselves under attack, they assumed their antagonists were a rival tribe and not the Dutch.

One Dutch settler heard the screams of the defenseless Indians all the way from the stockade in New Amsterdam. Babies were hacked to pieces in front of their mothers and thrown into a river, he claimed. Refugees came back to New Amsterdam "with their legs cut off, and some holding their entrails in their arms." The soldiers returned to New Amsterdam and boasted to Kieft—who sat out the "battle" from headquarters—that they had killed eighty Indians. He gave them handshakes all around.

Kieft's massacre was not only cruel, but stupid. Now all the Indian tribes surrounding New Amsterdam united in war against the whites. The settlers of Pavonia were forced to abandon their prosperous cattle and fruit farms and cross the Hudson to Manhattan. Over two years, the conflict known as "Kieft's War" escalated until both sides were committing acts of stomach-turning savagery. In one case, it was claimed, Kieft laughed as he watched his troops decapitate captured Indians—then kick around the severed heads like soccer balls.

Kieft claimed, without any evidence, that he had embarked on the foolish campaign against Indians only after the urging of Pavonia's farmers. The West India Company did not believe it. After the war's end, he was recalled to Amsterdam to face charges of mismanagement. His successor as director-general, Peter Stuyvesant, arrived in the New World and found to his horror that the inhabitants had "grown very wild and loose in their morals."

In 1647, as Kieft was on his way back to face justice in the Netherlands, his ship wrecked off the English coast and he drowned. The colonies he left behind survived him.

⇝ BLOOD WILL OUT ⇜

THOMAS LUTHERLAND, MURDERER
1652?–1692

IN MEDIEVAL TIMES, it was thought you could identify a murderer by gathering the suspects and lining them up to touch the victim's body. Superstition held that once in the presence of the guilty party, the dead person's wounds would open up and blood would ooze forth. This practice had a name—"Law of the Bier"—and followed English settlers to America, where it was employed in the investigation of New Jersey's first recorded murder mystery.

On November 12, 1691, just below the Quaker settlement of Salem on Delaware Bay, an empty riverboat was found beached, its contents looted and no one aboard. The vessel belonged to John Clark, a Philadelphia trader who sailed up and down the river to sell his goods, and who had last been seen in Salem the previous day. A posse of constables had no trouble tracking down the missing booty, which included a wheel of cheese, buttons, cloth, and "English goods." They were hidden under a haystack at the nearby home of a thirty-nine-year-old carpenter, Thomas Lutherland.

Lutherland's wife insisted he had slept at home the night of Clark's disappearance, and claimed he had lawfully bought the items for some wampum and silver coins. But this transaction did not show up in Clark's meticulous ledger. Salem's justices of the peace had another reason to be suspicious of Lutherland. He was a convicted felon. He had been transported from England and had gone on to commit other thieveries in Philadelphia. Lutherland had left behind a wife and child in the old country, and his current marriage was bigamous.

In January, Clark's body was found washed up on the Salem shore, strangulation marks around the throat. It was decided to subject the murder suspect to the Law of the Bier, so he was led into a room and told to touch the bloated corpse. He did so, swearing oaths that God should strike him dead if he had committed the killing. No bleeding occurred on the corpse's neck wound. Then Lutherland shouted out, a little too anxiously: "If I had murdered him, he would bleed afresh! Poor innocent man! Why should I destroy him?"

In court, Lutherland contradicted his earlier story by saying that, yes indeed, he had stolen most of those goods found in his haystack. But he swore he found them only after happening upon Clark's already empty boat; some other, unknown party must have committed the murder. The sheriff, prosecuting the case as king's attorney, ridiculed the defendant's constantly shifting stories, "like Irish quag-mires." The panel of jurors agreed, found Lutherland guilty, and ordered him to die.

Lutherland had five days to prepare his mortal soul for the afterlife. It was a prospect that, though he might have been a terrible sinner, he believed in. He gave a full confession, admitting he had choked the life out of Clark even as the victim cried out, "Spare my life and take my goods!" He blamed the devil's temptation for a life spent in "drunkenness, whoring, swearing, tempting young women to debauchery, and then leav[ing] them." He—or at least the clerk taking down this moral lesson—added: "I have been very disobedient to my parents, a great breaker of Sabbaths, which was the cause of my habit of sin. I had rather go to an ale-house than to any church. Pray young people take warning in my shamefull end."

An oxcart carried Lutherland to his appointment on Gallows Hill outside Salem, where, on February 23, 1692, he was hanged. The town justices then delivered a complete record of the case to a Philadelphia printer, who turned it into one of America's first true crime bestsellers. The pamphlet's title: "Blood Will Out."

From a distance of more than three hundred years, it is easy to laugh at the belief that dead people had magical properties to identify their killers. But the investigators who made Thomas Lutherland lay his hand upon the man he had killed were practicing an early form of forensic psychology. They thought he might show a guilty or panicky reaction, as he did. The "Law of the Bier" was more a test of the killer's reaction than of the victim's.

However primitive this custom may seem, it was not the most barbarous form of justice exercised in a town named Salem in 1692. Later that year, the court of Salem, Massachusetts, executed twenty people for the crime of witchcraft.

❖ DEAD MAN'S CHEST ❖

WILLIAM KIDD, PIRATE
1654?–1701

THE NAME CAPTAIN KIDD SAYS "PIRATE" as surely as a skull-and-crossbones flag identifies a ship filled with cutthroat buccaneers. But while many of literature's most recognizable pirates—Captain Hook and Long John Silver, for instance—are pure invention, Kidd was a real man. And legends that he left buried treasure on the Jersey Shore may even be true.

William Kidd fit the classic picture of a pirate in every swashbuckling aspect: He was tough, physically strong, ill-tempered, and ruthless in his pursuit of prizes on the high sea. Scottish by birth, he probably became a sailor at a young age. In 1690, he sailed to the new English colony of New York and established himself as a prominent privateer. He married

An old woodcut shows Captain William Kidd—whose name became synonymous with impiety and treachery—burying a Bible. Treasure hunters have searched the Jersey Shore in vain for three hundred years in hopes of digging up his buried loot.

a wealthy widow and earned a good living by trading in Caribbean ports. He also made occasional forays along the coast to hunt enemy French shipping.

In 1695, Kidd won the backing of New York's governor, the Earl of Bellomont, for a more ambitious sailing venture. He would take a gunboat into the pirate-infested Indian Ocean, capture a boatload of booty, and split the proceeds with the investors. Royal authorities in London approved his commission and dispatched him to hunt French vessels and "pirates, free-booters and sea-rovers" of all nations. The hidden partners included four Whig nobles close to King William III, and perhaps His Majesty himself. Kidd's ship, the thirty-four-gun *Adventure Galley*, sailed out of New York Harbor in September 1696.

There followed the first long run of bad luck in the captain's career. Kidd sailed for more than a year without once encountering a pirate ship. His stocks of food—and his hope of recouping the investment—ran low. Out of desperation, Kidd the pirate hunter turned pirate himself.

He captured six ships, four of them belonging to neutral powers or nations allied with England, and none of them pirates. His greatest haul, the *Quedah Merchant*, was trading with Britain's own East India Company and was brimming with gold, spices, and silks.

Tales soon reached London of Kidd turning pirate. His crew, it was said, performed cruel tortures on captured crew members and passengers—beating the men with the flats of their swords and raping the women. It is known that he personally killed one sailor by clubbing him with a bucket. Orders were sent to Bellomont, Kidd's own backer, to seize the pirate upon his arrival.

Kidd could have gone into hiding in the Caribbean, but he believed he could be proven innocent with the help of his powerful friends. In Curacao, he hired a smaller ship, the *San Antonio*, and sailed toward New York with his treasure in the hold. On June 3, 1699, in need of repairs and fresh water, the *San Antonio* anchored south of Cape May.

Captain Kidd's vessel here passed not only into Delaware Bay, but into New Jersey legend. It was later said that he buried his treasure somewhere on the coast. Possible locations for the hiding place have been identified at Cape May; Wildwood; a now-submerged island near Toms River; and another vanished place, "Money Island," in Raritan Bay. Two elm trees, "Kidd's Rangers," are said to serve as markers for Kidd's treasure at Cliffwood Beach in Monmouth County.

Another folk legend of the Pine Barrens holds that Kidd sailed on to Little Egg Harbor, where he fell in love with a farm girl known only as Amanda. A changed man, he vowed to give up his career as an outlaw and become a simple fisherman.

In reality, Kidd spent barely twenty-four hours off New Jersey—and there is no record that he set foot upon land there. While he was anchored in Delaware Bay, five "old pirates" rowed up to the ship. One of them recognized the captain and told him he was a wanted man. They brought Kidd news that another seafarer had gone on his own pirate venture in the Indian Ocean and secretly offloaded a booty of slaves, ivory, and gold at Sandy Hook. The daring move had set off a widespread alarm for pirates up and down the New Jersey coast, and Governor Jeremiah Basse had personally set off in a sloop to hunt pirates.

Kidd sailed to a hiding place off Long Island and sent messages to Governor Bellomont, offering to come ashore in exchange for a safe conduct pass. The governor lured Kidd to Boston, then had him arrested and shipped to London in irons. At the captain's trial for piracy in Admiralty Court, he pleaded that he had come by all his loot legally by the terms of his privateer commission. But pirates who had gladly slit throats under Kidd's command now testified against him.

Kidd was sentenced to hang, and on May 23, 1701, he was led to Execution Dock in London. In keeping with grisly custom, Kidd's body was hoisted to a gibbet overlooking the River Thames as a lesson to honest mariners. It remained there for years.

Captain Kidd brought no more than forty thousand pounds sterling worth of cargo back to America. Only a small portion of it was gold or silver, and most of that was dug up by the authorities from a hiding place in Long Island and confiscated. Still, the legend of a huge Captain Kidd hoard waiting to be rediscovered will probably live on as long as people keep telling pirate yarns.

❯ GOD SAVE THE QUEEN ❮

EDWARD HYDE, VISCOUNT CORNBURY, GOVERNOR
1661–1723

SALACIOUS POLITICAL GOSSIP doesn't get better than this: New Jersey's first royal governor was a man who liked to dress in women's clothing. He would speak before colonial assemblies and walk the streets in gown, stays, and petticoats. This strange behavior, he explained, allowed him to represent the person of his cousin, Queen Anne—making him a drag queen in the truest sense.

So goes the legend of Edward Hyde, Viscount Cornbury, Third Earl of Clarendon, and, supposedly, pioneer cross-dresser. Sadly, the whole thing is false. The scandalous rumor-mongering about Lord Cornbury apparently began with his political enemies in New Jersey. Through sheer repetition, and because listeners love a naughty story, the transvestite tale then worked its way into the historical record. It is still cited as truth today in many a reference work, despite a total lack of credibility.

This portrait hanging in the New-York Historical Society bears the label "Edward Hyde, Lord Cornbury." Recent scholarship casts doubt on the identification and on the tale that Cornbury was a transvestite.

To be sure, Cornbury was not the most admirable politician of his
era. His noble English lineage allowed him to buy an officer's commission in the army, and his greatest feat there was to help overthrow his
own commander, King James II. William II, who attained the throne
thanks largely to Cornbury's maneuvering, appointed him governor of
New York in 1701 as a reward. William's successor, Queen Anne, added
the governorship of New Jersey as a further plum.

New Jersey, then as now, was a squabbling patchwork of impossible-
to-govern interests, with the key difference being that it was actually split
into two governments. The colonies of East Jersey and West Jersey were
originally run by proprietors, or landowners, who were helpless to resolve
constant disputes with their tenants over deeds, rents, and religious tol-
erance. The proprietors appealed to Queen Anne to appoint a governor,
and Cornbury, a believer in vigorous royal authority, was chosen to set
things straight.

But instead of being a firm ruler, the queen's appointee came across
as a pompous ass. When he arrived at the port of New York in 1702,
the rustic colonials must have gaped at his equipage: 130 tons of silken
clothes, pewter dishes, tablecloths, curtains, oil paintings, and assorted
fripperies. Relations were not improved when, shortly afterward, public funds intended to build coastal defenses found their way into Cornbury's construction of a country retreat. (It was built on New York City's
Governors Island, which happens to be named for him.)

In New Jersey, Cornbury turned down what was most likely the first
bribe attempt in a rich history of New Jersey corruption: one hundred
pounds sterling in silver offered by an East Jersey proprietor. Perhaps it
was too cheap for his taste. Those opposed to the proprietors' land policies raised seven hundred pounds in a successful bid to make Cornbury
see things their way. The hated clique of his favorites came to be known
as the "Cornbury Ring" and controlled the collection of taxes and rents.
Just to alienate more New Jerseyans, Cornbury persecuted the Quakers
by denying them the right to hold public office.

In 1707, the fed-up New Jersey Assembly petitioned Queen Anne to
recall the governor. Letters to London from Assembly member Lewis

Morris, who had his own ax to grind—he had wanted the governor's job for himself—proved influential. Morris recounted a history of bribes, both true and rumored. To further outrage his correspondent, he passed on the story that Cornbury was "dressing publiqly in womans cloaths every day and putting a stop to all publique business while he is please-ing himselfe with that peculiar but detestable magot." (Maggot, in the eighteenth-century sense, meant a foppish whim and not an insect.)

Cornbury lost his job, came into financial ruin, and tumbled further into disgrace when he was sent to a debtor's prison in New York. But he was salvaged in 1710 when his father died, leaving him the title Earl of Clarendon and a fortune. The newly minted earl sailed back to England, where he became a respected diplomat and member of the Privy Council.

The stories about Cornbury "dressing publiqly in womans cloaths" got told and retold. Some embellishments got added long after he died. One of these details likely started as a joke: that the governor wore a dress in order to better represent Queen Anne in the New World. Pic-torial "evidence" of Cornbury's kinky habit even surfaced in the form of an eighteenth-century portrait of what looked like a heavy-jowled man in drag. It hangs in the New-York Historical Society with a label iden-tifying the person as the "half-witted" Lord Cornbury.

It has taken the research of a recent historian, Patricia Bonomi, to re-veal the transvestite business as nonsense. Only four letters written dur-ing Cornbury's lifetime accuse him of cross-dressing. No writer claims to witness the unusual habit firsthand, or provides a specific example. Had Cornbury actually done such a thing, it would have excited a sen-sation in the London press, which then as now was scandal-obsessed. As for the work depicting the supposed Cornbury in drag, no one knows who painted it or when. It is probably an unskillful (and ugly) portrait of a real woman.

History can sometimes be as titillating as the gossip column—but both need to run a correction now and then.

⇒ ON THE WARPATH ⇐

TOM QUICK, "INDIAN SLAYER"
1734–1796

FOR YEARS, TOM QUICK was celebrated as a folk hero who made the upper Delaware Valley in Pennsylvania, New Jersey, and New York safe for fellow white settlers in the 1700s. In best frontiersman style, he wore buckskins and a wild beard as he blazed the forest trails. It was said that he possessed superhuman strength with a hatchet, and invented the sport of fly fishing. An article in the *New York Times* referred to him as "the Paul Bunyan of New Jersey."

But the real basis for Quick's fame reveals a darker side to America's frontier. His nickname was "the Indian slayer," and accounts make him out to be a serial killer. It was said that over the course of his life he cold-bloodedly murdered ninety-nine Indians and declared, on his deathbed, "Bring me one more so I can make it an even hundred."

Much of Tom Quick's life is obscure and based on tales told many years after the fact. An account written by James E. Quinlan in 1851, *Tom Quick the Indian Slayer*, supplies almost all the known details of his life and is considered unreliable by modern historians.

His Dutch-born father, Thomas Sr., is recorded as one of the first white settlers in Milford, Pennsylvania, in 1733. It was Indian country, populated by Munsees of the Lenni Lenape nation. The Lenape were a peaceful tribe and lived side by side with white neighbors for years without violence. When Tom Jr. was born a year after his father's arrival, the Lenape came to the family's log cabin and celebrated the joyous occasion.

As a boy, Tom Jr.'s friends were of the same Indian tribe he would go on to decimate. He shunned book learning in order to hunt, fish, and explore trails with the Munsees. He grew up speaking the language of the Munsees fluently and could have passed for one.

But the French and Indian War proved to be a tragic turning point in Quick's history, and that of the Indians. That conflict, lasting from 1756 to 1763, pitted the French against the British colonial government for supremacy over North America. Both sides used Indians as pawns in the struggle, although most tribes sided with the French. White settlers, caught in the middle, fell victim to bloody Indian attacks.

Sometime during the war, a group of Indians ambushed the Quick family on the Jersey side of the Delaware River. The father fell dead from a rifle shot and was scalped. Tom Quick Jr. survived and swore revenge against all Indians.

Quick began his campaign of mass killing in seedy style—during a bar brawl. Quinlan's book recounts how he ran into a Munsee Indian named Muskwink at a tavern in Sullivan County, New York, in 1763. Quick cursed him out, and the drunken Muskwink responded by bragging that he had taken part in the murder of Quick's father. The Indian Slayer grabbed a musket from the fireplace, ordered Muskwink outdoors, and executed him. Then he coolly returned to the tavern, put back the gun, and finished his glass of rum.

No attempt was made to punish Quick for this crime. Indeed, many settlers, bitter at attacks by the "savages" during the French and Indian War, approved of such cruel reprisals. Throughout the 1760s, Quick proceeded to ambush and kill Indians, usually by luring away a lone traveler on a "hunting trip" and shooting him in the back. He would then return to white settlements with the deerskins that once belonged to his Indian victims, and crack his only recorded joke: "I shot one buck on top of another."

Sometime shortly after the murder of Muskwink, Quick carried out his most wanton deed. Crouching in the reeds overlooking a rapids called Butler's Rift, on the Delaware River in northwest New Jersey, he lay in wait for a sign of Indians. Eventually he spotted a canoe bearing an Indian man, woman, and their two children and stopped it at gunpoint. Quick shot the man, then tomahawked the woman and the eldest child in their skulls.

Quick decided to spare the infant's life and have it adopted by a white family. But, Quinlan wrote: "The fact suddenly thrust itself into his mind, that the child would in a few years become an Indian, and this so enraged him that he instantly dashed out its brains."

Later, Quick would justify his deed with the aphorism: "Nits make lice."

The Indian Slayer lived to be sixty-two. Though it is not known what he died of, legend has him succumbing to smallpox in 1796 as he croaked out his last, homicidal wish to kill "an even hundred." One folktale claims that a band of Indians, delighted that their arch foe was dead at last, dug up his bones as a trophy. They were unaware that the remains carried the smallpox, and so Quick was able to kill yet more Indians even in death.

Quick's life was puffed up—although certainly not whitewashed—in the popular history by Quinlan. Did he really kill anywhere close to ninety-nine Indians? Not likely. Only six murders are enumerated in Quinlan's history, and even these killings are not confirmed by contemporary sources.

But as the frontier became a distant and romanticized memory, the Quick legend lost much of its malign force. The killings of Indians were seen as having served a useful purpose, like felling the trees of a forest. In 1889, Quick's town of Milford dedicated a nine-foot-tall obelisk above a site believed to be his grave.

This resting place lay undisturbed for more than a century until one night in 1997 when unknown vandals used sledgehammers to smash the monument into pieces. No longer was Tom Quick such a folk hero.

⇛ BAD SEED ⇚

WILLIAM FRANKLIN, GOVERNOR AND LOYALIST
1731–1813

BENJAMIN FRANKLIN MAY HAVE BEEN the most beloved of all Founding Fathers, but not by his son. William Franklin rose from the great man's shadow to become governor of New Jersey, only to get thrown in prison for staying loyal to the crown during the Revolutionary War. Two years of captivity turned him into a bitter enemy both of the newly created United States and of his father, who refused to lift a finger to help him.

William Franklin sat for this portrait in London after fleeing post-Revolutionary America. His father, Benjamin, disinherited him with the comment that there would be no fortune to leave if William's Loyalists had won the war.

William's very birth was a scandal, because Benjamin happened not to be married at the time. The mother might have been Benjamin's future wife (as William said) or the denizen of a Philadelphia bawdy house (as a family friend believed). In either case, far from feeling shame in his illegitimate offspring, Benjamin Franklin—the most prominent statesman in the colonies—groomed him to be heir.

William Franklin got a first-rate education, attained the rank of army captain, and took the plum job of clerk to the Pennsylvania Assembly. When Benjamin conducted his experiments proving that lightning was a form of electricity, William designed and flew the famous kite. The young gentleman accompanied his father to London in 1759, going there to read law, and achieved notice in the royal court.

William inherited his father's smarts, ambition, roguish charm, and carelessness—he, too, fathered an out-of-wedlock child. But the pleasures of London life made him a "thorough courtier," in his father's disapproving words. Benjamin Franklin's visage was of appealing simplicity: bifocals, plain clothes, and long, stringy hair. William Franklin took to powdered wigs and silk handkerchiefs.

It was as much through his own connections as his father's name that William won appointment as New Jersey's royal governor in 1762. He had never been an inhabitant of that colony, and his advancement carried the stink of nepotism. John Adams called it an "insult to the morals of America, the elevation to the government of New Jersey of a base-born brat."

Actually, William Franklin was an exceptionally able governor. He built roads, abolished debtor's jails, chartered Rutgers University, and established America's first Indian reservation at Brotherton, Burlington County. But in 1768, a chest containing 6,750 pounds sterling was stolen from the house of Samuel Skinner, the East Jersey proprietary treasurer. The losses turned out to be virtually all the public funds in the colony. This catastrophe did not boost confidence in Governor Franklin's fiscal policies.

As the crisis of Parliament's taxation of the colonies came to a head, William Franklin tried to steer an impossible middle ground between his homeland and his king. Benjamin assumed his son would quit as royal governor and join him in the growing movement for colonial resistance. But the notion of the throne as ultimate source of law and liberty had been drilled into William in his law studies. He saw the independence movement as reckless radicalism.

At their last meeting before war separated them, William angrily chastised his father. "If you design to set the colonies in a flame, I hope you will take care to run away by the light of it," he said. "I have lost a son," Benjamin groaned.

Say this for William Franklin: he was brave. While every other royal governor fled his province or flipped to the revolutionaries, William remained on the job. In January 1776, he was placed under house arrest at his Perth Amboy mansion. Even in this condition, he could have ridden out the war in safety had he not written letters telling the British army where it could intercept arms shipments to the rebels. For this action, New Jersey's new Provincial Congress declared him "an enemy to the liberties of his country."

William was placed under arrest and marched north to Connecticut, because that state was a patriot stronghold far from his Tory friends back in New Jersey. The date of his arrival there must have rankled: July 4, 1776.

Still, it was comfortable treatment—William was put on parole and stayed in an unguarded house, free to write letters to whomever he wished. He promptly abused this privilege by mailing out thousands of papers offering "protection" to loyalists. This was essentially license for the Redcoats to loot and pillage the New England countryside, sparing the house of anyone who could produce one of Franklin's documents.

When the prisoner's efforts were exposed, the Continental Congress—whose members included Benjamin Franklin—ordered him put in solitary confinement in a jail notorious for its filth and overcrowding. William stayed there only a year before being allowed to go free in a prisoner-of-war exchange. But in that time, his wife, broken-hearted and reduced to a hand-to-mouth existence, fell ill and died at age forty-three.

William Franklin was understandably bitter, but it is hard to excuse what he did next. Settling in British-controlled New York City, he founded a group known as the Associated Loyalists to organize guerrilla missions behind patriot lines. The raids served no useful military purpose and won no hearts and minds. In atrocity after atrocity, Franklin's Tories stormed their way into farmhouses and shot patriot leaders—in one case shooting and wounding a five-year-old child.

The most breathtaking crime committed by the Associated Loyalists occurred in 1782 after they landed a brig, appropriately named the *Arrogant*, at Toms River. The town was put to the torch and twelve prisoners seized. One of them, Captain Joshua Huddy, was marched to a beach on Sandy Hook and summarily hanged to retaliate against the death of a British officer, Philip White. Huddy's dangling body was left for the patriots to discover, along with a taunting message pinned to his clothes. "UP GOES HUDDY for PHILIP WHITE," it read.

The United States flew into a rage. George Washington planned—but never carried out—the execution of a British officer, chosen by lot, to avenge Huddy. The Continental Congress demanded that William Franklin be turned over to them for justice. William took the course of many a Loyalist by sailing to safety in London. There he ended his days, praised as a "martyr to his principles."

Benjamin Franklin left few personal observations on this dramatic Oedipal aspect of his life. His popular *Autobiography*, originally undertaken as a life's lesson of thrift and hard work for his son, ended up making no mention of William whatsoever, except for one sentence praising his work as an aide in Pennsylvania. Benjamin cut William entirely out of his inheritance with the explanation that had the Loyalist side won, there would have been no estate left anyway.

Like the Civil War, if not on the same apocalyptic scale, the Revolution was a vicious "brother against brother" conflict. And in one famous case, father against son.

❧ LOYAL TO NO ONE ❧

JOE MULLINER, BANDIT
1750?–1781

WALK THROUGH THE New Jersey Pine Barrens, amid stunted trees, red streams, and eerie silences occasionally broken by screeching seagulls, and you might feel the presence of evil spirits. This is the home of the Jersey Devil, the legendary bat-winged, dragon-tailed creature that flies around frightening lone travelers. More earthbound terrors have also lurked here, none of them more notorious than the bandit Joseph Mulliner.

In the 1770s, before American independence, Mulliner started out as a coastal pilot. When the Revolutionary War broke out, he turned pirate. His small sloop was perfectly adapted to slip stealthily from the coves that dot the Jersey Shore around Egg Harbor. From these lairs, he preyed upon vulnerable merchant ships as they anchored at shore. Occasionally he took hostages among the crew and collected ransom from their relatives on land.

At some point Mulliner expanded his brigandage from sea to land. He recruited a band numbering anywhere from thirty to one hundred men and led them in robbing wagons, plundering farms, and burning houses. A swaggering giant of a man, reputed to stand six-foot-five, Mulliner wore a British officer's red uniform and carried a brace of pistols wherever he rode.

The Mulliner gang called themselves "Refugees," the term for soldiers who fought on the Loyalist side. Their real loyalty was only to themselves. The Revolutionary government had no power in much of New Jersey, including the sparsely populated Pine Barrens, and Mulliner's outlaws took full advantage. In fact, their victims included British sympathizers as well as patriots.

Their hideout was a place called Cold Spring Swamp, a spooky tangle of cedar wood and weeds on the Mullica River. There, it was said, Mulliner ingeniously nailed several cedars to a large log, on which he would paddle to and from the rendezvous point. If he thought he was being watched, he could quickly steer to a small island and be instantly camouflaged.

Local lore makes Joe Mulliner out to be an eighteenth-century Robin Hood who stole from the rich, gave to the poor, and made the Pine Barrens his personal Sherwood Forest. In fact, his robberies helped impoverish an already war-scarred countryside, and there is no record of his sharing the wealth with anyone but his fellow criminals.

Mulliner's career as a bandit came to an end in the summer of 1781, at a tavern in the hamlet of New Columbia (now Nesco). Legend says his love of pleasure was his downfall. Mulliner drank heavily, flirted with the ladies, and invited one pretty girl after another to dance. While dancing the night away, he failed to notice a company of patriot militia gathering outside. The soldiers, probably tipped off by one of Mulliner's confederates, disarmed and captured him.

Mulliner was tried for high treason, based on his professed loyalty to the crown. He was not then regarded as a folk hero. "When he came to trial," the *New Jersey Gazette* reported at the time, "it appeared the whole country, both Whigs and Tories, were against him." Mulliner was hanged in Burlington on August 8, 1781.

Inspired by legends that Mulliner buried his treasure, fortune-seekers periodically dig around the Mullica River. All have come up empty. But on a nearby barrier island where the pirate once lurked, entrepreneurs have come up with a modern way of separating travelers from their money. It's called Atlantic City.

⇒ BIG SHOT ⇐

AARON BURR, VICE PRESIDENT
1756–1836

A WEARY TRAVELER ONCE STOPPED at a roadside inn to discover a waxworks exhibit re-enacting the most shocking act of political hardball in U.S. history. There in miniature was Vice President Aaron Burr aiming his dueling pistol and Founding Father Alexander Hamilton falling dead on the rocky bluffs of Weehawken, New Jersey. Underneath was this bit of poetry:

Dapper, sly Aaron Burr is perhaps the only man to be indicted for both murder and treason—and beat both raps.

O BURR, O BURR, WHAT HAST THOU DONE?
THOU HAST SHOOTED DEAD GREAT HAMILTON.
YOU HID BEHIND A BUNCH OF THISTLE,
AND SHOOTED HIM DEAD WITH A GREAT HOSS PISTOL.

The lodger who came upon this tableau laughed uproariously when telling of his discovery. His name? Aaron Burr.

Contemporaries had no shortage of adjectives to describe Burr—"dangerous," "corrupt," and "Machiavellian" are some of the choicer ones—but getting to the heart of his personality is difficult. Even Burr, writing about himself in the third person, said, "We know not what to make of him." But why the Hamilton-Burr duel took place is no such mystery: it was a case of mutual hate and jealousy.

Aaron Burr was born in Newark of an intellectual and religious aristocracy. His maternal grandfather, Jonathan Edwards, was the foremost American preacher of the 1700s, and his father, Aaron Sr., was president of the College of New Jersey, now Princeton University. By sixteen, Aaron Jr. was himself a Princeton graduate. Instead of adopting his family's Presbyterian ethic, however, he was a doubter. "Great souls have little use for small morals," he once explained.

Burr chose law as a profession but interrupted his study to serve with distinction as a Revolutionary War officer. By the time America won its independence, he had relocated from New Jersey to set up a law practice in the growing city of New York.

Burr in his infamous duel with Alexander Hamilton. Historians still debate whether Hamilton shot to kill; there was no doubting Burr's deadly intent.

He and fellow New Yorker Hamilton moved in the same spheres as successful lawyers, popular socialites, and slick womanizers. Burr, who belonged to the Democratic-Republican party (confusingly, a predecessor to today's Democrats), masked his ambition behind an outward calm and self-effacing humor. Hamilton, of the rival Federalist party, was the more fiery and intellectual of the two. But while they were opposites politically, Hamilton and Burr to all appearances got along cordially.

Hamilton in the 1790s was a spectacular star, as Washington's first secretary of the Treasury and the virtual creator of America's capitalist economy. Burr also had political talents the likes of which the young republic had rarely seen. He got himself elected senator, unseating Hamilton's father-in-law, and set up a network of loyal operatives in the New York Legislature. In 1801, he advanced to vice president. He was never trusted by the new president, Thomas Jefferson, and for good reason—Burr had intrigued behind Jefferson's back to take the top job for himself.

Once in the second-highest office in the land, Burr began to form ties with his party's mortal foe, the Federalists. To the vice president, the New England Federalists proposed an audacious plan: secession of their states, together with New York, to form a "northern confederacy"—a breakaway American republic. Burr gave no commitments, but his silence indicated tacit support.

With this remarkable coalition behind him, Burr launched a campaign for governor of New York in early 1804. Hamilton was now out of office and politically floundering, but when he got wind of the irresponsible secession scheme, he did all in his power to thwart it. He told his Federalist allies in Albany not to vote for Burr, calling him "a dangerous man and not to be trusted." A man attending the meeting penned a newspaper piece claiming that Hamilton gave a "still more despicable opinion" of the vice president, but the writer never specified it.

Burr, to his great surprise and humiliation, lost the gubernatorial election. Seething, he read the article referring to the "despicable opinion" and wrote Hamilton a note demanding to know what it was. When Hamilton wrote back with an unsatisfactory reply, Burr invited him to an "interview."

This, of course, was the euphemism for a duel. Burr and Hamilton were well acquainted with these so-called affairs of honor. Burr had dueled Hamilton's brother-in-law five years earlier—both men missed— while Hamilton's nineteen-year-old son, Philip, had died shooting it out over an insult to his father. Duels were illegal, which is why New York gentlemen typically hashed out their differences in New Jersey, beyond the power of the city's authorities. In practice, though, almost no one was ever prosecuted for dueling. It was considered a useful social convention, a way to literally get rid of bad blood.

Had anyone been drawing up odds on the Hamilton-Burr duel, the smart money would have gone to the vice president. He practiced regularly with a pistol—firing into a man-sized target—and didn't miss a wink of sleep the week before his fateful encounter. Hamilton, by contrast, had written a friend that he intended to "throw away," or intentionally miss, his first fire.

Why would Burr want Hamilton dead over a vaguely written article about a "despicable opinion"? Why did Hamilton accept a challenge he might lose? One possible explanation is that both men were without a political future in the East. Each was exploring the possibility of relocating to the Mississippi River valley and establishing a new power base there. And this country wasn't big enough for the two of them.

On the hot, muggy morning of July 11, 1804, Burr was rowed across the Hudson to the bluffs of Weehawken. He and his second spent some time clearing twigs from the dueling ground before Hamilton arrived. Hamilton, as the challenged party, had the right to provide the weapons— smooth-barreled pistols with an enormous .56 caliber.

A coin was flipped to determine positions and who would give the order to fire. Hamilton won both tosses. The two men stood twenty feet away—Hamilton pausing to put on glasses—and leveled their pistols.

At the call of "Present!" both squeezed their triggers. Hamilton's pistol ball flew into the tree branches twelve feet above ground, although whether this was intentional or because of bad aim will never be known.

Burr's shot hit its target squarely—burrowing into Hamilton's midsection and cracking his spine.

"I fear this is a mortal wound, doctor," Hamilton told a physician as he lay trembling. He was right. Friends rowed him back to Manhattan, where he lingered in agony for a full day before dying.

By killing Hamilton, Burr thought he was salvaging his good name; instead, he had ruined it. The loser in this duel was simply too important and too popular. Burr was indicted in both New York and New Jersey for murder. But the authorities made no move to prosecute, and Burr continued to serve as vice president through the end of his term in 1805.

It took cool nerve to kill in a duel, but it took unmitigated gall for Burr to pursue his next project. He set out on a boat down the Mississippi River through what was an untamed wilderness. Along the way, he acquired a band of followers for an unspecified adventure. His likely plan was to separate the western territories from the U.S. government, creating a new republic with himself as president. Some witnesses thought he had a more Napoleonic dream: to overthrow Spanish rule in Mexico and make himself emperor. Jefferson had his old vice president arrested and hauled into court for a spectacular trial on charges of treason. He was acquitted in 1807, but the affair only deepened his disgrace.

His wealth squandered, his reputation in ruins, Burr never lost his rascally panache. (He produced at least two illegitimate offspring, and once commented: "When a lady sees fit to name me as the father of her children, why should I deny her that honor?") At age seventy-seven, he married a widow reputed to be the wealthiest woman in America and plundered her fortune. She sued for divorce on grounds of his adultery, and it was granted on the day Burr died.

History has not been kind to Burr, who is portrayed as America's original corrupt and venal pol, and a killer to boot. Hamilton's heirs have hardly been more forgiving. For the two hundredth anniversary of the Weehawken affair in 2004, the descendants of Burr and Hamilton were persuaded to get together on the historic New Jersey grounds as two male kinfolk re-enacted the duel. The handshakes were awkward, and the clans, like Hatfields and McCoys, stayed apart. One woman on the Hamilton side shared a bit of family wisdom with a reporter: "If you see a Burr, shoot him."

❖ IN THE ROUGH ❖

THE KILLERS OF BALTUS ROLL

LET OTHER GOLF COURSES NAME THEMSELVES after shady elms, green hills, and other inoffensive beauties of nature. Baltusrol Golf Club in Springfield, New Jersey, where Jack Nicklaus won two U.S. Opens, went for something sharper. The world-class course gets its name from a sensational murder case.

Baltus Roll, a modestly prosperous, sixty-one-year-old farmer, was the victim in an 1831 robbery-killing that shocked the New Jersey countryside. The old gentleman tilled the soil of land that would later be named for him, and lived with his wife on the mountaintop above.

Often passing by the remote farmhouse that icy winter of 1831 was a sleigh driver, Peter B. Davis. He was a hopeless debtor and drunk who had failed in the tavern-keeping business and just picked up an opium habit. Somehow, whether through the rumor mill or his own fevered imagination, Davis got the idea there was great wealth stashed in the Roll estate.

Davis sniffed around the taverns and bowling alleys near his home in Camptown (now Irvington), looking for a "good, resolute" partner in crime. He approached one man, Robert Montgomery, over a cup of cider. Montgomery later testified: "He said he knew an old man and woman living alone; they had neither chick nor child in the world; they had a thousand dollars of money; the world owed him a living and he was determined to have it."

Montgomery turned him down, so Davis recruited a ne'er-do-well named Lycidias Baldwin. On February 22, the two of them rode Davis's one-horse sleigh through the rainy night. Sometime between eleven and midnight, the Rolls were awakened by a knock, then the crashing-in of the door. Mrs. Roll (the trial and newspaper records give her no first name) later described the invaders as two men, including a tall one with heavy whiskers who talked through his nose. The duo lifted Roll from bed, punched him, threw him about the room, tore his clothes off, then led him outside and threatened to kill him if he didn't tell where he hid his fortune.

Roll had no treasure. But the killers would have none of his pleadings. They tortured him with ropes as Mrs. Roll watched in fear and helplessness. "The small man was at his feet tying him, and the large man at his head, choking him," she said. Roll gave one last gasp and died.

The terrified widow ran through the snow-covered woods, summoning help from neighbors. When she returned to the house with the Good Samaritans, they found Baltus Roll dead just inside the front gate, face down in a puddle. The house had been thoroughly ransacked, the mattress of the family bed slashed open. Footprints led from the body to the tracks of a horse sleigh.

The plot had never been particularly sophisticated, and it fell completely apart when the authorities got word of all the strange barroom conversations Davis had been having. A week after the murder, he stabbed himself in the chest, survived, and was taken into custody. Baldwin, learning of this, confessed the murder to several strangers and killed himself with an overdose of laudanum.

The trial of Davis, held in Newark over five days that summer, drew crowds of fascinated observers and was such a sensation that New Jersey's Supreme Court chief justice presided to ensure fairness. Unhappily for the prosecution, Mrs. Roll could not identify the defendant as the "heavy-whiskered" killer, while the confession of Baldwin was ruled hearsay and inadmissible. Davis was found not guilty. The verdict provoked widespread outrage, and in Newark the defendant was hanged in effigy.

Davis had no occasion to celebrate his good fortune. While being interrogated after his arrest, Davis had admitted signing his brother's name to a promissory note even as he denied murder. The judge sentenced him to an astonishing twenty-four years in prison for forgery, and Davis died shortly afterward in his cell.

Baltus Roll's farm passed over the years from one family to another until it ended up in the hands of Louis Keller, publisher of the *New York Social Register* and ardent golfer. In 1895, Keller developed the grounds into one of America's first challenging, Scottish-style golf courses. The name of Baltus Roll and the notoriety of the trial were still so strong in people's minds, and so well identified with the property in Springfield, that this became the club's name. The founder failed to get the spelling right—although, admittedly, "Baltusrol" has a more exotic sound to it than "Baltus Roll."

The old farmer's ghost is said to haunt the mountain where he lived, although no sightings have been recorded on the fairways or greens below—which is a surprise, considering that a hacker who loses his ball in Baltusrol's treacherous hazards could always assign the blame to a convenient bogeyman.

⤞ HELL FOR LEATHER ⤝

ANTOINE LeBLANC, MURDERER
1802–1833

SECRETED WITHIN THE LIBRARIES and curio cabinets of some of New Jersey's finest houses are souvenirs of an old murder case. Book covers, lampshades, change purses, and wallets are inscribed with the date in 1833 when a murderer named Antoine LeBlanc was hanged. The leather keepsakes belonged to LeBlanc, but not in their current form. They were made from skin carved off his body.

French immigrant Antoine LeBlanc was in America for a week before he became a triple murderer. Soon after this woodcut portrait, he was hanged, his body carved up, and the skin tanned into leather souvenirs. (Photo courtesy of the Morristown and Morris Township Library)

It might be thought just a ghoulish campfire tale if the historical record did not confirm every detail. LeBlanc, a thirty-one-year-old farmhand from the Moselle region of France, arrived on American shores on April 26, 1833. Back home he had formed an attachment to a beautiful young woman named Marie, but her parents rejected him as too low-bred. LeBlanc decided he would attain wealth in the New World, sail back home, and present himself as a more acceptable suitor.

Within a few days of his arrival, LeBlanc was hired through an employment agency to work at a farm in Morristown, New Jersey. His employers were Samuel and Sarah Sayre, a respected and well-off couple who were each about sixty years old. They were in special need of help because their black teenaged slave had run away just before spring planting.

LeBlanc apparently expected to do light tasks as a gardener. Instead, he found himself given the backbreaking labor of chopping wood and slopping the hogs. The farmhand spoke no English and the Sayres spoke no French. Other workers on the Sayre estate loathed the foreigner for his inability to communicate, his habit of smoking smelly cigars, and his disdain for personal hygiene. For his part, LeBlanc simmered with resentment. The only way he would make his fortune, he decided, was through sudden and violent action.

On the night of May 11, a Saturday, LeBlanc fortified himself with hard cider at a local tavern and walked home to the Sayre house. Catching Samuel Sayre upstairs shaving, LeBlanc pretended to be frightened and motioned in sign language for the old man to come down to the stables. There in the dark, LeBlanc clubbed Mr. Sayre a single, fatal blow in the back of the head with a spade.

He summoned Sarah Sayre with a similar ruse and swung away at her. But the first impact only injured her, and she fell to the ground screaming and pleading for her life. Blow after blow from a spade failed to silence her. Finally, as he later told an interpreter, "I kicked her on the head with my heavy-shod boots" until she breathed no more.

After burying the Sayres under a pile of manure, LeBlanc sneaked into the bedroom of their black servant, known only as Phoebe. She was still asleep when he rammed a pitchfork into her chest, killing her.

His murderous work done, LeBlanc used chisels to pry open every trunk and drawer in the house. Voraciously, he stuffed coins, silverware, linens—even a toothbrush and thimble—into pillowcases. Then he changed his bloody clothes for one of Samuel's suits and took off on a stolen horse.

LeBlanc's plan was to get to New York by Monday and set sail back for Europe—and Marie—before anyone had discovered the bodies. But greed was his undoing. He had stuffed too much swag into the pillowcases, and secured them too loosely to his saddle. Item after item dropped off the horse as he pounded his way along the Morristown-to-New York road. A sheriff's posse followed the trail to a Newark tavern. LeBlanc was surprised while sipping a morning refreshment, the bag of blood money at his side.

The killer offered up a full confession and the explanation, "I did it all for Marie." A jury needed all of twenty minutes to convict him. On September 6, LeBlanc was hanged on the Morristown village green before twelve thousand people, more than five times the town's population. Observers noted that most of the cheering crowd was female.

There had been mass murders before in New Jersey. But everything about LeBlanc's case—his status as a Catholic immigrant, the good standing of his victims, his lack of remorse—aroused a passionate loathing. Hanging wasn't good enough for him.

And so, after LeBlanc's body was cut down from the noose, it was taken to a local surgeon's office. There, Princeton professor Joseph Henry, the foremost American scientist of the era, began a bizarre, Frankenstein-like experiment. He hooked the corpse up to electrodes, ran a current through it, and was able to make LeBlanc's cold, dead eyes roll around in their sockets. The strange procedure proved nothing, exactly, except that current will make a dead person's eyes roll around in their sockets.

LeBlanc's ears were then cut off and given away as souvenirs. The skin was stripped away and sent to a Morristown tannery, which spared no effort in a grisly form of recycling. Wallets, book jackets, and simple strips of skin were hawked on the streets, many of them inscribed by the sheriff who had arrested LeBlanc. Some were passed down from generation to generation among New Jersey's most respected families.

One of the human skin wallets—a frail, green-brown piece of leather—was, in the early 2000s, still in the possession of a Morristown-area chief of police. It was described by a journalist who hunted down what remained of LeBlanc after a long series of inquiries and dead ends. He was also able to locate the hanged man's death mask. A smooth, expressionless, even gentle face, it betrays nothing of the savagery that he committed—and to which he, too, fell victim.

⇻ FOOL'S GOLD ⇺

RODMAN M. PRICE, GOVERNOR
1816–1894

JOWLY FACED AND MUSTACHIOED, Rodman McCamley Price stares back from his nineteenth-century portrait like the classic man of means. His résumé appeared highly distinguished, as an original Forty-Niner, a governor of New Jersey, and a top financier. But he was also a thorough-going crook who spent his last days in jail—and was so shameless that he stole from his own mother.

Civil War–era governor Rodman McCamley Price set the standard for future New Jersey politicians: he spent time in jail after ripping off the federal government, his creditors, and his own mother.

The son of a state senator from Sussex County, New Jersey, Price dropped out of Princeton and joined the Navy as a purser. In 1846, he had the good luck to be aboard a ship off Mexico's province of California at the outbreak of the Mexican War. He helped seize the city of San Francisco, was named its chief judge, and got the plum job of purser for the Pacific Squadron. By war's end, the United States had captured all of California and Price had won a reputation.

A greater fortune lay in wait. In 1849, word reached the East that gold had been discovered in California, and a horde of prospectors beat a trail westward. Price was sharp enough to know the real fortunes lay not in chancy mining claims, but in San Francisco real estate. He bought dozens of prime city lots that soared in value, earning him perhaps half a million dollars his first year. To make these transactions he used insider knowledge and, most likely, Navy funds. After he departed California, the federal government sued him for $88,000 it thought he misappropriated.

Both Price's cash and his accounts had a way of vanishing forever. On the voyage back to Washington, D.C., his steamboat exploded and sank. Price survived. He claimed to have lost all his financial records, which forever doomed Uncle Sam's attempts to get the missing funds back.

But the episode had no effect on his popularity, and he was welcomed to his new home of Hoboken, New Jersey, as a war hero. He was elected to the House of Representatives as a Democrat, served a single, undistinguished term, then won the race for governor in 1853.

As the state's chief executive, Price was basically competent. On the plus side, he founded Trenton Normal School, the state's first institution for the instruction of teachers. On the minus side, he let the mighty Camden and Amboy Railroad dictate his economic policy and he was fiercely proslavery. After stepping down as governor, he was a leading voice advocating blacks' "subordination to the superior race" of whites. In 1861, on the eve of the Civil War, Price made the astonishing proposal that New Jersey should secede and join the Confederate States. "I believe the Southern Confederacy permanent," he explained.

It wasn't, and neither was Price's wealth. He invested his California earnings in a Wall Street partnership that went bust. Hounded by creditors, he plunged recklessly in a series of failed ventures: a New York-to-Weehawken ferry, a quarrying business, land speculation in South Bergen. At one point he formed a company to build a New York City-to-New Jersey bridge. The plan anticipated the George Washington Bridge by fifty years, and was fifty years too soon to be feasible. This initiative, too, lost money.

To get out of his hole, Price handled family finances with the same sticky fingers he'd shown in the Navy. Upon his father's death, the ex-governor was named executor of the estate and helped himself to shares of the inheritance that didn't belong to him. A judge stepped in to bar Price from handling the funds, but not before $73,000 was plundered from the other heirs, including Price's own widowed mother. Afterward, a business rival had the temerity to point this out in a published tract. Price sued him for libel, and lost. It didn't help when a character witness testified about Price: "I am not conscious of having any animosity toward him, although I have no respect for him."

Price slid into personal bankruptcy, keeping the family homestead in the Ramapo mountains but little else. In his old age, he maintained that if only that steamboat hadn't burned up, those missing ledgers would prove the government owned *him* money. Thanks to influential friends in Washington, Congress agreed, and Price received a $60,000 cash settlement from Congress.

A woman named Emma Forrest learned of Price's windfall and sued. She had long accused Price of swindling her father in a California land deal, and the courts agreed with her. A judge issued a writ of attachment against the ex-governor, forbidding him from cashing out his $60,000 until he had paid Forrest. Price ignored the order and made drafts against the funds. One day in June 1893, he stepped off a train in the town of Oakland, near his home, and saw a detective waiting for him. He was under arrest for contempt of court.

Price spent a few days in the Hackensack jail before making bail. By this time, he was utterly destitute and in his dotage, and there seemed little point in putting this dull-eyed, white-haired old man through the rigors of trial. He died at home a year later, at seventy-eight, having dodged justice to the end.

✧ DOMESTIC DISTURBANCE ✧

BRIDGET DERGAN, MURDERER
1844–1867

"ALL THE AIR IS FILLED WITH BLOOD AND CRIME," Mark Twain wrote a friend with cynical delight in the spring of 1867. He had sailed from California to the East Coast just before a New Jersey domestic servant named Bridget Dergan stabbed her master's wife to death. It was arguably America's most sensational murder trial featuring a female defendant before Lizzie Borden, and Twain related the grisly particulars with relish. The trial has "a splendid interest," he wrote. "It is perfectly invaluable to me since I have become so bloodthirsty."

Barely literate and poor, Dergan labored in her native County Sligo, Ireland, as a milkmaid. Her first crime was committed at age twenty. After plundering some gold coins from her father's strongbox, she stole away in the night and boarded a ship to America.

Irish domestic Bridget Dergan, whose hanging in 1867 for the stabbing murder of her master's wife fascinated the newspapers and Mark Twain.

She arrived in New York in December 1864. Like many a female Irish immigrant of the time, her only job opportunity was that of a house-maid—indeed, the Irish servant named "Bridget" was a comical stereotype in popular literature. This flesh-and-blood Bridget worked only a few weeks at a time for various households in New York and New Jersey before she fell ill with sore eyes and fainting spells.

A doctor and Civil War veteran named William Coriell then generously paid a house call on her, diagnosed her with epilepsy, and urged a long bed rest. He refused to accept a fee and insisted she come work as his house servant. She would cook and clean for the doctor, his wife, and their newborn baby back at Newmarket, a rural town outside New Brunswick. When Dergan demurred, citing loyalty to her present master, Coriell pressed the point. "One good turn deserves another," he told her.

Over the next year, Dr. Coriell and his new maid Bridget grew scandalously close. Thirty-one-year-old Mary Ellen Coriell had no illusions about her husband's lechery. Her indignation exploded into a violent argument when Dr. Coriell suggested that Dergan sleep in the bedroom with them. The doctor finally agreed to let the maid go at the end of her agreed-upon four months of service; that date fell at the end of February 1867.

Dr. Coriell apologized to Bridget, and she claimed he said about his wife: "I wish she were out of the way." From this remark came Bridget Dergan's odd notion that she could take Mary Ellen Coriell's place as woman of the house. On February 25, 1867, Dr. Coriell left on an all-night house call to deliver a patient's child. Dergan waited until midnight, when Mrs. Coriell was sure to be asleep. Then she crept up the stairs, oil lamp in one hand and a butcher's knife in the other.

Durgan burst into the bedroom in a frenzy. She pulled Mrs. Coriell out of her bed and stabbed her a dozen times. The woman fought back, pleading, "Don't kill me, Bridget." Dergan brought every possible weapon into the attack. She clubbed her mistress with a baby chair, punched her, bit her on the neck. Finally, a whirlwind of stabbing thrusts finished off the 110-pound victim, and she dropped dead on the floor.

Dergan attempted to cover up her crime by pouring the contents of the lamp onto the bed covers and setting it aflame. She decided to save the eighteen-month-old baby—she would, after all, be its new mother—and fled into the snow and darkness. Breathless, she stopped at a neighbor's house. Some burglars or bandits had sneaked into the Coriell home, she said, and she had gotten out just in time.

The neighbor looked down at her skirts and saw an enormous bloodstain. Dergan immediately tried to fold fabric over the blotch, the first sign that she had committed less than the perfect crime.

The fire at the Coriell house did only minor damage, and a wealth of evidence implicated Dergan. A mold was taken of the bite marks on the dead woman's neck, and these matched the maid's teeth perfectly. Even a primitive form of fingerprinting helped the authorities. Dergan had cut her own hands with her wild swings of the knife, and the wounds matched perfectly with bloody marks on the bedroom walls. Her attempts to shift responsibility were absurd; she insisted that the bloodstains on her dress came from "my monthly courses."

Much of the fascination presented by her trial, then, lay not in the whodunit but in her salacious revelations about Dr. Coriell, such as his invitation to share the family boudoir. Only after she was found guilty of murder and sentenced to die would she admit her crime. Blandly, she said she thought she would get away with it because "the doctor liked me."

On August 30, 1867, Bridget Dergan was led to the gallows of the Middlesex County jail in New Brunswick before an eager crowd. Some spectators hollered "Down in front!" Others took wagers on whether she would be calm or hysterical. The ones betting on stoicism won. Dergan insisted on whispering her final words to a priest—"Don't let them Protestants know what I say"—and dropped silently to her death.

➤ DEATH ALLEY ➤

THE SEDUCER AND THE ABORTIONIST

ON AUGUST 26, 1871, the nude body of a young Paterson, New Jersey, woman was found stuffed into a baggage trunk at a New York City railroad station, and the politics of abortion would be changed for the next hundred years.

It was a mild and sunny Saturday afternoon, perfect conditions for a summer trip out of the city. Amid the crowds at the Hudson River Railroad Depot was a shabbily dressed woman who paid $22 for a ticket to Chicago. She appeared nervous as her trunk was taken off a hired horsecart and checked through. Then she disappeared. As all the passengers' luggage was being hauled to the platform, the lid of this trunk was jarred, and there was an overpowering stench.

The station master was quickly called over to make an inspection. Inside the trunk was a mass of bloodstained quilting and rags that, when

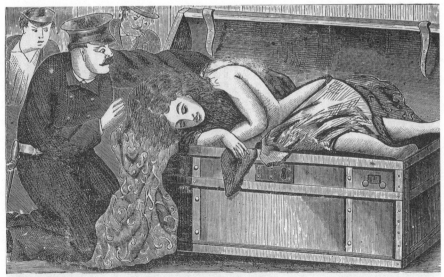

Opening of the MYSTERIOUS TRUNK, and horrible Discovery

A romanticized depiction of the "trunk mystery" of 1871—the discovery of Alice Bowlsby's body in a trunk after a botched abortion.

parted, revealed a dead woman. Her frail, petite body had been folded up against itself and roughly crammed into the 2¾-foot-by-1½-foot space. She had a tangled mass of light auburn hair and the rough hands of a worker. A coroner estimated that she was about twenty years old and had been dead three days. Cause of death was metroperitonitis, an inflammation of the uterus. It had been caused by medical malpractice during a "criminal violation of nature's laws"—an abortion.

The newspapers quickly called it the "trunk mystery." Who was the dead woman? And who had brought the trunk to the station? The body was laid out in a morgue for the public to examine, in hopes someone could provide identification. Crowds of the curious and prurient filed past the horrid spectacle.

Eventually, a cart driver led police to a Manhattan address where he had picked up a trunk and taken it to the station. This, he was sure, was the same trunk that contained the body. The resident of that address, one Dr. Jacob Rosenzweig, was put under arrest.

Detectives familiar with New York's underworld recognized him at once: Rosenzweig was an abortionist. His trade, though illegal, was widely tolerated under the city's Boss William Tweed. But the death of a patient in so shocking a manner rendered all political protections void. Rosenzweig was booked on a charge of manslaughter.

Police searched his plush doctor's office downtown, where they found various bloody scraps of fabric and false bosom pads that would later be linked to the late patient. Rosenzweig denied he'd lost any patients. Polish-born and thirty-nine, he was part of the first large wave of Jewish immigration to hit American shores. There was more than a whiff of prejudice in the *New York Times*'s description of him as "a fat, coarse and sensual-looking fellow, without any traces of refinement in person or manners." But he really was a quack: he had bought his diploma through the mail for $40.

The day after the arrest, an identification was finally made on the body. She was Alice Bowlsby, twenty-five and single. Her mother and two younger sisters, with whom she lived in Paterson, had noticed her absence since the weekend, when she was to have returned from a visit to an aunt in Newark. A family doctor went to New York on their behalf and, aghast, recognized the body.

Born in the small town of Troy Hills, New Jersey, Alice Bowlsby had followed her family to the growing industrial city of Paterson. Her father took to drink, walked out on the family, and left wife and daughter to fend for themselves as seamstresses. Alice worked a sewing machine and had no shortage of suitors.

One of these men was Walter Conklin, a dapper twenty-three-year-old clerk at the Dale silk factory and the son of a city alderman. He lived five blocks from Bowlsby and visited her often. From one such encounter she became pregnant. Conklin had courted many other young Paterson ladies and had promised marriage to one of them, who was not Bowlsby. The prospect of fathering an illegitimate child shook his comfortable world.

A notice in the *New York Herald* seemed to provide a way out: "Ladies in trouble guaranteed immediate relief, sure and safe; no fees required until perfectly satisfied; elegant rooms and nursing provided. Dr. Ascher." "Ascher" was a pseudonym for Rosenzweig. Conklin apparently showed the ad to Bowlsby and offered to pay for the abortion. She rode the train to New York on August 23, made her way to the doctor's office, and was not seen again until the grim discovery at the railroad station.

On August 31, the day that Bowlsby's identity was printed in the newspapers, Conklin made his way to the silk factory without his usual aplomb. There, in the isolation of a fireproof vault, he blew his brains out with a revolver. In his pocket was a neatly penned letter. It read: "I have long had a morbid idea of the worthlessness of life, and now to be obliged to testify in this affair and cause unpleasantness to my family is more than life is worth."

The newspapers turned the tragedy into part morality play, part circulation booster. No one missed the irony that these two lovers, who had sought to abort their child, ended up dying themselves. The *Times*, by coincidence, had earlier that year run a series of articles exposing the surreptitious world of abortionists. One of these stories, headlined "The Evil of Our Age," reported on a shady character who turned out to be Rosenzweig himself.

Rosenzweig was put on trial by a district attorney who made an emotional appeal to the jury. "O, what a fate is this!" he said. "How many unfortunate, erring young women have died lingering, agonizing deaths at the hands of these Dr. Aschers, who sticks a sign out in a Death Alley, allur[ing] the miserable into his lair?"

Rosenzweig was sentenced to the maximum at the time, seven years in prison. But impelled by publicity of the case, the New York Legislature passed a law making abortion a felony. Twenty years in prison was to be the punishment, whether the fetus, the mother, or both died. Other states followed suit, and a federal law was passed making it a crime to advertise any form of contraception. Many of these laws remained in force for the next century, until they were swept aside by the Supreme Court in the 1973 *Roe v. Wade* decision.

Ironically, New York's tough abortion law provided the basis for an appeal that got Rosenzweig sprung from prison. His lawyers argued that the new law had abolished the old, and therefore the prisoner could not be guilty of anything. After a year in prison, the doctor was a free man. As for the trunk-carrying woman who had tried to dispose of Bowlsby's body, she never was found.

❧ CRAZY LOVE ❧

CHARLES K. LANDIS,
TOWN FOUNDER AND KILLER
1833–1900

CREATING YOUR OWN TOWN has its privileges. Charles K. Landis was founder of Vineland in South Jersey, where he set all the utopian rules, including no alcohol, no fences, and a shade tree in front of every house. Streets and schools were named after him. He attained wealth and high public esteem. And when a local newspaper editor mocked him in print, Landis stormed into his office, killed him—and got away with it.

A Philadelphian by birth, Landis combined the qualities of the nineteenth-century social visionary and modern real estate developer.

He had already made several successes speculating in land when in 1861 he traveled to the empty swamplands of New Jersey forty miles south of Philadelphia. Here he would plant an ideal village. A surveyor looked toward the dreamer with the black beard and searching eyes and muttered: "The man is crazy."

Because Landis intended to surround the settlement with prosperous fruit orchards, he named his city Vineland. But despite this evocative name, no wine, or indeed any alcoholic beverage, could be sold. Landis was a prohibitionist who believed the "evil of drink" would cut into profits.

In flocked frugal homesteaders, including one ingenious dentist named Thomas Welch who, taking advantage of the dry laws, invented unfermented wine and sold it as Welch's grape juice. Those whose ideas offended Victorian sensibilities in other towns were welcome here, among them advocates of woman suffrage, spiritualism, and free love. Some women went about town wearing—gasp!—trousers.

Landis encouraged the unconventional atmosphere and reaped financial reward from the steady stream of settlers—all of whom had to lease homesteads from the founder. His town had an endorsement from no less than President Ulysses S. Grant, who paid an 1874 visit to Vineland and declared: "It is one of the greatest places for industry and prosperity and intelligence."

Charles K. Landis founded the town of Vineland, promoted women's rights and temperance, and got away with killing a newspaper editor who dared criticize him. (Special Collections and University Archives, Rutgers University Libraries)

Vineland's founder had idiosyncrasies to match his town. He wrote an ahead-of-its-time novel foretelling a rocket trip to Mars. On a trip to the Alps, he conversed with "the spirit of the mountain." Landis's wife, Clara, was a teenager when they married, and her father, a Navy commodore, was so violently opposed to the match he promised to shoot the groom on sight. Husband and wife fought, too. On one occasion, it was rumored, she took his gun and blasted away at the household furniture.

Landis made other enemies in town through his power to cancel leases and confiscate property at will, which he exercised as arbitrarily as a feudal lord. Dissent found a voice in Uri Carruth, editor of the weekly *Vineland Independent.* Chafing at Landis's "dictatorial" ways, Carruth ran article after article belittling him. At one public meeting, Landis denounced the *Independent* as "a low, dirty, nasty, scurrilous, scandalous sheet."

An article in the March 20, 1875, issue of the *Independent* particularly incensed him. This piece, written by Carruth, referred to "a prominent Vinelander" who could only be Landis. It dredged up the rumor about Clara Landis's target practice at home and claimed that ever since, the husband had been "galloping up and down, telling every man he met, confidentially, that his wife was crazy." The "wretch" was now trying to get her committed to an insane asylum.

Landis read the article in a slow, boiling rage. After giving himself two hours to make preparations, he walked to the offices of the *Independent* and asked a desk clerk to summon the editor. Carruth came in from off the street to see his nemesis draw a revolver. The editor dashed into the composing room to escape, but Landis followed him and fired a shot into the back of his head. As Carruth crumpled to the floor, Landis waved the offending news clipping and shouted: "My poor, crazy wife showed me this, and that is the result!"

Remarkably, Carruth battled for seven months with a bullet in his skull before dying. Landis went on trial for murder at the Cumberland County Courthouse in Bridgeton, where so many people wanted to watch that the tickets had to be rationed. His lawyer was Benjamin Williamson, who as state chancellor had been New Jersey's top judicial officer. Williamson offered this defense: Landis was not guilty by reason of insanity. Apparently, the critics who called him crazy had been right all along.

The month-long trial was filled with embarrassments for Landis. It was revealed that this civic leader, who forced teetotalism on others, himself enjoyed a tipple of wine now and then. To back up the insanity defense, the lawyers made much of his mystical visions, his paranoia, and his storms of rage. Prosecutors argued that this was proof not of debilitating mental illness, just a rotten personality. If Landis were to walk free because of insanity, state Attorney General Jacob Vanatta told the jury, it would be a type of insanity that "never occurs with anyone unless he is very rich or holds some high social position."

The jury deliberated for a day before reaching a verdict on February 5, 1876: Landis was not guilty and insane. Lucky for him, he required no confinement in an asylum and was liberated to take charge of Vineland once again.

Clara Landis, the maligned wife over whose honor Landis had committed his crime, never once showed up in court to support her husband. After the trial, she divorced him. But Landis's financial affairs did not suffer. He went on to make money off more real estate developments, including the Shore town of Sea Isle City, and lived another twenty-four years. In his model town of Vineland, Landis Park, Landis Intermediate School, and Landis Avenue are all named for him. Nothing was ever named for Carruth, New Jersey's martyr to the First Amendment.

✥ MOB RULE ✦

A LYNCHING IN NEW JERSEY

BETWEEN 1882 AND 1936, at least 3,383 African Americans were lynched—victims of a racial terror that helped to enforce white domination. In some southern towns, it became a sort of festivity: storm the jailhouse, torture and hang a black man, and take souvenir photographs of the corpse. Well over 90 percent of these extrajudicial murders occurred in the states of the Old Confederacy or on the western frontier. But in 1886, lynch law came to New Jersey.

The scene of this ugly episode was Eatontown, a prosperous farming village fifty miles south of New York City. A free black community had long lived here in peace with their white neighbors, but slavery was a living memory. Not until the end of the Civil War had New Jersey released the last of its African Americans from bondage. One of these citizens born a slave but freed at a young age was Samuel Johnson.

Johnson's short stature and athletic build made him a skilled jockey, one of the few professional careers open to a black man in the nineteenth century. He was well known to the racing fans at Monmouth Park, who nicknamed him "Mingo Jack" after a thoroughbred he rode. When his racing days were over, Johnson continued working in the stables as a groom. In the last year of his life, he was sixty-six but fit as a man twenty years younger.

On the afternoon of March 5, 1886, a twenty-four-year-old white woman named Angeline Herbert left her father's house to pay a visit on a neighbor. As she walked a trail through the thick piney woods, someone came up from behind her and swung a club at her. Two blows dropped her, semi-conscious, to the ground. The attacker then raped her.

Word of the crime was quickly relayed to Herbert's father, George, and to the Eatontown constable, Herman Liebenthal. The victim described the rapist as a short, black man, wearing a black jersey and blue overalls. The men assumed this man was Johnson, who lived just one and a half miles away. "I'll shoot him!" cried George.

Constable Liebenthal arrested Johnson at his house a few hours later—despite having no warrant. The jockey's wife and adult daughter insisted he had been at home the whole day. His clothes did not match those the rapist wore. "I don't know nothing about the business," Johnson protested as he was led away to jail.

From miles around, the people of Eatontown walked to the small, brick lockup and glowered in the direction of Johnson's cell. Some gathered in a nearby tavern. Mingo Jack was spoken of as a notorious pervert, and stories about him grew more outrageous with every drink. It was said that he was a highway bandit, and had once tried to rape a farmer's wife the previous summer.

"That nigger ought to be hung," a man said. Someone brought a clothesline to the bar, and another sat knotting a noose.

The constable was aware of all this. At 10 P.M., he went back to the lockup, lit a stove fire, and told Johnson that a lynch mob was forming against him. He later testified—dubiously—that the prisoner claimed he could take care of himself. And so the jailer locked the doors and walked away for the night, leaving his prisoner unguarded.

At about 11:30 P.M., the rumble of double-team wagons was heard throughout the center of Eatontown. Each vehicle contained men with murder on their minds. The mob numbered anywhere from forty to seventy-five people. Not one white onlooker made an effort to stop them. The blacks who lived near the jailhouse, mindful that their lives too were at stake, simply stayed silent.

The jailhouse door was made of heavy oak and was barred by a heavy padlock. It gave way in a matter of minutes to a crowd wielding sledge-hammers and hoes. The cell door was even easier to break down. Swinging their tools and fists, the surging mass of whites clubbed Johnson to death. His skull was broken in several places, and one eye came loose from its socket.

Like a trophy, Johnson's body was hung in triumph that night from the jailhouse door. Citizens who awoke to the macabre display were not particularly disgusted by it. The *New York Times* reported: "One young miss, after looking at the spot where Mingo Jack was found hanging, exclaimed: 'How interesting!'"

In the South, lynch mobs carried out their atrocities without fear of prosecution. To its credit, the state of New Jersey made efforts to find out who was in the mob that hanged Johnson. However, not one of ninety witnesses called before a coroner's jury in Eatontown that spring would admit he or she saw any act of violence. At times, the proceedings turned into farce. Once, a juror picked up a torn hat that was submitted as evidence—it had been left at the bloody scene by a lyncher—and dropped it on his own head, to the accompaniment of laughter.

Arrest warrants were issued against eight men. They included William Kelly, the man believed to have knotted the rope; Constable Liebenthal, who was charged with manslaughter for his neglect; and William Snedeker, who testified: "If I helped hang Mingo Jack I certainly would not have told about it. I have said I was glad the nigger was hanged, and I am glad yet." All charges were dropped when a Monmouth County grand jury failed to make indictments.

The killing of "Mingo Jack" Johnson—the only lynching carried out in New Jersey since the Revolutionary War—remains officially unsolved. Likewise, Angeline Herbert's rapist was never brought to justice, either. In 1888, a Philadelphia man named John Miller confessed on his deathbed that he committed the crime for which Mingo Jack was lynched. No one in Eatontown followed up on this.

⇝ RIPPING YARN ⇜

SEVERIN KLOSOWSKI,
JACK THE RIPPER SUSPECT
1865–1903

FOR YEARS, SCOTLAND YARD'S CHIEF INSPECTOR haunted the foggy alleys of London in search of the phantom who had terrorized the city by butchering its prostitutes. With time, the detective came to narrow down the suspects until he reached a startling conclusion. Jack the Ripper, he said, was a New Jersey hairstylist.

This man was Severin Antoniovich Klosowski, who lived in London at the time of the Ripper killings in 1888 and in Jersey City a few years later. He was convicted of killing three of his wives, but was never found guilty or even charged in the deaths of "Jack's" victims. However, many "Ripperologists" who have made a cottage industry out of trying to crack the case view him as an excellent candidate for history's most notorious serial killer.

A dark, glowering presence with a fierce walrus mustache, Klosowski was born in Poland, studied surgery there, and worked for a time at a

Warsaw hospital. At age twenty-three, he abandoned both his profession and his wife to move to London, where he set up shop as a barber. Ominously, the neighborhood where he lived was Whitechapel. Students of Jack the Ripper lore know it as the squalid, sinister slum in which five prostitutes were butchered in the late summer and fall of 1888.

The killings generally shared common traits. The stalker met his victims at nighttime in a secluded alley and presumably posed as a client of their services. Once alone with a woman, he killed with deep slashes to the throat. Other mutilations would follow on the woman's body, the violence growing more sadistic with each successive murder. Some victims had their internal organs sliced out and carefully placed around them.

Whatever Klosowski's alibi at the time, he was never questioned about it. In 1889, he married a fellow Pole, Lucy Baderski. (Since Klosowski was still legally married in Poland, this was bigamy.) In the spring of 1891, the couple boarded a ship for America to start a new life after the death of their baby from disease. He settled in Jersey City, opened a barbershop, and not once made the headlines.

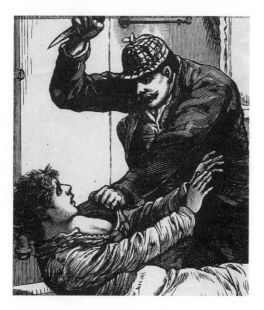

Jack the Ripper slaughtered five London prostitutes in the most famous unsolved murders in history. Some think he later emigrated to Jersey City.

Outwardly respectable, he was a batterer at home. Lucy would later reveal how she once discovered a knife hidden under his pillow while they lived in Jersey City. He told her he planned to cut her head off with it, then pointed to a spot in the room where he would bury her.

Understandably perturbed, Lucy ran out on her husband in February 1892. Klosowski re-immigrated to London four months later and contracted a series of additional bigamous marriages. From one of his wives, whose last name was Chapman, he took the alias "George Chapman." Then he married a talented pianist named Mary Spink. Together they opened a "musical barbershop" where customers had their hair cut to keyboard accompaniment.

Klosowski had previously skipped out on his wives by abandoning them. Mary he decided to get rid of permanently. In 1897, he went to a pharmacist and bought an ounce of antimony, a tasteless and odorless poison with deadly effects similar to arsenic. Sprinkled on Mary's food, in small doses and over time, it killed her. The attending doctor failed to detect foul play and diagnosed her as dying of consumption.

Klosowski used the same poison seasoning to kill two more wives. But he put far too much of the stuff into his last spouse and was arrested when shockingly high levels of antimony showed up in her autopsy. He was hanged on April 7, 1903.

Were the three poisonings his only murders? Scotland Yard's chief inspector, Frederick Abberline, who had been pounding the pavement investigating the Whitechapel killings fifteen years before, was intrigued by the Klosowski case. When the poisoner was brought into custody, Abberline told the arresting officer: "You've got Jack the Ripper at last!"

The inspector later outlined his theory for a London reporter. There was the coincidence of Klosowski's arrival in London before the Ripper killings began, and his departure after they ended. There was Klosowski's training as a surgeon, which fit the Ripper's technique of excising his victims' organs. There was the suspect's obvious misogyny. "The story told by 'Chapman's' wife of the attempt to murder her with a long knife while in America is not to be ignored," Abberline added.

A contemporary author, R. Michael Gordon, has built on this theory by claiming that Klosowski was responsible for four additional Jack the Ripper murders—in New York and New Jersey. In a 2003 book, *The American Murders of Jack the Ripper*, Gordon identified four women as being his victims. Among them were:

- Elizabeth Senior, seventy-three, who was found stabbed to death at home in Millburn, New Jersey, on January 31, 1892. The house had been burglarized and $45 stolen.
- Mary Anderson, a hotel servant who was shot in the back while walking to work along railroad tracks in Perth Amboy, New Jersey, on June 8, 1892. The killer also cut her throat.

There are numerous holes in Gordon's theory. Neither New Jersey case fits the Ripper's style—the stabbing of a streetwalker. Ripperologists are generally agreed there were five "canonical" victims in London. In none of those cases did Jack shoot a woman, steal money, or leave behind a victim older than forty-six.

And nothing but circumstantial evidence—the fact of Klosowski's residence in London and his surgical training—implicates him in any Ripper killing. Most damaging of all to his candidacy for Ripperdom was his modus operandi. Klosowski was known for slow, stealthy poisonings, nothing like the fevered cutting that the Ripper employed.

But who else could Jack the Ripper have been? Among the names put forward by amateur sleuths as the notorious killer are two of Queen Victoria's princely sons and Lewis Carroll, the beloved children's author. However outlandish the notion of a New Jersey Jack the Ripper, he surely outranks these suspects in plausibility.

❖ ARTFUL DODGER ❖

EMANUEL NINGER, COUNTERFEITER
1847–1924

THE STOUT, SANDY-BEARDED FELLOW with the German accent looked like just another prosperous farmer when he moved to the hamlet of Flagtown, just outside Somerville, New Jersey, in 1885. He dressed well, gave to local charities, and settled his wife and four children on a tidy, three-acre farm. Since he never did actual farming, the neighbors naturally wondered where his money came from. A Prussian army pension and a talent for playing the stock market, he explained. That was why he always took monthly railroad trips to New York City—to consult on his investments there.

Actually, Emanuel Ninger made his money by, well, making it. He was a counterfeiter, and perhaps the most artistically talented counterfeiter of all time. With a master's touch, he hand-painted his dollar bills instead of printing them. These creations, featuring beautiful brushwork and expertly copied portraits of Benjamin Franklin and Abraham Lincoln, drew admiration from art experts and are still furtively collected today.

Respectable family man Emanuel "Jim the Penman" Ninger in his mug shot after finally getting caught for passing counterfeit notes. (U.S. Secret Service/ National Archives)

The man the Secret Service called "the Penman" was born in Preum, a town in Germany's Rhineland. Ninger emigrated with his wife in 1882, settling at first in Hoboken, New Jersey, and taking on work as a sign painter. He struggled to support a growing family but soon hit upon a solution to their problems. With his creative talents, he could create wealth.

Ninger began by buying bond paper from the same mills that supplied the paper used for real currency. He cut the paper into squares and, to give it a properly worn appearance, soaked it in coffee—a technique counterfeiters still use today.

Almost all counterfeiters of the era used photoengraved plates to print their money. Ninger had a more artistic touch. Working at a light table, he put the bond paper above a bill and traced the design elements. Then he filled in the tracing with pen, stationer's ink, and a camel's hair brush. To simulate the security threads present in real bills, he ingeniously painted red and blue lines on the paper.

The product of this hard, criminal work was meager, by counterfeiting standards: perhaps only five $50 notes a month. But in his career, Ninger probably passed $40,000 worth of bills, making him a rich man for his time. His trips to New York were a means of passing the fakes under the cloak of anonymity. Typically, he spent them at saloons and groceries, eluding suspicion even though he asked for large sums in change.

The flow of good money in return for bad enabled Ninger and his family to buy their dream house in Flagtown. No one thought to connect this ideal neighbor with the stories of counterfeit money that filled New York newspapers beginning in 1891.

The Secret Service came to realize that all these hand-painted bills were coming from a single source. Agents called the unknown forger "Jim the Penman" and put examples of his work on exhibit at the Treasury in Washington, hoping someone might recognize the artist's hand. Every brushstroke was studied for clues. One puzzle was just why the counterfeiter got his details right, yet omitted the words "Engraved and printed at the Bureau of Engraving and Printing." A writer speculated this was "because the artist didn't care to burden his soul with unnecessary lies."

Further frustrating the investigators, many of Ninger's suckers didn't consider themselves victims. One bar on Wall Street proudly hung a pen-and-ink bill on its wall, while a man of leisure in Cincinnati collected others.

The "Penman" finally tripped up on March 28, 1896. On one of his New York trips, he tried to buy a bottle of Rhine wine at a downtown saloon by laying a $50 bill on the bar. He didn't notice that the fake note lay in a puddle. The bartender picked up the bill—and the wet ink smeared his fingers. Ninger was collared as he ran away.

Ninger's arrest was a source of relief to the Secret Service and distress to his admirers. A prominent educator named Silas Packard examined a Ninger $20 bill and called the work "little short of genius." "I don't know of any holder of his 'circulation' who would part with it for double its face value," he wrote. "He has not harmed anybody, not even the government, but has really conferred a favor on the public. The account of his rare achievements has filled many columns of the city press that would otherwise have been given over to domestic scandal."

When Ninger appeared in Manhattan court a month later, he pleaded guilty to counterfeiting and asked for the judge's mercy. It was a nervy gambit. First, Ninger's lawyer argued that all that painstaking penmanship had rendered his client nearly blind. Then, he took up Packard's thesis by saying the counterfeit bills were a benefit to society, since they were more valuable than real money.

The judge rejected this unusual argument, sentencing Ninger to six years in prison. Once the counterfeiter became a free man, he bought a farm in Oley, Pennsylvania, and lived the rest of his life with his family quietly and peacefully.

A 1909 law makes it illegal for anyone—whether counterfeiter or collector—to knowingly possess phony currency. The ban is so strict that today one cannot even possess counterfeit money from the Civil War era. Still, on today's black market, one of Ninger's $50 bills can reportedly be bought for a minimum of $1,000. "Jim the Penman" was proven right: his funny money was more valuable than the real thing.

Dead Wrong

INFAMOUS MURDERS

❧ SEA OF SORROW ❦

THE KILLING OF OCEY SNEAD

HER NAME WAS OCEY SNEAD, twenty-four years old, and even after she was reduced to an eighty-pound wraith, lying nude in the cold bath-tub water that drowned her, you could tell she once was beautiful.

Her long auburn hair floated ethereally; her dead brown eyes stared back at the doctor who'd been called to this sad scene in East Orange, New Jersey, on the afternoon of November 29, 1909. A pile of petticoats

Melancholy, emaciated Oceana "Ocey" Snead was found drowned in a bathtub in 1909.

lay near the tub, and on this pile was pinned a note. Ocey Snead's last letter told how she had lost a baby the previous year and desired to join that child in heaven. "When you read this I will have committed suicide," she wrote. "Do not grieve for me; rejoice with me that death brings a blessed relief from pain and suffering greater than I can bear." Funny thing, the doctor thought after reading the neatly penned note over and over. There wasn't a pen, or an inkwell, in the entire house.

In fact, there was hardly anything in the house: no furniture, no heat, no food beyond a few crumbs in the kitchen. This, and Ocey's starved condition, brought instant suspicion on the gray-haired woman who made the phone call reporting the suicide. Speaking in a soft southern accent, she identified herself as Virginia Wardlaw, the aunt of the deceased. She had been living in these grim quarters with her niece for the last week. Ocey had retired to the bathroom about twenty-four hours before Wardlaw saw fit to check on her and found her dead.

The East Orange police were very interested. Ocey had left $20,000 in life insurance money, which went to her blind and dying grandmother; to her mother; and to her mother's two sisters, of which Wardlaw was one. This established plenty of motive for foul play. But Wardlaw was

Snead's mother, Caroline Martin, in court before she went to prison for manslaughter. To many, it seemed she put her whole family— including her two black-clad sisters— under an evil spell.

offended that policemen should interrogate her, the proud flower of Georgia aristocracy, like a common criminal. Once at police headquarters, she clammed up. She wouldn't talk about Ocey's baby, insurance, or reason for living in this unheated house. Nor would she explain her garb, which was extraordinary even by the overdressed standards of 1909: all black, with voluminous, tent-like skirts, and three veils totally obscuring her face.

It took weeks of investigation to track down Ocey Snead's other relatives. She had indeed given birth to a baby the previous year, it turned out, and it was dead. Another baby had been born to her that summer, but it was dying in a New York City hospital. Ocey's husband was her first cousin. He had deserted her shortly before the birth of this second child, spooked by his wife's morose behavior and the haunting presence of her mother and aunts.

These three sisters lived in New York City, moving in and out of a succession of decaying boarding houses, each of them wearing the same dark clothing and heavy veils. One was Virginia Wardlaw, fifty-seven and unmarried. The others were two widows: Mary Snead, sixty-one, who was also the mother of Ocey's husband; and Caroline Martin, sixty-four, Ocey's mother. In Martin's possession, the police found a pile of writings that instantly incriminated her. They all appeared to be in Martin's handwriting, they were all signed "Ocey Snead," and they were all suicide notes.

A Gothic horror story now presented itself, with dark hints of mental illness and the occult. The Wellesley-educated Wardlaw had been headmistress of girls' schools in Tennessee and Virginia, but left each institution in a hurry, with both the accounts and buildings in shambles.

Wardlaw's sisters lived with her, often wandering the halls in threes, popping up in students' rooms and scaring them half to death. In the sisters' quarters, the blinds were perpetually shut, keeping the interiors as dark as their inhabitants' mourning raiment. Sometimes, it was rumored, they went out at night to the cemetery to hold seances.

The stout, bespectacled Martin, the oldest sister, seemed to hold hypnotic sway over her kin. Her daughter, who had the given name Oceana, was offspring of a marriage to a Confederate army colonel. Ocey seemed bright and cheerful in school. But at age fifteen she suddenly withdrew from classes. Afterward, she never seemed to leave the presence of her family. She was put into an arranged marriage with her cousin and moved to New York City at twenty-one.

There, her mother introduced her to morphine. Ocey wasted away, rousing from her torpor to write melancholy letters and sign her name to a series of wills pushed in front of her. A month before her death, she told a neighbor: "Please take me away from here. They are starving me to death and they will not give me any medicine."

Caroline Martin insisted to anyone who would listen that she was a loving mother, and that Ocey was the one who starved herself. Her suicide may have been tragic, Martin said, but it was of Ocey's own free will. The mother denied being the author of the suicide notes, even though she seemed morbidly proud of them. "It is the custom of educated and refined people to leave notes upon committing suicide," she said. "The illiterate and unrefined rarely do."

Prosecutors in Essex County, New Jersey, were unmoved. How likely was it that Ocey Snead, a weak shell of a woman doped on morphine, would have the force of will to drown herself in a foot of icy water? Their theory was that Martin had planned Ocey's death to collect on the insurance at a time when the family urgently needed money. She had written several suicide notes as practice, always getting her weak and pliable daughter to sign them, before escorting her to a cold death. The family history suggested a precedent: One of Ocey's cousins had died back in Tennessee when his nightclothes caught fire. He had been heavily insured, and Wardlaw was the beneficiary.

Martin was outraged at the unchivalrousness of the whole thing when she and her sisters were put in jail on the charge of Ocey's murder. At pretrial hearings, she exploded in frequent outbursts, damning her own lawyers as "black-hearted Republicans" like the Yankee soldiers who had violated old Dixie. Her sister Wardlaw chose to drop out of the proceedings by committing suicide. She secretly hid the daily meals delivered to her jail cell and starved herself, dying on August 9, 1910.

The trial of Caroline Martin and Mary Snead ended before it could begin. On January 23, 1911, Martin accepted an offer to plead no contest to manslaughter. She admitted dosing her daughter with the morphine and putting her into the tub—but shouted, even as the judge tried to silence her, that the death was an accident. Mary Snead, whose part in the conspiracy was hard to prove, was let go with all charges dropped.

Martin lingered behind bars for two years before dying in the State Hospital for the Insane, where she'd been transferred after her ravings and self-destructive behavior grew more pronounced. No one could be certain if it was suicide or simple illness. But like her daughter, Ocey Snead, she was gone from her strange world of sorrows.

⇒ ILL WILL ⇐

FRANCES CREIGHTON, POISONER
1899–1936

AS HER LOVED ONES FELL SICK, one by one, young Frances Creighton was always there to help. With a show of tenderness she sat at their bedsides, nursing them with hot drinks and pudding. And with a look of disbelief, she pondered just why each patient ended up dying anyway.

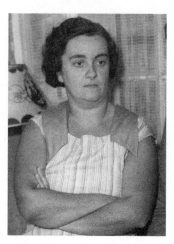

Frances Creighton in 1935, a decade after she escaped justice in the poisoning deaths of three family members. She would be executed months later for a fourth murder. (*New York Post*)

The neighbors in Newark had their own guesses about what killed Mrs. Creighton's mother-in-law, father-in-law, and brother between 1920 and 1923: deliberate poisoning. They were right, although it would take another decade and another victim to prove it.

The woman born Mary Frances Avery was plump and pale, with dark, hooded eyes and a face, one investigator later said, that looked like it "remembered an old sorrow." At fourteen she was orphaned and taken in by friends of the family, Walter and Anna Creighton. Their son, John, grew close to his young housemate. John and Frances married when both were nineteen.

The elder Creightons let the newlyweds live at their Newark home, but the honeymoon did not last. Frances was domineering, quarrelsome, and given to telling lies. This did not faze her spineless husband, who obeyed her orders with a "Yes, Fan." John's parents were made of sterner stuff. After the birth of Frances's daughter, Ruth, they chastised the young mother about the way she brought up her newborn. Dreadful scenes ensued.

A few days after everyone had seemingly kissed and made up, Frances insisted her mother-in-law try a cup of hot cocoa. Anna drank and became desperately ill. She lay in bed, vomiting and choking, for a week. By then she appeared to be recovering. But on December 1, 1920, Frances brought her a cup of coffee. The forty-seven-year-old woman gasped, unable to speak, and died with a look of terror on her face.

The Creightons' family doctor certified the cause of death as ptomaine poisoning. To neighbors, Frances said Anna got sick from eating a bad lobster salad.

If Walter Creighton ever had any suspicions about his wife's death, he never acted on them. But the following September, Mr. Creighton went to the Newark police to complain that his wallet had disappeared from home. Soon he was sick, too. He died on September 25, 1921, within forty-eight hours of being looked over by a doctor. Like his wife, he was forty-seven. John and Frances inherited the Creighton home, and the bulk of Walter's $9,868 estate.

Frances's teenaged brother, Charles Avery, who had long been under her thumb, now moved in with her. At Frances's urging, he bought a life insurance policy paying $1,000 and named her as sole beneficiary. At home, Charles scrubbed floors and tended to the toddler. Frances, pregnant with a second child, spent her afternoons holding tea socials. Neighborhood biddies tittered that her brother was the "maid."

Soon the gossips had more to talk about. Early in April 1923, Charles came down with agonizing stomach cramps. Frances had him confined to his bedroom and fed him coffee and chocolate pudding. A next-door neighbor eavesdropped as the teenager griped loudly about the awful taste. Then she heard John Creighton shout "No! N-o!" followed by Frances's laughter.

On April 20, about three weeks after coming down with his ailment, Charles died. He was eighteen. This time, the family doctor called for an autopsy. It found a fatal amount of arsenic. Both Frances and John were indicted on a charge of first-degree murder for causing the death of Charles Avery by poison.

But the case against the Creightons was deeply flawed. The Essex County prosecutor suspected Frances had spiked the pudding with a face powder made from arsenic, but could not find any such product. Her husband could not be tied to the poisonings at all. And Frances herself came across as the most sympathetic of defendants, a twenty-four-year-old mother still wearing mourning clothes. The trial in June 1923 lasted ten days, and the jury deliberated less than an hour. John and Frances Creighton were not guilty.

Within a few weeks, the authorities put Frances on trial a second time—this time for the murder of Anna Creighton. Her body had been exhumed along with Walter's, and trace amounts of arsenic had been found in it. (No charges were ever brought in Walter's death.) Fortunately for Frances, forensic science of that era was unreliable in proving arsenic poisoning, and she sat confidently throughout the trial. Only once did her wan countenance flush red—when it was revealed she had stolen the silk stockings intended to dress her mother-in-law's corpse. Nevertheless, she was acquitted again.

The Creightons were free but found Newark too hostile a place for them. By the 1930s, they were living in the Long Island, New York, town of Roosevelt, where few neighbors knew of their lurid past. It was an unusual living arrangement, even for Depression days. John Creighton had befriended a fellow World War I veteran named Everett Appelgate and invited him to live with him. Appelgate, his wife, Ada, and their daughter found room in a bungalow with all four Creightons.

In these cramped quarters, Everett Appelgate began an affair with Frances. It turned out, though, he was more interested in her daughter, Ruth, by now a pretty girl of fourteen. Appelgate bought her presents, drove her to school, and one night had sex with her. Frances knew of this illicit activity and chose to condone it. But Appelgate's wife, Ada, loudly complained—and, to one neighbor, confided the secret of Frances's "Jersey trouble." Within a few days, in September 1935, Ada was dead.

This time there was no confusion about what caused the death. An autopsy found ample evidence of arsenic, and Frances had just bought a household poison called Rough on Rats. Confronted by police, she admitted spooning the stuff into Ada's eggnog. Along the way, she blurted out a confession to killing her brother, Charles, back in 1923 because he was a "pervert." Appelgate was arrested as an accomplice, but Mr. Creighton was never charged.

Frances Creighton, who had borne up so well at her Newark trial, fainted in her cell on execution day, July 16, 1936. She had to be rolled into the Sing Sing death chamber on a wheelchair, strapped into the electric chair, and shocked into eternity while still unconscious. Appelgate followed to his own execution. Most likely, he was innocent of murder, but Creighton had insisted her lover was also her partner in crime—and this was enough to condemn him. So, even on her way out, she was able to take one more life with her.

❧ FALLEN IDOL ❦

GEORGE WHITE ROGERS, *MORRO CASTLE*
HERO AND KILLER
1899–1958

THE *Morro Castle*, THE FASTEST AND PROUDEST ocean liner making the Havana-to-New York run, was beating its way through a gale off the Jersey Shore when it went up in flames. The confused, blundering captain kept his vessel steaming into the wind, ensuring that the fire spread quickly. Crewmen abandoned ship without helping passengers. Ladies in evening gowns and men in tuxedos plunged screaming into the storm-tossed waters.

In those terrifying wee hours of September 8, 1934, one man kept his calm. Chief Radio Operator George White Rogers stayed at his post, tapping one SOS after another, even as the heat blistered his feet and turned his face a bright red. One hundred thirty-four people died in the conflagration of the *Morro Castle*, but many of the 320 survivors owed their lives to those distress calls.

Rogers won instant fame. His home city of Bayonne, New Jersey, gave him a gold medal, a vaudeville company invited him to tell his story on the stage, and a national radio association named him "Hero of the Year."

George White Rogers at the official inquest into the fire aboard the *Morro Castle*. Acclaimed as a hero for tapping out a desperate SOS, Rogers died in prison for a double murder. (*New York Post*)

But perhaps Rogers wasn't such a hero. Four years after his brave deeds, he tried to kill his boss with a package bomb. Later, he committed a double murder. Many historical sleuths now believe the *Morro Castle* fire was arson, and Rogers was the arsonist.

A nearly three hundred-pound man, Rogers had bad teeth, droopy lips, and gluttonous habits, like eating lemon rinds whole. In his hometown of Oakland, California, he was sent to a reformatory for being "unruly," and molested younger boys there. He enlisted in the Navy, where he was accused of several thefts. A 1920 explosion at the naval base in Newport, Rhode Island, injured Rogers and put him under suspicion of setting the blast himself. Nevertheless, he earned an honorable discharge.

Rogers had undeniable talent with a radio, and continued to serve in the merchant fleet. By 1934, he was chief radio operator aboard the *Morro Castle*, the pride of the Ward Line. It carried fun-loving passengers to the

After beaching off Asbury Park, the *Morro Castle* became a morbid tourist attraction. (*New York Post*)

swanky casinos of Havana, where they could party the Depression away night and day.

The evening of September 7, as the *Morro Castle* was on its return leg to New York, Captain Robert Wilmott died of an apparent heart attack. The first officer, William Warms, found himself in command of the ship just as it headed into the strong northeast gale. Then, at 2:15 A.M., as the *Morro Castle* was off Sea Girt, black smoke was seen pouring from a cabinet in the "B" deck writing room.

Rogers, who was not on watch, took initiative by rushing to the radio shack. There, he wrapped a wet towel around his massive head and repeatedly tapped out an SOS on the radio keys. This was all done without an order from the new captain, Warms, whose own decision to stay the course fanned the flames and made the disaster worse.

As panic swept the ship, many passengers—still woozy with drink—choked to death on smoke or burned up while trapped in their cabins. Those able to escape ended up freezing, and sometimes drowning, in the rough ocean. Bodies washed ashore from Belmar to Manasquan, and the charred hulk of the Morro Castle beached off Asbury Park, where it became a morbid tourist attraction.

Rogers was one of the last survivors to be picked up by rescue vessels. The Federal Bureau of Investigation, fully aware of his sketchy past, investigated whether he might have set the fire. But this never came out publicly, and the portly crewman was showered with kudos for his heroism. An official inquiry failed to determine a cause for the fire; the leading theory was that the varnish-soaked cabinet was ignited by sparks from a nearby smokestack.

Rogers, his fifteen minutes of fame over, started a radio repair shop. It burned down in an unsolved arson. Then he got a job as radio technician for the Bayonne Police Department. There, he grew resentful of his superior, Lt. Vincent Doyle, and jealous for a promotion. The cops on the beat took an immediate dislike to the new hire, with his immense waistline and bigger ego.

In 1938, Rogers left a package on Doyle's desk and stepped out to "mail a letter." Doyle opened his gift and was knocked over by an explosion that blew three fingers off his hand. Rogers was convicted and drew a twelve- to twenty-year sentence. After just three years, World War II intervened and he was granted parole so he could serve in the undermanned merchant marine.

Rogers later opened another electronics repair shop in Bayonne, and lost money. He and his wife were loners, but they did have two neighbor friends: eighty-three-year-old William Hummel and Hummel's unmarried daughter, Edith, fifty-eight. The old man had lent Rogers more than $7,000 to help him with his business. On June 19, 1953, with Rogers in the car with him, Hummel drove to his bank and withdrew $2,400. It was the last time anyone saw him alive.

On July 2, police walked into the Hummel home to find father and daughter murdered, their skulls bashed in with a hammer. The bodies had been lying there—Mr. Hummel downstairs, his daughter upstairs—for two weeks. Rogers's sloppiness proved his undoing. He had worn the same pair of pants for years, and those trousers now had telltale bloodstains on them. Rogers went on trial yet again, this time for the murder of the Hummels, and was given two life sentences.

No sooner had the cell doors clanged behind him at Trenton State Prison than dogged researchers began to rewrite the history of the *Morro Castle*. Doyle, the police lieutenant wounded by Rogers's bomb, was first to put forward the theory that his antagonist set the liner ablaze. He had the opportunity, he had the pyromaniacal background, and he had a motive: to make himself into a hero. Several authors have embraced this theory. Some even believe Captain Wilmott's death was no heart attack, but an act of poisoning by Rogers.

Rogers went to his grave claiming to be the hero of the *Morro Castle*. But before he died in prison in 1958, he could not resist muddying up this story. To one of his fellow inmates, he confided: "No one will ever know what happened on that ship."

❧ WITH A VENGEANCE ❧

HOWARD UNRUH, RAMPAGE MURDERER
1921–

ON THE MORNING HE SETTLED ALL HIS SCORES, Howard Unruh dressed up in a brown, tropical worsted suit, straightened his neat little bow tie, and loaded a clip of bullets into a Luger pistol. Behind him in his Camden, New Jersey, apartment he left two documents he'd been poring over. One was a Bible, left open to St. Matthew's exhortation: "Ye shall hear of wars and rumors of wars: See that ye be not troubled." The other was a list of neighbors, who, Unruh was certain, were laughing at him behind his back. Next to each name he had written the notation "retal," for retaliate.

Unruh, a quiet, lanky man of twenty-eight who lived with his mother, was about to begin America's first gun rampage in which the shooter targeted complete strangers. It was September 6, 1949, and within twenty minutes thirteen people would be dead or dying.

A combat veteran of World War II, Unruh knew how to kill expertly. He had achieved marksman status in the Army, and as a civilian he took

After Howard Unruh's murder of thirteen neighbors, Camden police found this photograph of him with his fondest possessions. "I'd have killed a thousand if I'd had bullets enough," he said.

his Luger to the basement every day for target practice. Before turning the neighborhood into a killing ground, Unruh had reconnoitered it thoroughly. He carried extra ammunition and had determined the optimal time to begin: 9:30 A.M., when the shopkeepers of River Avenue would be opening for business. His first bullet was aimed at a bread deliveryman, sitting in a parked truck. It was a wild shot, and missed. Unruh's aim got better as he went on.

John Pilarchik, twenty-seven, was first to die. He was busily at work in his shoe repair shop when two bullets cut him down. The second and third victims were next door in a barbershop. The barber, Clark Hoover, thirty-three, was giving a back-to-school haircut to a six-year-old boy, who sat smiling on a hobby horse when Unruh stepped inside. "I've got something for you, Clarkie," Unruh said, then fired twice. Haircutter and boy fell dead almost simultaneously.

Ignoring the screams of the boy's mother, Unruh left. He next zeroed in on the neighbors at the top of his enemies list, the Cohens. They owned a pharmacy and lived above the shop, next door to Unruh. The previous day, they had taken down a gate in their backyard that allowed him access to his own house. This so enraged Unruh that he later claimed it set off his murder spree.

Unruh walked to the drugstore and shot to death a man standing in the doorway—"He didn't get out of my way" was the killer's later explanation. Unruh then fatally shot Maurice Cohen, thirty-nine; wife Rose, thirty-eight; and Maurice's sixty-three-year-old mother, Minnie, who dropped as she ran for a telephone upstairs. Twelve-year-old Charles Cohen saved himself by hiding in a closet.

Reloading his Luger, Unruh stepped outside in search of new prey. He fired at a woman who was hanging laundry in her backyard with her son, hitting them both with nonfatal wounds. A motorist slowed to witness the carnage; Unruh poked his pistol into the man's open window and shot him dead. Then he walked to another car stopped at a red light. Three shots through the windshield instantly killed the woman behind the wheel and her sixty-six-year-old mother, and left the driver's twelve-year-old son dying.

As the sound of gunfire reverberated up and down River Avenue, shock gave way to hysteria. Men and women ran through the streets screaming, while store owners barricaded themselves inside. "He's killing everyone!" someone shouted from a window. A bar owner stepped outside with his own pistol and shot Unruh in the buttocks. The killer reacted as if he'd been bitten by a gnat, and kept going.

Next, Unruh stormed the tailor shop owned by another man on his hit list, Thomas Zegrino. The tailor was away on business, but Zegrino's twenty-nine-year-old wife of three weeks, Helga, was there. She died from a single shot.

Unruh walked outside and fired one last bullet—at a two-year-old boy looking at him through a window. The boy died, becoming the thirteenth and final life taken in the Camden massacre. Then the gunman heard sirens and went home.

From the number of casualties, the police assumed that an army of killers was on the loose. Gingerly they made their way to the Unruh house. Officers aimed shotguns and rifles at his second-story room and barked orders for his surrender. Unruh's phone rang. It was the editor of the *Camden Evening Courier*, who had found the shooter's name in the phone book.

"I want to know what they're doing to you down there," the editor said.

"They haven't done anything to me," Unruh said. "I'm doing plenty to them."

"How many have you killed?"

"I don't know. It looks like a pretty good score."

Unruh hung up with an "I'm busy" as a can of tear gas flew through his window. He stepped out, hands up and unarmed. At the police station, he gave the district attorney a blow-by-blow account of whom he'd killed and how. Only after he had been sitting at a desk for several minutes did the investigators notice a trickle of blood from where he'd been shot by the tavern owner.

For years, Unruh had concealed his murderous rage behind a pair of glasses and a shy, unassuming demeanor. Just like practically every future rampage gunman for whom he set the mold, he kept to himself. He went to the Lutheran church every Sunday and read his dog-eared Bible over and over. As a hobby he collected model trains, and guns. The Luger he used to slaughter his neighbors was a war souvenir he bought at a local shop.

Unruh had seen war and served his country honorably. Fellow soldiers in his tank unit remembered one thing odd about him. Every time he saw the corpse of a German, he wrote an entry in his diary describing it in morbid detail.

After returning home from the Army, he became increasingly withdrawn, silent, and enigmatic. He noticed odd and quizzical glances from his neighbors, which convinced him they were having laughs at his expense. Unruh, who never had a girlfriend, was certain his neighbors were "thinking of him as a homosexual," according to a later psychiatric report.

Without a job, he sat at home nursing his grudges. The night before his attack, he finished scribbling the "retal" list. He also went to a movie theater in Philadelphia, where he sat through a double feature and got the idea that Barbara Stanwyck was one of his persecutors.

Clearly he was deranged, but his deed was confounding to a public not familiar with the modern-day mass murderer. His family insisted Unruh's mania was a product of his war experience. But the psychiatrists found his mental breakdown was more gradual, with no single cause. They diagnosed him with "dementia praecox," or severe paranoid delusions, and ruled him mentally unfit for trial.

Unruh was not particularly pleased by the turn of events that saved him from the electric chair. He insisted on his own sanity. Unruh's rationale: he had many enemies, was not certain who they were, and found it was better to kill everyone to be sure his enemies died, too. "I'd have killed a thousand if I'd had bullets enough," he said calmly.

Unruh never went to trial, but he never went free, either. Into his late eighties, he remained locked up in Trenton Psychiatric Hospital, a senile, white-haired patient who read from a Bible and muttered passages to himself.

☞ BADMAN ☜

ERNEST INGENITO, MASS KILLER
1924–1995

IT HAD BEEN A YEAR SINCE Howard Unruh's massacre on the streets of Camden, and the last place expecting the madness to repeat itself was the placid region of South Jersey scrub forest and fruit orchards just twenty miles south. But on November 17, 1950, the pleasantly named hamlet of Piney Hollow echoed to the explosion of pistol fire as another lone gunman went rampaging. By the time he was finished, five innocents lay dead.

Ernest Ingenito worked in a television repair shop, but the technology that truly fascinated him was guns. The husky hothead, twenty-six, had accumulated quite the collection of them since being dishonorably discharged from the Army for fighting. His rages—he once beat up a short-order cook for burning his toast—and his persistent affairs broke up Ingenito's marriage.

Ernest Ingenito spent twenty-six years in prison for the rampage killings of five people in 1950. He is shown here in 1994 after he went back to jail for child sex abuse. (*The Trentonian* / Emma Lee)

That summer of 1950, wife Theresa left him and moved back in with her parents, who owned a truck farm a few miles away. Ernie seethed over being denied visits to his children, a baby and a two-year-old. Calls to various lawyers were no use. One fateful Friday night, he piled his arsenal—a carbine, a Mauser, a Luger, and a .32-caliber revolver—into a Ford sedan and roared off toward the in-laws' home.

Theresa opened the door and tried to shoo her husband away. "Do you love me?" he asked, but got no response. He went back to his car, strapped the Luger and .32 to his belt and stormed back inside. "You don't want me to see the kids? This is what you get!" he shouted triumphantly. Theresa ran to protect the children—the baby in a crib, the toddler cowering in a bathroom. But Ernie shot her before she could get there. The petite, pretty woman fell—dead, he thought. In fact, the bullet had hit her in the shoulder and she lived. He never went after the kids.

Theresa's parents were not so lucky. Ernie had come to hate them as much as his wife, blaming them for the failed marriage. He shot his father-in-law, Michael Mazzoli, forty-four, to death in the dining room. Theresa's mother, Pearl, forty-five, ran screaming out the back door, bound for her own parents' home next door. Ernie came racing after her. By now, he had decided that every last member of the Mazzoli family deserved to die.

The sequence of killings in the home of Theresa's grandparents was unclear in the confusion and hysteria. Five people were shot. Ernie hunted Pearl Mazzoli to her hiding place in a closet and shot her "full of holes," as he later bragged. Pearl's mother, Theresa Pioppi, seventy-two, was gunned down nearby. John Pioppi, forty-six, Theresa's uncle, came at the gunman with a knife; Ingenito coolly shot him down. John's sister-in-law, Marion, twenty-eight, fell dead in the living room. Only one shooting victim in the Mazzoli house survived: Marion's nine-year-old daughter, Jean.

It was 9:30 P.M., and Ernie Ingenito's bloodlust was far from sated. He got back into his Ford and drove two miles to the town of Minotola, home of his wife's other uncle and aunt. With the shout, "I cleaned out the rest of the family. I came here to get you," Ernie stormed the house. Hilda and Frank Mazzoli fell, badly but not mortally wounded. For once showing mercy, the shooter spared their children and drove away.

By then, the alert had gone out for a mad gunman, and dozens of New Jersey troopers were hitting the highways. Just after 1 A.M., police halted Ingenito's car at a roadblock. He made a weak effort to slice one of his wrists with a tin can lid before being handcuffed. By his arraignment at daybreak, Ingenito had calmed down. He told the judge: "I did it. I don't want to talk anymore."

Prosecutors wanted to send him to the electric chair for five murders. But in January 1951, a jury recommended mercy after hearing evidence that Ingenito may have suffered from mental illness. There was no provision for life imprisonment without parole at the time, so Ingenito was able to earn his freedom twenty-four years later.

Utterly remorseless, even proud of being a mass murderer, he moved to Trenton and resumed his violent behavior. He took a liking to the eight-year-old daughter of one girlfriend and subjected the child to a regular ordeal of rape. To intimidate her, he would pull out a favorite true crime book—Jay Robert Nash's *Bloodletters and Badmen*—and flip to the three pages devoted to him. Eventually, however, this girl found the courage to report Ingenito to the authorities. At age seventy, he was put back in his natural habitat of prison, and died there a year later.

❧ OLD WOUNDS ☙

ROBERT ZARINSKY, SERIAL KILLER
1940–

A COLD, PUNISHING RAIN WAS FALLING on the night eighteen-year-old Robert Zarinsky staggered home, drenched and oozing blood from his thigh. With him was cousin Theodore Schiffer, wounded even more badly in the chest. Under the light of a single bulb, Zarinsky's mother used a pair of tweezers and a tongue depresser to dig bullets out of the two youths. How did they get the injuries? Robert was asked, and he smiled. "I shot a cop," he said. "I got pissed off 'cause he shot Teddy."

It was November 28, 1958, the day that Rahway, New Jersey, police officer Charles Bernoskie died shooting it out with two unknown burglars at a Pontiac dealership. The next morning's headlines were full of the story, and they made Robert's father, Julius, throw up back home in the neighboring city of Linden. But Veronica, the domineering matriarch of the Zarinsky household, announced: "Nobody's to know of this." The order to maintain silence also fell upon the other Zarinsky child, sixteen-year-old Judith, who had watched as her two relatives underwent their crude surgeries. She agreed to take the secret to the grave.

Really, there was no choice. Robert was mom's enforcer, with Judith as his personal punching bag. He was big brother in more than age: a fanatic for weightlifting, he packed two hundred pounds of muscle onto a five-foot-six body. He called himself a Nazi, enjoyed setting fires, and fantasized about becoming dictator of New Jersey. One school psychiatrist wrote that he "seeks to gain status and prove his masculinity by association with delinquent groups."

In the 1960s, Robert Zarinsky married and inherited his father's produce business. But he never settled down. The young man liked to cruise in a ragtop convertible, often stopping to chat up teenaged girls. On August 11, 1969, two twelve-year-olds in Atlantic Highlands, New Jersey, reported that a car pulled up to them and a beefy man with muttonchop

Robert Zarinsky became the
first man in New Jersey history
to be convicted of murder without
the victim's body being found.
(New Jersey Department of Corrections)

sideburns tried to pick them up. Two weeks later, on August 25, Rosemary Calandriello vanished.

She was seventeen, and had stepped out barefoot from her Atlantic Highlands home on a scorching afternoon to buy some ice pops. She was last seen getting into a convertible with a sideburned driver who matched the description given by the twelve-year-olds. Fortunately, those girls had thought to write down the license plate number of the stranger, and this number was Zarinsky's. A search of his convertible was enough to make the cops shiver. The inside door handles had been pulled off and lay under the seats—a perfect setup to trap a passenger. Also in the car was a pair of panties and a bloody hammer.

But Rosemary's body never turned up, and the police decided that if you didn't have a corpse, you didn't have a case. Frustrated, they sent the evidence from Zarinsky's car to the FBI labs to see if the experts could make anything of it. The feds made a startling discovery: a hair on the bloody hammer belonged not to Rosemary, but to another seventeen-year-old girl named Linda Balabanow. She had disappeared five months before Rosemary, and her body ended up in the Raritan River. She had been choked to death with an electrical wire, still knotted around her neck.

The police were certain Zarinsky did it. But forensic science was in its infancy, and the detectives didn't think the hair match-up was solid enough. As they hesitated, bodies kept turning up, always an hour's drive from the Zarinsky home in Linden. Ann Logan, nineteen, was found sexually assaulted and strangled in 1973. The following year, two bodies were found next to each other on a dirt road: Joanne Delardo, fifteen, and Donna Carlucci, fourteen.

"We have to get this guy off the streets," one prosecutor seethed after this last discovery. Desperate, the Monmouth County authorities used what circumstantial evidence they had to indict Zarinsky for the six-year-old Rosemary disappearance. They caught a lucky break. Putting Zarinsky in jail created new evidence, for soon he was confiding to jail informers about how he could make bodies disappear into the ocean. He was found guilty in Monmouth County court in April 1975. It was the first time in New Jersey history that a man was convicted of murder without a corpse.

Prosecutors could not pin any of the other teen murders on Zarinsky. They had not even thought to connect him to the shooting of Officer Bernoskie. Then came the spring of 1999. Zarinsky, still serving a ninety-eight-years-to-life sentence, complained he wasn't getting the inheritance from his recently deceased mother. Serial killer or not, he was the rightful owner. Thousands of dollars had been drained from his accounts, and Zarinsky blamed his sister, Judith, for it.

Judith was questioned on suspicion of fraud. In her quest for leniency, she let spill that forty-year-old family secret. She told police about Robert's boast about shooting Officer Bernoskie back in 1958, and told the police where they could find the bullet scar on him. Police went to Zarinsky's cousin, Theodore Schiffer, and he admitted his part in the deadly burglary. The coldest case in Rahway police records, so cold it was practically forgotten, was suddenly solved.

In the spring of 2001, Zarinsky went on trial for murder. He was now sixty-one and likely to stay in prison for the rest of his life, no matter the outcome of this trial. The prosecutors, and Bernoskie's family, simply wanted an old wrong to be righted.

It was not to be. During the long gap between crime and prosecution, fingerprints and other key evidence from the burgled car dealership were lost. The jury reached a verdict of not guilty, even as several members of the panel made disgusted faces. They thought he was the killer, but weren't convinced beyond a reasonable doubt.

❧ SEEING THE DEVIL ❧

THOMAS TRANTINO, COP KILLER
1938–

THIRTY-EIGHT YEARS BEHIND BARS. Nine parole applications denied. By the time Thomas Trantino left prison in 2001, he had achieved these totals, both of them unsurpassed by any other inmate in the New Jersey penal system. It is harder to quantify emotion, but Trantino was probably also the most despised cop killer in state history. What could one man do to earn such hatred?

August 26, 1963, was a day that would echo painfully for years afterward in the working-class town of Lodi, New Jersey. The Angel Lounge, on the "Sin Strip" of Route 46, was throbbing all night with raucous laughter, excited shouting, and blaring music. On two occasions a pair of patrol officers showed up, asking the bartender to keep things quiet. At 2:30 A.M. came a report of more noise: gunshots. The same two policemen, Peter Voto and Gary Tedesco, arrived at the door. No one had been shot; it was just a drunk showing off, firing into the floor. "How many times do I have to come here?" the beefy, no-nonsense Voto asked.

Inside the Angel Lounge were three low-level hoodlums and four young female hangers-on. Trantino, twenty-six, was there to celebrate the score of his life. This Brooklyn kid with a hawklike nose and a pimply face had become a heroin addict at fifteen and a convicted robber at twenty-one. In prison, he acquired a nickname—"Rabbi Tom," because of his mixed Jewish-Italian parentage—and a future partner in crime, Frank Falco. After Trantino's release, he got married, had a baby, and fell promptly back into his old career as a stickup man. Before heading to the Angel Lounge, he, Falco, and a cohort had robbed $2,000 in cash and jewelry from a Brooklyn apartment.

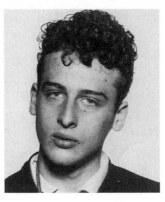

Thomas Trantino in his mug shot after he and a cohort murdered two police officers. He was turned down for parole a record nine times. (New York Police Department)

Ten whiskey cocktails later, Trantino was feeling invincible. He was the one who had been showing off with his .38-caliber revolver, heedless of the dangerous attention it would bring. He was still on parole and was known by the New York Police Department as a menace. The others, Falco and Anthony Cassarino, were wanted for a loanshark murder in Manhattan.

The two cops checked Cassarino's identification and, not realizing they had a criminal in their hands, let him leave the bar. Then Voto saw a gun wrapped in a towel on the bar. No one would give a straight answer about who owned it, so he asked his partner, Tedesco, to call for backup. Voto, a forty-year-old veteran sergeant, found himself at severe disadvantage. Tedesco, twenty-two, was a probationary officer and did not carry a gun. Trantino was armed and willing to kill.

Voto felt the barrel of a gun press the back of his head and an arm slip around his neck. "Don't move or you're dead!" Trantino shouted. He pistol-whipped Voto so viciously that the gun's plastic grip broke apart. Falco then grabbed the immobilized sergeant's service pistol and trained it on Tedesco.

"Strip!" the gunmen shouted. It was a technique they used in get-aways: force the victim to undress, slowing his pursuit. The cops complied, getting on their knees and pulling their shirts off. But an impatient Trantino made a split-second decision to commit cold-blooded murder. He fired two shots into Voto's head and one into his back, shouting ecstatically: "We are going for broke! We are burning all the way!" Falco joined in the slaughter, cutting down the helpless, nearly naked Tedesco.

The murderers made it out of the Angel Lounge and fled to New York City. Two days later, New York detectives tracked Falco, twenty-five, to a Midtown hotel and shot him to death in his room. According to the official version, they had no choice: he threw a bottle at the arresting officer and grabbed for the cop's gun. Trantino heard this news and made the decision that night to save his own skin. Accompanied by a lawyer and a reporter, he walked into a police station and surrendered.

The murder trial of Thomas Trantino took place the following February. The women at the bar, including Trantino's mistress, all identified him as Voto's killer. Trantino himself took the stand to claim he couldn't remember a thing. One of his few memories from the Angel Lounge was an explosion in his ear, and a kaleidoscope of colors. "I saw Falco . . . he looked like a devil," Trantino said.

The jury found Trantino guilty of first-degree murder, with no recommendation for mercy, and a judge sentenced him to die in the electric chair. But the death penalty was becoming a thing of the past. Judges granted every stay of execution that Trantino sought. Finally, in 1972, the New Jersey Supreme Court invalidated the state's capital punishment law. Trantino's death judgment became a life term. Under sentencing guidelines, he was eligible for parole in 1980—after just seventeen years behind bars.

The lucky prisoner prepared himself for life on the outside, studying for a college degree in education and psychology. He published a book of his writings, *Lock the Lock*, sprinkled with primal scream poetry and such laments as: "I don't know my son / I don't know where all my sperm has gone." To interviewers, he insisted he was innocent. He expected to be released from prison as his due. Relatives of the slain Lodi police officers girded for a fight. Supported by police fraternal groups throughout the United States, they helped convince the New Jersey Parole Board not to grant Trantino parole on his first try. Or his second. Or his third through ninth attempts.

It was an older, wiser Trantino who pursued parole throughout the 1990s. This time, he claimed to be remorseful and admitted he carried out the cop killings—even though he said he didn't remember them. He told of the counseling work he was doing with younger convicts in the prison system, discouraging them from drugs and violence, and holding himself up as a cautionary tale.

The parole board would not free him, but in 2001 the state Supreme Court did—ruling that political pressure was arbitrarily keeping Trantino locked up. For the Lodi families, it was a stunning defeat. No one felt it more bitterly than Voto's brother Andrew, who had become the Lodi police chief. He said he had one vow for the killer: "Trantino, I hate your guts and I'll follow you to the grave."

❧ SPELLBINDING ❧

CARL COPPOLINO, POISONER
1932–

GAUNT AND BEAK-NOSED, with hollow, brooding eyes, Dr. Carl Coppolino did not look the part of the sixties swinger. The reason he cast such a hypnotic spell on women was simple: he was a hypnotist. But the young doctor from Middletown Township, New Jersey, pursued more than just sexual conquests, one cast-off mistress said. He also used his spellbinding skills to murder.

As an anesthesiologist at Riverview Hospital in Red Bank, Coppolino had a promising career that went off track due to his unbalanced behavior. Jealous of a nurse, he wrote notes threatening to mutilate her. Hospital administrators wanted to fire him, but in early 1963 he beat them to the punch by retiring on disability insurance. He claimed to have coronary disease. It later turned out that he took digitalis, a drug that mimics the symptoms of heart attacks.

A retiree at age thirty-one, Coppolino did not lack for income. He had studied hypnosis, and wrote paperbacks promoting this method as

Dr. Carl Coppolino and his second wife, Mary, celebrate after his acquittal for murder in Freehold in December 1966. He was not so lucky at a second trial. (*New York Post* / Terence McCarten)

a means of weight loss and quitting smoking. Furthermore, his wife, Carmela, was an M.D. herself and earned a good living doing research at the pharmaceutical manufacturer Hoffman-La Roche. Carl stayed home with their two children. To alleviate the tedium, he pursued a hobby of suburban men everywhere: chasing after a neighbor's wife.

The wife was Marjorie Farber, who lived across the road from him in Middletown. Eighteen years older than Carl, but still attractive, she let the doctor hypnotize her so she could kick her cigarette habit. This turned into a full-blown affair. Carmela turned a blind eye to the cheating. Marge's husband, a fifty-two-year-old retired Army officer named William Farber, was apparently not so approving. But we'll never know for sure. On July 30, 1963, he died in his bed.

Carmela, believing Carl's explanation that Farber had died of a heart attack, filled out the death certificate, identifying the cause of death as a heart attack. The following year, the Coppolinos moved to Sarasota, Florida—and Marge followed them there.

The love triangle became a quadrilateral when Carl began romancing not just Marge but a thirty-eight-year-old divorcee, Mary Gibson. Carmela confided to her father that Carl had asked for a divorce and that she refused him. Not long after this came tragedy. At 6:00 in the morning on August 28, 1965, Carl made an urgent call to a doctor friend. Carmela was dead. The death certificate listed this as a heart attack, too.

Coppolino was now free to take up the lover of his choice, Mary Gibson or Marge Farber. He chose Mary, wedding her just twenty-two days after his first wife's death. This looked like an astute match, for Mary had a sizeable income from investments and was good with Carl's children. At least, it might have been astute, had the marriage not sent a jilted Marge into a rage.

This woman scorned went to police with an incredible tale. Neither Colonel Farber nor Carmela Coppolino had died natural deaths, Marge said; they had been murdered. She identified Coppolino as the killer in both cases. Back in 1963, he had been an accomplice in her own husband's death. Coppolino had given her a muscle relaxant used in surgery, whose name she couldn't remember, and a syringe. He had told Marge this substance would kill by paralyzing the lungs, and urged her to stick the needle in William Farber's leg while he slept.

Mesmerized by his hypnotism, she complied, but the injection succeeded only in making her husband violently ill. Coppolino came to the home, under the guise of treating William for a heart attack, and gave him another shot. This did nothing, either, and the doctor muttered: "He is a hard one to kill." Then he took a pillow and smothered the colonel to death.

Mrs. Coppolino had probably died the same way, Marge said, either poisoned, smothered, or both. The authorities found it hard to believe. But the elements of Marge's story held up. Coppolino had in fact requested vials of succinylcholine, a muscle relaxant, from a hospital where he used to work. He had done so twice, once just before Farber's death, and again just before Carmela's. He had given a dubious story for the purchases: the drugs were for experiments on cats. His infidelities gave him plenty of motive to have both victims out of the way. He also had a $65,000 insurance policy on Carmela.

Investigators quietly exhumed both bodies, first Carmela from her grave in Boonton, New Jersey, then Colonel Farber from Arlington National Cemetery, for new autopsies. Carmela's body showed a hypodermic needle track in her left buttock, but no trace of poison. On Farber's corpse, examiners found a double fracture of the larynx, evidence of strangulation. Coppolino was indicted for murder.

Coppolino attended his trial, held in December 1966 in the Monmouth County courthouse in Freehold, wearing a sharkskin suit and a cocky smile. His confidence was well placed, for his defense lawyer was the flamboyant, feisty F. Lee Bailey. Just months before, Bailey had won acquittal for Sam Sheppard, another famous doctor accused of murdering his wife. He aggressively challenged every bit of medical evidence, suggesting that Farber's larynx damage might have been caused by the shovels of undertakers.

Bailey also slashed away at the state's star witness, Marge Farber. Her claim of hypnosis was dubious, he said, and she exuded a hateful jealousy for Coppolino. "She wants this man so badly that she would sit on his lap in the electric chair while somebody pulled the switch, just to make sure he dies," Bailey growled.

In just over four hours, the Freehold jury reached its verdict: not guilty. Coppolino was now bound over for a second trial, in Florida, but his odds looked even better there. Prosecutors had evidence of physical violence in the Farber murder, and a witness. For the death of Mrs. Coppolino they had neither. Succinylcholine was indeed a virtually untraceable drug, as the doctor had told Marge. Once absorbed by the blood, it breaks down into succinic acid and choline, two chemicals naturally present in the body.

To the rescue of prosecutors came Dr. Milton Helpern, chief medical examiner of New York City. Helpern's staff of chemists spent months analyzing the presence of the poison's two natural components before confirming there were abnormal levels of it in Carmela Coppolino's brain. It was the first autopsy in medical history to name succinylcholine as a cause of death.

On April 28, 1967, the Florida jury found Dr. Coppolino guilty. It was a curious verdict: he was convicted of murder in the second degree, not the first. Second-degree murder is supposed to apply to crimes that are not premeditated. Carmela's poisoning had been a cold-blooded deed. The jury, uncertain of the medical facts, compromised.

Coppolino served thirteen years in a Florida prison before parole was granted, on the condition that he never resume the practice of medicine again. At least the doctor knew how to heal himself. His supposedly weak heart defied medical science, growing stronger over the years and enabling him to live well into old age.

❖ FAMILY MAN ❖

JOHN LIST, MASS KILLER
1925–

"MILD-MANNERED ACCOUNTANT"—the phrase could have been invented to describe John Emil List, a man who stared at rows of numbers every day through thick glasses, barely looking up from his desk. At home in Westfield, New Jersey, he timidly shrank from contact with the neighbors, people who laughed at his habit of wearing suit and tie whenever he went outdoors, even to mow the lawn. Wouldn't he show them all. On November 9, 1971, this mild-mannered accountant murdered his wife, three children, and mother, then vanished into a new identity for seventeen years.

Westfield, a pleasant and peaceful commuter town, came to be so identified with its most infamous event that local wags called it "Listfield." But the Lists ended up there only by happenstance. Originally from a small town in Michigan, John List bopped from one corporate middle-management job to another. In 1965, he caught what he thought was the break of his life when a bank in Jersey City hired him as vice president. The family savings went into buying their dream home, a rambling,

John Emil List with wife, Helen, and children (from left) Patricia, John, and Frederick a few months before he shot them all and vanished into a new life.

nineteen-room Victorian mansion. This was one of the many quaint if shabby old estates that gave Westfield such charm, and inspired one of the town's most famous citizens, cartoonist Charles Addams, to draw the setting for his *Addams Family.*

The List family, if less outwardly morbid than Addams's creation, came to have its troubles too. John's wife, Helen, had been infected with syphilis by her first husband, and the ravages of the disease often left her bedridden. John's aging mother, Alma, moved into a spare room, creating endless friction with a daughter-in-law she despised.

The three kids were healthy enough. But eldest daughter, Patty, was a bit of a rebel, by her dad's standards anyway, because she liked to write folk songs and bring home long-haired boyfriends. The two boys, John F. and Frederick, were good-natured and obedient, often in their Scout uniforms. But they were two extra mouths to feed, and John List was having a hard time making ends meet.

After only a year at the bank, List was fired. He set up his own financial planning business at home, but his icy personality did not attract clients. By 1971, he was three months behind on his mortgage and the creaking Victorian was falling into disrepair. Meanwhile, the generation gap between father and daughter got worse with her talk about going into an acting career. John List, whose one social outlet was to teach Sunday school at the Lutheran church, thought this was akin to her becoming a prostitute.

At age forty-seven, at a bumpy crossroads in life that some men might experience as a midlife crisis, John List decided to kill his entire family. It was no rash deed; he apparently began planning the massacre in May 1971 and waited six months to strike. Mass murder would serve the dual purpose of shedding List's money burden and ensuring that all his kids' souls were saved. He figured that they were still young, relatively innocent, and likely to go to heaven. With impeccable logic he decided to spare himself execution. As a killer, he needed to redeem his sins before dying.

At 7 A.M. on the cold day of November 7, List saw the children off to school. At 8 A.M., he walked up to his wife, Helen, forty-five, who was having toast and coffee over the breakfast table. She said, "Good morning." He pulled a 9mm German-made Steyr pistol and shot her in the face. Then he walked up to Alma, eighty-five, who was still lying in bed. She barely had time to ask what that noise was downstairs before he shot her, too.

The house was vast, with thick walls, and no neighbor heard the echoing gunfire. Now List went to work covering his tracks. He wrote notes to the kids' schools explaining they would be gone to visit relatives in North Carolina. He had the post office stop delivering mail. He drove to his dead mother's bank and cashed out her bonds.

One by one, as the kids came home from school, their father was waiting for them. Patty, sixteen, arrived first, dismissed early from Westfield High because she felt ill. John shot her in the jaw as she walked into the house through a side entrance. Frederick arrived next, and was killed with a head shot. John List's aim was not quite as steady on his oldest son and namesake. The younger John saw danger coming and ducked the first shot, but his father killed him with nine bullets.

List dragged his youngest four victims into the house's ballroom and laid them out on the floor, tucked into sleeping bags. Alma's body stayed upstairs because John found her big-boned body too heavy to carry.

The killer then typed a series of explanatory notes and left them behind on a desk. Each letter wrapped the deed in self-pitying sanctimony. To his pastor, List wrote that "I wasn't earning anywhere near enough to support us." He went on: "I leave myself in the hands of God's justice and mercy. I don't doubt that He is able to help us, but apparently he saw fit not to answer my prayers the way I had hoped that they would be answered. This makes me think that perhaps it was for the best as far as the children's souls are concerned."

John List slept one last night in this house filled with corpses, then drove off the next morning to disappear.

Owing to List's preventive measures and an uncurious community, the bodies were not discovered for another month. A neighbor, who had seen the Lists' lights slowly winking off as the bulbs burned out, finally called the police on December 7. Patrol officers arrived to shine flashlights over the massacre scene, made all the more gruesome by hymnal music still playing from a radio.

The police knew who did it. But where did John List go? Investigators mailed "Wanted" posters across the nation, to nothing but dead ends. The murder house turned into a ghoulish tourist attraction, invaded periodically at night by thrill-seeking teens, until an arsonist torched it.

It was not until 1989 that the John List case was cracked by an episode of the television show *America's Most Wanted*, which featured a sculptor's bust showing what an older List might look like. A woman in Colorado recognized this man as an old neighbor named Robert P. Clark, who had since moved to Midlothian, Virginia. FBI agents found Clark there on June 1 and held him for the outstanding New Jersey murder warrant.

While authorities had been following leads in Europe and South America, John List had resumed life as an accountant here in America. He stole the name Robert Clark from an old college classmate, flew to Denver, and began a new life in a cheap trailer park. He was careful to fly under the radar of government record bureaus by not buying a car or a house. In 1985, List married a woman he met at a church social who knew nothing of his homicidal past and thought his first wife had died of cancer. They never had children.

For a time, Robert Clark denied he was John List, a claim he went on making even after a fingerprint match proved he was lying. Eventually, his defense strategy switched tactics. The lead lawyer argued that List's hypocritical notes pleading poverty proved he cared for his family and killed them "with love in his heart."

Jurors intently listened to this, then found John List guilty of first-degree murder. Locked away for five consecutive life terms, List grew increasingly happy in prison because it was such a safe, orderly place. Approaching eighty, John List told a TV interviewer he fully expected to go to heaven and was looking forward to joining his family there.

➤ MAD WORLD ◄

JOSEPH KALLINGER, SERIAL KILLER
1936–1996

IT WAS JOSEPH KALLINGER'S STATED OBJECTIVE to murder every living soul on planet Earth. Since the world population in the mid-1970s was 3 billion, more or less, this was a difficult plan requiring money and a partner. To get the cash, he conceived a series of home-invasion robberies, and as a cohort he enlisted his thirteen-year-old son. Once Kallinger had concluded his divinely decreed "global massacre," he could then reign as God.

Mass murder sprees are rarely so ambitious. But Kallinger was quite serious, as the suburbs of New Jersey discovered to their horror beginning on November 22, 1974.

Joseph Kallinger at his cobbler's shop in 1973 with his wife, Elizabeth, and son Joseph Jr. Soon afterward, Kallinger killed the boy and took his other son on a campaign of "global massacre." (*Philadelphia Bulletin* / Temple University Archives)

It was a cold afternoon, and a twenty-one-year-old housewife in Lindenwold, ten miles outside Philadelphia, had just tucked in her two babies for a nap. A knock came from her door and she answered to see a skinny, adolescent boy asking if she'd buy cuff links. No, she said. Half an hour later, the boy returned, this time with a swarthy, malodorous, middle-aged man wearing a suit and tie, who forced his way inside. This robber held a knife to her throat and said, "Don't make a sound or I'll cut you." He tied her up, forced her to perform oral sex on him, and made off with thousands of dollars in cash and jewelry.

Over the next seven weeks, the strange duo continued their house raids, growing more savage on each occasion. They struck in Harrisburg, Pennsylvania; Baltimore, Maryland; and Dumont, New Jersey. On each occasion, the man singled out a house on a quiet suburban street, where a young, pretty woman lived. He or his young companion gained entry by claiming to be a salesman. The father tied up the woman, waved a knife and a revolver, and demanded valuables. He usually disrobed his victims and sexually assaulted them. The small, apprentice robber gathered loot.

On January 8, 1975, came the most vicious rampage yet. This time, the man and boy stormed a house in Leonia, New Jersey, and held eight people hostage. Some were stripped naked and painfully hog-tied. A nurse, Maria Fasching, arrived amid the mayhem to care for the bedridden family matriarch. Fasching was led at knifepoint to the basement and saw a friend lying tied up, his pants down around his ankles.

The ill-smelling man told her to perform oral sex on this captive. "No!" she screamed. The attacker slit her throat, ear to ear. "I'm drowning!" were her last words as blood filled her lungs and coursed onto her white nurse's dress. She died a week before her twenty-second birthday.

Fleeing through the back yards, the throat-slasher tore off his blood-soaked shirt and tie and threw them to the ground. The shirt yielded a laundry label, "KALINGER," and Jersey police traced it to Philadelphia. Computers failed to find anyone with that last name, but the Philadelphia police had a helpful suggestion. Surely, they said, this must be Joseph Kallinger.

"Crazy Joe" was what the neighbors called him in Philadelphia. Kallinger, thirty-nine, was a shoe repairman who labored at a home workshop, where he kept the shades perpetually drawn to ward off perceived CIA spies. In addition to fixing his customers' shoes, he performed thousands of experiments on the soles. The perfect sole, he believed, would align the brain with the heel and serve a heavenly purpose.

Whenever Kallinger felt his right palm itch, which was often, he beat one of his seven children. Once he had branded his daughter with a red-hot spatula and gone to jail for it. The previous summer, another of his children, Joey, fourteen, had been found dead in the rubble of a vacant factory. Philadelphia police thought Joseph Sr. had killed him but had no evidence. The next oldest child was Michael, thirteen. This was the skinny boy that the home invasion victims picked from lineups as the attacker's apprentice.

There was no mystery about who committed the robbery wave: Joseph Kallinger and son Michael. But the "why" required delving into Joseph's mind, a shadowy realm where fantasy and sadistic evil coexisted. He was a schizophrenic who talked of ghostly visions and cackled to himself. But much of this behavior was affected, as if he wanted to impress psychiatrists with how crazy he was. His beliefs seemed utterly irrational, yet there was calm cunning in the way he cased his victims' houses and made swift escapes. Mentally ill or not, he understood his actions were wrong.

Michael was classified as a juvenile offender and given a short stay in a reformatory. His father got no such lenient treatment. Prosecutors in three states wanted him imprisoned for life. He went on trial, first in Harrisburg and then in Bergen County. Banking on an insanity defense, he played the part of courtroom madman to the hilt—windmilling his arms, whistling, and, at one point, breaking his eyeglass lens and trying to slash his wrist with the jagged edge. Jurors found him sane and guilty. He was given thirty years in prison in Pennsylvania, life in New Jersey.

Intrigued by the headline-making case, the writer Flora Rheta Schreiber sought out Kallinger for jailhouse interviews. Her previous book had been the bestseller *Sybil*, about a woman with multiple personalities, and

Schreiber found Kallinger just as fascinating. Her 1983 book about him, *The Shoemaker*, dropped a bombshell. In it, Kallinger confessed the murder of his son Joey nine years earlier. He had chained the teenager to a ladder and drowned him in a pool. A month before that, he revealed, he had committed a murder in which the police never suspected him. This was a nine-year-old boy named José Collazo, whom he lured to a Philadelphia warehouse, castrated with a shoe-leather knife, and left bleeding to death.

In *The Shoemaker*, Kallinger detailed his plan for the "global massacre" of all of Earth's inhabitants. The notion was inspired, he said, by a God who was disappointed that the experiments with brain-healing shoes had failed. "I knew I had to destroy the world, to kill every man, woman and child in it," Schreiber quoted him as saying. "That was God's command to me."

As a prison lifer, Kallinger had more than enough time to prove he truly was a mental case. He got into frequent fights with inmates, took to eating paper clips and staples, and died at age fifty-nine from choking on his vomit. The sister of Maria Fasching, the young nurse Kallinger had butchered two decades earlier, gave a newspaper reporter this eulogy: "The world is just a little better place now that he's dead."

➹ MODEL PRISONER ➷

ROBERT RELDAN, SERIAL KILLER
1940–

FOR THE JADED PUBLIC OF THE 1970S, deadbolting its doors against surging crime and growing ever more disgusted by the joke of revolving-door justice, the New Jersey prison system had a reassuring message. Criminals can be rehabilitated, they said, and Robert Reldan is proof.

He had served just four years for a violent knifepoint rape, but the doctors at Rahway prison said he was now cured of his unnatural urges and ready for parole. Well-spoken, with angular good looks and penetrating black eyes, this model inmate—"model graduate," the education-minded authorities preferred to call him—was also the perfect choice to go on David Frost's television special about crime. Please understand us, Reldan told a national audience that spring of 1975. We sex offenders are suffering from an illness. We need to be treated, not locked away to rot.

Robert Reldan was an unusual prisoner, and not just in his ability to be a glib TV personality. His aunt was Lillian Booth, a millionaire many times over from early investments in what became IBM, and he enjoyed a childhood of privilege in the wealthy Bergen County enclave of Closter. Aunt Lillian paid for his European vacations, flying lessons, and scuba expeditions. But the family money only made him greedy for more.

Starting at age sixteen, he embarked on a career as a purse snatcher, using the money for expensive clothes his parents wouldn't buy him. Over the years, Reldan's crimes became more violent. He turned to sexual attacks, enjoying the feeling of choking women with their own pantyhose. By the time Reldan earned his prison release in May 1975, he had served two stints for rape. New Jerseyans were about to find out if this experiment in "graduating" prisoners was a success.

That October 6, the police in Haworth, New Jersey, got a panicky call. Jonathan Heynes, an engineer, said his newlywed wife, Susan, twenty-eight, was missing from home. She was homesick for their native England,

A child of privilege, Robert Reldan grew up to become a rapist and serial killer. (Bergen County Sheriff's Office)

and the police at first thought maybe she had just flown there on a whim. That possibility was ruled out when she failed to turn up anywhere in Britain or the United States. Ten days later, another young woman vanished. Her name was also Susan—Susan Reeve, twenty-two. She had last been spotted getting off a bus near the home in Demarest she shared with her mother and father, the latter a prominent lawyer. It was just two miles from the previous disappearance.

Police assumed the worst, that the two Susans were victims of a serial killer. Teams of bloodhounds sniffed the rolling woodland of Bergen County, amid country clubs and secluded estates, without success. On October 27, a hiker found Heynes's nude body in the woods of Rockland County, New York. The next day, Reeve's body, also naked, was found nearby. She had been strangled and raped. In the case of Heynes, decomposition was too far along to ascertain a sex attack.

The police quickly zeroed in on Robert Reldan as a suspect. They had never been that enamored by his performance on the David Frost show, and there were convincing reasons to investigate him for the murders. He lived in Tenafly, near where both Susans were last sighted, and his modus operandi of choking and rape was well established. Finding probable cause to search his home would be a problem. But Reldan made it easy for them. On Halloween, he was caught red-handed burglarizing a house.

The murder evidence against Reldan, back in jail after five months of freedom, looked overwhelming. Wisps of hair were vacuumed from the floorboards of his car, and they matched the hair of both victims. In addition, he had sold Susan Heynes's engagement ring at a pawnshop. Confronted with this failure of sex offender re-education, the head of the program was crestfallen. "He conned me," the official sighed.

But Reldan had many tricks left, and he applied his devious mind to going free. He tried to enroll a fellow con in a plot to murder his wealthy Aunt Lillian and inherit her money for his trial defense. The conspirator turned out to be an undercover detective. At Reldan's trial for the Susan killings, held in the Hackensack courthouse in 1979, he figured out a way to mail cash-stuffed envelopes to each of the jurors. When this did not have the desired effect of a mistrial, Reldan plotted escape. He sprayed a smuggled can of Mace into the face of a sheriff's deputy, jumped out a window, stole a car, and hightailed it out of New Jersey. Within hours, a roadblock cornered him in New York state. Two days later, he was found guilty of double murder.

In 1986, Reldan won a retrial based on the fact that prosecutors had improperly told a jury of his previous rapes. It was deft lawyering. But in the courtroom his vanity got the best of him. He insisted on representing himself as his own attorney, counting on his charm to win over the jurors. Instead, they convicted him again.

Reldan served out a life sentence in the maximum-security prison in Trenton. Never again would he be invited to appear on any TV specials, but he was able to exercise his considerable charisma on pen pals and prison groupies. Faithfully, they published the many poems he wrote, telling how harsh life was on the inside.

✎ BAD FAITH ✎

ROBERT O. MARSHALL, WIFE KILLER
1939–

SALESMANSHIP GAVE ROBERT O. MARSHALL the sweet life he flaunted, with a house in the most desirable section of Toms River, New Jersey, a country club membership, and a knockout wife who reared three handsome sons. He had a lucrative business brokering life insurance, and he poured all his considerable skills of persuasion into the task. On September 7, 1984, however, Marshall had to pitch the biggest sale of his life—convincing the State Police he didn't murder his wife—and he just couldn't close.

This was the story Marshall told: It was just after midnight, and he was driving home with wife Maria after a night playing blackjack at Atlantic City. He felt a tire on his Cadillac Eldorado go "wishy-washy" and pulled over to a picnic area in the Garden State Parkway median. While he leaned down to examine the damaged sidewall, some robber after his casino winnings clubbed him on the head, knocking him out. He awoke to find Maria dead in the front seat, two bullet holes in her back.

Marshall thought the authorities would accept this version of events, no questions asked, because of his social prominence around town. He was badly mistaken. The police wanted to know why a tire that felt soft had actually been neatly slashed. They wanted to know why Marshall, instead of stopping at a nearby, well-lit toll plaza, had made for the dark woods around Oyster Creek. Most of all, the police wanted to know about the $1.5 million in life insurance policies that Robert owned on Maria, a housewife who earned no income.

The marriage of Robert, forty-four at the time of the murder, to Maria, forty-two, was less happy than it appeared. They'd made a beautiful couple. He was a Navy veteran with a square jaw and piercing dark eyes; she was a blonde with a warm, loving smile.

Many people around Toms River regarded Robert as pushy and arrogant, but it was hard to argue with success. He volunteered for the United Way and was a tennis partner with John Russo, the state Senate president.

The "Ken and Barbie" of Toms River, Robert Marshall and wife Maria seemed to have it all. His killing of her—by use of a hit man—came to embody the dark side of New Jersey's suburbs in the 1980s.

Maria was mother hen for their sons' high school swim team, attending every meet and leaving encouraging notes in oldest boy Robby's underwear drawer each morning. When acquaintances called Robert and Maria "Ken and Barbie," it wasn't entirely mocking.

But Robert, with the same restlessness he brought to his twelve-hour workdays, grew bored with this comfortable marriage. At a Fourth of July barbecue in 1983, where he'd been tooling around in his boat—named *Double Down*, after his favorite pastime of blackjack—he met a high school principal named Saran Kraushaar. Recklessly, Robert plunged into an affair with this married woman. Between gifts for the mistress, casino losses, and a home equity loan Robert forged in Maria's name, he fell $300,000 in debt. Maria knew all this but chose not to confront her husband about it.

Sometime in late 1983, Kraushaar would later testify, Robert told her he wanted to "get rid of" his wife and asked if she knew anyone who could "take care of it." She thought it was a joke, but Robert was deadly serious. His plan was to put out a contract on Maria's life, freeing him to marry Kraushaar and collect a small fortune in insurance.

Either at a Toms River party or from some other connections in low places, Robert got in touch with a crew from rural Louisiana who specialized in construction equipment thefts. A former deputy sheriff turned crook, Billy Wayne McKinnon, was the key contact in the murder conspiracy. Robert told him he wanted Maria shot, and the death made to look like a random robbery.

McKinnon suggested the fake holdup take place on the highway, and said Robert himself should take a bullet in the leg to make it look authentic. With typical self-preservation, Robert recoiled at the idea and said he should instead be hit on the head—but not too hard, or he might become "an idiot for the rest of his life."

For his part, Robert admitted he had dealings with McKinnon—but claimed he'd hired the Louisianan as a private investigator because he suspected *Maria* of bad faith. Cash was missing from his gambling fund, he claimed, and he wanted to find out what had happened to it. This made little sense by any cost-benefit analysis, because the supposedly missing money amounted to $3,500, and Robert paid his "investigator" a minimum of $6,300.

On September 7, 1984, therefore, the police had plenty of reasons to be suspicious of Robert Marshall and his not-especially-convincing grieving widower act. With the law closing in, Marshall retreated to the same motel where he had many a tryst with his mistress. There, he recorded a tape insisting on his innocence but saying he'd be found guilty anyway. He dropped thirty sleeping pills into a Coke, then conveniently fell asleep before taking a sip.

That December, Marshall was formally charged with murder solicitation. Because of publicity, the trial was moved from Ocean County, where the crime took place, to Atlantic County. Among the courtroom spectators was the author Joe McGinniss, who wrote the true crime book *Blind Faith* about the case and transformed Robert Marshall into a symbol of all the sordid lusts lurking behind tidy suburban facades.

The two-month trial in early 1986 exposed Robert Marshall, would-be civic pillar, as a greedy sociopath. The most devastating blow was the testimony of McKinnon, who agreed to turn state's evidence. Marshall himself was a terrible witness. Asked by a prosecutor what became of Maria's body, Marshall had to admit her ashes were still in a cardboard box at the funeral home.

It took a jury six hours to convict Robert Marshall of murder. After just an hour and a half of further deliberations, on March 5, it sentenced him to death by lethal injection. This made Marshall by far the wealthiest man on New Jersey's death row, and the only one not to commit a killing by his own hand. In 2004, after blitzing the courts with appeals for eighteen years, Marshall finally succeeded in overturning his death sentence on the grounds of incompetent counsel. He was resentenced to life in prison with parole eligibility in 2014.

Who was the actual hit man? McKinnon denied he did it, but then he had to or the prosecutors never would have given him a sweet deal of just five years in prison. Instead, McKinnon fingered one of his underworld acquaintances, Larry Thompson, as the killer. The same jury that convicted Marshall, however, found Thompson not guilty.

In the end, the only man besides Marshall to rot in prison for the murder conspiracy was a hardware store clerk without a previous criminal record named Robert Cumber. This man's only role was to mention Marshall's name to McKinnon, apparently not aware a murder was in the works. The prosecutors offered to let him plead guilty to a minor offense, but he turned it down and was sentenced to thirty years for murder. Cumber was not released until 2006, when Governor Richard Codey commuted the term, calling it "unconscionable." Whoever pulled the trigger on Maria Marshall remains unknown to history.

⇾ LOCKED BOX ⇽

ARTHUR SEALE, 1947– AND
IRENE JACQUELINE SEALE, 1947–,
HUSBAND-AND-WIFE KIDNAPPERS

ON MAY 1, 1992, TWO DAYS AFTER the president of Exxon International vanished from the driveway of his home in Morris Township, New Jersey, the police searching for him got their first clue. A note from a group calling itself "Warriors of the Rainbow" claimed it had kidnapped him. They demanded an $18.5 million ransom for his return.

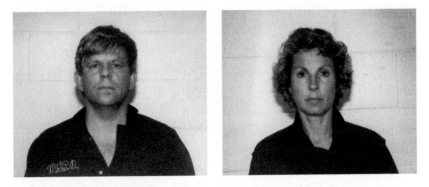

Arthur and Jacqueline Seale in their 1992 mug shots, after blundering their way into FBI custody during a ransom drop. The married couple kidnapped an Exxon executive and accidentally killed him. (Federal Bureau of Investigation)

Because the environmental group Greenpeace had a ship called the *Rainbow Warrior*, and because Exxon was reaping bad publicity from the recent spill of its *Exxon Valdez* oil tanker, the crime looked to be the work of environmental radicals.

This assumption was wrong. The abductors were not a new terrorist group, but a couple from the New Jersey suburbs. Arthur and Jacqueline Seale were not stirred by vengeance for a corporation's wrongs, but by their own greed. They were not professionals, either, and this would have grim consequences for the target of their get-rich-quick scheme.

High school sweethearts from Hillside, New Jersey, they had long been accustomed to living well. Arthur was an ex-cop and worked in the security department of Exxon. He was paid well for it, enough to buy a $400,000 house and put two teenagers in private school. Jackie ran a local winery. Blond, tan, and fit, they looked like the perfect professional couple.

In 1987, Arthur quit Exxon to pursue a personal adventure. The family moved to Hilton Head, South Carolina, and sank their life savings into an interior design store. The business failed, and in defiance of all logic, the Seales relocated to yet another expensive playground for the rich: Vail, Colorado. Neither husband nor wife could find a job there. Humiliated, they moved back to New Jersey to live with Arthur's parents. By early 1992, they were forty-five and $750,000 in debt.

As the Seales bickered and ducked lawsuits by their creditors, they both yearned to return to their old yuppie lifestyle. It was Arthur who chose the means to this end. Among his tasks at Exxon was developing the company plan to protect executives from kidnapping and assassination while abroad. He still had a company directory listing every executive's home address. Why not use his expertise about kidnapping to become a kidnapper himself? Jackie agreed: it just might work.

Sidney Reso, fifty-seven, was president of Exxon International, the arm of Exxon that operated outside North America. Modest and soft-spoken, he shunned use of the company limousine and drove himself the short distance to work every day at Exxon headquarters. Arthur Seale knew all this and decided Reso would be the perfect victim.

The morning of April 29, 1992, Reso kissed his wife goodbye, drove the length of his two hundred-foot driveway, and stepped out of the idling car to pick up the morning paper. Arthur, wearing a ski mask, and Jackie, at the wheel of a parked van, were there waiting for him. The masked man pointed a handgun at the executive and ordered him toward the van. Reso complied, until he saw where the Seales intended him to lie down. It was a homemade coffin. With all his might, he tried to break free. A shot rang out. By accident or out of panic, Arthur had shot him in the left forearm.

The bleeding, moaning Reso was now handcuffed and stuffed into the snug, wooden box. The Seales drove him to a self-storage facility ten miles away, locked him into a shed, and later returned with gauze and antiseptic to treat his wound. They came back the next day to feed him a meager ration of water, vitamins, and a tangerine. "What's happening? What do you want?" he gasped. "Nothing personal," Arthur said. "Just dealing with Exxon."

The Seales ordered Reso to speak into a tape recorder to prove he was alive and being treated well. But by his second day of captivity he was already dying. The coffin had air holes, but as it sat in an unventilated metal shed, the temperature inside rose to 100 degrees. Reso lay prone, alone with his fears and festering wound. When the Seales checked on him the morning of May 3, the fourth day of captivity, they found him dead.

There was no pause for mourning. Later that day, the kidnappers drove Reso's body fifty miles south, to a sandy stretch of pines off the Garden State Parkway, and buried him. Arthur took the box home and burned it. Then they sat down to write more of their "Warriors of the Rainbow" ransom notes.

Unaware of Sidney Reso's end, his loved ones tried everything in their power to bring him back safely. His wife, Patricia, made televised appeals for his release. Exxon gathered the cash for a ransom. Finally, the kidnappers made a phone call giving the FBI instructions on where to deliver the cash. It was a complex itinerary through Morris and Somerset counties, with FBI agents being instructed to drive from one site to

another on the night of June 18 before dropping off a suitcase filled with
$100 bills.

The Seales' plan was elaborate, not brilliant. They intended to make
calls by pay phones as part of their cat-and-mouse game, but failed to
anticipate that the FBI had staked out as many phones as possible in
Morris County. The surveillance paid off when an agent spotted a suspicious man talking into a phone at the same time other agents were receiving a call from the kidnapper. After a pursuit by car, FBI agents pounced
on both Seales.

Inside the family Mercedes, the authorities found bullets, latex gloves,
and the Exxon directory with Reso's address. They also discovered that
the Seales had recently acquired passports and tried to set up bank
accounts in Switzerland and Pakistan. Both husband and wife kept silent
for ten days. Then, with the prospect of a life sentence hanging over her,
Jackie cracked. Somberly, she walked federal agents to Reso's grave.

Jackie maintained that she took part unwillingly in Arthur's kidnapping scheme and the cruel hoax to pretend Reso was still alive. She was
a battered wife, she said, living in fear of Arthur's terrible rages. Prosecutors did not believe her, but agreed to seek a lenient murder sentence
because of her cooperation. She received life in prison, with a chance of
parole after twenty years.

Arthur pleaded guilty. His sentence—125 years to life—guaranteed
that he, like Reso, was doomed to die in captivity. The difference was, a
judge told him, "You will not be bound, gagged, shot, or placed in a
coffin." From prison, Arthur Seale wrote repeated letters to Reso's widow
begging forgiveness. He never got an answer.

⋇ MONSTER NEXT DOOR ⋇

JESSE TIMMENDEQUAS, MEGAN'S KILLER
1961–

THE LURE WAS A PUPPY. Seven-year-old Megan Kanka loved them, even
more than she loved mint chocolate chip ice cream or her doll collection

or bicycling around her neighborhood of split-levels in Hamilton Township, New Jersey. So when the man who lived across the street offered her the chance to come see his Labrador retriever, she ignored whatever creepy vibes may have come from his bad skin, greasy mop of hair, and nervous demeanor. Eagerly, she went into his house.

Anyone who has heard of Megan's Law will know what happened next on that sunny summer afternoon in 1994. The man holding out the lure was a pedophile who raped and murdered her. Megan's name lives on, as the inspiration for the national law to track and protect against sexual offenders upon their release from prison. Not so well known is the name of her killer, Jesse Timmendequas.

The man who committed the most notorious child murder since the Lindbergh kidnapping grew up amid "Tobacco Road"-style squalor and neglect. His borderline-retarded mother conceived Jesse, one of her ten

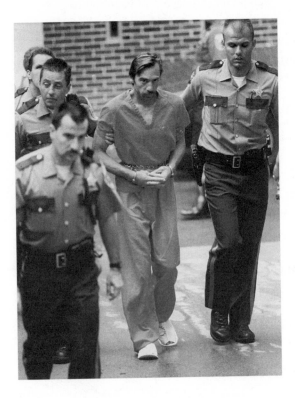

Jesse Timmendequas being led to his arraignment. Once confronted by police, he quickly confessed to Megan's murder and asked for a Band-Aid to cover the spot where she bit him.
(*The Trentonian* / Craig Orosz)

children by seven fathers, while her husband was in prison for burglary. The brood moved around central New Jersey twenty-one times, at one time living in a car.

The family name was the father's alias, copied off an Indian tombstone before he abandoned the children. When Jesse Timmendequas was later facing the death penalty, his defense lawyers would say this father had raped him and tortured his pets.

By elementary school, Timmendequas was a "frightened little rabbit with glasses," in the report of one teacher. By his late teens, a sexual longing for small children was surging within him. He was nineteen and living in Piscataway when he approached a five-year-old girl, enticed her to a duck pond, and pulled down her pants. After serving a year in jail, he stalked a seven-year-old girl, choked her nearly to death, and ran away, thinking wrongly that he had killed her. For this crime, Timmendequas plea-bargained and was sentenced to ten years in prison.

His term was served at the Adult Diagnostic and Treatment Center in Avenel, New Jersey's special prison that provides psychiatric care for sexual offenders. Avenel's many critics called it little more than a cushy frat house for perverts. Timmendequas, for one, saw no rehabilitation there.

Megan Kanka, seven, had the misfortune to live next door to a convicted sex offender. Her 1994 murder led to Megan's Law.

He blew off his therapy sessions and befriended two other hard-core pedophiles. Once Timmendequas served out his sentence, he moved in with the ex-cons.

Their house, 27 Barbara Lee Drive in the Trenton suburb of Hamilton, was diagonally across the street from the Kanka family, whose solid, middle-class lifestyle couldn't have provided more of a contrast with Timmendequas's sordid existence. Parents Richard, an electrical contractor, and Maureen, a stay-at-home mother raising three children, had moved to this neighborhood for its safety. Rumors circulated about the strange inhabitants of No. 27, but the Kankas did not credit them.

Timmendequas, now thirty-three and employed as a landscaper, had managed to stay on the right side of the law until he saw the Kankas' daughter, Megan. He later told police that she aroused sexual desires in him, and "I would get sweaty palms and my heart would race." On July 29, 1994, this girl with blond hair and rosy cheeks was walking to a friend's house when she saw Timmendequas on his lawn cleaning a cabin cruiser he had just bought. Perky and inquisitive, she stopped to ask about the boat. The conversation then turned to Timmendequas's black Lab.

The neighbor Megan knew only as "Jesse" escorted her upstairs, past the sleeping form of his friend's mother, an Alzheimer's sufferer. They went into his bedroom, he began touching her, and she screamed. Timmendequas choked Megan with a belt, and she fought back hard, biting his hand. But the forty-pound Megan was no match for a man four times her size. He raped and sodomized her on the floor. Then he strangled her. It took her five minutes to die.

The dead girl bled from the mouth, so Timmendequas wrapped plastic bags around her head to avoid stains. He stuffed her body into a toy box and drove it to a park. Before discarding her body amid the weeds, he molested Megan one last time.

When Megan failed to return home that evening, neighbors pitched in to help the police in their search. Among them was Timmendequas himself, who handed out fliers bearing Megan's picture. But after canvassing Barbara Lee Drive, investigators became suspicious of this man with a criminal record. They took him in for questioning, where, chain-smoking and visibly trembling, he admitted being Megan's killer. His confession showed no trace of remorse, but much fear. At one point, he sniveled about the bite he'd suffered and asked for a Band-Aid.

Detectives arrived at the Kanka home the evening of July 30 to break the news that Megan's body had been found in the park. "All I could hear was the crying and wailing from the house," Maureen recalled later. "I just sat there. I couldn't react. I was just numb. My little girl was dead."

Only two days later, however, Maureen Kanka was in public, speaking out for a state law that would require community notification any time a child molester was let out of prison. The Megan murder instantly seared itself into the national consciousness, coming to symbolize every parent's worst nightmare. Families had a right to know about the dangers that might lurk in their neighborhoods, the Kankas and an army of supporters argued. Little more than three months after the crime, Megan's Law went on the books in New Jersey.

The law's provisions, which require convicted sex offenders to register with the authorities wherever they move, have been contested ever since by civil libertarians. They argue that the law amounts to persecution of those who've already served out their sentences, and that it encourages vigilante action against them. In the end, however, politicians found it hard to dispute Maureen Kanka's argument: If she had known her neighbor was a pedophile, Megan would still be alive.

Justice moved slower than politics. Timmendequas did not go on trial for capital murder until May 1997, a year after President Bill Clinton signed a federal version of Megan's Law. Defense lawyers, confronted with a case they could not win, argued that the name "Megan" should not even be mentioned because of the emotional pull it would have on jurors. They lost that argument.

The defense strategy seemed aimless, even counterproductive. During summations, one of Timmendequas's lawyers, Barbara Lependorf, said that Megan had brought on her own murder by approaching the molester. "Jesse didn't suggest it," she told the jury. "He was minding his own business." This version of events provoked wonderment and scorn, and failed to help Timmendequas. He was found guilty.

The same jury then sat to hear arguments on whether Timmendequas should be sentenced to live or die. Timmendequas's lawyers, hoping to show some hint of humanity within the monster, brought up evidence that he'd suffered harrowing and nonstop abuse. In a videotaped statement, Jesse's brother Paul painted their father as a nasty drunk, sadist, and rapist. But it later came out that he contradicted himself on key details of this abuse, and even thought Jesse deserved death.

On June 22, 1997, the jury pronounced its sentence: death. Timmendequas went to death row in Trenton with the prospect of remaining alive for many years, thanks to the lengthy appeal process. From the jurors, he had only the tiniest flickering of sympathy. "One of the thoughts that went through my mind was, what a waste of a human life," one of them said afterward. "But that doesn't excuse what he did to Megan."

✣ THOU SHALT NOT ✣

FRED NEULANDER, KILLER AND RABBI
1941–

THOU SHALT NOT KILL. Thou shalt not commit adultery. Rabbi Fred Neulander had preached on the Ten Commandments often, but in September 1994 the O. J. Simpson case turned his mind to the Jewish prohibition on *loshen hara,* or gossip. "Voyeurs," he called aficionados of the courtroom coverage, eager for "gory details or fanciful theories." Writing in the newsletter of his synagogue, M'kor Shalom in Cherry Hill, the largest Reform temple in South Jersey, he lectured: "How shallow our lives must be if another's travails and machinations filled our world."

Two months later, Rabbi Neulander had new reasons to wish away the voyeurs. On November 1, he arrived home to find his wife Carol lying dead on the living room floor, her head bashed in by an intruder. At first, neighbors feared a psychopathic burglar was in their midst. Then the speculation: maybe the rabbi did it.

Preposterous, idle chatter, defenders of Rabbi Neulander said. Here was a man who, at fifty-three, not only had no criminal record, but was a respected teacher and moral leader. In Cherry Hill, a sprawling and shapeless suburb that was one-third Jewish, his temple provided a community center. His sermons were pedantic and pompous, it was true, and the short, bull-necked cleric often erupted in bullying rages. But egotism was a fault of many clergymen, and Neulander backed up his words with charity to the homeless.

He had an outwardly loving relationship with shy, warm-hearted Carol, fifty-two. She was the quiet half of the marriage, but had still parlayed her housewifely kitchen skills into a million-dollar bakery business. Together the Neulanders had raised three handsome children, all bound for college and high-paying professions.

But the gossip wouldn't stop, especially when the Cherry Hill police stopped treating Rabbi Neulander as a bereaved husband and started treating him as their number one suspect. On the 911 call Neulander made after finding Carol dead, he blurted: "Do I touch her or should I do anything . . . I don't think so." Why would a caring husband not even

At his 2001 trial for murdering his wife, Rabbi Fred Neulander got lucky when a jury deadlocked. At his second trial, he lectured the jurors on the Bible and morality. They spared his life anyway. (Photo © *The Star-Ledger.* All rights reserved)

touch a wife in distress? Within a week of the murder, Neulander was telling friends it would never be solved. Was this a prediction or a hope?

Rabbi Neulander, it turned out, had a lot to hide. Bored by family life, he used his pulpit at M'kor Shalom to seduce women. Many had fallen into spiritual crisis and trusted the rabbi as mentor; he returned their reverence by preying on them. One such woman was Elaine Soncini, a Philadelphia radio personality. Depressed after her husband's death, she approached the rabbi about converting to Judaism. They began daily liaisons, and soon she was asking him about marriage. Fred couldn't do that, he told her in the summer of 1994: divorcing Carol would be a *shanda*, a scandal. But don't worry, she might be out of the way by New Year's.

The revelations of Neulander's philandering were enough for M'kor Shalom to ease him out of his rabbi post in February 1995. But they did not add up to a murder case. Neulander had an airtight alibi. On the Tuesday of the murder, he was visibly at his temple. And the rabbi, unlike that other notorious wife-murder suspect O. J., was actively trying to pursue the real killers. He hired a private eye and temple congregant, Leonard Jenoff, to investigate the case. Jenoff promptly made a nuisance of himself, paying visits to newspaper editors, sometimes providing sketches of a suspect drawn by psychics, sometimes suggesting that "Maybe it was the Jewish Mafia."

Carol Neulander's last word was "Why?" when a hit man clubbed her over the head at her Cherry Hill home.

If Neulander committed a murder, he had obviously hired a hit man. But the police didn't have the identity of this mysterious figure. Nor did they have fingerprints or a murder weapon. Nevertheless, four years after Carol Neulander's death, Fred was indicted for her murder. As the wheels of Camden County justice ground slowly toward a trial, *Philadelphia Inquirer* reporter Nancy Phillips kept bugging Jenoff to tell her more. Finally in May 2000, he agreed to spill his guts, on the condition they meet in public, at a diner.

Phillips brought the Camden County prosecutor along with her. Jenoff, picking at his fruit salad, took a long time to get to the point. Then he dropped a bombshell. *I* was the hit man, he said. The rabbi had said he wanted Carol eliminated because she was "an enemy of Israel." Jenoff, regarding Neulander as a holy man, agreed to perform the mission. To help carry out the assassination, Jenoff recruited a subcontractor— a twenty-year-old heroin addict named Paul Daniels, whom the hard-drinking private eye had met at a twelve-step program.

Together they had bluffed their way into the Neulander home. When Carol's back was turned, Jenoff clubbed her over the head with a lead pipe. "Why?" she screamed. Daniels administered three more deadly blows, blood and brains flying everywhere.

Jenoff confessed partly from overwhelming guilt, but also out of resentment—the rabbi had, after all, paid little more than half of the promised $30,000. By pleading guilty to manslaughter, Jenoff and Daniels were both guaranteed relatively light prison terms. Neulander went on trial for murder, and dodged a bullet in 2001 when the jury deadlocked and caused a mistrial. A second trial followed a year later, with defense lawyers succeeding in their bid to move to Monmouth County because of extensive local publicity.

Neulander appeared to have momentum. But his eldest son Matthew had made up his mind that his father was guilty, and he was a devastating witness. He told the jury how his father—whom he referred to not as "dad" but "Fred"—had threatened to divorce Carol in bitter arguments. Fred, he said, acted detached and unemotional about Carol's murder. The prosecutor asked Matthew, an emergency medical technician, how many people he'd met who had suffered a traumatic loss. Hundreds, Matthew said.

"How many reacted as your father did?"

"None."

On November 20, 2002, a jury found Fred Neulander guilty of first-degree murder after deliberating for four days. During the sentencing phase of the trial, he had the opportunity to speak in his own defense and almost doomed himself with his chutzpah.

"I miss her and I loved her and I love her," he said of the wife he'd had murdered. He admitted his adultery had been "disgraceful," then paused and added, as if propounding a great truth: "And note that that's a theological word, disgraceful." The jurors were repulsed. But Fred and Carol's loved ones both wanted his life spared. Their message was heeded, and the jury voted for life imprisonment. Neulander would be eligible for parole at age eighty-eight.

The rabbi went off to prison utterly unrepentant, refusing to confess to murder or speculate on who did it. He might have broken God's commandments, but he would never be a gossiper.

➤ MURDER BY DESIGN ❧

ANDREW CUNANAN, CROSS-COUNTRY SPREE KILLER 1969–1997

MAYBE HE LIKED THE THRILL OF MURDER, or the fantasy of revenge. Maybe he felt that targeting celebrities, such as fashion designer and gay icon Gianni Versace, gave his own wasted life a celebrity of its own. Nobody will ever know what drove Andrew Philip Cunanan to go off on a four-state killing expedition in 1997. But the motive for one of his murders, which he committed in an isolated Civil War cemetery in South Jersey, is well established. Andrew Cunanan needed a car.

It was May 9, two months before Cunanan achieved tabloid fame as Versace's assassin, but the pursuit of the gay spree killer was already a hot story. He was wanted in the murders of two of his ex-lovers in Minnesota. One man had been bashed in the head with a hammer, the other shot and dumped on the side of the road. From there, the twenty-seven-year-old Cunanan had sped off in a stolen car, invaded the home of a prominent Chicago developer, and decapitated him with a band saw. The fugitive then drove off in the dead man's Lexus.

Because the Lexus was equipped with a car phone, police could use radio triangulation techniques to pinpoint Cunanan's location. But the authorities let slip this information to the news media, which ran with the story. Driving south on the New Jersey Turnpike on this Friday afternoon, Cunanan heard a news report about himself. He pulled over, snapped off the antenna, and frantically tried to tear out the wiring.

Correctly reasoning that the phone signal could still be traced, he stopped at a tourist information booth and asked about nearby historic sites. Cunanan got a brochure about Finns Point National Cemetery, an isolated, marshy triangle of land hugging Delaware Bay in nearby Pennsville, New Jersey. It was the burial ground for two thousand soldiers of both the Union and Confederate armies. Before the day was out, one more body would lie there.

In a cross-country rampage in 1997, Andrew Cunanan killed victims in Minnesota, Illinois, and New Jersey before assassinating fashion designer Gianni Versace in Miami Beach. (Federal Bureau of Investigation)

William Reese, forty-five, was an electrician by training but a Civil War buff first and foremost. For twenty years he had dressed in the blue uniform of the 14th Brooklyn Militia at battle re-enactments, growing a scraggly black beard to enhance the authenticity. As full-time superintendent of Finns Point, he knew all the mournful stories behind the historic graves. Every day, Reese left his wife and child at home and drove his pickup to the farmhouse that served as center for his one-man caretaking operation. This red Chevy caught Cunanan's attention as he drove down the remote road to Finns Point, desperate to unload his own vehicle.

Cunanan knocked on the office door at about 3:30 P.M. He brandished a .40-caliber pistol and demanded the keys to the pickup. Then he ordered Reese to kneel, and fired a single shot into the back of his skull.

The killing of Reese bumped Cunanan's death toll up to four and put his name on the FBI's Ten Most Wanted list. But the leak about the Lexus car phone was not the first of police blunders. The FBI's behavioral science unit was not asked to profile him until weeks too late. If they had done so, they might have divined that his destination was the gay party scene of Miami's South Beach neighborhood.

Growing up in San Diego, the handsome, olive-skinned son of a Filipino father and Italian-American mother, Cunanan had long aspired to be at the glamorous center of the gay elite. Openly homosexual since his teens, he spun charming lies about his fabulous wealth and breeding. He liked to drop Versace's name, although he apparently never knew the Italian trend-setter. Far from being the trust fund baby he posed as, Cunanan was a broke college dropout with no job prospects.

Dealing in methamphetamines gave him the cash to fuel his purchases of expensive designer clothes and hundreds of videos of violent pornography. For a while, he prostituted himself as a kept boy to a millionaire. But in 1996, his sugar daddy kicked him out, upset by Cunanan's other affairs.

Cunanan's first murder took place on April 27, 1997. Each successive killing must have given him greater confidence. Eventually, he lashed out at the one man who, for him, symbolized the status Cunanan could only pretend to: Gianni Versace.

Cunanan arrived in South Beach the day after Reese's murder, still driving the stolen pickup. There he raised cash by peddling drugs and pawning a stolen gold coin. On July 15, he showed up at the gate in front of Versace's estate. The fifty-one-year-old millionaire was returning from his morning trip to the newsstand. He never saw his ambusher step up to him and fire two shots into his head.

The Versace murder made headlines around the world and turned Cunanan into a criminal legend. Witnesses started seeing him everywhere, from an okra farm in Arkansas to a Kmart in New Hampshire.

One of the biggest manhunts in U.S. history ended at the time and place of Cunanan's choosing. Abandoning his motel, he broke into a houseboat and holed up there for nine days. On July 24, the police got a tip about a burglar and laid siege to the moored vessel as television helicopters hovered overhead. After four hours, a squad charged inside, firing tear gas canisters, to discover a body seated on a couch. It was Cunanan.

The killer had shot himself through the mouth with a .40-caliber pistol—the same weapon he had used to execute Reese and Versace. Whatever the dark secrets that drove him to mass murder, they died with him.

❧ STEEL CAGE MATCH ❦

AMBROSE HARRIS VS.
ROBERT "MUDMAN" SIMON

DEATH ROW WASN'T BIG ENOUGH for the two of them. Ambrose Harris and Robert "Mudman" Simon were the two meanest men in the meanest wing of Trenton state prison, capable of striking fear into their fellow murderers with a single menacing gesture. Simon, a motorcycle gangster and white racist, had a hypnotic glare that his own lawyer called "Charles Manson-like." Harris, a black psychopath, was built like a linebacker and filled with sadistic rage.

Since New Jersey enacted a new capital punishment law in 1982, more than fifty-five people have been sentenced to die. But only one has been executed—and it wasn't by the state. It happened on September 7, 1999, when Simon, forty-nine, and Harris, forty-seven, met each other in the steel cage that constituted death row's recreation room. "Let's get it on," Simon growled, and the two charged at each other like wild beasts. It would be a fight to the death.

They called him the "Mudman" because he once accepted a prison dare to eat a sandwich containing human feces. He was disgusting, dangerous, and proud of it. As a leader of the Warlocks gang centered in the town of Jim Thorpe, Pennsylvania, he grew a beard halfway down to his enormous beer belly and swaggered about, openly toting guns. Simon had a special hatred for blacks and Puerto Ricans, and targeted them in bar brawls.

In the mid-1970s, young women who hung out with the Warlocks began to disappear. The body of nineteen-year-old Beth Dusenberg was found in an abandoned strip mine in 1981, seven years after her murder. Simon had shot her in the head because she refused to have group sex with the gang. He went to prison, where he slashed a fellow inmate to death and avoided any penalty for it by claiming self-defense.

Ambrose Harris sodomized and murdered a young woman for the fun of it. Before being sentenced to death, he told her parents they should apologize to him. (*The Trentonian* / Bob Castelli)

The Pennsylvania parole board released Simon after he served a little more than half of his twenty-year sentence. Eleven weeks later, he murdered again. On April 3, 1995, a patrol officer in Franklin Township in South Jersey pulled Simon over on a routine traffic stop. He was unaware that the driver had just stolen some guns. As the cop filled out paperwork for a ticket, Simon shot him in the neck and head. For this crime, there would be no leniency. The Mudman was sentenced to die.

Like Simon, Ambrose Harris had spent most of his adult life in prison. His mother was a convicted murderer, and at an early age he took to gang fighting on the Trenton streets. At eleven, Harris was committed to a mental hospital for "pre-psychotic" tendencies. At fourteen, he was questioned in a mugging murder. His chosen profession was armed robbery, and the New Jersey prison system gave him a higher education in violence.

The morning of December 17, 1992, Harris had been out on parole for six months when he decided to commit a carjacking as casually as one might hail a cab. Accompanied by a girlfriend, he staked out a Trenton parking lot. They picked out the driver of a sporty red Toyota MR2 as an easy target.

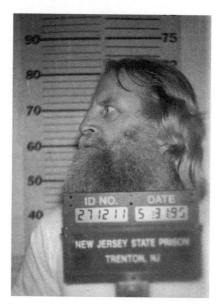

Robert "Mudman" Simon was Harris's equal in depravity. The state wouldn't execute either of them—but in 1999 they fought to the death. (New Jersey Department of Corrections)

She was Kristin Huggins, twenty-two, a recent art school graduate showing up for her first professional job—to paint a mural. Harris stuffed her into the trunk, drove her to a secluded rail corridor, and raped her. Sobbing, she told him she was a virgin and wanted to live. Harris was unmoved. "I've got to pop her because she'll tell," he told his girlfriend. Then he shot Huggins twice in the head.

When the murder was finally solved, it seemed to fulfill every white suburbanite's worst nightmare about Trenton. Harris lived up to his vicious image every day at his murder trial, shouting, spitting, and flipping his middle finger at the judge. He worked hard to get the death sentence that his jury pronounced on him.

Harris, Simon, and the other dozen-odd inmates on death row lived a life of near-total isolation. Twenty-one hours a day were spent confined in solitary cells. In the time they were permitted outside, they had to walk out of their cell naked before submitting to a strip search. Because of the liberal number of appeals allowed them, the time spent before death by lethal injection could amount to decades, not years.

In this isolated world, Mudman was the alpha male. He got second helpings of food before anyone else and taunted other inmates during recreation time. One of his fellow murderers, Jesse Timmendequas—the pedophile who killed seven-year-old Megan Kanka of "Megan's Law" fame—was so scared by Simon's chants of "Jesse, come out and play!" that he would never leave his cell.

But Harris was not one to be messed with, either. With no other entertainments, he lifted weights and did three thousand push-ups a day until he had built himself into a 270-pound behemoth. His cell adjoined Simon's, and he grew increasingly irritated at the loudmouth next door with the annoying habit of banging his metal cup against the floor all day to kill cockroaches. "I'm going to take care of this problem," Harris once muttered to fellow death row inmate Robert O. Marshall, the wife killer of *Blind Faith* notoriety.

The same thing was on Simon's mind. September 7, 1999, was the day scheduled for an exterminator to fumigate four of the prisoners' cells, and all were led together into the steel cage. The guards remained on the outside, looking in. Marshall and another inmate played chess. Then Simon and Harris ran at each other, and the death match began.

It was no contest. Harris outweighed Simon by sixty pounds and had advantages of height, reach, and pure homicidal rage. After Simon threw two swings that missed, Harris dropped his opponent to the concrete floor with a hammer-like punch. Then he climbed atop a card table, leaped down, and stomped on Simon's head. The guards, who were not armed, did not enter the cage or try to break up the fight. Harris jumped again and again onto the Mudman until the unconscious man's eyeballs and teeth popped out and blood splattered ten feet in every direction. After about one minute, Harris stepped back, gave a "black brotherhood" salute to another inmate, and allowed the guards to handcuff him. "Ambrose ain't no punk," he said.

Like Simon before him, Harris pleaded self-defense to a prison killing and got away with it when a jury found him not guilty of murder. More good news came his way in 2006, when the state declared a moratorium on its death penalty, making it increasingly unlikely that he or any other inmate would ever suffer lethal injection. In time, the killing of Mudman Simon may well be the last execution to take place on New Jersey's death row.

⇸ No Angel ⇷

Charles Cullen,
Nurse and Serial Killer
1960–

THEY WERE CANCER SUFFERERS, BURN WARD PATIENTS, and great-grandparents in their nineties. Each quiet death attracted its share of private grief but no public suspicion. Not, that is, until a woman named Helen Dean summoned her son, Larry, to her bed at Warren Hospital in Phillipsburg, New Jersey, on August 30, 1993. "He stuck me," she moaned. "That sneaky male nurse."

Helen Dean's accusation was brushed off. She seemed physically fine, especially at age ninety-one, after a successful breast cancer surgery. Her angry insistence that a hospital staffer injected her sounded like a classic old person's paranoia. She was released from the hospital the next day, went home—and promptly died. Larry angrily called the Warren County prosecutor's office. That "sneaky nurse," he told them, was named Charles Cullen. Helen Dean had been murdered, and Cullen was the murderer.

Nothing happened. Tests of Helen's blood and tissues were run for more than a hundred foreign substances, without one positive match. Cullen passed a lie detector test. He was hardly a model employee, it was true. The hospital knew all about his two suicide attempts and his conviction for breaking into the home of a coworker. But he was off the hook for murder, and he kept his job. No one reviewed the records of other patients who had died suspiciously while in Cullen's care, even though by this time there were plenty of them.

When Cullen left Warren Hospital four months later, it was on his own terms. There were many more hospitals and nursing homes willing to hire him. None wanted to confront the possibility he might be an "angel of death" who felt compelled to execute his patients, and none suspected he would turn out to be New Jersey's worst recorded serial killer.

With a body count of up to forty, nurse Charles Cullen was New Jersey's worst serial killer. (Photo © *The Star-Ledger.* All rights reserved)

At the ten medical institutions Cullen worked for over the next ten years in New Jersey and in Pennsylvania's Lehigh Valley, the same pattern of poor performance repeated itself. He would drag his personal miseries to work with him and get into quarrels with fellow nurses. He would barge into the rooms of patients he was not assigned to. More ominously, he would also steal medications and give patients injections he was not authorized to perform.

At each job, he was fired after a year or less. Just as predictably, the hospital or nursing home that fired him would not tell other employers of his awful work record. The bosses who let Cullen go were too fearful of being sued for exposing his secrets, and the bosses who hired him were too desperate to fill night-shift jobs. One nurse in Allentown, Pennsylvania, was even fired after blowing the whistle on him.

In June 2003, electronics did what human common sense failed to do. They caught Charles Cullen. The computerized medicine cabinet at Somerset Medical Center in Somerville showed Cullen had ordered a dose of a heart medicine called digoxin for a patient who had not been prescribed the drug. The computers also showed he reviewed the records of a patient who was not his. This patient, the Reverend Florian Gall, sixty-eight, Roman Catholic vicar of Hunterdon County, died the next day. The cause was heart failure, but tests showed he had high levels of digoxin in his blood.

The hospital ordered tests on more patients who had died in recent weeks. In four of them the tests found "abnormal lab values," meaning high levels of digoxin or low blood sugar that could only have been caused by an insulin overdose. Even then, with the head of New Jersey's Poison Control Center screaming for action, Somerset Hospital hesitated to fire Cullen. Finally, in October, he was let go and the police were called in.

On December 12, county detectives rousted Cullen from a restaurant in Somerville and asked him to submit to an interrogation. He came along, wearing his usual sad-eyed and grumpy countenance. Cullen had a lifetime's worth of guilt to unload, and over the next six hours he did so.

The number of patients he had murdered was somewhere between thirty and forty. He'd had a long career, after all, and there were so many patients along the way; he could be forgiven for not remembering the exact death toll. Cullen said he typically poisoned their bloodstreams either with needles or by tampering with bags of intravenous fluid. His drugs of choice were insulin and digoxin, which was what killed both Reverend Gall and Helen Dean. Because it was a medicine, digoxin was not one of the one hundred poisons tested for in Dean's death.

Cullen struggled to justify his monstrous deed. Like other angels of death, medical workers who exploited patients' trust in order to execute them, he claimed he was doing something merciful. Cullen, a high school dropout from West Orange who served in the Navy, had gone to nursing school to ease the pain of the suffering. At his first job, at St. Barnabas Medical Center in Livingston, he worked among burn victims. The experience of scraping their skin and seeing their useless limbs amputated left him nauseated and depressed. They were "just slowly being chopped away and so it was a very dehumanizing process," he said piously.

To restore the patients' "humanity," Cullen robbed them of their life. His first known victim, a Jersey City judge being treated for sunburn at St. Barnabas, was given a lethal injection in 1988. The nurse's last known murder was that of Reverend Gall fifteen years later.

Cullen's rationale may have been euthanasia, but his confession made clear that he really desired to exercise control over those weaker than him. In his own life control was lacking. He had gone through divorce, and then a bankruptcy when he fell $66,000 behind on his child support. He had made up to twenty half-hearted suicide attempts, starting at age nine. "I kept going into these deep depressions and I would say that that was part of it," he told the police, the word "it" serving as a euphemism for his murders.

To find out how many people Cullen killed, the police needed his cooperation in going over medical records. He granted them this cooperation in exchange for his life. Cullen pleaded guilty to a total of twenty-three homicides—even though the actual number was certainly higher—and the judicial system gave him a life term in prison instead of the death penalty.

"I wish I would have taken my own life a long time ago so I wouldn't, would have, what I did," Cullen told the police after his arrest. "You know, maybe if I was nine years old and would have had to die that day, all these lives, including my family, wouldn't be affected in this way." For once, the victims of Charles Cullen had something to agree with him about.

Mob Paradise

THE JERSEY UNDERWORLD

❯ THIRST FOR POWER ❮

WAXEY GORDON, RACKETS CHIEF
1889–1952

"WAXEY," IT WAS SAID, came from the wax-like smoothness of his stubby fingers as they glided into the pocket of a mark and came up holding a wallet. "Gordon" was a tribute to some other once-famous street tough, in whose footsteps he followed on New York's Lower East Side. Put together, the name "Waxey Gordon" struck fear into this Jewish ghetto in a way his real name of Irving Wexler never could.

Waxey Gordon, seen after his release from prison in 1940, fell from kingpin of a New Jersey-based bootlegging empire to street-level heroin pusher.
(*New York Post*)

But all the pickpocketing and leg-breaking never could have made Waxey Gordon the New Jersey millionaire that he became. It took the U.S. Constitution to do that.

When Prohibition was enacted in 1920, Gordon was among the visionary few to grasp the enormous profit potential in supplying the nation with liquor. That year, he struck a deal with Arnold Rothstein, the consummate underworld fixer. Rothstein chartered a cargo ship filled with Scotch from Great Britain. Gordon was given a $175,000 bankroll and the charge of warehousing and retailing the hooch.

Rothstein eventually grew fearful that the federal authorities would crack down on this racket, and allowed his junior partner to buy him out. Suddenly Gordon found himself in charge of the mightiest rum-running empire on the East Coast. Bribes and firepower ensured his authority. In 1925, he was arrested for bootlegging when one of his ships' captains squealed. The skipper was soon found shot to death in his hotel room. It was conveniently ruled a suicide, and all charges against Waxey were dropped.

Flush with cash, Gordon expanded from supply into production. By 1930, he had muscled his way into controlling whiskey cutting plants in Philadelphia and breweries in the North Jersey cities of Paterson, Elizabeth, Union City, and Harrison. Under Prohibition, the breweries were allowed to stay open so long as their beer had an alcoholic content no greater than one-half of 1 percent. Gordon's employees made near beer for one hour a day, then spent the next twenty-three hours brewing the real thing.

At each location, tubes carried the beer underground, through the municipal sewers and into a garage located a discreet distance away. There, the product was piped into barrels and loaded onto trucks. Good beer should be aged in vats for two to three months, but the greedy Gordon directed that it sit for just forty-eight hours before going into the pipe-lines. His future nemesis, prosecutor Thomas Dewey, observed: "The public had to be thirsty to drink Waxey Gordon's stuff."

Gordon commanded the fear if not the love of his goons, who called him "The Louse." Behind his back, of course. He was five-foot-six, with a thick body, a bulbous skull, and a gruffness that exploded into violence if he was crossed. He kept up the pretense of an honest businessman and married family man, once splurging $4,200 on a library of the classics. It was never read, or even opened.

Gordon listed his residence as the Alexander Hamilton Hotel in Paterson, and he had a Jersey Shore summer home in Bradley Beach. But he fit right in with Broadway society, where he cavorted with showgirls half his age. He wore monogrammed silk underwear, and loose, pin-striped suits made by Al Capone's tailor.

This was not the only trait Gordon shared with Chicago's mob chief-tain. Both gangsters also had a casual attitude toward paying their taxes. Capone was eventually sent to prison for tax evasion, and it occurred to federal prosecutors that this was the ideal way to put Gordon away, too.

In 1930, it was estimated, Gordon earned $1.34 million from beer alone, and paid $10.76 in income tax. Dewey, the young new U.S. attorney for Manhattan, sent his agents to Gordon's bank in Hoboken to go over the bootlegger's accounts. They were told to sit and wait, and in the mean-time gangsters arrived through the back door, withdrew their deposits, and took with them all records of the dirty money. Gordon had invested millions in the Jersey banks, and in the Great Depression the bankers were not willing to lose his business.

In the spring of 1933, Gordon suddenly found himself fighting on a new flank. Rival beer baron Dutch Schultz declared war and went about hijacking Gordon's beer trucks and picking off members of his crew. On April 12, an assassin stormed Gordon's hotel suite in Elizabeth and gunned down two of his top aides. The top man himself escaped, squeezing his bulk through a window. But he was now in fear for his life. When he was arrested the following month on a tax evasion rap, he was glad to have the protection of a jail cell.

At his Manhattan federal trial, Waxey Gordon portrayed himself as a mere salesman for the beer distribution business. All those millions of dollars the government said he had? It really belonged to the two gangsters slain in Elizabeth, now forever silent and unable to testify. "I've got only two vices," he said. "One is for beautiful clothes and the other is for a beautiful home."

On cross-examination, Dewey savaged him. He read from paperwork Gordon had filed in Asbury Park, which permitted him to carry a pistol: "Reason for application—'Carried large sums of money on person for business purposes.' Is that right?"

"At times, yes," Gordon said, avoiding eye contact.

"I suppose the money wasn't yours."

"It wasn't."

The jury went back to deliberate on December 1, and came back fifty-one minutes later to find Gordon guilty as charged. He was immediately sentenced to ten years in prison. The ironies of the following week couldn't be crueler. On December 5, Prohibition was repealed. The same day, Waxey Gordon's nineteen-year-old son, Theodore, came racing from medical school in North Carolina to New York, hoping to plead with the judge to reduce the sentence. Along the way, his car spun out of his control and he was killed.

A grayer, wobblier Waxey emerged from prison in 1940. "Waxey Gordon is dead," he told reporters. "From now on, it's Irving Wexler, salesman." But he had nothing legitimate to sell. In 1951, he tried to peddle a package of heroin on the streets of Manhattan, then sagged in disbelief when the buyer announced himself as a federal narcotics agent. "Shoot me," Gordon pleaded. "Don't take me in for junk." His death wish was granted soon enough. Waxey Gordon was sent to Alcatraz, where he expired after just one year of captivity.

❧ CHOP HOUSE ❧

DUTCH SCHULTZ, BEER BARON
1902–1935

THE DUTCHMAN HAD A TEMPER. Everyone in gangland knew that. There was that night he smashed a peanut bowl and jabbed the shards into a disrespectful punk for telling a joke about some chorus girl. And the time he tortured a rival bootlegger by wrapping gonorrhea-infected rags around his eyes, blinding him for life. Wild and vicious stuff, but what Dutch Schultz was proposing in the fall of 1935 was sheer madness. New York state's newly appointed racket-busting prosecutor, Thomas Dewey, was aiming to topple the crime syndicate's leadership. Schultz's solution: put a hit on Dewey.

Every other gang chief—New York's Lucky Luciano, Meyer Lansky, and Lepke Buchalter, and New Jersey's Longie Zwillman—was incredulous. Mobsters killing mobsters was perfectly legitimate. They had set up their own contracting arm, Murder Inc., for this purpose. But you didn't gun down policemen, and certainly not America's most respected law officer after J. Edgar Hoover. A dead Dewey would kill their political protection just as surely.

Dutch Schultz (left) leaves an upstate New York courtroom in August 1935 after his acquittal for tax evasion. He soon afterward decided to eliminate his problems by plotting to murder New York prosecutor Thomas Dewey. (*New York Post*)

Two months later, Schultz lies rambling on his deathbed at Newark City Hospital after the rest of the underworld decided Dewey should live. (*New York Daily News*)

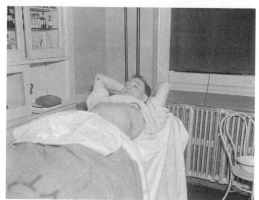

Schultz stuck to his guns. As the crusading young U.S. attorney for New York, Dewey had already brought down Schultz's old rival, Waxey Gordon, for tax evasion. Then, in 1935, the Dutchman himself was indicted for the same thing. He beat that rap, then exiled himself to New Jersey to avoid the constant hassling from New York. From the safe distance of the Robert Treat Hotel in Newark, where starstruck staff and newsmen fawned over him, the thirty-three-year-old racketeer plotted his next murderous move.

Brains and nerve drove Dutch Schultz to the top of the underworld, even if he did lack impulse control. He was born Arthur Flegenheimer in the South Bronx, where he ran with the various Jewish gang youths who regarded their striving immigrant parents as suckers. Because Flegenheimer was an improbable name for a gangster, and didn't fit nicely into headlines, the young hood adopted the moniker of Dutch Schultz.

Reading about his own feats was one of Schultz's few vanities. The sleepy-eyed fellow was handsome—"like Bing Crosby with his nose bashed in," an intimate recalled—but skimped on expenses by wearing shoddy, ill-fitting suits. The contrast with his sharp-dressed mob colleagues couldn't be clearer. "Only queers wear silk shirts," Schultz once said.

By the early 1930s, Schultz had virtually cornered beer bootlegging in the Bronx, New Jersey, and Manhattan's West Side. From there, he muscled into the restaurant unions and seized Harlem's policy racket— the street lottery based on guessing sequences of three numbers. With a human adding machine named Otto "Abbadabba" Berman by Schultz's side, this last enterprise turned into a Depression-proof gold mine. Schultz's path to power was littered with the corpses of his enemies: Legs Diamond, Vincent "Mad Dog" Coll, and Schultz's own lieutenant, "Bo" Weinberg. This last unfortunate was suspected of mob treason, and Schultz took savage delight in revenge. The Dutchman reportedly trussed up Weinberg, encased him in cement, and personally chucked him into the Hudson.

Would Dewey himself now fall to the Dutchman's fury? A Murder Inc. team actually scouted the U.S. attorney's comings and goings from his Fifth Avenue apartment. Mob assassin Albert Anastasia, posing as a father teaching his son to ride a bicycle, shadowed the prosecutor every morning. Finally he judged his mission would be impossibly messy. Too many witnesses, too many innocent bystanders.

The mob syndicate came to realize that Anastasia was right, and that this, the most audacious hit plot in mob history, could come to no good. If the Dutchman persisted in his mad assassination talk, Dewey might get word. Besides, Schultz himself might inadvertently spill their secrets if he went on trial.

So, instead of whacking Dewey, the mob chose to make Schultz himself their target.

Getting to the big man was no problem. Everyone knew he spent nights in the back dining room of the Palace Chop House, around the block from his hotel in Newark. Late on October 23, 1935, he was there as usual, going over betting slips. Sitting at the round table with him were Berman and Schultz's two most trusted bodyguards, Bernard "Lulu" Rosencrantz and Abe Landau. It was just the four of them at 10:15 P.M. when they got the unexpected call.

The two assassins had the advantage of surprise, if not numbers. One entered the front door carrying a pistol. He nodded silently to the bartender, who understood exactly what to do: drop and say nothing. Behind the first hit man came his tall, strapping partner, his overcoat concealing a sawed-off shotgun. They barged their way into the back room and opened up a loud and smoky fusillade.

The shots found their mark, piercing Berman, Rosencrantz, and Landau before any of them could stand up. But Schultz wasn't there. The first hit man bounded into the men's room and caught him standing at the urinal. It was an embarrassing way for Schultz to make his last stand. A single .45 slug went through the midsection.

Landau and Rosencrantz, perforated by ten wounds between them, managed to struggle to their feet. Wildly, they shot back at their assassins. The invaders beat a retreat the way they came, hopping into a car driven by a wheelman known to history only as "Piggy." In an amazing feat of endurance, Landau stumbled to the street, aimed his Smith &

Wesson .45 at the getaway vehicle, and blazed away. Then, dizzy from blood loss, he dropped to the pavement.

All four victims of the Palace Chop House slaughter still breathed when the police got there. They were taken to Newark City Hospital, where they died, one after the other. It was the deadliest gangland rubout ever to take place on a day other than Valentine's Day.

Schultz, in agony as peritonitis attacked his wounded stomach, lingered for nearly a day. "Tell us who did it," a policeman said. "It was somebody that didn't like me, I guess," the Dutchman spat back. But over the next few hours, afflicted by delirium and the demons of a dying man, Schultz slowly grew talkative. Soon he was babbling endlessly—so much so, the police called for a stenographer to sit at his bedside and type down every word he said. The hope was that he'd spill some clues to aid Dewey's rackets crackdown.

But no bombshells emerged, just the strangest free-association prose this side of James Joyce: "Oh, oh, dog biscuit, and when he is happy he doesn't get snappy. . . . You can play jacks, and girls do that with a soft ball and do tricks with it. I take all events into consideration. No. No. And it is no. It is confused and it says no. A boy has never wept, nor dashed a thousand kim."

Dutch Schultz died at 6:40 P.M. on October 24. His rambling drivel offered no clues about the killers. Yet, six years later, the authorities did catch them. The man with the pistol was Charlie "the Bug" Workman, who did twenty-three years in a New Jersey prison for his crime. The shotgunner was Emanuel "Mendy" Weiss, who ended up being executed in New York for an unrelated murder.

In the wake of the Dutch Schultz rubout, the New York prosecutors managed to put away most of his rival gang leaders. Luciano went to prison and was deported; Murder Inc.'s boss, Buchalter, went to the electric chair. Some mob aficionados take this as proof that Schultz was right, that assassinating Dewey—who went on to become New York governor and came within a hair's breadth of becoming president— would have been in everyone's best interest.

Dewey himself learned what happened five years later from a district attorney's investigator. He heard the tale impassively until it came to the detail about the assassin teaching a youngster how to ride a bicycle. Dewey's eyes widened. He remembered that boy, and in that moment realized that the mob had saved his life.

❧ LAST LAUGH ❧

WILLIE MORETTI, UNDERBOSS
1894–1951

WILLIE MORETTI WAS A GAMBLING MAN who liked sure things. In the mid-1930s he discovered a scrawny young singer from Hoboken named Frank Sinatra and placed a bet on the kid's future.

When Sinatra got booked into all the best nightclubs of North Jersey, he had Moretti to thank. From there, his talent and connections got him a seven-year personal services contract with Tommy Dorsey's band. The budding star soon wanted to begin a solo career, the story goes, but Dorsey refused to free him from the contract. A couple of Moretti's henchmen shortly paid the bandleader a visit. One of them put a contract release in front of Dorsey, stuck a gun barrel into his mouth, and assured him either his brains or his signature would be on that piece of paper. Dorsey signed.

There is, admittedly, no evidence that the business with the contract happened. The tale of Sinatra's Mafia-assisted career entered pop culture

Willie Moretti and wife. "They're good people," he said of his underworld cohorts. "I think bad people ought to be behind bars and these fellows aren't behind bars yet." (*New York Post*)

through hearsay. It became legend when *The Godfather* author Mario Puzo wrote how Don Vito Corleone made a certain bandleader "an offer he couldn't refuse." Sinatra was always steamed about any hint that his friends' violence helped his rise to the top. But the fact was that Moretti ruled New Jersey on behalf of the mob, and he had a special relationship with Ol' Blue Eyes. Sinatra performed at the wedding of one of Moretti's daughters. For that matter, so did Dean Martin, Jerry Lewis, and Milton Berle.

Willie Moretti liked to entertain as much as he liked entertainers. He was called the laughing boy of the underworld, and his wisecracks helped liven up an otherwise grim business. A roly-poly five-foot-four, he spun yarns and belly-laughed at his own jokes. The biggest chortles came from the time in 1931 when he rubbed out a double-crossing bootlegger named William Brady in Hackensack. As Moretti's machine gun hosed him down, Brady screamed: "I'll pay! I'll pay!"

Anyone who knew Moretti in middle age found it hard to believe he was once a ninety-eight-pound featherweight boxer. The tough pug was born Guarino Moretti in Harlem and fought under the name "Willie

Willie Moretti, dead. The good-natured gangster was rubbed out in a "mercy killing" to stop his babbling. (*New York Post* / Barney Stein)

Moore." Young Moretti started to fill out his tiny frame when Prohibition put food on his table. He settled in East Paterson, New Jersey, in 1927 and became a professional rumrunner, loyally busting heads for booze baron Waxey Gordon. After Gordon was sent away to prison in 1933, Moretti assumed control of most of North Jersey's rackets.

When New York kingpin Frank Costello got married, Moretti stood up as his best man. He also served the big man as his underboss and top earner. Moretti's laundry business was a cover for a profitable enterprise in union rackets and gambling.

Moretti preferred the racetrack to the card tables, and was a habitue of the $100 betting window at Monmouth Park. He claimed all his income came from gambling, and he consistently beat the odds because he had a system. "Bet 'em to place and show," he explained when investigators quizzed him about his wealth. "You've got three ways of winning. Come down to the track some time and I'll show you."

As the cash rolled in, Moretti spent lavishly and well. Politicians and judges took their cut, of course. For himself, he bought a stately house in Hasbrouck Heights and a summer retreat in the Shore town of Deal. Along with his brother Sal, a horse trainer, he also purchased a thoroughbred farm. As a wink of mischief, he named one of his prized racers Muscle In.

Moretti never missed Sunday Mass, and he sent each of his daughters to the best universities. When he heard his protégé Sinatra planned to divorce first wife Nancy, the mobster wired him a telegram: "REMEMBER YOU HAVE A DECENT WIFE AND CHILDREN. YOU SHOULD BE VERY HAPPY." Of course, Moretti betrayed his own wedding vows with regularity. At some point, he contracted syphilis from one of the many prostitutes he slept with. By the 1940s it was wasting his brain.

Moretti had his lucid moments, but the rest of the Mafia had to worry about him in the closing months of 1950. Senator Estes Kefauver, in pursuit both of the mob and the Democratic presidential nomination, formed a committee to investigate organized crime. Moretti glibly offered opinions to all the newspapers that he was just a rougher sort of businessman, and anyway, everyone has a racket.

On December 13, he went to testify before Kefauver and fellow senators in Washington. Most mobsters on the hot seat invoked their Fifth Amendment right to not testify and seethed with grouchy, hateful stares. Moretti spoke volubly, with Runyonesque color. It was some much-needed comic relief amid a moment of national drama.

Was Moretti a member of the Mafia? "No, I am not a member, as I do not have a membership card."

Had he been friends with such characters as Al Capone and Lucky Luciano? "They're good people. I think bad people ought to be behind bars and these fellows aren't behind bars yet."

How did he take care of political protection? "I don't operate politically. If I did, I'd be sitting where you are—a congressman."

It was a bravura performance, and one senator even thanked Moretti for offering such frank answers. The crime syndicate was less impressed. Fellow mobster Vito Genovese argued that Moretti had to be silenced—at the point of a gun. He was bound to crack up, Genovese told Costello, and break the oath of *omerta*. Genovese was playing a double game, for he stood to replace Moretti as Costello's underboss. But an anguished Costello approved the hit anyway, rationalizing it as a "mercy killing."

On October 4, 1951, Moretti awoke at 9 A.M., sipped a coffee, and changed out of his silk pajamas into a snappy suit. Into his pockets he stuffed a roll of $2,000 in hundreds and fifties. He tossed his racing form and binoculars into the back of his Cadillac and headed for a day at the track in Jamaica, Queens.

But first, some business to transact. Moretti had a date at one of his favorite hangouts—Joe's Elbow Room restaurant in Cliffside Park—for what he believed would be a sit-down with mob chief Albert Anastasia. Anastasia's boys showed up, but the boss himself was running late. Moretti did not attach any significance to this.

The four other diners chatted in Italian with Moretti over orange juice and cake. At 11:25 A.M., the waitress retreated into the kitchen. This was the moment for Moretti's execution. Two members of the hit squad pulled .38-caliber revolvers and aimed squarely for his bald skull. Moretti had no time to react before he was falling from his chair and onto the tiled floor, forcibly retired at age fifty-seven.

The police investigating his murder later got a special chuckle out of the sure-thing bet he had circled in his tip sheet. It was a horse named Auditing, who finished fourth and out of the money that afternoon. So much for Willie's system.

☆ KISS OF DEATH ☆
VITO GENOVESE, FAMILY BOSS
1897–1969

THE CAREER OF VITO GENOVESE offers living, backstabbing proof that there is no honor among thieves. The code of *omerta* decreed absolute silence; Genovese dropped dimes in order to get his boss Lucky Luciano out of the way. Heroin-pushing was a no-no; Genovese raked in millions by importing the drugs from Italy by the shipload. This remorseless godfather also coveted another man's spouse so greedily that he killed the hapless husband and married the widow twelve days later. However, this was perfectly OK by the Mafia's rules of sexual morality, because the victim was not a made man.

Vito Genovese flashes a toothy smile that belied his cold-blooded nature. The feared boss's villa in Middletown, New Jersey, is now a public park. (*New York Post* / Louis Liotta)

To neighbors in Atlantic Highlands, New Jersey, the nattily dressed fellow walking the streets of their small town looked like any other businessman. He described himself as a scrap paper dealer. In reality Genovese was head and namesake of the mightiest of New York's five crime families. Ready to do his bidding was an army of 450 followers in the gambling, loansharking, and labor rackets.

An immigrant from Naples, Genovese made his bones by helping to rub out the last of the Mustache Pete bosses in 1931. Afterward, he was Luciano's feared underboss and enforcer. In mid-decade he began building his dream home in the suburbs: a lavish hillside retreat in Middletown, New Jersey, landscaped like an Italian villa with weeping hemlocks and terraced pools. (Today, it remains a beautifully tended expanse of gardens, the jewel of the Monmouth County park system.)

Genovese's icy eyes, concealed by dark sunglasses, never blinked as he ordered up a murder. One of his soldiers, Joe Valachi, later recalled: "If you went to him and told him about some guy doing wrong, he would have the guy killed. And then he would have you killed for telling on the guy." It was just such a murder—of one of his own assassins—that led New York prosecutors to begin investigating him in 1937. Genovese quickly fled to Italy with $750,000 in his suitcase.

With typical duplicity, the mob boss first allied himself with Benito Mussolini, becoming drug dealer to Il Duce's son-in-law. Then, when the tide of World War II shifted, Genovese offered his mob services to the Allied occupation forces. A bright Army intelligence officer with the amazing name of Orange Dickey determined Genovese was the same mobster wanted for murder in New York, and had him arrested. But the district attorney's only witness ended up dead of poisoning, which, intriguingly enough, occurred while he was being held in protective custody in a jail cell. A furious judge said he was forced to let the defendant go, and thundered: "You have thwarted justice time and again." Genovese grinned.

The mob leader resumed control of his rackets and settled himself again in New Jersey, this time from a plush homestead in the Shore town of Atlantic Highlands. There, Vito and Anna Genovese dined on gold and platinum plates and enjoyed what was hardly a conventional Mafia marriage. Not only had Genovese arranged to have her husband murdered, police informers claimed she was a bisexual who frequented mob-owned gay bars in Greenwich Village—and Don Vito fully approved. Come the 1950s, however, Anna tired of the life of a mob matron and filed for divorce. In the settlement that followed, Vito retreated to a humble clapboard cottage elsewhere in Atlantic Highlands.

The collapse of the Genovese marriage was an embarrassment. But the main roadblocks to his resuming his place at the top of the mob universe lay elsewhere. One of these roadblocks was Luciano. The once all-powerful gangster had been deported from the United States, but he sought restoration to his old throne by convening a mob conference in Havana in 1946. Genovese, one of the attendees, apparently tipped off newspapermen about what was going on. Under the glare of scrutiny, the Cuban government ordered the not-so-lucky Lucky out of their country.

The other obstacle to Genovese's becoming boss of his family was the man Luciano had designated as successor, Frank Costello. Genovese complained bitterly that he was the rightful heir. Finally he took action in May 1957 by sending his three hundred-pound torpedo Vincent "Chin" Gigante to gun down Costello. The hit man's bullet only creased his target's skull, but Costello got the message and unconditionally yielded control of the family to Genovese. As a follow-up later that year, Genovese arranged for the spectacular murder of the next-most-powerful Mafia head, Albert Anastasia. There was talk that Genovese aimed to be not just boss, but boss of bosses.

First order of business, Genovese determined, was to invest heavily in the heroin business. The crusty old dons had once shunned this action because even corrupt police refused to grant protection, but it was the undoubted wave of the criminal future. Genovese called for a national syndicate meeting to ratify his decision to enter the drug trade and divvy up the spoils. The site of this spectacularly ill-fated summit, on November 14, 1957, was the small upstate New York town of Apalachin. No sooner had the broad-shouldered, cigar-chomping Mafiosi pulled up in their limousines than they found, much to their surprise, state troopers waiting for them. Genovese was among the rogue's gallery of mobsters who tried to make a break for it through the surrounding farmland, only to be thrown into jail.

No charges stuck to the boss—his only apparent crime was to consort with other criminals—but the shame was tremendous. The Apalachin episode caught the attention of a U.S. Senate subcommittee investigating the rackets, and of a young counsel on that panel named Robert F. Kennedy.

The federal probe into Genovese's affairs ended up getting a push from an unexpected source. The semi-retired Frank Costello, still smarting from his bullet nick, always was quicker to go to his wits than a gun for revenge. Now he served up some gangland justice. Costello, in collaboration with Luciano and Meyer Lansky, directed Genovese to a get-rich-quick heroin deal that turned out to be a setup. The would-be boss of bosses became a federal prisoner, sentenced to fifteen years.

Genovese, utterly paranoid, convinced himself that his cellmate and old underling, Joe Valachi, was part of the conspiracy that had ratted him out. One day, Genovese planted a kiss on Valachi's cheek as a trick to take him into his confidences. Another prisoner muttered to him: "The kiss of death."

Valachi had never before dreamed of violating his sacred oath of *omerta*. But with the threat of murder hanging over him, he became the first made mobster ever to give total cooperation to the federal authorities. Eventually the reading public was enlightened to the existence of the terms Cosa Nostra, Five Families, consigliere, and capo through Valachi's testimony. Genovese died behind bars, and the secret life he swore to uphold was no secret anymore.

✤ IF LOOKS COULD KILL ✦

JOE ADONIS (GIUSEPPE DOTO), CAPO
1902–1972

LIKE A PROSPECTOR, Joe Adonis looked west and saw gold. The gambling kingpin was feeling the pinch from a reformist New York City administration in 1944 when he crossed the George Washington Bridge into organized crime's new frontier. Here he set up a chain of illegal gambling palaces that raked in millions. A panel of U.S. senators later asked Adonis why he had moved to New Jersey. He deadpanned: "I liked the climate better."

True enough, and not because Adonis's brick mansion in Fort Lee put him at nine hundred feet above sea level. The gangster was a friend of the Bergen County prosecutor and chief of detectives, along with various local police chiefs. The mayor of the neighboring town of Cliffside Park served as Adonis's lawyer. They looked after Adonis well and were rewarded with his dirty money. In that cozy corner of suburbia, the politicians could rationalize that they were giving the working man a harmless pleasure. Few cared to know that Adonis was a capo under Mafia boss Frank Costello, and got there by murder.

Joe Adonis had a beguiling way about him that made all his wrongs seem right. His real name was Giuseppe Antonio Doto. A pal's slip of the tongue gave him the moniker Adonis, but it was perfect. The young Brooklyn hood's swarthy, finely molded face and rippling physique made him look as much Greek god as Italian mobster. Proud of his looks, Adonis preened in front of mirrors, dressed in tailored suits, and romanced a harem of showgirls.

Joe Adonis shows off his killer good looks in a New York Police Department mug shot. The public face of gangsterism in the early 1950s, he took the rap for higher-ups. (New York Police Department)

Adonis had connections in high and low places. His childhood friends included two future mob bosses, Lucky Luciano and Albert Anastasia. On their behalf, he joined the hit squad that in 1931 assassinated Joe Masseria, pretender to the title "Boss of Bosses." The bloody move helped consolidate crime syndicate rule over New York, with Adonis in charge of floating crap games, slot machines, and bookmaking. On the side, he dabbled in the legitimate business of vending machines and trucking.

In the 1940s, Mayor Fiorello La Guardia, a *paisan* Adonis once supported, turned against the gambling rackets and campaigned to smash the one-armed bandits that were corrupting the city's youth. This was the atmosphere that sent Adonis into exile in the comfortable climes of Fort Lee. New Jersey was ruled by Costello's garrulous underboss Willie Moretti. The two were pals, and Adonis was godfather to one of Moretti's daughters. Now, Joey set to work running the mob's dice and roulette games.

At first, these dives were shabby barns, the floors covered with sawdust. Adonis had the golden touch to transform them. His showpiece gambling hall in Lodi was, from its outside appearance, a shabby garage. But the interior was a plush casino, with a restaurant in which steak dinners were served by waiters in white jackets.

Suckers from New York were escorted here by fleets of limousines. They rubbed shoulders with New Jersey judges and businessmen from old-money families, who plunged as heavily as anyone at the card tables. The heavy debts often went unpaid, but this was just fine for Adonis. He was always looking for favors to cash in.

In the wake of Adonis's move to his new home, the locals noticed a succession of thick-necked, scar-faced men buying up expensive property, too. Soon Fort Lee was the most celebrated Mafia suburb since Al Capone's Cicero, Illinois. Among those who moved in were a boss (Anastasia), an underboss (Anthony "Tony Bender" Strollo), and a future boss (Tommy Eboli).

Adonis did not rank especially high in the organizational charts compared to these men. But he was conspicuous thanks to his glad-handing and charisma. In 1951, he was called to testify before Senator Estes Kefauver's committee on organized crime. When asked if he had heard of the Mafia—not if he was a member, just had heard of it—Adonis replied: "It is entirely fictitious."

Even without Adonis's cooperation, the Kefauver committee had no problem exposing the gambling going on all over North Jersey. This led to one of those periodic outcries for reform that inconvenienced the mob from time to time. Adonis was indicted for conspiracy and promotion of gambling shortly after testifying in Washington, and the national crime syndicate directed him to take the rap. Adonis did so, refusing to implicate any other Mafiosi as he entered a plea of no contest.

Adonis was all set to go free and assume control of his enterprises when he left Trenton prison in 1953. Then the federal government found a new weapon against him. He had a certificate showing he was born in Passaic, New Jersey, in 1902, but investigators discovered it was a fake and that he was really born in a town outside Naples. The government ordered him deported as an undesirable alien to Italy.

In his native land, Adonis was just as undesirable. The Italian police kept constant tabs on him, certain he was still up to no good. Finally, a court ordered him into internal exile on the grounds he remained a Mafia leader. "I'm a sick man," he sputtered in his last appearance in court, at age seventy. "If you send me to exile, it'll kill me." Adonis was correct. Banished to a remote town on the Adriatic Sea, he died of a bad heart four months later.

❧ CLIPPED ❦

ALBERT ANASTASIA, FAMILY BOSS
1902–1957

YOU COULD TAKE ALBERT ANASTASIA out of Brooklyn, but you couldn't take Brooklyn out of Anastasia. The Lord High Executioner of Murder Inc. had advanced himself from contract killer to Mafia boss and traded his railroad flat near the docks for a splendid estate in Fort

Lee, New Jersey. One night in 1952 he plopped down in front of his television and saw a salesman named Arnold Schuster telling the thrilling
story of how he had spotted the famous bank robber Willie Sutton on
a Brooklyn subway. Schuster had promptly told the police, who collared
America's most-wanted fugitive. Anastasia fumed. Sutton wasn't mobbed
up in the slightest, but it was the principle of the thing that stirred the
don's rage. Law-abiding behavior, breaking out on his old streets!

"I can't stand squealers!" Anastasia rasped to his minions. "Pop him!"
His wish was their command. The following week, Schuster, twenty-
four, was walking home when a shadowy gunman slew him with a shot
in each eye. The crime aroused national outrage, yet went unsolved for
more than a decade—until the Cosa Nostra turncoat Joe Valachi relayed
the tale of how Albert Anastasia had an innocent man killed on an angry
whim.

Mob bosses have achieved high body counts over the years, but it is
doubtful any of them found as much pleasure as Anastasia did in killing. The broad-beamed, bull-like stevedore from Italy's Calabria region
notched his first murder in 1921, shooting a fellow dockworker. He was
sentenced to death but went free on the combination of a technicality, the
untimely demise of one witness, and another's flight out of the country.

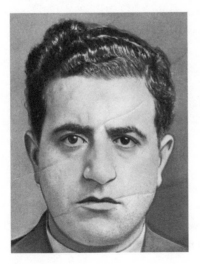

Albert Anastasia, in his New York
Police Department mug shot, was called
"Lord High Executioner" of Murder Inc.
(New York Police Department)

After that, no earthly law could stop the young Mafioso. He killed by gun, knife, garrotte, and a signature specialty: hammering an ice pick into the ear. He was so good at his job, New York's crime syndicate appointed him chief executive officer of their assassination business, Murder Inc. The papers called him Lord High Executioner, but fellow mobsters had a nickname more fitting to his homicidal mania: The Mad Hatter.

With the help of his three brothers, all equally stone-cold dock-workers, Anastasia seized control of the unions on the Brooklyn waterfront. This gave the Anastasia boys the life-or-death power to determine who worked and who didn't in the trough of the Great Depression. When a daring young longshoreman blew the whistle on this racket in 1939, Anastasia strangled him and had his body dumped in a lime pit by the Passaic River in New Jersey. Two years later, Murder Inc. assassin Abe Reles turned state's evidence and began linking Anastasia to thirty mob hits. For his trouble, Reles found himself pitched out the window of a hotel room guarded by six policemen—the "canary who could sing but couldn't fly."

Anastasia served for twenty years as loyal No. 2 to the family boss, Vincent Mangano. When the Lord High Executioner began itching for the top job, you can guess what happened to Mangano. He vanished

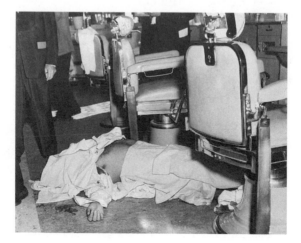

In 1957, Anastasia left his Fort Lee home for an appointment with the barber and never came back. (AP/Wide World Photos)

sometime in 1951, and has never been found. Anastasia was an expert at body disposal, too.

The heads of New York's other four families would normally have disapproved of such an unsanctioned murder, but Anastasia was given their blessing to become the new boss. Frank Costello, most powerful of the dons, felt he needed the unstable gang lord as a counterweight to his nemesis, Vito Genovese.

As for any effective CEO, the cash flowed in. In 1947, Anastasia bought his thirty-four-room, five-bath house done up in Spanish stucco and perched on Fort Lee's breathtaking Palisades over the Hudson River. Two Dobermans roamed the lawn, gnashing their jaws from behind an iron fence. The interior was done up in Mafia Baroque, with mirrored crystal tables and a lacquered grand piano bearing oriental designs. On one wall hung a painting of a Roman gladiator beheading a foe.

The lavish expense that went into these living quarters caught the attention of the U.S. attorney's office in Newark, which tried to nail Anastasia for tax evasion. Their key witness, the building contractor who installed Anastasia's plumbing, ended up vanishing along with his wife from a home filled with bloodstains. Anastasia pleaded guilty in 1955 to tax evasion and served a year in prison, but it is unlikely he would have gotten what amounted to a plea bargain if the prosecution's case hadn't suffered such a hard blow.

Soon after Anastasia regained his freedom, the underworld was ready to forcibly retire him. It wasn't so much his excessive killings, or the hit against Arnold Schuster, although the exiled boss Lucky Luciano did complain that Anastasia was "startin' to see himself like some guy in the gangster movies."

The fatal problem was that Anastasia's gangland ally Costello was now in retirement. Without this bedrock in place, two mob insurgents, Vito Genovese and Carlo Gambino, felt free to take on the don. The Lord High Executioner was always a muscleman, not a chess master, and he could not so much as glimpse his opponents' next move.

On October 25, 1957, Anastasia squeezed into the back of his big, black Lincoln and told his driver to take him to the barber at the

Park Sheraton hotel in Manhattan. The chauffeur-bodyguard dropped off Anastasia, parked the car in a garage, and chose that time to take a leisurely stroll instead of catching up with his boss. In the barber's chair, Anastasia sat back and submitted his scruffy neck to the electric clippers. He relaxed and shut his eyes as the glass doors opened up behind him.

Two well-dressed men, overcoats covering the bottom halves of their faces, strode in purposefully. The barber stepped to one side, and the intruders leveled pistols at the bulky figure sitting there like a perfect target and fired away. Anastasia, his back and arm pierced by three bullets, managed to wrest himself upright, kicking free the chair's footstand. In the mirror he saw the reflection of his killers, and instinctively lunged at these phantoms. Two more slugs buried themselves in his skull and he went down for good.

Albert Anastasia, who had escaped electrocution as a young man, met his death in another type of chair, at age fifty-five. Fate was poetic—and silly. Anastasia's property was sold for taxes, and the plush home of the most feared mob boss in America ended up in the hands of the wackiest comedian in America, Buddy Hackett.

❧ SILENT PARTNER ❧

ABNER "LONGIE" ZWILLMAN, GANGSTER
1904–1959

ONCE THERE WAS A POOR JEWISH BOY from the slums of Newark who rose to become a powerful and wealthy gangster. Politicians sought his counsel, a glamorous movie star fell for him, and the Italians who ran the national crime syndicate made him a member of the club. It's enough to make you believe in the American dream.

Abner Zwillman was the name of this striver, but friends called him "Longie." The nickname hinted at the physical toughness behind his success. At six-foot-two, he was known in his neighborhood as *der langer,* Yiddish for "the tall one." The swarthy, wiry bruiser could always be called upon to combat teenaged Irish bullies whenever they hassled Jewish street peddlers.

At fourteen, Zwillman was an all-around strong-arm man as well as a numbers runner. When Prohibition came, he rode shotgun for shipments of illegal liquor landing at Port Newark. Eventually he became the chief supplier of beer for Newark.

To counter inroads on his rackets, Zwillman aimed a few particularly low blows. Once, he hunted down a rival bootlegger to a restaurant and shot him in the testicles. Another time, he viciously blackjacked a double-crossing underling and told the police he was sorry the man didn't die. Zwillman spent six months in jail for the latter assault in 1930, but it was the last conviction on his record.

With the repeal of Prohibition in 1933, Zwillman was one of those farsighted gangsters willing to break down ethnic barriers and eager to find new outlets for enterprise. His fellow rumrunner and good friend Willie Moretti vouched for him with the Lucky Luciano crime family of New York, and Luciano's boys provided him with muscle. In return,

Abner "Longie" Zwillman in 1938, when he had begun transforming himself from unabashed gangster to Newark businessman.
(*New York Post*)

Zwillman was a tremendous earner through his street lottery, vending machine rackets, and control of the movie projectionist and stagehand unions.

His bookmaking racket was not especially kosher. Prime gambling season was the World Series, which typically took place during the Jewish high holy days—so Zwillman's runners blithely stopped by synagogues to take bets on the ball games.

Zwillman attracted gangsters of all ethnicities, to whom he was a wise rabbi. Allies in higher places made Zwillman probably the best-protected mobster of his era. He was friends with both Harold Hoffman, the crooked Republican governor of New Jersey, and Frank Hague, the crooked Democratic boss of New Jersey. He personally engineered the election of Newark's mayor, and he offered $300,000 to a gubernatorial candidate in return for the right to name the next state attorney general. (In that case, Zwillman was refused.) To further court good will, Zwillman's Third Ward Political Club donated generously to Jewish charities and distributed free turkeys every Thanksgiving.

Longie had a rough edge during bootlegger days. But in his mature years he came to understand the importance of looking almost respectable in a crowd of not-at-all respectables. This high school dropout hired a tutor to help him speak proper English, read the classics, and became a bigger fan of opera than most of his Italian cohorts.

His immaculately cut suits, slick hair, and rugged good looks were popular with the ladies. For a time he dated Jean Harlow, and reportedly he impressed his wiseguy buddies by keeping a strand of her hair in his wallet. It came from a part of Harlow's body that was not her head and offered proof that she was no natural blond. His womanizing ended when he met a prominent socialite named Mary Mendels Steinbach. Zwillman married her and settled into a twenty-room house, built of ivy-covered stone in West Orange. Together, they raised two children to be law-abiding citizens.

The front for Zwillman's activity was a cigarette vending machine company called Public Service Tobacco. With the vast amounts of un-reported cash this business pulled in, he was free to diversify his portfolio by investing in legitimate industries: the Hudson Tubes railroad, now known as the PATH train, and the Sands casino in Las Vegas.

Few were fooled by his facade. Newspapers called him "The Al Capone of New Jersey" and identified him as one of the "Big Six" who controlled the mob. The others, supposedly, were Meyer Lansky, Bugsy Siegel, Joe Adonis, Frank Costello, and Lucky Luciano. Actually, Costello and Luciano controlled Mafia families; the other four did not. But Zwillman was a highly influential racketeer, and friends with all the above mobsters. He was a natural target for Senator Estes Kefauver's organized crime committee, and on March 26, 1951, he testified before it.

Zwillman portrayed himself as an honest businessman who had made money from bootlegging, sure, but that wasn't a crime anymore, was it? Flashes of his charm and humor broke through at times. He got laughs by denying that he was a silent partner in various shady businesses: "They accuse me of owning places. I walk into a restaurant, and I own the restaurant."

But television audiences were less swayed by Zwillman's quick wit than they were by his damning silences. On forty-one occasions he refused to answer questions on the grounds that they might incriminate him.

The U.S. attorney's office in Newark built a tax evasion case against Zwillman, digging up evidence he had cheated Uncle Sam out of $55,146 in one year alone. A jury heard this case in 1956 and deadlocked on it, causing a mistrial. This victory was purchased at a hard price. Zwillman's underworld cronies had bribed two of the jurors to hold out for acquittal. In January 1959, indictments came down against two Zwillman-connected hoodlums for jury tampering, and it became obvious Longie himself would be charged next. Depressed and anxious, the big man visited a doctor and was diagnosed with advanced heart disease.

At 2 A.M. on February 26, 1959, Zwillman woke up his wife by loudly pacing their floor, complaining of insomnia. He had drunk two bottles of Kentucky bourbon, but it had had no effect, and he suggested they both take tranquilizers. She went back to sleep. After awakening, she couldn't find him and walked down to the basement. Hanging from a crossbeam was the lifeless form of Longie Zwillman.

Zwillman had committed suicide, and he'd done it the hard way. He had looped the plastic clothesline three times around his throat, tied the rope over a crossbeam, and bent his knees to tauten his noose. The unusual manner of the death caused speculation that this was no suicide at all, but a gangland execution.

But the mob does not kill people in such bizarre fashion, and Zwillman had reason to feel suicidal. "I'm paying for it now," he had said toward the tail end of his American-dream career. "I wouldn't do it again for ten million dollars."

❧ BURYING THEIR DIFFERENCES ❧

ANTHONY "TONY PRO" PROVENZANO, CAPO AND TEAMSTERS LEADER 1917–1988

FENWAY PARK IN BOSTON may have its Green Monster, Wrigley Field in Chicago its ivy, but New Jersey sports fans are not deprived of tradition. They can always point to the goalposts at Giants Stadium and say that's where Jimmy Hoffa is buried.

Jimmy Hoffa, at the peak of his power in 1957, relied on Jersey Teamsters boss Tony Provenzano as his East Coast mainstay. Jealousy would undo their alliance. (*New York Post* / Barney Stein)

The tale that Hoffa's body was mixed into concrete and sunk into the Meadowlands, there to be trod upon in countless touchdown runs and end zone dances, is perhaps the best known of New Jersey's urban legends. The labor leader vanished in Detroit in 1975, at the same time the football stadium was under construction. But why would his killers go to all that expense of shipping his mortal remains such a distance? Most experts discount the idea as a grim joke. However, there is indeed a Garden State connection to Hoffa's disappearance, and his name is Anthony "Tony Pro" Provenzano.

Provenzano, the leader of the New Jersey Teamsters, was the strongest ally of Hoffa, the International Brotherhood of Teamsters president. Like Hoffa, Tony Pro was short and stubby, with ham fists and a personality to match. Provenzano began working as a union driver out of Hackensack in 1934, when he was sixteen.

He rose over the next twenty-five years from shop steward to Local 560 president to vice president of the Teamsters International Brotherhood. Provenzano had organizing ability and unflinching toughness. But more importantly, he was a capo in the Genovese crime family.

"Tony Pro" Provenzano (center) remains the top suspect in arranging Hoffa's murder. (*New York Post* / Frank Leonardo)

Tony Pro built a strong loanshark and bookmaking business along his routes, and added a lucrative income from shaking down the family owned trucking companies of Hudson and Bergen counties. The firms got protection against costly slowdowns, Genovese soldiers got no-show jobs, and the workers got the shaft. By the early 1960s, Provenzano's eleven thousand-member Local 560—based, appropriately enough, in Union City—gained the reputation as the most corrupt local within the Teamsters.

Provenzano earned a salary higher even than Hoffa's, and did not hide it. His sprawling ranch house in Clifton was the gift of a trucking company executive, and he dressed like a mobster right out of the movies, in sharkskin suits and a blinding pinky ring.

Provenzano and Hoffa got along like best friends. Tony Pro needed Hoffa in power to get loans from the Teamster pension fund, and Hoffa needed Tony Pro's muscle. "Let us bury our differences," Hoffa once said in a gesture toward union dissidents, and Provenzano did the burying.

In 1961, Local 560's secretary-treasurer, Anthony "Three Finger Brown" Castellito, made noises about reform. Two of Tony Pro's button men, Harold "Kayo" Konigsberg and Salvatore "Sally Bugs" Briguglio, strangled him. The body was then run through a garbage shredder.

Two years later, Provenzano went on federal trial for extorting $17,000 from a trucking company. One of the listed witnesses was a union member named Walter Glockner, but he never got a chance to testify. He fell dead on the streets of Hoboken, shot in the back, the week the trial began. With a shrug, Tony Pro told reporters: "He was accident-prone."

Provenzano was often indicted but had a skill at beating the rap. But in 1963 he was finally found guilty of extortion in federal court in Newark and sentenced to seven years in prison. It was the first great success of Attorney General Robert F. Kennedy's "Get Hoffa Squad," which he had formed to purge the Teamsters of mob influence. A year later came a greater feat: Hoffa was found guilty of bribery and jury tampering.

The top Teamsters ended up in the same penitentiary in Lewisburg, Pennsylvania—a notoriously cushy Club Fed for mobsters. Tony Pro's connections and rank as prison capo provided Hoffa with a pampered life. In return, the Jersey Teamster expected Hoffa to help him with a problem. As a convicted extortionist, Provenzano was barred from collecting his union pension, and he wanted Hoffa's help in restoring it. Tony Pro was stunned when Hoffa told him rules were rules. "It's because of people like you that I got into trouble in the first place," Hoffa said.

Provenzano did not take this rejection well. He got into frequent screaming matches with his former friend and was heard offering to single-handedly tear out Hoffa's guts.

Once freed from prison in 1971, Hoffa promptly began lobbying to get back his old job as Teamster president. Talking like a reformer, he vowed to call in all the union's bad loans. He also made vague threats against Provenzano, whom he blamed for blocking his path back to power. Hoffa was operating under the dangerous delusion that he was bigger than the mob.

On July 30, 1975, Hoffa had an appointment to meet two key figures in a peace meeting: Detroit mobster "Tony Jack" Giacalone and Provenzano. Neither man showed up. Seething, Hoffa kept waiting at the meeting spot, a restaurant near his home turf in the Detroit suburb of Bloomfield Hills. At about 2:45 P.M., a maroon 1975 Mercury pulled into the parking lot, and Hoffa got inside. From that point, Hoffa vanished from history and into legend.

Provenzano had a solid alibi for that afternoon: he was back at Local 560 headquarters in Union City, playing rummy. However, the FBI came to the certainty he had ordered a hit on Hoffa. Pennsylvania mob boss Russell Bufalino gave the OK, and Provenzano dispatched the gunmen. Memos in FBI files identify the murder suspects as Sally Bugs Briguglio; his brother, Gabriel; two other New Jersey brothers, Stephen and Thomas Andretta; and two Hoffa confidants, Frank "The Irishman" Sheeran and Chuckie O'Brien.

Ordered to testify before a grand jury, Provenzano kept silent. Sally Bugs talked to a reporter, hinted at knowing something, and was quickly rubbed out.

No one was ever brought to justice for the Hoffa hit, but Provenzano paid dearly. The Hoffa probe uncovered Tony Pro's 1961 murder of the union insurgent and his plunder of the pension fund, and for these crimes he drew a life sentence. He died in a federal prison at age seventy-one.

So what happened to Hoffa? It became the favorite guessing game of gangland, with a succession of mob convicts each claiming to have insider's knowledge. Probably the most compelling story is offered by Sheeran, who was a dying man when he confessed to being Hoffa's assassin in a 2004 book.

Sheeran, a professional hit man, claimed that a hit squad drove Hoffa away from the restaurant. When they arrived at a deserted house outside Detroit, Sheeran shot Hoffa twice in the back of the head. The body, Sheeran speculated, was sent to a Detroit crematorium. However, he couldn't be sure. So the guessing goes on, with Giants Stadium still in the game.

⤞ SECRET GARDEN ⤝

RUGGIERO "RICHIE THE BOOT" BOIARDO, BOSS OF NEWARK
1891–1984

LIKE A FEUDAL LORD, gang kingpin Ruggiero "Richie the Boot" Boiardo reigned in splendor, and wanted the world to know it.

The road past his home in Livingston, New Jersey, was flanked by a pedestal on which stood a dozen painted busts of his family, staring blank-eyed like porcelain dolls. A statue of Boiardo himself, astride a white horse, towered above them. Vegetables and flowers grew in a grassy expanse marked by a sign, "Godfather's Garden." A long driveway through the woods led to his sprawling citadel, a stone mansion that *Life* magazine called "Transylvanian traditional" and featured in a 1967 photo spread.

Somewhere on these seventeen acres, it was rumored, lay an incinerator where Boiardo disposed of his foes. "Stay away from there," one of his lieutenants, Anthony "Little Pussy" Russo, once said with a shudder.

The overlord of this eerie estate was no recluse, but a talkative, wisecracking mover and shaker. Boiardo liked to claim he was the inspiration for Mario Puzo's *The Godfather*, for which he offered no proof, but his long life story did bear certain resemblances to Don Vito Corleone. Like the fictional godfather, Boiardo was Sicilian-born, built a bootlegging empire in America, and formed partnerships with powerful politicians.

He settled in Newark at age nineteen. After Prohibition, he quit his job driving a milk truck in favor of supplying the harder stuff: rum, whiskey, beer. His nickname, "the Boot," derived not from footwear but from the pay telephones in which he transacted business. If you asked where Richie was, the answer would come: "Richie's in the booth." In Newarkese, this became "Richie the Boot."

Through ruthless intimidation, Boiardo became the chief supplier of booze in the Italian First Ward. In 1930, he foolishly waged a territorial war with Newark's more powerful Jewish gangster "Longie" Zwillman. The two were a study in contrasts: Zwillman, suave and quiet, kept to the shadows, while the beefy, boisterous Boiardo preferred to party in style. Diamonds seemed to drip from his clothes, most noticeably on his $5,000 studded belt. The Zwillman-Boiardo conflict ended when a shotgun blast fired by an unknown assassin filled Boiardo with lead. The diamond belt probably saved his life, deflecting the full force of the blast. Taught his lesson, Boiardo made lasting peace with Zwillman.

Although he was regarded as the loser of this particular war, Boiardo's underworld stature grew with time. He consolidated his power in the First Ward, even after relocating to the suburbs, and formed an alliance

"Richie the Boot" Boiardo (left) at one of his final court appearances, in 1979. The Newark crime lord trumped justice into his nineties. (Photo © *The Star-Ledger.* All rights reserved)

with the Genovese crime family. In the 1950s, as Zwillman squirmed under a battery of indictments that drove him to suicide, Boiardo inherited virtually all the rackets of New Jersey's largest city.

Boiardo's son, "Tony Boy," owned a contracting company whose contracts were largely fictional and existed solely to collect kickbacks from the Newark government. Under Mayor Hugh Addonizio in the 1960s, the Boiardos took a piece of all public works projects. As once-proud Newark fell apart, its infrastructure crumbling and its neighborhoods torched by race rioters, tax money was helping Richie the Boot to lay down tiles and build swimming pools at his castle.

Boiardo played the kindly patriarch, but his own lieutenants chafed under his rule. In 1963, an FBI wiretap caught "Little Pussy" Russo calling Richie the Boot "the most treacherous [obscenity] in the world," and both father and son "weasels." Richie was a "nut," Russo said, using his backyard crematorium not only to dispose of his own murder victims, but also corpses supplied by the New York families.

"Ray, I seen too many," Russo told Genovese capo Angelo "Ray" DeCarlo. "You know how many guys we hit that way up there?"

"What about the big furnace he's got back there?" DeCarlo said.

"That's what I'm trying to tell you! Before you go up there . . ."

"The big iron grate."

"He used to put them on there and burn them."

Even with these words on tape, law enforcement authorities speculated the body-burning story was just mob boasting and storytelling. Why, after all, would a boss put evidence of a murder right on his property? Yet there is no doubt Boiardo was a killer. Tony Boy was caught on another wiretap gleefully recalling how his father murdered a hapless victim known only as the "little Jew." "The Boot hit him with a hammer," the younger Boiardo said. "The guy goes up and he comes down. So I got a crowbar this big, Ray. Eight shots in the head!"

The wiretap transcripts, leaked to *Life* magazine for the same article that featured Boiardo's Mafia manor, put pressure on the state of New Jersey to finally take action against him. He was indicted on a gambling rap and sent off to prison at age eighty. To reporters, he laughed it off.

"They call me a crook," he said. "Everybody's got a job, some good, some bad." A year's relaxing stay at a state prison farm did nothing to persuade him to retire. In 1979, Russo was found shot to death in a spa in Long Branch, and many suspected Boiardo had Little Pussy whacked for his big mouth.

That same year, the state of New Jersey made its first attempt to indict gangsters on specific charges of operating a Mafia syndicate. A fading, withered Boiardo was among them—at age eighty-nine, the oldest mobster ever to be put on trial, anywhere. Pleading ill health, he had the charges dismissed. He died four years later, having outlived his son and every other vestige of New Jersey's swaggering gangland glory years.

❖ THANKS A MILLION ❖

NEWSBOY MORIARTY, NUMBERS KING
1910–1979

IN THE HISTORY OF THE NUMBERS RACKET, no one has made a better score. On July 3, 1962, two carpenters repairing a dingy row of garages in Jersey City came across an abandoned 1947 Plymouth. Inside, they saw some envelopes addressed to one Joseph Vincent Moriarty—a.k.a.

"Newsboy" Moriarty, sour-faced as usual in a Jersey City mug shot from 1960. Two years later, he lost a million dollars. (Jersey City Police Department)

Newsboy Moriarty, street lottery king of Hudson County—and this was more than enough to convince them that the shabby old sedan might be worth combing through.

Using crowbars, the workmen pried the trunk. A cloud of dust parted to reveal two leather bags and a tool box, and in these containers was a mountain of cash. The bills were smelly, moldy, even rotting around the edges, but they were beautiful. The total: $2,438,119.

Newsboy Moriarty had come into his fortune one nickel at a time. As a youth he hawked newspapers on the streets of Jersey City, an enterprise that offered perfect cover for collecting betting slips from his customers. Enthusiasts put down five- and ten-cent wagers in hopes of hitting "the number"—a daily three-digit combination, typically drawn from the last number in the parimutuel handle of three pre-selected horse races. Moriarty was a natural for the business, with mathematical skill, industriousness, and a reputation for always paying off.

Most importantly, he had the backing of Jersey City's all-powerful mayor, Frank Hague. Boss Hague was a killjoy who clamped down on booze and prostitution but extended toleration toward his only vice, gambling. Moriarty's honest reputation and Irish background gained him political favor. Under both Hague and the boss's equally corrupt successor, John V. Kenny, the police took their cut of Moriarty's receipts. Some cops even moonlighted as numbers runners for him.

Although he came to rake in $5 million to $8 million a year, Moriarty's racket was strictly independent. The Italian Mafia made no moves against him, wary of offending his political protectors. Moriarty was arrested forty-seven times for gambling, but most of these busts were strictly for show—afterward, he would get back his cash and policy slips. Not trusting banks, Moriarty stuffed bills into an assortment of hiding places—his fireplace flue, floorboards, car trunks.

This self-made millionaire led a lifestyle less like a gangster and more like the blue-collar Joes who made up so much of his clientele. A lifelong bachelor, he lived with his mother and two sisters in a modest brownstone. He wore ill-fitting pants, always seemed to have two days' growth of beard, and made his pickups in rattling jalopies. The sour expression on his face matched his sour stomach, for which he was always gulping down pills.

Moriarty forever cemented his reputation as an honest bookie after September 15, 1958, when a Jersey Central commuter train plunged off a drawbridge and into Newark Bay, killing forty-four people. The next day's front pages all pictured a railroad car dangling over the water with "932" stenciled on its side. Seeing this as a providential sign, hundreds of policy players bet 9-3-2 the following day, and 9-3-2 was the winning number. Bookies up and down the East Coast were wiped out, but the Newsboy paid all winners. He was even able to extend loans to other gambling kingpins outside of Hudson County and cut into the New York mob's action.

With opportunity came danger. "Trigger Mike" Coppola, the homicidal numbers boss of the Genovese mob, began putting pressure on this rogue operator to kick back to him. After hiding out for a time, Moriarty was arrested for possession of betting slips and sentenced to serve a short term in Trenton state prison. The word was, he was happy to go into the big house and be safe from the long arm of underworld justice.

If this was the plan, it backfired spectacularly. Just a few months after Moriarty entered prison came the discovery of his $2.4 million in the back of the Plymouth. The public-spirited workers who made the find immediately alerted the FBI. Within hours, the Jersey City police went on their own expedition. In a nearby garage they found $168,000, although there is reason to suspect this number was understated. Jersey City lore has it that of the four policemen who hauled the cash out in duffel bags, all retired comfortably within a year.

The hoopla over "Moriarty's millions" set off a treasure hunt to dwarf any expedition for a pirate hoard. Children and adventure seekers from Weehawken to Bayonne began tearing up garages in futile quests for more of the gambler's stash. Nothing was ever found.

From prison, Moriarty denied he was the unlawful owner of the $2 million-plus. All the evidence, including the car's registration (to Moriarty's girlfriend) and the medical folder inside (Moriarty's chest X-rays) indicated otherwise. Finally he was paid a visit by an Internal Revenue

Service agent who convinced him that the treasure was lost to him, anyway; should he 'fess up, he could at least satisfy a huge tax lien against
him. The Newsboy promptly filed a tax return claiming $2.4 million in
income—and seeking a $212,000 rebate. He didn't get it.

A free man again, Moriarty shrugged off the huge loss as just another
cost of business. But the 1970s were even unkinder to him than the 1960s
had been. Gangsters kidnapped him and tortured him with a blowtorch.
Reform administrations in Jersey City withdrew his political cover. Worst
of all, the all-too-legal New Jersey Lottery robbed the numbers racket
of its once-loyal customers. Suffering from Parkinson's and a weak heart,
Moriarty was hobbling on a cane when he endured his last gambling
arrest, a few months before his death in February 1979. Why would
you possibly still be at this criminal enterprise? a judge asked him. The
Newsboy could only respond: "It's part of my life."

❧ IN HIS OWN WORDS ❦

SIMONE RIZZO "SAM THE PLUMBER" DECAVALCANTE, FAMILY BOSS 1913–1997

THE PLUMBING AND HEATING supply industry does not always provide scintillating conversation, and the FBI agents who overheard Sam
DeCavalcante talking about this business fought boredom nearly every
day. But sometimes the wiretaps on New Jersey's only homegrown crime
boss produced a riveting mini-drama. One such moment occurred in 1963.
DeCavalcante was shooting the bull with Cosa Nostra cohort Angelo
"Ray" DeCarlo, and the topic turned to what the mob did best—murder.

"Ray, you told me years ago about the guy where you said, 'Let me hit
you clean,'" DeCavalcante said.

"That's right," DeCarlo said. "So the guy went for it. There was me,
Zip and Johnny Russell. So we took the guy out in the woods. . . . I said,
look, Itchy was the kid's name. I said, 'You gotta go, why not let me hit
you in the heart and you won't feel a thing.' He said, 'I'm innocent, Ray,

but if you've gotta do it.' So I hit him in the heart and it went right through him."

Both remembered the rubout of legendary New Jersey mobster Willie Moretti, and they agreed that he deserved a better fate than to be shot in the face. "It leaves a bad taste," DeCavalcante said. "We're out to protect people."

When the transcripts of the FBI's DeCavalcante recordings were revealed in court in 1969, the public got its first glimpse at the everyday life of a Mafia don. The story was a national sensation, and a severe blow to DeCavalcante's dignity. His image was that of a ramrod-straight businessman, with iron-gray hair and somber suits to match. He never cursed, and he chewed out subordinates who failed to wear neckties. The boss despised his underworld nickname of "Sam the Plumber," much preferring the aristocratic "The Count," or "Princeton Sam." Now DeCavalcante, who lived in Princeton and hoped the township's Ivy League cachet would rub off on him, was caught on tape discussing the ungentlemanly art of murder.

A bootlegger's son, Simone Rizzo DeCavalcante grew up in Trenton, where street lotteries and speakeasies were a fact of life. When Sam was

Simone "Sam the Plumber" DeCavalcante glowers at the camera on his way to court in 1969. He preferred the nickname "Princeton Sam." (*New York Post* / Arty Pomerantz)

just twenty-two, his own father inducted him into the mob. Their largely Sicilian outfit was little-known and liked it that way. New York wiseguys called this family the "Jersey farmers," with a hint of contempt. With perhaps fifty made men, the farmers weren't one-fifth the size of the smallest of New York's Five Families. But they dominated the building trades of Union and Middlesex counties, and expanded into the Shore during the 1950s development boom there.

DeCavalcante, who ascended to boss in 1962, enhanced his reputation by serving as a roving ambassador to the New York mob. He carried messages from one rival family to another, smoothed over ruffled feathers, and generally tried to promote peace. There are those who insist that DeCavalcante, with his pencil-thin mustache, regal air, and talent for conciliation, served as the model for Marlon Brando's don in *The Godfather*.

The 1960s were a time for the underworld to be on guard. John F. Kennedy was in the White House, and his bulldog brother Robert, the attorney general, had declared war on organized crime. Without court authorization, agents wiretapped the social clubs and business offices of Mafiosi across the nation. The first New Jersey bug went into a restaurant where Genovese capo DeCarlo did business. This produced leads pointing to DeCavalcante as a major player in loansharking, and another microphone was successfully tucked near his desk in his Kenilworth, New Jersey, office.

The whole operation was illegal. But the FBI felt that breaking the law was worth it. Their intelligence would unravel the intrigues of gangland and flesh out the FBI's organizational charts, telling who was who in the national syndicate.

Some of the nuggets were golden. DeCavalcante spoke again and again of the "Commission," the nine-member panel whose word was final on all the national rackets. He feared that the Commission's vendetta against renegade crime boss "Joe Bananas" Bonanno would start "World War III." He griped that Bonanno's son, a crazy "bedbug," was unfit to be captain. He bragged of averting a bloody move against Bonanno operations on the West Coast: "We were supposed to hit some people out there but we straightened that out—Carlo [Gambino] and I straightened it out."

Sometimes Sam's generous nature shone through. Discussing the shakedown of a contractor, he explained how his predecessor as boss had demanded contractors pay him 75 percent of the money they saved by freezing out union labor. DeCavalcante only asked for 50 percent. He counted mayors and state legislators as his friends, and a mayor of Elizabeth was caught on tape in one meeting. Once, DeCavalcante called up the police chief of Kenilworth. "Listen, chief, I need a favor," he said. "The problem is my cousin. . . . He's working for me now and he takes care of the payroll. We'd like to get him a gun permit for this area. We're trying to stop crime."

Being a crime lord had its banal moments as well. DeCavalcante moaned about the expense of putting his children through college, and complained about his gastrointestinal woes. He had an affair with his comely Jewish secretary, Harriet Gold—FBI agents jotted down "Sam and Harriet making whoopee again" in one transcript—and could talk to her in Yiddish. He was a watcher of Steve Allen's TV show but disliked *The Man from U.N.C.L.E.*

In 1965, President Lyndon Johnson ordered an end to all FBI eavesdropping, and the DeCavalcante papers might have been forever kept under wraps. But after Sam the Plumber was indicted on a federal charge of extortion, his lawyers demanded full discovery of any wiretaps that might be used as evidence against him. To their amazement, the government complied, and to DeCavalcante's horror, the once-classified transcripts were filed as public documents. The candid conversations about racketeering, corruption, and killing filled thirteen volumes and made headlines for weeks.

But the tapes, the product of the FBI's own lawbreaking, could never be admitted in court. DeCavalcante beat the extortion rap, although he did serve fifteen months in prison after pleading guilty to a gambling charge. In the late 1970s, he retired to Florida, living out the rest of his comfortable life there. Few mob bosses have suffered such public humiliation, but then few have been as fortunate to live and prosper, as DeCavalcante did, to the age of eighty-four.

❧ EL PADRINO ❧

JOSE MIGUEL BATTLE, CUBAN GANGSTER
1930–

THINK OF CUBAN GANGSTERS, and the over-the-top character played by Al Pacino in *Scarface* comes to mind—maniacally screaming "Say hello to my little friend!" as he sprays his enemies with machine-gun fire. But the real-life godfather of the Cuban-American Mafia, Jose Miguel Battle, had the icy calm and business acumen of a corporate officer. And the base of his power was a community of Cuban exiles in North Jersey who feared him as they would a dictator.

Battle began his career as a vice officer with the Havana police under Cuban strongman Fulgencio Batista. Nominally a man of the law, he safeguarded the plush gaming palaces that American gangsters Santo Trafficante and Meyer Lansky built in Havana. Upon Fidel Castro's seizure of power in 1959, Battle joined the flood of exiles who settled in Florida. Like many Cubans, he yearned for Castro's overthrow—not necessarily to restore freedom but to bring back gang power.

When a CIA-backed exile army landed at the Bay of Pigs in 1961, Battle was there as a company commander. It was a fiasco, of course, but Battle fought furiously for two days before his unit was captured.

Jose Miguel Battle, in a playful moment with a pet monkey, reigned unchallenged as CEO of the Cuban crime "corporation" for forty years. (Historical Museum of Southern Florida)

In prison, he demanded discipline from his soldiers and respect from their captors. Once, he slapped a guard across the face for mistreating his men.

By the time Battle went free after two years of captivity and was shipped to the United States, he had earned a hero's laurels. He was soft-spoken, dignified, tall, and built like a linebacker. He donated generously to charities. But friends did not call him *el padrino*—"the godfather"—for his personal qualities. What inspired respect were his mob connections.

In the late 1960s, Battle moved from Miami to a high-rise in Union City, New Jersey, to begin his new career: boss of a crime syndicate known as "the corporation." He was no insurgent. Success was assured by a mutual-assistance pact with the Genovese family and its New Jersey capo, "Bayonne Joe" Zicarelli. Battle was given a franchise over one-time Italian Mafia strongholds in Hudson County that were now home to Latino immigrants. In return, he gladly kicked back a share to the dons. Protection was guaranteed by Union City's mayor, William Musto, and the notoriously corrupt police department of West New York.

The corporation's business was *bolita* ("little ball"), a street lottery in which players chose three random numbers drawn from racetrack handles. Bets were placed in bodegas and Spanish-speaking bars up and down Bergenline Avenue—center of America's largest concentration of Cubans outside Florida. Even in the age of state lotteries, bolita drew faithful twenty-five-cent and $1 players—thanks to the game's 600-to-1 payoffs and untaxed income.

In the 1970s, the corporation expanded by building betting parlors throughout the Puerto Rican neighborhoods of New York and large operations throughout the Miami area. Battle was a heavy gambler himself, frequenting cockfights and playing for up to forty-eight straight hours at poker. He was never in danger of losing his shirt. By one estimate, he was personally worth $250 million.

As much as $2 million flowed his way every week from betting operations, and it was supplemented by tribute from drug dealers and truck hijackers. To disguise his earnings, Battle invented an ingenious form of money laundering. His mobsters would locate winners of the official

Puerto Rican lottery, buy their tickets from them, and report the jack-pots as legitimate income.

Battle's authority was enforced by gun and firebomb. Interlopers who set up betting operations were burned out of business in a series of arsons in New York City from 1983 to 1985; among the eight people killed was a three-year-old girl. After Battle had a falling-out with his chief hit man, Ernesto Torres, he went to great lengths for revenge. A car bomb failed to kill the enforcer outside his Cliffside Park, New Jersey, apartment in 1975, but a few months later a bullet between the eyes did the job. Another time, Battle had a rival murdered by sending a male assassin, wearing a nurse's dress, to shoot him to death in his hospital bed.

El padrino escaped prosecution for years because he preyed upon Spanish-speakers who didn't trust the authorities and were terrified of his wrath. By the 1980s, Battle was behaving like an international crime lord. He moved to a walled estate in southern Dade County, Florida, and flew frequently to Europe, where he kept secret bank accounts, and Peru, where he had $1 million invested in a casino.

Battle was an old and ailing man in 2006 when the law finally made a successful takeover of his corporation. He, son Jose Jr., and two other officers of his mob were all convicted of a racketeering conspiracy that included thirteen murders. But *el padrino* was never to serve a day in prison; because of his failing kidneys, a Miami federal judge agreed to postpone his sentence indefinitely. Instead of dying in a blaze of glory like "Scarface," Battle faded into old age and powerlessness after a forty-year reign.

❧ COWBOY STYLE ❧

NICODEMO "LITTLE NICKY" SCARFO, FAMILY BOSS
1929–

ATLANTIC CITY HAD ONCE BEEN a mob paradise, flush with tourist money, wide open for illegal dice games, and host to a historic gangland convention that drew Al Capone and Lucky Luciano. But by the mid-1960s the beach town was a decaying wreck. It must have seemed like Siberian exile for Nicodemo "Little Nicky" Scarfo.

He had been an effective capo in the Philadelphia family of Angelo Bruno—a hothead who stood only five-foot-five, was touchy about it, and liked to prove his manhood with violence. Then, in 1963, he killed a bar patron in a meaningless fight over a stool. Bruno decided a punishment was in order. Once Scarfo completed a short prison stay for manslaughter, the boss decreed, he must quit Philadelphia and redeem himself in Atlantic City.

For a decade, Scarfo did as told by operating what few piddling rackets remained there. He sold pornography, shook down the construction unions, and squeezed whatever life blood was left from a once-glorious resort. Then, in 1976, he hit a jackpot. New Jersey voters approved a referendum to legalize gambling casinos in Atlantic City. All of a sudden, the streets whose names inspired the game Monopoly were a land of opportunity, and all the cash was real. Atlantic City was no longer mob exile, but the focus of action.

Nicodemo Scarfo, sharply dressed and well coiffed as always, in court before the racketeering trial that put him away for life. (Reprinted with permission of the *Press of Atlantic City*)

Governor Brendan Byrne issued a warning to the mob: "Keep your filthy hands out of Atlantic City." He might as well have commanded the waves to retreat. Scarfo had the cement industry in his pocket, and Resorts International, Caesars, Bally, Tropicana, and Harrah's could not build their pleasure palaces without paying million-dollar tributes to him.

The diminutive mobster also ran Local 54, the union that supplied the casinos with bartenders, waiters, card dealers, and janitors. When a union leader named John McCullough tried to get in on the action, Scarfo sent some men disguised as florists to his home. Instead of roses, they delivered six gunshots to McCullough's head and neck.

"One day I'm gonna own this place," Scarfo told one visitor to his apartment house as they surveyed the rising Atlantic City skyline. He could be excused his arrogance, because his ascent in New Jersey coincided with a spectacular Philadelphia mob war that eliminated everybody above him. Angelo Bruno, known as the Docile Don because he so rarely resorted to violence, was first to go. On March 21, 1980, an assassin stuck a shotgun into the back window of Bruno's car in South Philadelphia and blasted a hole in the sixty-nine-year-old boss's head. Bruno's successor, Philip Testa, lasted a year before a nail bomb blew him to bits.

Bodies began turning up in car trunks and dumps all over the City of Brotherly Love. It was mob war on a scale unseen since Chicago in the 1920s, with touches of savagery and symbolism. The treacherous underboss who arranged the hit on Bruno was found dead with dollar bills stuffed in his anus. It was a Sicilian message: don't be greedy.

Scarfo did not launch the war. Other, renegade mobsters in the Philadelphia mob were behind the hits on Bruno and Testa. But with his proven ruthlessness, Scarfo was ideally situated to step over the bodies and take over the family. In 1981, at age fifty-three, he won the backing of the Mafia's national commission to become the new boss.

Scarfo quickly set new rules, opening up a booming trade in methamphetamines that his predecessor Bruno had strictly forbidden. The new boss also decreed that all bookies and loansharks in Philadelphia pay him a street tax. Cars filled with his thugs, brandishing pistols and baseball bats, hunted down those who withheld payment. To solidify his position in Atlantic City, Scarfo simply bought the government. He paid $150,000 in bribes to ensure that the mayor, Michael Matthews, would steer municipal contracts the mob's way.

For twenty years, the "books"—membership rolls in the mob—had been closed. Scarfo opened them up, inducting a crew of young, homicidal lieutenants. Unlike the old dons, who carefully insulated themselves from the dirty work, Scarfo joined his hit men in many a mission. He took a sadistic glee in meting out death. "I *love* this," he once said when wrapping up a corpse for disposal. The boss also relished it whenever his hits became the top story of the day on local television news. "Nicky liked cowboy style," said one of his cohorts, Nick Caramandi. "He liked broad daylight, restaurants or busy street corners. . . . He liked a lotta noise to scare people."

Mob etiquette about never harming a "civilian" went out the window. In order to intimidate a man who dared testify about Scarfo's personal role in a murder, Scarfo ordered that witness's father eliminated. Gunmen wounded the man in a botched hit in 1982 in the Shore town of Wildwood. He did not die, but the case made headlines—and all the stories carefully described the hit man's jogging suit. For the next few days, Scarfo and his deputies paraded around Atlantic City wearing identical jogging suits, as if to flaunt their responsibility.

The boss modeled himself on an old-time Hollywood gangster. He wore designer suits, feathered his hair into a salt-and-pepper pompadour, and put lifts in his shoes. Any mention of his "Little Nicky" moniker drove him into a rage.

It took very little to provoke Nicky to homicide. Salvatore Testa, son of the murdered old boss Phil, had been Scarfo's loyal field general on the streets of Philadelphia, carrying out a number of Wild West slayings. But in 1984, Testa broke off his engagement to the daughter of Scarfo's underboss. Scarfo considered this a deadly insult and began to imagine that the charismatic, twenty-eight-year-old Testa was recruiting his own soldiers behind the boss's back. It wasn't true, but Scarfo didn't like to take chances. He had Testa's own friends shoot him to death.

This murder was just one of perhaps twenty that Scarfo ordered during his career, but it was a turning point. Scarfo's soldiers could now never be sure whether their own boss would have them killed. Loyalty was no guarantee of survival; Sal Testa had been as loyal as anyone, and his reward was an early grave.

Talking to the federal investigators was once unthinkable among Scarfo's band of outlaws, but now it seemed rational. And the FBI was closing in. They had wrung a guilty plea from Matthews for bribery, and they had uncovered the Scarfo mob's corruption of the Philadelphia City Council. Three made men agreed to testify that Scarfo was the center of a web of murder conspiracies. One of them was Scarfo's own underboss and nephew.

In November 1988, a federal jury in Philadelphia convicted Scarfo and sixteen members of his crime family under statutes of the Racketeer Influenced and Corrupt Organizations (RICO) Act. His sentence, fifty-five years, ensured he would never be paroled unless he reached the improbable age of 104. It was a far more permanent exile than being sent to the ghettoes of Atlantic City.

❧ WHO'S SORRY NOW? ❧

GEORGE FRANCONERO, CONNIE FRANCIS'S BROTHER 1940–1981

TWO YEARS OF AGE, and little else, separated Concetta Franconero from her baby brother Georgie. They wore matching clothes and played together on the streets of Newark's Ironbound neighborhood; he provided the cheering section when she practiced accordion. She went on the radio at age nine, where Arthur Godfrey gave her an easier-to-pronounce name and set her on the path to stardom as Connie Francis.

Just after her twentieth birthday in 1958, Connie recorded "Who's Sorry Now?," an updated rock version of an old standard, and sold a million records. Soon she was America's top female vocalist, a Hollywood actress, and a Vegas headliner. From New Jersey came a letter from George: "Write if you get work."

The wry joke, the gentle tease, was George Franconero's way of gaining popularity. But behind the sense of humor was a jealousy. He didn't want to live in Connie Francis's shadow forever. Other important friends were going to make his career for him, and they happened to be in the mob.

A "C" student, Franconero worked himself through Seton Hall University and graduated from the law school there. At first, he struggled along as a $125-a-week assistant in the Essex County prosecutor's office. Then his connections came through for him—some of the same tough guys who often hung around Connie Francis. By the late 1960s, Franconero was a partner in a top-flight law firm (another partner was a future governor, Brendan Byrne) and had a very important client, Teamsters Local 945.

This was the garbage union, with control of the most profitable hauling routes in North Jersey. Organized crime ran it, of course, making so much money that Local 945 was called the crown jewel of the Genovese crime family. All the dirty money had to be laundered, which is where Franconero came in. He deposited the pension funds in a variety of family owned banks, then served as front man for a series of fraudulent loans backed by these deposits. The money—$4.7 million of it from one institution, the Bank of Bloomfield—went back to the mob disguised as legitimate earnings.

Franconero indulged in other scams centering on the mall boom. One parcel of land that looked ripe for development was owned by the township of Rockaway, New Jersey. Franconero and a partner used forged affidavits to claim they held the property rights. When builders sought to put the Rockaway Townsquare Mall there, they paid Franconero $95,000 in a settlement rather than fight the phony claim.

The 1970s were growth years for the mob. The Mafia was finding new and innovative ways to infiltrate legitimate business such as banks, insurance companies, and construction firms. By abetting these infiltrators, Franconero gave himself, his wife, and his two children a good living.

They moved to a large ranch house in North Caldwell, the affluent Newark suburb that would later be home to the fictional Tony Soprano.

Franconero was also carrying a $500,000 debt, a burden that his mobster associates fully exploited for their favors. "Georgie wasn't a criminal, but a victim," Connie Francis wrote. "He was manipulated by people far shrewder than he ever was, people who took advantage of his deeply rooted weaknesses. . . . Tragically, doing anything at all for others gave him the feeling of self-worth that he lacked."

In 1977, as Franconero's banks inevitably went bust, the federal government uncovered the frauds. The lawyer pleaded guilty to a relatively minor charge, submitting a false bank application, and drew a light sentence of probation. But this agreement did not immunize him from state charges, and he was eventually also found guilty of fraud for the mall scheme. Disgrace and disbarment followed. Free on appeal and fighting to fend off a three-year prison sentence, Franconero supported his family as a furniture salesman.

By then, however, prison was not his greatest fear. The Teamsters played rough. Two successive Local 945 presidents had vanished into unknown mob cemeteries, and the present leader, Joseph Campisano, was convicted in 1979 of racketeering. Franconero was rumored to have supplied the U.S. attorney's office the information it needed to prosecute that case. Offered a place in the Witness Protection Program, Franconero turned it down, unwilling to uproot himself from his loved ones. He had no illusions about what would happen to him. "You can't talk about them and expect to stay alive," he said.

On March 6, 1981, the morning after a winter storm, Franconero walked out of his home bundled in a heavy overcoat. As he stood on the driveway, brushing the snow off his car's windshield, two men emerged from hiding behind a row of bushes. They pointed .32-caliber pistols at his head from twenty feet away and fired, accurately. Franconero dropped into a snowbank, his dead hand still clutching the snow brush.

For Connie, who endured three divorces, a rape, and a stay in a mental institution, the loss of George was an especially cruel blow. Her memoir, *Who's Sorry Now?*, is dedicated to her brother: "Oh, sweetheart, for as long as I live, I'll wonder what I could have done to change your life." Seeking justice for the murder, however, was something else. Connie Francis would not sing. When an FBI agent asked her if she had any idea who killed Franconero, she answered: "I have ideas, sir, but they'll remain locked in my head—and my heart—forever."

❧ COLD BLOODED ☙

RICHARD "THE ICEMAN" KUKLINSKI, KILLER
1936–2006

TWO YEARS HAD PASSED since Louis Masgay vanished in New Jersey. When his body turned up in 1983, shot and wrapped in garbage bags, it was fresh, as if he'd just died. The coroner puzzled over this oddity until he carved open the victim's heart and discovered ice crystals inside. Whoever killed Masgay had kept the body frozen for those two years, in an attempt to disguise the time of death. From then forward, the New Jersey authorities had a name for their most wanted, most elusive killer: the Iceman.

Richard Kuklinski possessed the coldbloodedness to match his nickname. Although he claimed to have murdered one hundred people in the course of his career, he was no serial killer who did it for kicks. Every

Richard Kuklinski, convicted
of multiple murders in the 1980s,
turned himself into a prison legend
as a supposed Mafia hit man.
(New Jersey Department of Corrections)

death was "just business," he said. Victims were typically lured by a prom-ise of nonexistent drugs or weapons at a cut-rate price. Kuklinski took the money, then killed his suckers by gun or cyanide. Taking a human life stirred no feeling in the Iceman, although thinking about it later might elicit an occasional chuckle.

As a child in a Jersey City housing project, Kuklinski suffered at the hands of bullies. He grew up to become a six-foot-four, 275-pound ox of a man who acted out revenge fantasies through violence. Through his job at a film laboratory, he got into the business of selling pornographic movies. This work introduced him to the Gambino crime family in the late 1970s. Kuklinski claimed to have been tutored by the Gambinos' chief assassin, Roy DeMeo, in a Brooklyn "chop shop" for body disposal, al-though mob experts are dubious about this.

Kuklinski's first known murder for profit came on January 31, 1980, when he promised to deliver a cache of porn to a mob hanger-on named George Malliband. When Malliband showed up for the exchange, Kuk-linski greeted him with four bullets in his chest. The killer then stuffed the body into a fifty-five-gallon drum and rolled it into a Jersey City waste dump.

The Iceman baited his victims on the hook of their own greed. The killing of Masgay was typical. Kuklinski told him he had a huge supply of blank videotapes, an expensive new technology in the early 1980s. Mas-gay, a businessman from Pennsylvania, was desperate to buy. Kuklinski stood him up again and again, each missed appointment only whetting Masgay's appetite. The gullible buyer worried he would miss the bar-gain of a lifetime and upped his offer from $50,000 to $95,000. Finally Kuklinski kept his word, meeting Masgay on July 1, 1981.

The buyer suspected nothing as he headed with Kuklinski to a ware-house outside Little Ferry, New Jersey. Kuklinski shot him and stuffed the body into an industrial freezer kept in the warehouse. He dumped the corpse two years later.

Kuklinski indulged in nonviolent crime as well. For a time he bought and sold stolen cars from a gang. When he feared the police were closing in on them, Kuklinski urged two of the crooks to go on the lam, putting

them up in a series of motels and bringing them their meals. They had
no idea that the Iceman merely wanted them out of the way. Kuklinski
served one of the thieves a hamburger laced with cyanide. The victim ate
half of it before keeling over. Kuklinski and the second thief then finished him off by strangling him with a lamp cord. A month later, the
cohort was himself dispatched with another cyanide-poisoned meal.

A professional killer must keep his family life insulated from work, and
Kuklinski guarded his own with ferocity. Criminal associates were forbidden, on pain of death, from visiting the split-level in Dumont, New
Jersey, he shared with his wife and three children. Barbara Kuklinski believed her husband was a currency trader and didn't question the source
of their wealth or his reasons for staying out all night.

The Iceman never let physical evidence connect him to a crime. But
at least three of his business associates, including the one who ended
up in the freezer, had made repeated phone calls to him before they vanished. State authorities took note of this coincidence, but could not
build a murder case on it. To do that, an undercover federal agent named
Dominick Polifrone was recruited.

Polifrone posed as a mob-connected drug dealer who could provide
Kuklinski with cyanide in exchange for guns. The two met repeatedly in
the fall of 1986 at the Vince Lombardi rest stop on the New Jersey Turnpike, where the agent's hidden wire recorded Kuklinski explaining what
he'd do with the cyanide. "I just have a few problems I want to dispose
of," he said. "I have some rats I want to get rid of."

Polifrone knew he was in dangerous territory. Kuklinski was probably
planning to kill him, like all the other suckers. Fortunately for the nervy
lawman, he had enough of the Iceman's own chilling words on tape to nail
him for murder conspiracy. On December 18, the State Police descended
on Kuklinski's home and arrested him. It took all their strength to sub-
due the fifty-one-year-old suspect; their shackles didn't fit around his
massive ankles.

At first, Kuklinski denied everything. But a 1988 trial ended in his conviction for two counts of murder: the fellow criminals he had poisoned
in their motel rooms. Put away in Trenton state prison for life, Kuklinski

decided to plead guilty to three other murders. His ego grew along with his sentence. In 1993, he happily sat for an interview televised on HBO. Now he claimed to be not merely a five-time convicted killer, but a master hit man responsible for one hundred murders.

The Iceman claimed to have earned $10,000 per hit. He boasted he was the assassin of both Jimmy Hoffa and Gambino crime boss Paul Castellano. Once, he flew to Hawaii to kill a mobster by tossing him from a hotel window. Another victim was blown to bits by a remote-controlled toy car that Kuklinski packed with plastic explosive. One man marked for death pleaded to Kuklinski for mercy. "He was please-God-ing all over the place," the killer remembered, speaking in a calm, flat voice. "So I told him he could have half an hour to pray to God, and if God could come down and change the circumstances, he'd [live]. But God never showed up."

The police have never been able to sift truth from fantasy in the Iceman's tales. Most of his contract-killing stories lack the ring of truth, to put it mildly, and mob figures disavowed any knowledge of Kuklinski. Still, he pleaded guilty to a long-forgotten New Jersey mob hit in 2003, and another meaningless thirty years were added to his life sentence. By the time his ailing heart and kidneys failed him in 2006, the Iceman had attained icon status as one of the most famous, feared killers of his time. It was probably enough to make him die a happy man.

⟫ CODE OF SILENCE ⟪

ANTHONY "TUMAC" ACCETTURO,
CRIME BOSS
1939–

"AS FAR BACK AS I CAN REMEMBER, I always wanted to be a gangster," the character Henry Hill says in the movie *Goodfellas*. His words found an echo when another wiseguy of his generation, Anthony Accetturo, explained the mystique of his chosen profession. Joining this thing of ours, he said, was "a dream, like some people want to become a doctor."

By the mid-1980s, Accetturo's dream had come true. He was New Jersey boss for the Lucchese crime family, and a millionaire. His blood oath to the Mafia seemed like the wisest life choice a man could make. Then, just like Henry Hill, he watched his world fall apart.

Accetturo was from Orange, New Jersey, but he found his calling a few miles away in Newark's gritty Ironbound section. He looted vending machines of coins, ran with a street gang of delinquents, and made betting collections for the Luccheses. His nickname, "Tumac," came from a movie caveman played by Victor Mature. Accetturo did not share Mature's famously fine physique—if anything, the Jersey kid was built like a bowling ball—but he had a caveman's barbarity in pummeling his foes to a pulp.

Accetturo was handy with a fist or a gun, and it was rumored that he murdered twenty-eight black interlopers who defied the mob by operating independent rackets in Newark. The violence had its effect, and Accetturo prospered even as his city fell apart from racial violence and drugs. Soon he was a suburbanite, living in wealthy, tree-lined Livingston.

The Luccheses, a relatively small operator in New Jersey compared to the Genoveses, Gambinos, DeCavalcantes, and the Philadelphia mob, grew rapidly once they abandoned the Mafia's traditional squeamishness about drug dealing. Their bold move owed everything to Accetturo. After he was promoted to capo in 1976, making him the Luccheses'

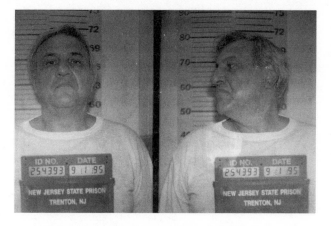

The defiant sneer on New Jersey capo Anthony "Tumac" Accetturo's mug shot can't hide the fact that he ratted out all his associates. (New Jersey Department of Corrections)

effective boss of New Jersey, Accetturo gave his blessing to a booming trade in heroin and cocaine. He also established a mail-order business selling worthless rocks as "investment" gems, penetrated the boardwalk concession stands of Point Pleasant Beach, and entered the illegal video poker industry.

The front man in this latter venture, a respected building contractor in Toms River, refused to kick in his fair share. Three of Tumac's stocking-masked thugs cornered him in his garage to play a non-friendly game of golf. They knocked him down, swung clubs into his skull, and killed him with blows that left divots in the concrete floor.

The war room for Accetturo's empire was a Newark luncheonette, Hole in the Wall, where a picture of Al Capone hung in a place of honor. Accetturo phoned the place regularly with coded instructions, insulating himself from the dirty work. When he was arrested in Florida in 1980 for fixing horse races, he faked mental illness to duck a trial. It was rather outlandish—Accetturo was forty-two and claiming to have Alzheimer's—but it worked.

Accetturo felt no fear when the federal government issued indictments against him in 1985 under the RICO Act. Prosecutors unwisely chose to put twenty Lucchese underlings on trial along with Accetturo. The proceedings grew into a circus, with the wiseguys in the role of clowns. One defendant shouted out so many sarcastic asides, the judge admonished him: "This isn't Dial-a-Joke!"

The trial in Newark lasted for seventeen months, a record in the federal courts. Prosecutors feared they would lose the case because the jury resented them for the tedium. However, Accetturo did not gamble on the outcome. He bribed a juror with $100,000. All the defendants were acquitted and walked free in August 1988.

Accetturo had little time to celebrate his victory. For years, he had kicked back no more than $10,000 a year to the Lucchese bosses in New York. But in the middle of the RICO trial in 1988, two rapacious new leaders took over the family: Vic Amuso and Anthony "Gaspipe" Casso. They demanded a full half of Accetturo's multi-million-dollar earnings. He refused.

Amuso and Casso did not earn their nicknames "the psycho twins" for nothing. They issued a chilling order: "Wipe out New Jersey." With glee, Casso drew up a list of thirty Lucchese mobsters from the Garden State and dispatched assassins to kill them all. At the top of the list was Accetturo.

Gang wars happen as a matter of course, and Tumac hunkered down for a few years in safe houses. Then he learned that Casso had handed out photographs of Accetturo's wife and grown son and ordered hit men to kill them, too. This was against the mob code as Accetturo understood it. To protect himself, he now had no choice but to give up—but not to Casso. He would turn state's witness.

When Accetturo became a cooperator in 1993, it was the first significant mob defection in New Jersey history. Where the feds failed, the state successfully rolled up the remnants of the tattered Lucchese organization. In doing so, they could thank Amuso and Casso. Not one of the thirty people on the hit list was killed, but the fear engendered by the psycho twins had sown seeds of distrust throughout the family.

Investigators were certain Accetturo conspired in thirteen killings, but they never prosecuted him for murder. Instead, he drew a sentence for racketeering and left prison in 2003. The boss realized that there was no code of mob honor worth defending any more. "They had no training, no honor," Accetturo said of Casso's crew. "All they want to do is kill, kill, get what you can, even if you didn't earn it."

✸ VIOLENT EPISODE ✦

VINCENT "VINNY OCEAN" PALERMO,
FAMILY BOSS
1949–

The Sopranos WAS JUST A few episodes old in 1999, and already characters were getting whacked left and right, the wiseguy dialogue was crackling, and the raves were pouring in. Television at its best, the critics agreed:

a brilliant, serio-comic exploration of psychology and the state of the American family today.

From the streets came a more earthy analysis. "Hey, what's this fucking thing, 'Sopranos?'" Joseph "Tin Ear" Sclafani, a soldier in the New Jersey-based DeCavalcante crime family, was overheard saying on an FBI informant's wire. "What the fuck are they? Is that supposed to be us?"

"You are in there, they mentioned your name in there," said Anthony Rotondo, his capo. "Every show you watch, more and more you pick up somebody. Every show."

"Yeah, I caught it one night," chimed in a mob associate, Ralph Guarino. "I didn't think it was really that bad."

Then, from Rotondo, a capsule review: "What characters. Great acting."

These real-life mobsters could afford to be amused, even flattered, by *The Sopranos*. For years, their DeCavalcante outfit had been overshadowed by New York's Five Families. But in the economic boom of the 1990s, they started earning cash, and respect.

It was a decade when the DeCavalcantes expanded from their base in North Jersey into the big leagues of New York City. They pioneered the Wall Street "pump and dump" scam, in which crooked brokers touted worthless stock, then peddled it to suckers once the value peaked. One man, above all others, was responsible for this success: acting boss Vincent "Vinny Ocean" Palermo.

Vincent "Vinny Ocean" Palermo, whose DeCavalcante underlings liked to think of themselves as the real "Sopranos." (New York Police Department)

Although chieftain of a New Jersey family, Palermo never lived there. He grew up in Brooklyn, swiping goods from the docks and putting the money back onto the streets in the form of usurious loans. He sold stolen seafood at his own store, Ocean Fish, which gave him his nickname. The family's namesake boss, Sam DeCavalcante, made Palermo a sworn member of the mob in 1976, thanks to the young man's wise decision to marry Sam's niece.

Short and compact, with a square jaw running to flab in middle age, Palermo was a mobster for modern times. Like Tony Soprano, he broke legs without pity, then drove back to the suburbs like any other working dad. At his waterfront home in Island Park, Long Island, he put on family barbecues and helped his five children with their homework.

Vinny Ocean achieved his status through loyalty. Sometime in the 1980s, family boss John Riggi sent him word that a suspicious car was parked outside his Linden, New Jersey, home. Palermo and his crew assumed these were gangland assassins. They drove out to Linden, ready to open fire, when a pickup truck came at them, headlights flashing. It was the family consigliere, shouting, "Forget about it—it's the FBI sitting there! Leave!"

In 1992, boss Riggi was sent away to prison, and designated a friend of John Gotti's, John "Johnny Boy" D'Amato, to run things in his absence. D'Amato got to enjoy his status as acting boss for only a few months. Palermo engineered his execution, which took place in the back of a car in Brooklyn. The body, and the car, vanished into an auto-salvage yard. Ever thrifty, the gunmen fished out $5,000 from D'Amato's pockets as reimbursement for the lost vehicle.

Recognized now as acting boss, Palermo used his New York crews to pull in million-dollar earnings. Money poured in from boiler rooms on Wall Street and strip clubs in Queens, as well as the traditional Jersey labor rackets. Palermo began talks with *Penthouse* publisher Bob Guccione about opening an "upscale" topless bar in Atlantic City. In 1998, DeCavalcante associates pulled off their biggest heist, robbing $1.1 million from the World Trade Center.

It was an easy score, but it led directly to the downfall of Vinny Ocean and his family. The FBI quickly tracked down the robbery's mastermind, a DeCavalcante associate named Ralph Guarino. He was easily flipped, and agreed to wear a wire for the feds.

It was Guarino who captured for posterity his fellow wiseguys' reviews of *The Sopranos.* To prove himself a good earner, he turned over to the boss a batch of supposedly stolen cell phones. These phones were bugged, allowing FBI agents to hear every word as Vinny Ocean implicated himself in a variety of crimes. Once, Guarino talked with Palermo about an underling that the boss considered a loose-lipped, degenerate gambler. "Kiss and make up," Guarino said. "Yeah, I'll kiss," Palermo said. He meant the kiss of death: the subject of his wrath was later found a bullet-ridden corpse.

With a treasure of incriminating tapes, federal agents took down the DeCavalcante family on December 2, 1999. Twenty-one capos, soldiers, associates, and the boss himself were all arrested. Vinny Ocean, given the choice between life in prison and violating his sacred oath of *omerta*, made the easy call. He agreed to testify for the prosecution against two of his capos and the consigliere, thereby becoming the first DeCavalcante boss to betray his organization.

Palermo re-emerged on the witness stand at the racketeering trial in May 2003. He showed no nervousness or shame as he recounted his various murders. One revelation was particularly stunning. Prosecutors asked Palermo to explain why his fellow capos sanctioned the hit on D'Amato back in 1992—the murder that allowed Vinny Ocean to become boss in the first place. It was because D'Amato had a reputation for visiting swinger clubs and having sex with men. "Nobody's gonna respect us if we have a gay homosexual boss sitting down discussing La Cosa Nostra business," Palermo said.

The following year, *The Sopranos* aired a show outing one of its most fearsome fictional mobsters as gay. It was, the critics agreed, one of the best episodes ever.

Power Corrupts

POLITICIANS AND OTHER CROOKS

✦ YES, BOSS ✦

FRANK HAGUE, MAYOR OF JERSEY CITY
1876–1956

FRANK HAGUE DIDN'T BECOME the most powerful man in New Jersey by book learning, and his every spoken word proved it. As mayor of Jersey City, he liked to boast of ruling "the most moralist city in America," by which he meant the most moral. In 1939, he ridiculed a foe by saying: "Why, he don't even know it's the nineteenth century." And yet, for all his butchery of the English language, Hague uttered four pithy words that summed up a philosophy of governance: "I am the law!"

Frank Hague, seen here on the day he declared "I am the law" in 1937. The boss of Hudson County accused those who dared criticize his money-grubbing and dictatorial ways of being communists.
(*New York Post*)

Few people in U.S. history have held political power so long or so absolutely. Hague reigned in Jersey City from 1917 to 1947, stuffing ballot boxes and cracking heads to ensure he won every election. As Democratic boss of Hudson County, his power extended to Trenton and Washington, where he chose governors and members of Congress to do his bidding. Public employees kicked back 3 percent of their salaries to the boss, enabling him to live lavishly half the year at the Jersey Shore and in Florida. Hague made no excuses for his tactics, which he said were those of a reformer.

Hague was a reformer, at least in the beginning. Born to immigrant Irish parents, he grew up in poverty in Jersey City's teeming tenement district known as the Horseshoe. A two-fisted troublemaker, he was expelled from the sixth grade as incorrigible. Street gangs, pool halls, and boxing gyms were his milieu, and from there it was a short step to ward politics. He was elected to his first post, constable, at twenty-four.

Marriage and fatherhood tamed his wilder instincts. He quit drinking and hanging out in bars, and was elected commissioner of public safety in 1913 on a platform of cleaning up Jersey City's red-light districts. Hague was good to his word. Soon, the police department was raiding notorious houses and sharply reducing street crime. Hague purged hundreds of officers for graft or incompetence. His mass firings ensured discipline, and a department that owed fealty to him alone. Voters responded by making him mayor within four years. His insurgent Democrats were known as the "Unbossed" ticket.

Hague was an energetic and activist chief executive. The poor and the immigrants cheered him when he doubled the tax assessments on the mighty railroad companies, who had long enjoyed special favors in Jersey City. He built the seven towers of the Jersey City Medical Center, the third-largest municipal hospital in the world, providing health care without charge.

Unlike the stereotypical Irish city boss, Hague was no back-slapper with a story for all occasions. Harsh and humorless, he projected angry righteousness rather than charm. The ruddy-faced patriarch had a boxer's tall and trim physique, and even in his sixties he was known to punch out those who tried his patience. Hague's sole vice was betting the horses, so gambling was the one type of "clean" crime allowed in his city. Of course, Hague took his cut.

Jersey City was a model of good, efficient government, or so Hague said. All his public initiatives required a large public payroll, and some of the jobs created were curious ones. Jersey City soon became the only municipality in America to have an organist for the jail, and a chaplain for the roads department. Through patronage, Hague built a base of city employees totally subordinate to his will.

Stories were rife of dead voters being resurrected to vote the Democratic ticket. However, Hague didn't need to invent vote totals when he could just use raw force. Nightstick-wielding cops fended off independent poll watchers. A Democrat named John Longo tried twice to run on a reform platform against Hague, and was twice jailed on trumped-up charges.

Enforcing loyalty was not just a job for Election Day. A squad of plainclothes police, known as the Zeppelins because they furtively hovered in all neighborhoods, acted as an intelligence arm to sniff out potential opposition. Anyone speaking poorly of the Hague regime might be hit with a higher tax assessment or an arrest for disorderly conduct.

Hague considered labor unions a threat to his power. When activists from the leftist Committee for Industrial Organization handed out literature in Jersey City in 1937, the mayor's goon squads forcibly put them on ferries back to New York City. Unflattering articles about the episode were published in *Time* and *Life* magazines, so Hague banned them from newsstands. "We hear about constitutional rights, free speech and the free press," he thundered. "Every time I hear these words I say to myself, 'That man is a Red, that man is a Communist.' You never hear a real American talk like that."

Mayor of Jersey City was the choicest of several hats that Hague wore. He also served as chairman of the Hudson County Democratic Committee, by which means he controlled county as well as city patronage. With Hudson turning in reliably huge Democratic majorities, no party candidate could hope to become governor, senator, or congressman without Hague's blessing. President Franklin D. Roosevelt owed his overwhelming margins in New Jersey to the power of the Hudson machine. Hague, in turn, was given control over the vast flow of New Deal money into New Jersey.

The 3 percent of pay that government employees handed over to Hague was supposed to fund Democratic election efforts. But as the boss grew comfortable in power, he pocketed more and more of his "take" of $1 million a year. His villas in Palm Beach and Miami Beach, his Park Avenue rental, and his summer home in Deal, New Jersey, couldn't be accounted for on a $7,500 mayor's salary. The thievery from the public till was colossal, but no grand jury would examine it so long as Hague controlled the prosecutor's office.

Hague retired as mayor at age seventy-one in 1947, but he made it clear he would continue to run Jersey City behind the scenes when he handpicked his nephew, Frank Hague Eggers, to succeed him. The voters might have accepted this flagrant nepotism had it not been for their city's all-too-obvious decline.

Property taxes had spiraled out of control to pay for Hague's no-show jobs. Services were a mess, with garbage collection still being done by horse cart. Hague rallied his troops for one last, heroic get-out-the-vote effort, but fraud was no longer an option. A Republican, Alfred Driscoll, now sat in the governor's office, and he ensured that state troopers guarded the voting machines.

The election of 1949 spelled the end for the Hague machine. A one-time loyalist named John V. Kenny saw the opportune time to rebel, and defeated Eggers in a rout. He took power as both mayor and Democratic Party chieftain, vowing real reform. Instead, he went on to reign supreme over Hudson County politics for the next twenty-two years, growing rich by selling his office to the Mafia. Hague was no longer the law. But good old-fashioned greed still ruled.

❧ LIVING LARGE ❧

ENOCH "NUCKY" JOHNSON,
BOSS OF ATLANTIC CITY
1883–1968

THE TOWERING BULK OF A MAN in his white suit and shiny spats strode Atlantic City's Boardwalk like he owned the place, because he did. For nearly thirty years, Nucky Johnson was political boss of the East Coast's most splendid resort. Every brothel, betting parlor, and speakeasy in town paid tribute to him, and under his overlordship they grew rich. When the likes of Al Capone and Lucky Luciano arranged a historic gangland convention in 1929 to divide up America's rackets, Atlantic City was the natural choice for a gathering place. The sun, sand, and salt air would refresh them, but they headed down the Shore for one reason: Nucky let them.

Enoch Lewis Johnson, high-living hedonist, unashamed friend to mobsters, hustlers, and gamblers, came from rural WASP roots. His parents, of English-Scotch ancestry, farmed the sandy soil of the Pine Barrens. Johnson's father became the Atlantic County sheriff, and passed the job to Nucky as a family heirloom. In 1909, the young man of twenty-five was sworn into office; just two years later he became chairman of the county Republican Party.

Nucky Johnson is the picture of elegance, from his tailored suit to his pinky ring, even as he awaits the guilty verdict in his 1941 tax evasion trial. (Reprinted with permission of the *Press of Atlantic City*)

Atlantic City was undergoing explosive growth as a resort, and visitors found they could get away with all manner of naughtiness. Besides the scandalous thrill of looking at bathing beauties in those new one-piece swimsuits, you could visit a den of prostitution or throw your money away at a floating crap game.

The sheriff's job would have been a challenge for the most diligent of law enforcement officials. Johnson wasn't diligent, and he didn't scruple to enforce the law. Instead, he continued the longstanding tradition of pay-to-play. The operators of notorious houses would pay weekly protection money to the police, with Johnson getting the lion's share. For the appearance of law and order, he might stage a raid now and then, with pimps forced to pay a fine. The amounts of those fines were then duly deducted from Nucky's payoff.

The arrangement was great for everyone—the tourists, the cops, the hoteliers, everyone but the joyless hypocrites who didn't know how to have a good time. "We have whiskey, wine, women, song and slot machines," Johnson once said, in a classic explanation of why organized crime exists. "I won't deny it and I won't apologize for it. If the majority of the people didn't want them, they wouldn't be profitable and they wouldn't exist. The fact that they do exist proves to me that the people want them."

Johnson held power by being creative on Election Day. Atlantic City had a high transient population of hotel workers who lived there only in the high season, and Johnson was padding the voter rolls with thousands of their names. Every election, these citizens were recorded as voting the GOP line *en masse*, regardless of whether they actually cast a ballot. In 1911, the Democratic reform administration of New Jersey governor Woodrow Wilson had Johnson removed as sheriff and indicted him for voter fraud. A friendly hometown jury promptly acquitted him.

The boss didn't stay unemployed long. He was appointed county treasurer and held the job for nearly thirty years without performing any of its duties. Johnson's real task was to run Atlantic City's rackets and its vote-producing machine. Thanks to him, the GOP rolled up absurdly high majorities that often swung the governor's race their way.

Johnson's steady stream of payoff money turned into a gusher when Prohibition became law in 1920. His domain included some of the Jersey Shore's best coves in which rumrunners could hide. Nucky's police guaranteed protection for smuggled booze. Gangsters such as Luciano, Joe Adonis, and Longie Zwillman showed their gratitude by wining and dining Nucky when they were in town.

Johnson was only in his thirties when his wife died, and after a decent period of mourning he discovered he enjoyed the bachelor's life. The boss arose every afternoon in his hotel suite at the crack of 4 P.M. He ate up to a dozen fried eggs for breakfast, donned one of his hundred suits, pinned a fresh red carnation to his lapel, and went out to the Boardwalk to hold court with followers. Then he bounded into his powder-blue limousine and made the rounds of Atlantic City night life.

At six-foot-one and close to 250 pounds, with a ruddy bald head and a booming, jovial voice, Nucky was the center of attention at every club. A showgirl was always on his arm, while headliners such as Sophie Tucker and Jimmy Durante sat at his table. Johnson handed out $400 tips along with bon mots. His most quoted aphorism was a complaint that his best dates were already taken by smooth young musicians: "Every time I kiss a blonde, I taste a saxophone."

Never one to care what society thought of him, Johnson was at his most daring during the gangster conference of May 1929. According to gangland legend, the event got off to a rocky start when the mobsters tried to check into a restricted hotel, using Anglo-Saxon aliases that Johnson had supplied. A hotel clerk took one look at them and refused to put them up. Nucky came to the rescue, ordering the crowd of heavies back into their limousines and spiriting them to his own hotel, the Ritz-Carlton.

The Atlantic City conference was a landmark in mob history, forging the first successful links in what became a national crime syndicate. The event was less fortuitous for Johnson. A newspaper photographer snapped him walking the Boardwalk with Capone, and no one believed it when the boss claimed the picture was a forgery. A barrage of bad publicity followed. In the late 1930s, the administration of Franklin D.

Roosevelt went after the boss. Treasury agents investigated him for the same crime that nailed Capone—tax evasion. He was an easy target, for he lived like a millionaire while drawing a county salary of $6,000.

Johnson went on trial in Camden federal court in July 1941. His defense was a nervy one. He admitted collecting $155,000 from the gambling rackets and never reporting it to the Internal Revenue Service, but claimed it wasn't income because all the cash went to the county political machine. Flabbergasted, the prosecutor asked Johnson: Isn't gambling a crime? "If you get caught," Johnson said.

The jury deliberated just five hours before reaching a verdict, and Johnson's pink face went pale as he heard "guilty." He only served four years of his ten-year sentence, but when he shambled back to the Boardwalk, he was a noticeably grayer and poorer man. He died at eighty-five, too soon to see the state of New Jersey legalize casino gambling in Atlantic City.

The industry that made Johnson rich went legitimate, with profits undreamed of in his day. Yet any old-timer who walked inside the resort town's vast and sterile gaming palaces, echoing to the din of thousands of bleeping video slots, had to agree: Nucky did it with style.

❧ UNEARTHLY GLOW ❧

THE RADIUM GIRLS

NO SMOKESTACKS BELCHED FOUL AIR, no whirring machinery threatened to tear off a limb. The United States Radium Corporation factory that opened in Orange, New Jersey, in 1916 was to all appearances clean, quiet, well lighted, and safe. The company made wristwatches with glow-in-the-dark faces and hired young women at good wages to do the work. They sat at a long table, delicately using a brush tipped with radium to paint numbers and hands on the watch dials. After a few strokes, the hairs on the paintbrush lost their shape. When this happened, the painters followed their instructions to put the brush to their lips and wet it to a fine point.

After a while, it wasn't just the wristwatches that emitted a spectral glow. Radium dust clung to the workers' hair and clothes and bathed them in light in the nighttime. The women—mostly between ages sixteen and twenty-one—found this to be a delightful lark. Some of them painted the wondrous ingredient onto their buttons and nails to surprise their dates. One teenager rubbed it on her teeth to give herself an electric smile.

To early twentieth-century science, radioactivity was an amazing if poorly understood phenomenon. Marie Curie, who discovered radium and coined the term "radioactivity," thought it might be a boon to humankind, perhaps even curing disease. (Instead, she died of radium-caused anemia.) Druggists sold radium pills and potions. As a sideline, U.S. Radium marketed radium residue as "hygienic" sand for children's play boxes. But even in that innocent age, some experts understood that radium could damage skin and tissue. Chemists who worked in the company's laboratory wore masks and handled the radioactive matter with tongs.

A 1926 cartoon shows Death's skeletons handing the "radium girls" of Orange, New Jersey, their radioactive paint. By 1933, thirty-eight women were dead. (University of Medicine and Dentistry of New Jersey Libraries, Harrison S. Martland, MD Papers [PC/1])

The young women in the painting studios were given no such protections from the radium they habitually licked and inhaled and touched. "I think I pointed [the brush] with my lips about six times to every watch dial," remembered one painter, Grace Fryer, who was hired at fifteen. "It didn't taste funny. It didn't have any taste." Sometimes, a worker might ask if this odorless, tasteless substance was dangerous. The answer came back: no.

But the reassurances were false. The radium, even in infinitesimal quantities, was poison. Once ingested, it plated itself onto the teeth and bones, where it bombarded cells with radiation. Tumors, bone decay, anemia, and a variety of cancers were the agonizing result.

The first signs of radium poisoning manifested themselves in 1922 when a number of young women began visiting dentist's offices in Essex County to complain of toothaches and swollen gums. In some cases, dentists extracted a diseased tooth only to tear out a mass of jawbone as well. Tissues and bone marrow had been eaten away by infection. A mysterious new ailment, "jaw rot," was diagnosed.

Other horrifying cases emerged. One woman's leg snapped while she was dancing at a ballroom. Another had two miscarriages and suffered so much bone loss that one of her legs became four inches shorter than the other. Some died of unknown ailments, and the cause of death was wrongly recorded as syphilis. The cases had a common thread: all the sufferers had once worked as dial painters. In 1924, a workers' advocacy group, the New Jersey Consumers League, began an investigation. It got no help from the state Labor Department or from U.S. Radium, neither of which considered radiation poisoning to be real.

"This is not an occupational disease," said the corporation's president, Arthur Roeder. He suggested that the women brought about their own illnesses, either from hysteria or bad dental hygiene. U.S. Radium brought in a professor from Harvard University to study the patients. When the expert concluded that their symptoms were caused by radium exposure, Roeder threatened to sue him if he released his study. U.S. Radium then lied to the Consumers League, claiming the Harvard results showed no harm from radium. A more compliant expert was brought on to examine the "jaw rot" sufferers and tell them their health was just fine.

It was the death of a male chemist, not a female laborer, that finally exposed the truth. Harrison Martland, chief medical examiner of Essex County, ran the thirty-six-year-old man's bones under an electroscope. The machine found an extraordinary level of radioactivity. Similar tests run on U.S. Radium workers found that they were all radioactive. In one case, a radiation expert was able to wrap film around a patient's leg and make an image of her radium-coated bones from the X-ray-like gamma waves emanating from inside.

U.S. Radium quietly settled three of the workers' cases for cash payments and hoped to avoid any publicity. But in 1926 it was sued by five women badly ill from jaw rot or cancer. The company defended itself by pointing out that the two-year statute of limitations to claim a workplace injury had long since elapsed. It was a Catch-22 for the victims: radiation sickness and cancer almost always take more than two years to develop.

Newspapers played up the story of the doomed "radium girls" and their battle against a seemingly soulless business behemoth. Fryer, who remembered wetting her lips on the radium six times per watch dial, lost all her teeth, underwent seventeen operations, and had to walk with a brace and a cane. She could barely raise her arm to take the oath on the witness stand. "It hurts to smile, but still I smile anyway," she told a reporter.

Others did not hide their bitterness. One of the plaintiffs, Katherine Schaub, noted that hundreds of radium victims were not joining the lawsuit. "They're afraid of losing their boyfriends and the good times," she said. "They know it isn't rheumatism they've got . . . God—what fools—pathetic fools!"

U.S. Radium used delaying tactics throughout the civil trial, provoking suspicions that it simply wanted the radium girls to die off before they could collect damages. Finally, in June 1928, it reached a settlement to provide the five women with $15,000 each, plus a $600 yearly pension and all medical expenses. It refused to admit wrongdoing and vowed to fight any other lawsuits. The company vice president, Howard Barker, complained of being victimized by "propaganda." A decade later, he died of cancer most likely caused by radium exposure.

The complete death toll from U.S. Radium is impossible to calculate with any precision. In 1933, Schaub, thirty-one, and Fryer, thirty-five, both died; that made thirty-eight fatalities blamed on the poisoned brushes. Some victims survived, crippled for life by bone lesions; others made it into their nineties before dying of causes related to their exposure as teenagers. Their very graves remain highly radioactive, and will stay that way for fifteen hundred years.

❖ WITHOUT A CLUE ❖

ELLIS PARKER, BURLINGTON COUNTY CHIEF OF DETECTIVES 1871–1940

EVERY ARMY INVESTIGATOR at Fort Dix, New Jersey, was stumped. A soldier from the base had vanished in September 1921 and turned up dead three months later. Any of the men in his unit could have done it. Into the mystery trudged the Burlington County chief of detectives, Ellis Parker. He interrogated all 175 suspects and found only one who

Ellis Parker strikes a Sherlockian pose in the 1930s. His reckless pursuit of the "real killer" in the Lindbergh baby case destroyed his career. (William Fullerton, www.fullterton1.com)

remembered where he was on the day of the disappearance. Promptly, this man was arrested as the killer. Only the guilty party, Parker reasoned, would come up with an alibi so long after the fact. "There isn't any perfect crime," he said, "because there isn't any foolproof lie."

It was one case among many that earned Parker a reputation as a crime-solver without parallel. The newspapers called him the "cornfield Sherlock Holmes" and "the local detective with the worldwide reputation." It was said that he cracked all but ten of his 286 murder cases. Parker's homespun appearance and folksy wit completed the portrait of a colorful sleuth. But it was sometimes whispered that he wasn't as amazing as his champions claimed, that he rushed to conclusions and routinely roughed up his suspects. The doubters were right. When Parker came across the one big crime he couldn't solve, he went to jail for his illegal tactics.

A Quaker from a long-established family, Parker started out as head of a posse tracking down horse thieves. He was so good at it that the county hired him as detective in 1892. It was the beginning of a forty-five-year career. Burlington was a rural bailiwick, but Parker had a genius for getting attention. Whenever he made an arrest, he was sure to publicize it, with maximum credit to himself. Soon, police departments from as far away as California sought his help on their cases.

He could have stepped right out of a novel. Parker did his crime-solving from a cluttered office in the county courthouse in Mount Holly, directly across from the home where he lived with his wife and eight children. Bald, pudgy, and stumpy, he wore rumpled suits and ties that hung crookedly. A pipe always seemed to be protruding from his squinty face. Between puffs, he offered up aphorisms such as: "There are two types of witnesses: the kind that won't say anything, and the kind that want to say everything."

Parker kept abreast of all advances in the science of criminology, but he preferred to crack a case by old-fashioned methods. Sometimes this took the form of rounding up everyone remotely connected to the victim, throwing them in jail, and waiting to see who broke first. In one murder case from 1931, he became convinced that one of the victim's employees, a man named Charles Powell, was involved. But he had no proof. "I finally decided that the only thing I could do was kidnap Powell, in a perfectly legal manner," he later said in an interview. After three weeks of captivity, Powell confessed and was found guilty. Parker failed to tell his interviewer that this "killer" was eventually ruled insane.

Stories about the detective got good rides in the New York papers, but he wasn't page one material. Then, in 1932, came Parker's chance to solve the kidnapping and murder of the Lindbergh baby. It was a crime that stunned the world, and led Congress to pass the "Lindbergh law" making kidnapping a federal offense. The shocking deed happened in Hopewell, New Jersey, outside Parker's county, but he offered his investigative services to the State Police anyway. They turned him down. Seething with resentment, Parker insisted they were hopeless blunderers and on the wrong track. When Bruno Hauptmann was convicted of the crime, the detective insisted he was innocent.

Governor Harold Hoffman agreed. In December 1935, he asked Parker to reopen the investigation. The detective grasped at dubious leads: The Lindbergh baby had never died at all! He had been murdered by a "rich degenerate"! A "stoop-shouldered man" did it! Nothing panned out. Parker was always surprisingly well connected to underworld characters, and he asked one of them—a disbarred Trenton lawyer named Paul Wendel—to help him find the real killer. Wendel agreed, but with no success. He was still working on the case when he vanished from a Manhattan street in February 1936.

On March 29, Wendel reappeared in surprising fashion—in jail. Parker declared he had solved the Lindbergh case, and was charging his prisoner as the killer. The detective produced a confession, in which Wendel told how he snatched the infant from the Lindbergh home and took it home to Trenton. The baby died in a fall from his crib, and Wendel disposed of the body. The dramatic turn of events seemed to vindicate Hauptmann, who was given a reprieve just two days before his scheduled execution.

But when state prosecutors questioned Wendel, he denied having anything to do with Lindbergh. He said he had been kidnapped by a gang of five men, among whom was Ellis Parker's son. The captors drove him to a house in Brooklyn and locked him in a dark basement. There, they blistered his face with a light bulb and kicked him about the body as he screamed in agony. Only one thing would make the torture stop, they said: "You are going to confess to the kidnapping of the Lindbergh baby." Wendel did so. The gang then drove him to a sanitarium near Parker's home in Mount Holly. The hostage was forced to rewrite his statement until it seemed believable. Six drafts and seven weeks later, Parker was able to announce Wendel's arrest.

It was obvious that the badly bruised prisoner had been framed. Hauptmann went to the electric chair, while Wendel was cleared. Parker protested, but now he had to worry about another kidnapping case—the one building against him.

Ellis Parker Sr. and Jr. were indicted later that year on federal kidnapping charges and put on trial in Newark in 1937. Their own strongarm men, unsavory characters with connections to the Trenton underworld, testified against them. As evidence, the government introduced records of long-distance calls Parker had made to the kidnappers in New York. Just as the sleuth said, there were no foolproof lies.

Ellis Parker drew a six-year sentence for kidnapping, while his son got three years. A prosecutor called him "engulfed by an ego complex which made him feel he was one of the greatest detectives in the world," while the judge blasted him for "feeling that you are above the law." The old man petitioned for a pardon but was still in prison in 1940 when he died at sixty-eight. His son, a fellow inmate, was at his bedside.

As his reward for cracking the Lindbergh case, it was said, Parker expected to land a book deal and perhaps even replace J. Edgar Hoover as head of the FBI. Instead, he got another historical recognition. He was among the first defendants to be convicted of violating the Lindbergh law.

❖ CHILD OF DESTINY ❖

HAROLD HOFFMAN, GOVERNOR
1896–1954

HAROLD HOFFMAN WAS POISED to make history when he took office in 1935 as New Jersey's youngest governor. A fleshy, bumptious glad-hander hailed as "the child of destiny," he promised to battle the Great Depression and clean up Trenton's mess of a fiscal system. His Republican Party talked of putting him up as a dark horse candidate for vice president, or even president.

Governor Hoffman did make history, but not in a way his admirers imagined. In 1954, with his heart failing and one month to live, he wrote a letter to his daughter and sealed it in an envelope marked: "DO NOT OPEN UNTIL MY DEATH." He was a thief, he said. He'd been dipping into the public treasury for nearly thirty years, and his total take added up to $300,000.

A successful embezzler needs to win the boss's confidence, and Hoffman had certainly swindled his bosses—the voters—virtually from the moment he first held public office.

Former governor Harold Hoffman in 1952, two years before he died and left a confession from beyond the grave to being an embezzler. (*New York Post*)

He was born in the small city of South Amboy, to a family descended from New Jersey's first Dutch settlers. At twelve, he was a precocious sports columnist for the local paper; at twenty-one, he was an Army captain serving in World War I. By 1926, he was both a successful candidate for the House of Representatives and the president and principal stockholder of a local bank, the South Amboy Trust.

In his campaign for Congress, Hoffman had been promised $17,000 in campaign contributions, and spent it sight unseen. The man who made him the promise—Senator Hamilton Fish Kean, grandfather of former governor Thomas Kean—then coughed up only $2,500. Hoffman fell deeply in debt, but continued to throw lavish parties and stock a bar full of bootleg liquor in his Washington apartment. To keep himself afloat, he took advantage of being president of a bank, making the first of many plunders into its deposits.

After two terms, Hoffman chose to leave Congress and run for the unglamorous post of state Commissioner of Motor Vehicles. It looked like a puzzling comedown, but there was logic behind this decision: Having control of a state government bureau gave Hoffman unlimited access to cash. Every month, he would steal up to $50,000.

In 1934, Hoffman ran for governor and narrowly won. It was a stunning result—a Republican, only thirty-eight, winning a traditionally Democratic state at the peak of President Franklin D. Roosevelt's popularity. One of Hoffman's assets was likability: he was a jolly fat man (five-foot-seven, 210 pounds) with a self-deprecating sense of humor. He loved the circus and loved to act the clown. At fund-raisers for the Circus Saints and Sinners, a group that supported retired circus performers, he delighted in dressing up in baggy-pants costumes and spritzing dignitaries with seltzer water.

The Hoffman administration seemed like a circus as well. To raise money for Depression relief, the governor rushed a hugely unpopular sales tax through the Legislature. The move alienated his own party without any practical result, since he repealed the tax within eight months. In 1936, he meddled disastrously in the Lindbergh baby kidnapping case by insisting that Bruno Hauptmann was not guilty. Hoffman said he was crusading for justice; a more cynical interpretation holds that he was angling for national headlines, and for his political future.

Hot-tempered and intolerant of any criticism, Hoffman lashed out—literally—at his opponents. Once he decked a reporter whom he outweighed by ninety pounds and knocked him out cold.

Being the most prominent man in New Jersey did not make Hoffman cautious about his embezzlement habits. He kept stealing—with one final plunge for $35,000 in 1937—and looting other accounts to fill the ones he had emptied. Throughout, he acted with an outwardly unruffled conscience. "If what he'd done had ever worried him," one friend later said, "he must have got used to it, like a man can get used to a wearing a wooden leg."

Governors at the time were barred from succeeding themselves, so Hoffman could not run in the 1937 election. He solved that problem in his last days in office by creating a new commission to handle unemployment compensation. His appointed commissioners turned around and elected a director—Hoffman.

In his new job, Hoffman apparently made no further embezzlements. Instead, he contented himself by covering up his earlier thefts. More than $15 million in state funds, meant for jobless compensation or for disability, were furtively juggled around and hidden by phony ledger statements and forgeries. Hoffmann then deposited the money in non-interest-bearing accounts at South Amboy Trust.

In 1954, a Democratic governor, Robert Meyner, took office. Troubled by reports of people getting their unemployment checks late, Meyner ordered a complete audit of Hoffman's division. What he discovered stunned him. Hoffman had signed illegal contracts paying exorbitant rates for state office space, and rigged other bids to favor companies owned by his friends. Then there were the accounting irregularities that suggested embezzlement. Meyner suspended Hoffman from the unemployment bureau on March 18, but kept quiet as to the reason why.

The governor was apparently hoping Hoffman would just bow out gracefully. But Hoffman was a dying man. In May, he carefully penned his testament to his daughter. On June 3, he trudged into his Manhattan apartment, one that the Circus Saints and Sinners had given him rent-free. As he bent down to untie his shoelaces, he fell dead of a heart attack.

Ada Leonard, Hoffman's daughter, opened the letter after the funeral. In it, Hoffman revealed how he had embezzled a total of $300,000. He tried to pay it back, and would have succeeded but for "a certain state official, unnamed but dead," who blackmailed him for $150,000. The letter did not name the blackmailer, and that person's identity—or whether that person even existed—remains a secret of New Jersey history.

Excuse-making and self-pity mixed with contriteness. Hoffman insisted that "no single person has actually been hurt by my default," which was true only if one does not consider taxpayers to be people. Yes, he used public money to reward his friends—but this was a strength, because "I have had an almost uncontrollable urge to help other people."

"Never let any of your sons enter politics," he wrote to Ada. "It is a lousy game. In order to be elected, you must necessarily accept favors from a large number of people. If you attempt to repay them after being elected to office, it becomes wrongdoing. If you don't, you are an ingrate."

In New Jersey government, Hoffman left an important legacy—by robbing the taxpayers blind, he ensured that every agency would have strict audits in the future. His hometown of South Amboy, filled with quick-to-forgive, quick-to-forget neighbors, remembered him in another way. They named the high school after him.

❧ RED-FACED ❧

J. PARNELL THOMAS, CONGRESSMAN
1895–1970

"ARE YOU OR HAVE YOU ever been a member of the Communist party?"

The questioner's face, ruddy even in times of calm, was turning bright red. Representative J. Parnell Thomas, Republican of New Jersey, had called congressional hearings to expose communism in Hollywood. But the witness in the hot seat on October 30, 1947, refused to play along.

Screenwriter Ring Lardner Jr., the namesake son of a famous humorist, was using his own dry wit to drive Thomas crazy.

"I could answer exactly the way you want, Mr. Chairman," Lardner said.

"It is a very simple question. Anybody would be proud to answer it—any real American would be proud to answer the question. Are you now or have you ever been a member of the Communist party?"

"I could answer it, but if I did, I would hate myself in the morning."

"Leave the witness chair," Thomas barked. Lardner protested, and the congressman banged his gavel. "Leave the witness chair!"

The sergeant-at-arms lifted Lardner by the arms. "I think I am leaving by force," he gasped.

Before there was Joseph McCarthy or McCarthyism, J. Parnell Thomas held center stage as Washington's foremost and feistiest scourge of communists. His dramatic inquiry sent Lardner and nine of his film industry colleagues to jail for contempt of Congress, while frightening Hollywood

"We Got To Burn The Evil Spirits Out Of Her"

Herblock cartoon of House Un-American Activities Committee witch hunters J. Parnell Thomas (N.J.), Karl Mundt (S.D.), and an obscure House freshman named Richard Nixon (Calif.) in 1948. (A 1948 Herblock Cartoon, copyright by the Herb Block Foundation. HERBLOCK, © 1948 The Washington Post Company)

into setting up its infamous blacklist. But Thomas, who grandstanded as a defender of Americanism and champion of law and order, turned out to be something else: a thief. The next time he and Lardner set eyes upon each other, they were inmates in the same federal prison.

Thomas was born John Feeney, the son of a Democratic politician in Jersey City, but shed both the Irish family name and party affiliation after his father's death. He never belonged to a church; after serving in World War I, he made patriotism his faith. His old house in the bedroom community of Allendale, New Jersey, was a shrine to Americana: engravings, antique guns, and genealogical charts tracing his mother's line back to Noah Webster. He worked as an insurance salesman in New York City and served from 1926 to 1930 as mayor of Allendale.

Even when Franklin D. Roosevelt was at the peak of his national popularity, Thomas's affluent county of Bergen was solidly Republican. Thomas scorned the New Deal as "just another form of socialism," akin to Nazism or communism, and advocated a return to business-friendly government. On this platform, he was elected to the state Assembly (1934) and U.S. Congress (1936).

In Thomas's freshman term in Washington, he joined the newly created House Un-American Activities Committee (HUAC). He took the chairmanship in January 1947 and gained a national platform as denouncer of subversive elements. He charged that nuclear scientists working on the Manhattan Project had been in contact with "persons outside the United States." The claim was widely ridiculed, but turned out to be right. Several spies, including Julius and Ethel Rosenberg, were later convicted of passing atomic secrets to the Soviets. One hard-charging young HUAC member, Representative Richard M. Nixon, helped expose the State Department official Alger Hiss as a spy.

But Thomas's definitions of "parlor pinks" and "fellow travelers" were applied with a dangerously broad brush. He called the distinguished nuclear physicist Edward Condon the "weakest link" in American security. Unions, colleges, even churches came under his microscope. To one committee witness, he asked this question about the most all-American of entertainers: "Would you say that Frank Sinatra is a communist?"

Short, balding, and round, Thomas achieved a more dignified stature
at the committee table by sitting on a phone book cushioned by a pillow. When witnesses balked at his trademark question—"Are you now
or have you ever been a member of the Communist party?"—he rapped
away with his gavel. The congressman seemed always to be red with exas-
peration, one observer noted, even in black and white newsreels.

In the fall of 1947, Thomas launched his blockbuster investigation into
communism in the movies. Interviews with Hollywood's leading lights,
among them Gary Cooper and Ronald Reagan, brought forth the names
of nineteen suspected communists. Out of that group, seven screenwrit-
ers, two producers, and one director were identified as "card-carrying"
members of the party. Subpoenaed to testify before HUAC, the "Hollywood Ten" chose to refuse any questions about whether they were communists. (In fact, they all were.)

The Hollywood Ten believed the First Amendment would protect
their right of free speech. But the Bill of Rights went out the window in
Thomas's hearing room. "We will determine what rights you have," the
chairman declared. Witness after witness refused to speak about their
political beliefs, so Thomas kept the sergeant-at-arms busy hauling them
away. Lardner made his stand calmly but firmly. Others sputtered back a
fiercer defiance, such as the writer Dalton Trumbo, who shouted: "This
is the beginning of an American concentration camp!"

The House of Representatives cited all ten for contempt, and they
were hauled off to prison. Hollywood quickly pledged not to hire them
back. A similar ban was slapped on anyone else who refused to cooperate
with investigations—which meant betraying colleagues by naming names.
It was the beginning of a blacklist that lasted into the mid-1960s and
ruined the careers of innocent and guilty alike. Lardner, a genuine communist, outlasted the purge to later become the Oscar-winning script-
writer of the movie *M*A*S*H*. Others, whose only crime was protecting
their friends, never got a second chance to hold a job.

Thomas's scorched-earth tactics infuriated liberals everywhere—and
one of them, columnist Drew Pearson, had a secret to reveal. Thomas
was illegally padding his payroll. In 1940, he had hired his secretary's

niece for a phantom job as stenographer; she cashed her paychecks, kept a small sum, and kicked the balance back to Thomas. Thomas added another no-show job a few years later. In all, the scam netted him about $8,000, and for this amount he forfeited his career.

Thomas was indicted by the federal government in November 1948. The congressman called it a trumped-up charge and "a new low in politics." But with his secretary ready to testify against him, he knew he was a beaten man. Thomas entered a plea of no contest to fraud and conspiracy, and drew a sentence of six to eighteen months behind bars.

At the minimum-security federal penitentiary in Danbury, Connecticut, Thomas was given what he called pleasurable duty: running the prison's chicken farm. One day he looked up to see Lardner, a fellow inmate, walking by. The two never spoke, but Thomas had a memorable encounter with another of the Hollywood Ten he had sent to prison. The ex-congressman saw the man, Lester Cole, cutting grass one day and hollered: "Hey, Bolshie, I see you've still got your sickle. Where's your hammer?" Cole eyed his tormentor cleaning the coops and responded: "And I see you're still picking up chickenshit."

✢ FIRED ✢

HUGH ADDONIZIO, MAYOR OF NEWARK
1914–1981

AN ORANGE GLOW FROM a hundred burning buildings lit up the night sky and reflected in the shattered storefront glass littering the streets. Newark, proud, gritty old Newark, was in flames, put to the torch by rioters, and Mayor Hugh Addonizio quivered as he watched the destruction. When the State Police and National Guard came to him for the order to take back the streets, he was the very picture of despair. "It's all gone," was all he could say. "The whole town is gone."

The urban warfare that devastated Newark from July 12–16, 1967, was among the deadliest race riots of a riotous decade. Twenty-six people were killed and entire neighborhoods of New Jersey's largest city were left a smoking wasteland. Among the casualties were the political careers of Newark's leaders. An investigation later determined that the riots had been caused in large part by minority rage at a City Hall where everything was for sale to rich crooks. The corruption went right up to Addonizio himself, and he went to jail for it.

Once, he had been the type of ethnic, liberal Democrat hailed as the future of urban America. The son of Italian immigrants, Addonizio earned a football scholarship to Fordham University, landed at Normandy Beach, and won the Bronze Star. His war hero record caught the notice of Newark's Democratic Party organization, which ran him for Congress in 1948. At thirty-four, he was elected in an upset.

In the House, Addonizio amassed a reliably liberal voting record and no major achievements. In 1962, in the middle of his seventh term, he entered the race for mayor of Newark. Addonizio told the voters he wanted to repair the decay afflicting his hometown, but privately offered this assessment: "There's no money in Washington, but you can make a million dollars as mayor of Newark."

Mayor Hugh Addonizio faces some tough questions after the Newark riots of 1967. Three years later he was in prison. (*New York Post*)

These homegrown fortunes came courtesy of the Mafia, which ran the only growth industries in town: gambling and loansharking. Addonizio himself bet recklessly at horses and cards, and incurred heavy losses that put him in hock to the mob. His friends, including mob kingpin Anthony "Tony Boy" Boiardo, were always willing to forgive the debts.

The gangsters affectionately called their protégé "the pope," because his squat stature, balding head, and jowly face gave him a certain resemblance to John XXIII. They paid for Addonizio's Caribbean vacations and donated heavily to his campaign. In turn, they expected favors. FBI wiretaps caught Genovese capo Angelo "Ray" DeCarlo bragging about the new mayor: "He'll give us the city."

Addonizio fulfilled their every expectation. Construction firms doing city business drew up fictitious budgets and paid ten cents of every dollar to dummy companies run by the mob. Shoddily built sewer lines crumbled and schools fell into disrepair. But others got rich. At least five City Council members, the municipal judge, the corporation counsel, and, of course, Addonizio himself, got a percentage of the graft.

Those Newark citizens who did not join the flight to the suburbs were rewarded with a decline appalling even by the standards of 1960s urban blight. Homeowners paid the second-highest property tax rates of any city, behind only Boston. One-third of the housing stock was substandard. Newark had the highest crime, infant mortality, and venereal disease rates in the United States.

Bearing the brunt of this social disaster were African Americans, more than half of Newark's population. Addonizio wooed their votes in 1962 with promises to spend more on housing and social programs. In office, he doled out patronage and a share of the rackets to favored black community leaders. The less influential poor simmered in their prison-like projects and rat-infested tenements, radicalized by the slogan "Black power." As the 1960s wore on, one city after another erupted in race rioting—Los Angeles, Chicago, Cleveland. In the spring of 1967, Addonizio pointed out hopefully that "we haven't had any racial conflict."

He spoke too soon. The long, hot summer of 1967 was the ugliest season of racial violence in U.S. history, and Newark's turn came on July 12.

The spark to the powder keg came from the largely white Newark Police Department. A black cab driver was roughed up while being arrested for a traffic violation, and a crowd gathered outside the Fourth Precinct, as if to storm the gates and free him.

"Police brutality!" they shouted. Angry young men hurled epithets, then rocks and bottles, at the cops guarding the station door. Suddenly, bands of troublemakers broke free from the crowd. They surged downtown, broke plate glass windows, and scooped up merchandise. Liquor, furniture, and television sets disappeared from the stores, triumphantly carried away in a surreal party atmosphere. When the rioters sensed the police would not stop them, they began setting fires as well.

In the moment of crisis, the leadership waffled. The disturbances were "isolated incidents," Addonizio told reporters. Two days passed before he finally sought the help of Governor Richard Hughes, by which time the streets had been given up to anarchy.

Things got distinctly uglier after a police officer was killed, the victim of a rioter's potshot. Troops riding the streets in armored personnel carriers and police in their squad cars began spraying bullets everywhere, out of panic and vengefulness. At times, police radios crackled with the alarm: "Hold your fire! You're shooting at each other!"

The final toll was put at $10 million in property damage, more than a thousand injured, and twenty-six killed. Of the dead, twenty-four were black, and the majority of those were innocent bystanders to the mayhem. A blue-ribbon state panel, set up by Hughes to investigate the riots, criticized the police tactics. The commission cited a cause of the riots as "the pervasive feeling of corruption" and called for a grand jury to look into it. Addonizio promised a thorough investigation. "If there are corrupt men in government, let's find them," he said.

The mayor was as stunned as anyone when the federal government did just that. In December 1969, Addonizio, nine former or current city officials, and "Tony Boy" Boiardo were all indicted for extortion. The charges came just as the mayor kicked off his race for a third term. The campaign was among the most bizarre in any city's history. By day, he sat in the Trenton federal courthouse, hearing contractors testify of being shaken down by the mob. In the evening, he motored back to Newark to hold rallies.

Despite his energy, the mayor lost both fights. On June 16, 1970, he was defeated in the election by Kenneth Gibson, who became the first black mayor of a large northeastern city. A month later, Addonizio was convicted of all sixty-four counts against him.

The judge handed Addonizio a ten-year sentence, a $25,000 fine, and a tongue-lashing. The ex-mayor's crimes were so devastating, he said, that "It is impossible to the estimate the impact upon . . . the decent citizens of Newark and indeed the citizens of New Jersey in terms of their frustration, despair and disillusionment."

❧ ARABIAN NIGHTS ❧

THE ABSCAM CROOKS

IN THE FLORIDA SUN, it was hard to say which glinted brighter: the dagger's steel blade, or the face of the man receiving it as a gift of friendship. On March 22, 1979, Angelo Errichetti, mayor of Camden, New Jersey, and all-around Democratic political fixer, climbed aboard a yacht and was ushered into the royal presence of Emir Yassir Habib. The

The rogues gallery of Abscam bribe-takers included chain-smoking Camden mayor Angelo Errichetti, who unwittingly led fellow politicians into the trap. (*New York Post* / Louis Liotta)

dignified Arab with dagger in hand reigned over some emirate or sheik-
dom or whatever. Errichetti didn't know—all he cared about was the
green on the man's dollar bills. The emir's agents had already delivered
the mayor $25,000, and he expected millions more. In return, Errichetti
had pledged to support their plan to build an Atlantic City casino and
to deliver them a stable of bribe-accepting members of Congress.

Now this silent potentate in a white burnoose showed his apprecia-
tion of the corrupt deal. With a flourish straight out the Arabian Nights,
he handed Errichetti a gleaming knife that had been in his royal family
for centuries. "I will treasure it," Errichetti said, tears welling in his normally jaded eyes. "Friendship is everything."

Here is the secret of the con game: the mark *wants* to believe. It doesn't
matter how smart or successful or powerful the victims, because once
they catch the whiff of big money, all their defenses fall. The street-
smart Errichetti never guessed that his priceless dagger was actually a
$2.75 souvenir bought at a flea market. Nor did he suspect that Emir
Yassir Habib was really Richard Farhardt, an undercover FBI agent from
Ohio, or that hidden video cameras had captured the dagger ceremony
and the transfer of the bribes.

It was one of the absurd lowlights of Abscam, the FBI sting operation that rocked Washington in 1980, led to the convictions of eight congressmen, and sent public trust in government plunging to new depths.
And nowhere did the scandal hit harder than in New Jersey, where

Harrison Williams poses
with an FBI agent in the
role of "Sheik Yassir
Habib." Williams became
only the second U.S.
senator in history to go
to prison. (Photo courtesy
of the Federal Bureau of
Investigation)

Errichetti unwittingly dragged a U.S. senator, congressman, state legislator, and several middlemen into the quicksand with him.

Operation Abscam wasn't so much a trap as a honey pot: offer free sweets and see how many crooks fly in. It began in 1978 when a convicted swindler named Mel Weinberg offered to become an informant for the FBI. In exchange for avoiding prison, Weinberg would rope in his old criminal contacts by offering to fence their goods. In this way, stolen art, forged certificates of deposit, and other commodities of organized crime could all be recovered.

It was Weinberg's idea to pose as the chief business agent of an oil-rich sheik. The FBI set up a front company for him run by a fictitious Sheik Abdul—source of the code name Abscam. The late 1970s were a boom time for the Arab oil states, and none of the hustlers doing business with Abdul Enterprises suspected it was a setup. To each one, the fast-talking Weinberg explained that the sheiks were sitting on piles of money burning holes in their pockets. Weinberg would invite crooks to various hotel rooms in and around New York City to sell their illicit goods. FBI agents posing as the sheik's American stooges were always waiting there, along with hidden cameras.

Abscam was humming along in this manner when an underworld figure introduced Weinberg to Mayor Errichetti in December 1978. With no prompting, Errichetti offered to sell forged securities and let the sheiks use the Camden seaport for drug smuggling. He dropped hints of his mob connections. Then he upped the ante: "I'll give you Atlantic City." Errichetti was a state senator as well as being a mayor, he explained, and "owned" four of the five members of the state Casino Control Commission. Casino licenses were on sale for $400,000. Done, the FBI actors said, handing him a down payment of $25,000. Errichetti could hardly believe his luck. "This is the most fuckin' unbelievable thing I've ever seen in my whole life, and I'm fifty years old," he exulted.

A man of his word, the mayor produced a member of the casino panel at a subsequent meeting, and split a $100,000 bribe with him. Weinberg asked Errichetti if there were any other New Jersey politicians this easy to get along with. To the FBI men's astonishment, the mayor offered up the name of U.S. Senator Harrison Williams, a fellow New Jersey Democrat and the respected chairman of the Senate Labor Committee.

The grave and dignified Williams accompanied Errichetti on the trip to the emir's yacht in Delray Beach, Florida, and watched the absurd ceremony of the dagger without blinking. After much hemming and hawing, Williams then got to business with Sheik Yassir. He wanted the Arabs to invest $100 million for a titanium mine in which he was a silent partner. Although Williams was too skittish to handle cash—he used a bagman lawyer for that—he was recorded bragging that he could use influence with President Jimmy Carter to OK the mine deal.

Errichetti's magic soon rounded up more members of Congress. Frank Thompson of Trenton, the No. 5 ranking Democrat in the House leadership, came to the sheik and left with a suitcase containing $50,000. Representative Ozzie Myers of Philadelphia was handed the same amount and was asked if he could sponsor an immigration bill allowing Emir Yassir to stay in the United States. It's a deal, Myers said, offering this civics lesson: "Money talks in this business and bullshit walks."

Soon, so many members of Congress emerged with their hands out that the FBI rented an expensive house in Washington in which to accommodate them. Bribes were passed in a living room stocked with furnishings borrowed from the Smithsonian, and under bright lights installed to enable the primitive video technology to do its work. If anyone got suspicious about the intensity of this light, the FBI actors explained that the sheik missed the desert sun of his homeland.

Abscam was forced to fold its tents when various newspapers got wind of the scandal and prepared to publish stories. On February 2, 1980, FBI agents fanned out across Washington and New Jersey to notify the politicians they were targets of an investigation, and that all those sheiks they had been meeting were really undercover men. When the politicians recovered from their stunned silences, it was time to dream up a defense. This was not easy, as videotape does not lie. However, one of the Abscam criminals, state senator Joe Maressa of Camden County, offered an ingenious excuse: "I thought it would be patriotic to take some of the OPEC money and get it back to the United States."

The rest of the men caught in the net thought harder and cried with one voice: Entrapment! We didn't want to take bribes; the feds enticed us into it. The public decided otherwise. None of the indicted officials held onto their jobs past the 1980 elections, and all were eventually convicted by juries. (One Florida congressman's conviction was overturned on appeal.) Harrison Williams, who became the second U.S. senator in history to go to prison, argued to the end of his days that the FBI tactics were illegal.

Mel Weinberg, the rogue who weaved the net in which even bigger rogues were caught, had the perfect rebuttal. "Nobody twisted anybody's arm to take the bread," he said. "We said it was there if they wanted it. They knocked each other over tryin' to be first on the bread line."

⇒ SNOW JOB ⇐

JOHNS-MANVILLE AND THE
GREAT ASBESTOS COVER-UP

"SNOWMEN," THE WORKERS AT THE Johns-Manville asbestos plant in the company town of Manville, New Jersey, called themselves. Powdery, white asbestos fibers covered their skin every day at work and clung stubbornly to their clothes. Sometimes the asbestos blowing away from the factory fell like snowflakes and kids tried to catch it on their tongues.

No one complained. By the 1930s, Johns-Manville Corporation—one of the blue-chip manufacturing giants whose stock prices made up the Dow Jones Industrial Average—had built itself an image as a company that cared. Workers received good wages along with free physical exams and chest X-rays. But the workers were not told what was in those X-rays. Thousands of them were gravely ill.

All the snow-like asbestos fibers they breathed into their lungs stayed there permanently, leaving hideous black dots. Some workers would suffocate from the lung-scarring ailment known as asbestosis. Others were doomed to die from mesothelioma, a cancer of the chest lining, or other types of cancer. The deadly effects spread far beyond the factory walls:

Johns-Manville asbestos sickened shipbuilders in Texas, pipefitters in California, construction workers in Tennessee. By the early twenty-first century, there were at least 350,000 victims in one of the worst corporate horror stories in U.S. history.

Company namesake Henry Johns was fascinated with the magical qualities of a mineral that would not burn. He obtained the first patent for asbestos insulation in 1868, and tinkered endlessly with the product in his basement lab in Brooklyn. But he, like many an asbestos worker, paid the price. His death in 1898 was attributed to "dust phthisis pneumonitis"—a condition medical science would later call asbestosis.

Johns-Manville was incorporated three years after Johns's death when his heirs merged the firm with a Milwaukee plumbing supplier, Manville

Workers on the factory floor in the early 1950s in Manville, New Jersey, chalky asbestos dust all over their clothes. It was Johns-Manville company policy not to tell them what their lung X-rays showed. (Neil Ranauro Collection, Special Collections and University Archives, Rutgers University Libraries)

Company. Ground was broken in 1912 for the company's main plant in Hillsborough Township, New Jersey. Five thousand people would be employed here by mid-century, weaving asbestos fibers into fabrics and insulation. An entirely new town came into being, taking the name Manville. New Jersey became the leading asbestos-producing state thanks not only to Manville but to companies such as Raybestos in Passaic, National Gypsum in Millington, and Baldwin-Ehret-Hill in Trenton.

Johns-Manville marketed asbestos as the "mineral of a thousand uses" that would insulate just about anything against heat—roofing tiles, clothes, brakes, and the steampipes and stoves aboard ships. In 1939, *Time* magazine ran a glowing cover story about Johns-Manville president Lewis Brown that cited his company as "the outstanding public relations success" of the corporate world. The same year, the Johns-Manville pavilion at the New York World's Fair dazzled visitors with its futuristic asbestos house and giant statue of Asbestos Man. Like a superhero, he stood in a real, flaming pit, unsinged thanks to his asbestos suit.

Of course, real men who exposed themselves to asbestos were risking their health. In 1924, a medical journal published the first article identifying a new disease, asbestosis, and linking asbestos fibers with lung disease. Shortly afterward, Metropolitan Life Insurance found that Johns-Manville workers were "risks to be selected with great care."

The grim evidence of asbestos's deadly effects grew throughout the 1930s. Johns-Manville responded with a massive cover-up. A 1933 Met Life study of asbestosis at the Manville plant was rewritten to remove its "darker tones" at the urging of company's counsel. Johns-Manville's director of health then ordered that X-rays showing lung damage be withheld from asbestos workers who believed themselves able-bodied. In a memorandum, he explained: "As long as the man is not disabled it is felt that he should not be told of his condition so that he can live and work in peace and the Company can benefit by his many years of experience."

In the early 1950s, a doctor named Irving Selikoff opened a clinic in Paterson, New Jersey, and was alarmed to find seventeen patients suffering from lung scarring. All seventeen worked at the nearby Union

Asbestos & Rubber Company. After a larger study of New Jersey asbestos workers, he announced his findings in 1964. Many were afflicted with mesothelioma, a newly discovered cancer that only existed in people who breathed in asbestos fibers.

Over twenty years, 36 percent of Selikoff's study group was dead or dying of mesothelioma or another type of cancer, and another 9 percent had nonfatal asbestosis. And these were just the workers in New Jersey and New York. Perhaps 4 million people in all were exposed to asbestos, mostly by working in the shipping industry during World War II.

When the first product-liability lawsuits began to hit the company in the late 1960s, Johns-Manville aggressively defended itself by arguing that its knowledge of asbestos disease only dated from 1964. But this line of defense crumbled as lawyers obtained Johns-Manville correspondence over the years.

One lawyer in Paterson gave a devastating deposition claiming he knew about the X-rays and approached the company president about it in the late 1940s. "Mr. Brown, do you mean to tell me you would let them work until they dropped dead?" the lawyer asked. The response: "Yes, we save a lot of money that way."

Small wonder that civil juries across America began to reward asbestos workers with million-dollar awards and to sock Johns-Manville with punitive damages. By 1982, the company—now renamed Manville Corporation—was earning a profit of $60 million on sales of $2 billion. But it was being hit with new lawsuits at a rate of five hundred a month, and each settlement cost an average $40,000. At that rate, Manville was likely to see all its assets depleted in a few years.

On August 26, 1982, Manville filed for Chapter 11 bankruptcy protection. All existing litigation was immediately frozen, and all new suits prevented from being filed. Claimants protested loudly. "They're hoping we die off," said one Manville retiree suffering from asbestosis.

However bad it looked, Manville's bankruptcy maneuver allowed it to continue earning money that went into the pockets of its victims. By the late 1980s, it had split into two entities: Denver-based Manville Corporation and a trust that existed solely to pay off asbestos victims. The asbestos litigation industry was meanwhile expected to cost American business more than $200 billion by the time the last claim was settled.

Little of this cash was of benefit to fading asbestos towns like Manville, New Jersey. In 1985, the last buildings of the Johns-Manville factory closed, throwing eighteen hundred employees out of work.

The lucky ones lost only their salaries. One widow spoke for the less fortunate asbestos workers, who were dying at a rate of ten thousand a year. "He tried to get well," she told Dr. Selikoff. "He loved life and he wanted to live for me and the kids. He laid down and when his last breath went out, he called me and said, 'Honey, I'm dying.' Then he died."

❧ DEEP COVER ❧

DAVID FRIEDLAND, STATE SENATOR
1938–

AS FATE WOULD HAVE IT, David Friedland—union lawyer, the New Jersey Legislature's flashy defender of the working class, and a milliondollar thief of Teamster pension funds—made his grand exit on Labor Day. It was September 2, 1985, and Friedland, staring down the looming

David Friedland, resurrected
after playing dead for two years,
in custody in 1987. (*New York Post* /
Charles Wenzelberg)

inevitability of a seven-year prison sentence, was downing Percodan and booze at his Bahamas condo. He was groggy but game for one last swim in paradise before both summer and freedom came to an end. So Friedland slipped on a scuba suit and sailed out for a dive in the ocean. Twelve hours later, night had fallen and there was no Friedland in sight.

A tragic accident, his loved ones agreed: one more victim of the Labor Day tradition of dying drunk and reckless. But without a body, more skeptical types—and this included practically everyone outside his immediate family—had their questions. Was Friedland really gone? Or had this slick and shadowy con man pulled off the ultimate swindle by faking his own death?

He was, after all, a man who had resurrected his career more than once. Friedland was just twenty-six when elected to the state Assembly from Jersey City in 1965. He was popular with the voters and a reliable tool of the utterly corrupt Hudson County Democratic machine. Three years into his tenure, the state's top organized-crime fighter labeled him "entirely too comfortable with organized crime." Friedland huffed with outrage and threatened to sue for libel before quietly accepting a six-month suspension of his law license. The charge was true: Friedland had been bagman for a $6,500 bribe that squelched a court charge against waterfront racketeer John DiGilio.

Not that it mattered to the voters of Hudson County, who accepted bare-knuckle politics and organized crime as facts of life. They cheered when he was named Assembly Democratic minority leader in 1969, regularly re-elected him, and advanced him to the state Senate in 1978. Friedland winkingly acknowledged his shady reputation and flaunted it with a hip panache. With bushy hair, sideburns, and modish suits, he was the State House's class clown. Once, he proposed making the state fish the catfish because it was the only creature able to survive New Jersey's polluted waters. Another time, he called for the Statue of Liberty to be placed on a swivel, so it could face Jersey City once in a while.

In the Legislature, Friedland was a reliably liberal vote for a higher minimum wage, tougher environmental standards, and more spending on the urban poor. He also lived a high life removed from his blue-collar constituents, skiing in the Swiss Alps, scuba diving in the Caribbean, and staying in condos in Miami Beach and Grand Bahama Island. Friedland's shady law practice bankrolled his jet-setting. As attorney for New Jersey Teamsters Local 701, Friedland arranged to secretly loan $4 million from its pension fund to a California investor named Barry Marlin. In payment, Marlin sent David Friedland $360,000 stuffed into a satchel.

The plunder left behind many victims, not just the Teamsters. Marlin's real estate deal was a gigantic pyramid scheme. It wiped out the life savings of more than a thousand people, among them several widows and a quadriplegic. Friedland went to trial on federal extortion charges and was found guilty in 1980. Sentenced to seven years in prison, Friedland offered the U.S. attorney's office a deal: let him wear a wire and catch other Hudson County officials admitting their part in corrupt deals. On one secret mission, he caught his close friend, the mayor of Weehawken, blabbing about bribery. The federal authorities prepared to recommend a sentence reduction for their star stool pigeon.

But Friedland, having betrayed his friend, had no problems betraying the government, too. The corruption cases resulting from his testimony took years to wend their way through the courts, and in that time Friedland discovered other uses for Teamsters money. Even while out of a public job, he arranged for front men to illegally borrow $20 million from the pension fund, of which Friedland peeled off at least $1 million for his Swiss bank account. The feds were slow to realize what was happening, but they finally took his leniency deal off the table in 1985. He was due to go to prison September 23.

By then, however, Friedland had done his vanishing act off the Bahamas. An air-sea search failed to find the body, and the missing man's lawyer seemed to rule out all hope of finding it. "He swam downward, thinking he was swimming upward," the lawyer explained.

In fact, Friedland was an experienced scuba diver, and even when drunk he knew up from down. The U.S. Marshals Service suspected he had staged the accident and put him atop their most wanted list.

They were right. Well before Friedland disappeared under the Atlantic's blue waters, he had an escape plan. First, he swam to a getaway boat anchored a few hundred feet away. Then he sailed to a rendezvous back on land with his girlfriend, a photographer named Colette Golighty. They flew to Spain under false passports and spent the next few months touring Europe and safariing in Africa. As an alias, the ex-senator claimed to be a Greek peach farmer. To fund his world tour, Friedland simply withdrew from his Swiss account.

In December 1987, word came from the Maldive Islands, a tropical archipelago in the Indian Ocean, that Friedland was operating a chain of diving shops there. He had publicized his business with a postcard showing him feeding a fish to a shark. For an international fugitive, this was either a taunting gesture or simply stupid. The Maldive authorities threw him in jail, where Friedland failed in one last gambit to escape justice. He begged to be allowed to convert from Judaism to Islam, so that the largely Muslim Maldives could not legally extradite him.

"I had a good time," was all Friedland would say upon his return in handcuffs to the United States after twenty-eight months on the lam. He paid a price for it: the penalty for his flight was a far harsher sentence— fifteen years in prison—than he would have faced if he'd stayed put. Upon becoming a free man once again, Friedland relocated to Florida and took up a new job—selling cemetery lots. It was a job to which he brought unique qualifications. How many other people can say they've risen from the dead?

❧ PUSHING HIS LUCK ❦

NICHOLAS BISSELL, SOMERSET COUNTY PROSECUTOR 1947–1996

NICHOLAS BISSELL KNEW HOW unlikely it was to survive as a fugitive with the national media on your trail. The man once considered New Jersey's most hard-nosed county prosecutor loved to go on *America's Most Wanted,* look into the television camera, and tell his quarry that you can run, but you can't hide. When Bissell himself went on the lam in

November 1996 rather than go to prison for abuse of his Somerset County office, his tough-guy words must have been ringing in his ears.

Federal marshals finally caught up with Bissell in a sixteen-dollar-a-night casino hotel in a dusty Nevada town. Cowering on the floor between his bed and the wall, he leveled a gun to his head. The lawmen tried to talk him down. Think about your two teenaged daughters, they told him. "We'll take you in," one said. "There doesn't need to be any problems." Bissell lowered his pistol for a moment. Just like when he was prosecutor, the choice of life or death was in his hands.

Bissell liked being in charge. In 1982, when Governor Thomas Kean appointed him Somerset prosecutor, he was just thirty-five and full of energy. Bissell seemed always to be in the courthouse rather than behind a desk, an unusual take-charge attitude in a job where nitty-gritty trial work is usually farmed out to underlings. He won convictions in tough murder cases, and unflinchingly called for the death penalty for the worst offenders.

Colleagues in Somerset, a wealthy expanse of horse farms and millionaire estates, thought of this Republican law-and-order man as incorruptible. He seemed to prove his independence by putting two Franklin Township police officers on trial for brutality. Once he sent a public official to prison and commented to an aide: "If that happened to me, I'd eat a gun."

Nicholas Bissell, photographed in 1990, played up his law-and-order credentials before being exposed as a shakedown artist. (*The Trentonian* / Emma Lee)

Bissell's appetites were huge, whether for headlines or the chili dogs and hamburgers that swelled his once-trim five-foot-nine frame to two hundred pounds. But nothing matched his lust for gambling. With his wife, Barbara, who worked for him in a clerical job, Bissell took frequent trips to casinos in Atlantic City and the Bahamas. Between 1989 and 1995, the Bissells blew at least $41,680 on these gambling jaunts. While he showed every sign of a bad habit, Bissell had less tolerance for other addictions. A crusader against drugs, he took advantage of civil forfeiture laws to seize assets from dime-bag dealers and big-time smugglers alike. In just one year, Somerset collected $1.1 million this way—more than most of New Jersey's heavily urbanized counties.

It was all an official shakedown. Bissell became so obsessed with forfeiture, he based decisions about whom to prosecute on how much his office could earn. Soon, the money was finding its way into Bissell's pockets, and he was spending it on hotel bills and racket club memberships. Blinded by greed, he bought a gasoline station in a partnership with his wife and the brother of his chief of detectives. Bissell stole every cent of his partner's investment while skimming $140,000 from the business.

Bissell's pattern of thievery emerged when a man caught in a minor marijuana bust came to the authorities with an astonishing tale. He'd been forced to give up two parcels of property in a forfeiture proceeding, the man said. Then this land had been sold by the county for one-tenth its value, and the buyer was none other than Bissell's chief of detectives. In 1995, the prosecutor was stripped of his office and charged with fraud, embezzlement, and official misconduct. With foolhardy arrogance, he insisted on serving as his own lawyer at his federal trial in Newark. Both he and his wife were convicted on May 31, 1996, on all thirty counts.

The judge called Bissell a slippery liar, adding: "I'm not satisfied I can trust him to appear for sentencing." However, the defendant was granted $100,000 bail and ordered to stay under home arrest with an electronic monitoring bracelet around his ankle. Bissell endured this humiliation all summer while he quietly sold off his furniture and china. On November 18, two days before a sentencing where he expected to receive ten years in prison, Bissell made his escape. He sliced off his high-tech ball and chain and drove away from his Montgomery Township home in a Jeep Cherokee.

Behind him he left a note stating that he intended to kill himself. Federal authorities dismissed it as a stunt to win sympathy and launched an international manhunt. But Governor Christie Whitman knew Bissell well from when she was a member of the Somerset County legislature (known in New Jersey as the Board of Chosen Freeholders), and she worried that he meant business. She made a radio appeal: "Nick, turn yourself in. . . . You do have responsibilities, you do have children, and this is really, really tearing them apart."

Bissell ran for three thousand miles before he ended up in Laughlin, Nevada. The man who once castigated criminal "crybabies" and "jerks" in court was now a shambling wreck himself, hiring strippers to do lap dances in his hotel room and gambling away his remaining cash at the $5 card tables. Early on the morning of November 26, eight days into his run, he heard a knock on his door and the words: "Police, open the door."

Bissell wouldn't budge, so the squad of U.S. marshals in their bulletproof vests kicked in the door. He sat there on the floor, cradling a .38-caliber Walther. "I'm not going to hurt anybody," he told them. "But I'm not going to be taken." For twelve minutes, the dialogue went on, the marshals urging Bissell to think of his family, the ex-prosecutor shaking his head. His last words were: "I can't do ten years." That said, he put the barrel in his mouth and pulled the trigger.

☛ MAN'S MAN ☚

MILTON MILAN, MAYOR OF CAMDEN
1963–

TEENAGERS FALLING DEAD in drive-by shootings, crumbling buildings given up to crackheads, neighborhoods devoid of jobs and hope—this was the ugly image of Camden, poorest city in New Jersey and murder capital of the United States. But on July 1, 1997, the sounds reverberating through downtown were cheers, not gunfire. Milton Milan, a brash, brawny community activist of thirty-four, was being sworn in as Camden's first Hispanic mayor, and it seemed his energy could finally bring the revival his hometown dreamed of. "*Viva* Milton Milan!" his supporters shouted. "Milton's in the house!"

But instead of being a revolutionary, Milan turned out to be a traditionalist, and not in the way voters desired. Like two of his four immediate predecessors as mayor, Milan became a convicted felon. Mob ties had a long and dishonorable history among Camden politicians, but Milan took things one sinister step forward. Not only did he take regular payoffs from the Mafia, he sold his office to the drug gangs.

The fall of Milton Milan dashed what could have been an up-from-the-bootstraps tale of urban success. The Puerto Rican boy grew up in poverty with a single mother on welfare. His North Camden was a rough but lively place, he once recalled, of "nets with no rims, playing handball, playing in front of the fire hydrants in the summer, fights on the streets, brushes with the law, the friends who either died or were arrested."

Milan dropped out of high school and joined the Marines, where he learned to operate heavy equipment. With these marketable skills, he was able to return to Camden, set himself up in construction, and use his persuasive personality to win city contracts for affordable housing. In business, the six-footer retained the swagger and the macho edge of the streets. "I have a pair," he liked to brag.

Milton Milan, large
and in charge of Camden,
liked to boast "I have a
pair." He went to prison
for racketeering.
(Photo © *The Star-Ledger.*

As a high achiever who remained close to his roots, Milan won the admiration of the Hispanic community. He was elected to City Council in 1995, relying more on charisma than organizational skill. The Camden County Democratic Party recognized his vote-getting potential in a city that was now more than one-third Hispanic, and backed him for mayor two years later.

In the closing weeks of the 1997 campaign, Milan was blindsided when fliers started popping up all over the city. The anonymous sheets accused him of being a drug dealer and a friend of Jose "J.R." Rivera, a thug linked to twenty murders who operated an open-air cocaine bazaar called "The Alley." Milan denounced the accusation as a smear and an anti-Hispanic slur. He shrugged off the hard blow to win 40 percent of the vote, a solid victory in a crowded field of candidates.

But the charges against Milan were true. Convicted drug dealers would later testify for the federal government that Milan bought packets of cocaine in the late 1980s; one acquaintance identified him a street-level seller. The mayor was not merely a friend of Rivera, but a client. Once, he had borrowed $65,000 of Rivera's drug money to finance his construction business. There were even shadowy hints that Milan was himself a murderer. In 1988, he was questioned by police about the shooting of a heroin dealer, and reportedly failed a lie detector test.

Never one to discriminate, Milan did business as readily with the Italian mob as with neighborhood pushers. In 1996, while he was still a councilman, he began taking cash envelopes from mobsters sent his way by Philadelphia family boss Ralph Natale. Eventually his mob take amounted to $30,000. Natale was caught telling a wire-wearing informant: "This guy, the mayor, sweetheart this guy, you'll love him. . . . He's a man's man. Smart . . . and looking to make money."

The very night of Milan's inauguration, with Camden celebrating the spirit of rebirth in the air, the new mayor was taking one of his cash envelopes, Natale said on the recording. Other construction firms were rewarded with city contracts on the condition that they do expensive remodeling work on Milan's house and supply him with cars.

With no real interest in the daily grind of governance, Milan let Camden's already woeful fiscal situation slide further into crisis. In the mayor's first year, Governor Christie Whitman appointed a state board to monitor the city's budget. By the time Milan left office, the state had taken over all city functions.

In the late 1990s, Camden's murder rate was consistently one of the ten highest in America. In response, the State Police began cracking down hard on "The Alley"—not just arresting the small-fry dealers, but threatening them with life sentences in order to get them to finger their higher-ups. Eventually this strategy, along with the federal probe of Natale, paid off. Names were named, and the top man at City Hall was identified as chief protector of the drug trade. In March 2000, Milan was indicted on racketeering charges.

"I'm going to fight," Milan said, refusing to resign. "I've always been a fighter." But at the trial, prosecutors offered two devastating witnesses against him: Rivera and Natale. They both told how Milan had gladly become the tool of both the traditional mob and the inner-city gangs. After a five-week trial, Milan was found guilty on December 21, 2000, on fourteen of nineteen counts.

Bowed and tearful, having lost fifty pounds, Milan appeared the following June to be sentenced to seven years in prison. "People believed in me and trusted in me," he told the judge. "I'm sorry to them, to my family and to my children." The convicted racketeer then quietly walked off to his fate, a smaller person in every way.

❧ THE FIX WAS IN ❧

ROBERT W. LEE, BOXING OFFICIAL
1934–

"I COULD HAVE BEEN A CONTENDER!" The lament of Marlon Brando's Hoboken, New Jersey, longshoreman in *On the Waterfront* speaks to the dashed hopes of all boxers who took a dive on the mob's orders. But by the end of the twentieth century, there was a more sophisticated way to rig the game. Promoters could make payoffs not to the fighters them-selves, but to the organizations that sanctioned the bouts and awarded the championship belts. No one in the murky alphabet soup of sanc-tioning bodies—WBC, WBA, and IBF—played this game more brazenly than the founder of the International Boxing Federation, Robert W. Lee.

Bob Lee carried the swagger of the streets and packed 220 pounds on his five-foot-eight frame. But he "never broke a sweat in the gym or took a punch," as a federal official said. Bureaucratic power, not muscle power, made him a big man in boxing. He had been the first black officer on the Scotch Plains, New Jersey, police department, and in 1978 was named assistant boxing commissioner to regulate a sport that had suddenly become resurgent in Atlantic City casinos.

More a booster than a watchdog, Lee allowed promoters to collect only half the state tax on gate receipts, and boxers to enter the ring with only cursory checkups on their health. In 1981, Lee accepted an envelope stuffed with $3,000 from a man who wanted to obtain a promoter's license. The bribe-payer was an FBI informant. Lee ducked indictment, but he was suspended by the boxing commission. Discrimination, he claimed. Lee could play the race card dramatically, even poetically: "If you're white, you're right. If you're black, get back."

Ethics violations or not, Lee took up the cause of boxing reform. He formed a third major sanctioning group in 1983—the International

International Boxing
Federation founder
Robert W. Lee (center)
after being indicted for
racketeering in 1999.
(*New York Post* /
Michael Norcia)

Boxing Federation—with offices in East Orange, New Jersey. Its acronym, a neat reversal of the FBI, was the IBF. Lee pledged to look out for boxers in a largely African American and Latino sport. At last, they would be free from the slavery of biased rankings and exorbitant sanctioning fees.

That was the theory. In reality, promoters—dominated by Don King with his bellowing sales pitch and exploding hair—were the real kings of the sport and made the decisions about who fought whom. Lee and his IBF simply went along with their whims.

In every weight class, the IBF maintained a monthly list of the top fifteen contenders, with the No. 1 man guaranteed a shot at the title. A boxer's place on the list depended partly on talent, partly on how much his manager paid up. By the 1990s, rankings in each weight class were for sale, from flyweight ($1,000) to heavyweight ($100,000). Lee claimed to be fighting for blacks but inflated the rankings of "great white hopes" on King's theory that they drew a better gate. Pale-skinned lummoxes such as Francois Botha stayed high in the IBF rankings by virtue of facing even more hapless challengers.

The results of these corrupt rankings drew scorn from the fans. After forty-five-year-old George Foreman won the IBF's heavyweight championship in a shocking upset in 1994, his handlers insisted that they hand-pick an easy opponent for his first title defense. Lee moved an unexceptional German boxer named Axel Schulz up the rankings in exchange for $100,000. Foreman struggled throughout the supposedly easy match, and observers thought Schulz had won. But the popular, roly-poly champ was awarded the decision anyway, along with his $10 million purse. The victims in this and other charades were not just the fans. Honest pugilists who refused to play by the federation's dubious rules were stripped of their titles and denied a chance at purses.

Federal investigators were able to bring down Bob Lee by persuading one of his closest underlings to turn on him. This informant, C. Douglas Beavers, was chairman of the IBF's rankings committee and personal bagman to both Lee and his son, Robert Jr. Beavers collected bribes from various promoters, referred to by code names: King was "Fuzzy-Wuzzy."

Cash drops were made to Lee in a hotel room in Virginia that was rigged with video. On December 18, 1997, Beavers came by with $5,000 wrapped in cellophane and taped to his leg. "Christmas cheer," he said as he handed the package to Lee.

Federal agents hoped that, confronted with the evidence, Lee would flip against the real target of their corruption investigation, Don King. But the IBF president refused to cooperate. Robert Sr., sixty-five, and Robert Jr., thirty-eight, were indicted in 1999 on federal racketeering charges alleging they collected $338,000 in bribes. The IBF was placed under a federal monitor, the first time a remedy for mob-riddled labor unions had been applied to a sporting organization.

The Lees' trial, held in Newark federal court from April to August 2000, hinged on Robert Sr.'s claim that all those payoffs were not really bribes but "tips." "Boxing is—let's face it—show business," argued their lawyer, Gerald Krovatin. The jury gave the defendants a split decision. Lee Jr. was cleared on all counts, and Lee Sr. was acquitted of the most serious counts of bribery. However, he was found guilty of interstate travel to aid racketeering, money laundering, and filing a false tax return. His penalty was twenty-two months in prison and a lifetime ban from boxing.

Beset by scandal, the sport of boxing fell into decline in the 2000s, losing ground to the cheerfully fake world of professional wrestling and the gory pastime of ultimate fighting. That's show business.

❧ PASSING THE TORCH ❧

ROBERT TORRICELLI, SENATOR
1951–

JUST A FEW MONTHS into his first term, Senator Robert Guy Torricelli of New Jersey was already blitzing the Sunday morning TV talk shows, raising millions of dollars for the Democratic Party, and burning with the intensity that gave him his nickname, "The Torch." In July 1997, he took his seat on the Senate Government Affairs Committee as it began hearings to investigate whether Chinese interests had illegally funneled money into President Bill Clinton's re-election campaign. Freshmen members of these panels are generally seen and not heard, but Torricelli spoke up as a defender of the White House.

The senator warned against ethnic stereotyping of Asians by walking back in history to the Senate Kefauver hearings into the Mafia, which he claimed painted an unfair portrait of Italian Americans. "It is among the first memories I have of government of the U.S. and probably the first hearing of the U.S. Senate I ever witnessed," Torricelli said passionately. "It was only on a flickering television screen, but I will never forget it and even if I tried, my family would never allow me."

In politics, shading the truth is not necessarily a crime, although it can turn embarrassing. Fact-checking by reporters revealed that the Kefauver hearings ended on August 22, 1951, when the senator was five days old. He must have been a prodigy indeed to retain such a memory. However, Torricelli's faulty childhood memories turned out to be trivial compared to his ethical woes. As irony would have it, the crisis came when a Chinese-born businessman admitted illegally raising funds for Torricelli and showering him with expensive gifts. The whiff of scandal extinguished the Torch's career.

Robert Torricelli in 2002 after he withdrew from his Senate re-election race because of a gifts scandal. "When did we become such an unforgiving people?" he asked. (*New York Post* / David Rentas)

Other kids collected baseball cards; young Robert Torricelli, growing up in Franklin Lakes, New Jersey, amassed history books and record albums of great speeches. At Rutgers University, Torricelli stood out for his anything-to-win mentality. Booted out of student government for vote fraud his first year, he came back to be elected president his junior and senior years. After getting a law degree, he was elected to Congress from his home county of Bergen in 1982, at age thirty-one.

Quickly he gained a reputation as a nervy publicity-seeker unafraid to make enemies. He was an especially irritating gadfly to the Ronald Reagan foreign policy team, which he blasted as being too hawkishly anti-communist in Central America. Then, in 1992, he became one of Congress's fiercest foes of Fidel Castro and sponsored a law tightening the U.S. embargo on Cuba. Torricelli called it a sign of his independence. Others noted that he took up his interest in the embargo only after his congressional district was redrawn to include Cuban voters.

Torricelli evolved in other ways. After divorcing in 1989, the one-time nerd bloomed into a robust ladies' man with an alluring wit and smoldering confidence. He dated Mick Jagger's ex-wife Bianca, the Democratic fund-raiser Patricia Duff, models, and journalists. Hobnobbing with the rich and powerful gave him a taste for luxury. Torricelli wrapped his doughy build in fine suits and moussed the graying hair back from his high forehead.

In 1996, Torricelli put all this ego and energy into the next step of an ambitious career: running for U.S. Senate. He won by amassing a $9 million war chest. In the Senate, he became Clinton's attack dog, ardently defending him on television during the sex-and-impeachment debate. But the qualities that lit up the small screen made Torricelli look like a preening jerk in person. Torricelli's own Democratic colleague from New Jersey, Senator Frank Lautenberg, made no secret of his disdain for him. When they talked, which was rare, Torricelli screamed things such as "I'm going to cut your balls off!"

Liked or disliked, Torricelli was respected as the Democratic Party's best earner. Where many elected officials loathe the routine of chatting up wealthy business people for donations, Torricelli found himself in his natural element. In an unprecedented honor for a freshman, he got the chairmanship of the Democratic Senate Campaign Committee. He obliterated all records by raising $87.2 million for Senate candidates in 2000. Against all expectations, the Democrats picked up five seats.

It should have been the Torch's finest hour, but there were signs his political skills were slipping. Bored with the Senate, he made moves in the summer of 2000 to run for governor, only to withdraw from the race when all the county bosses he counted on for endorsements went for James McGreevey instead. Then, a Justice Department investigation into political fund-raising—the same issue that Torricelli had been so indignant about back in 1997—began to center on an importer from Cresskill, New Jersey, named David Chang. He had donated $52,000 in illegal checks to the 1996 Torricelli campaign—dodging the limits on individual contributions by compelling business associates to become "straw donors" on his behalf.

With the threat of serious prison time hanging over his head, Chang accused Torricelli of causing all his woes. Chang said the candidate had hit him up for cash and promised to use his Senate influence to make his donations worth it. Chang said he bought Torricelli a dozen Italian suits, an $8,100 Rolex watch, Tiffany cuff links, a bronze statuette, a television set, and earrings for his girlfriend.

Torricelli admitted accepting the television, statuette, and earrings, but said he received no "illegal gifts" and did nothing special on Chang's behalf. His version of events was challenged by reporting in the *New York Times*. Stories revealed that Torricelli *did* lobby aggressively for Chang. He took the businessman with him to meet South Korea's finance minister and urged that Chang be allowed to buy an insurance company for $1.5 billion from the Seoul government.

In January 2002, the U.S. attorney's office in New York announced Torricelli would not be indicted, and the senator called himself vindicated. But that summer, as Torricelli headed into a re-election campaign, the Senate Ethics Committee "severely admonished" him for his relationship with Chang. Torricelli himself had become the issue, and out of nowhere his Republican challenger led in the polls.

On September 30, thirty-five days before the election, Torricelli made the bitter decision to drop out of the race. To succeed him on the ballot, the Democrats tapped his old nemesis Lautenberg, who had retired from the Senate two years before. Without Torricelli's ethical baggage, Lautenberg won.

"When did we become such an unforgiving people?" Torricelli asked in his bowing-out speech. "When did we stop believing and trusting in each other?" Never, as it turned out. As an ex-senator, Torricelli parlayed his talent for drumming up dollars into a new career as a business consultant. Governors, casino owners, and developers all went to him for his wisdom. "In Oregon, Torricelli would be finished," marveled the political scientist Larry Sabato. "But in New Jersey, there's no telling where he might end up."

❧ SOME FRIEND YOU ARE ❧

ROBERT JANISZEWSKI,
HUDSON COUNTY EXECUTIVE
1945–

THE DEMOCRATIC ORGANIZATION of Hudson County, New Jersey, prized disciples such as Barney Doyle, a ward leader who helped get out the vote and in return earned the patronage job of superintendent of weights and measures. After his swearing-in ceremony in 1949, a reporter asked him: "Barney, how many ounces in a pound?" "Aw, gimme a break," Doyle said. "I just got this job."

Loyalty to the Democratic machine translated into power in Hudson, and once you got in office you were expected to take care of your friends and yourself. It was in this tradition that Robert C. Janiszewski of Jersey City began his service as county executive in 1988. But Janiszewski's loyalty would have its breaking point, as his friends and sponsors would sadly learn.

His political life was formed through friendships, most importantly with a kid who lived a block away in Jersey City named Paul Byrne. From the time they were both four, "Bobby J." and Paul served as altar boys together, played stickball together, and hung out on stoops together. Janisewski grew up to become a teacher but itched for a political career. The savvy Byrne turned into his personal consultant, arranging the campaign financing to put Janiszewski in power.

No one had the illusion Janiszewski was a reformer. He had served quietly on the county Board of Chosen Freeholders (1972–1978) and in the state Assembly (1978–1984), voting as party leaders told him. But he had political pull and energy, and once he became county executive there were high hopes for him. His first term as executive coincided with a gentrification boom that turned the once-shabby Hudson riverfront into the "Gold Coast." Janiszewski plowed newfound revenue from property taxes into parks and education.

Janiszewski's local power was immense and spilled into the state and national arenas. He was simultaneously county executive, chairman of the county Democratic Party, and a board member on the Port Authority of New York and New Jersey. In 1992, he earned a sheaf of IOUs by chairing Bill Clinton's winning presidential campaign in New Jersey.

The chain-smoking executive with the wispy mustache cut a striking figure. A devotee of hot dog stands, he was always wolfing down wieners and guzzling black coffee—yet never seemed to add weight to his stringy form. He owned a $300,000 condominium on the riverfront and ski resort homes in upstate New York and Colorado.

Robert Janiszewski behind his desk and a stack of New Jersey laws that he broke. (Courtesy of the Hudson Reporter Newspaper Group, Hoboken, N.J.)

The basic rule of rewarding friends and punishing enemies prevailed in Hudson County. It was a regular practice to shelve the low bidder on a contract and award the deal instead to some deep-pocketed political contributor. So long as a politician did not personally enrich himself, this was legal. Janiszewski played the game of "clean graft" to perfection. But he collected dirty graft, too. The county executive who earned a $114,000 salary collected untold hundreds of thousands of dollars in bribes.

The money came from developers, auditors, bond underwriters, and other vendors doing business with Hudson County, with Byrne serving as middleman. With time, however, Janiszewski got careless and shed his insulation. He began cramming envelopes of cash into a work file cabinet. He took his payoffs in the very sanctum of the Hudson County Courthouse, where his offices were located. Once, he gave a speech for a hundred guests while secretly worrying that someone might notice his pocket bulge.

Janiszewski finally overreached himself by demanding $30,000 in bribes from Dr. Oscar Sandoval, a psychiatrist, in return for $2 million in contracts to provide counseling at the county jail. The house of detention, a cesspool of patronage, was under sharp government scrutiny in the late 1990s. Investigators from the U.S. attorney's office convinced Sandoval to turn informer.

In November 2000, the doctor lured Janiszewski to an Atlantic City hotel room and slapped a cash envelope in front of him. Janiszewski was seized by a fear that a microphone might be hidden nearby. Rather than speak, he wrote on a pad of paper: "Not now. Later." The county executive had not counted on hidden cameras, which videotaped him scribbling his incriminating words.

Janiszewski was given an extraordinary deal. He could avoid immediate arrest, even stay in office, by turning cooperating witness. The executive agreed, becoming the highest-ranking official in New Jersey to be an informant. Federal agents wired his car for sound, and in the following eight months he recorded more than sixty conversations implicating politicians and developers in a web of crooked deals. He resigned on September 6, 2001, by which time the U.S. attorney was preparing multiple indictments.

Seven people were convicted of corruption crimes thanks to Janiszew-ski's secret tapes and testimony. The mayor of Hoboken and two mem-bers of the Board of Freeholders—among them Sandoval's girlfriend, Nidia Davila-Colon—went to prison. Even Byrne found himself under indictment, done in by his best friend's secret tapes. "This is the politi-cal equivalent of John Gotti ratting out his bookies," said the old insider Byrne, by now blind from diabetes. "I wouldn't rat out my worst enemy, even if I could get my eyes back."

On May 6, 2005, Janiszewski reported to federal prison in Pennsyl-vania to begin a forty-one-month sentence. On the very same day, Paul Byrne died at home, still awaiting his sentence. In one of his last inter-views, the dying man had said: "I have no expectation of going to heaven when I die. I do expect an extended stay in purgatory."

✦ OUT ✦

JAMES MCGREEVEY, GOVERNOR
1957–

ON THE HUMID AFTERNOON of August 12, 2004, perspiration and tears were streaming down the faces of several aides to New Jersey governor James McGreevey. Reporters at the State House learned that a "major announcement" was looming. From the supercharged air of crisis, it was a good guess that the governor was resigning. A danger had always been there that scandal might drive McGreevey from office. The question was, which scandal?

This was an administration, one columnist wrote, that "accomplished the remarkable feat of lowering ethical standards in the state capital." The Democratic governor's chief fund-raiser was a sexual blackmailer. McGreevey was caught by a wire-wearing informant reportedly giving his blessing to an extortionate land deal. And observers were still won-dering why two years earlier McGreevey had hired an Israeli man with no apparent credentials to be his adviser on terrorism.

"Good afternoon," McGreevey began his press conference, flanked by his parents and wife, Dina. "Throughout my life, I have grappled with my own identity, who I am. As a young child, I often felt ambivalent about myself, in fact, confused."

Reporters leaned forward in their chairs. Across America, cable news television viewers phoned their friends to clue them into the spectacle unfolding live. Was he saying . . . ?

"At a point in every person's life, one has to look deeply into the mirror of one's soul and decide one's unique truth in the world, not as we may want to see it or hope to see it, but as it is.

"And so my truth is that I am a gay American."

A gasp went up from the crowd. And the bombshells kept dropping. McGreevey, a twice-married father of two, said he had engaged in a "foolish" affair with another man. The disclosures would harm "my family and my ability to govern," so he would resign, effective November 15. Later, it emerged his affair had been with the same man he had hired as his homeland security adviser.

Bright, personable, tireless, and possessed of exceptional work habits, McGreevey once seemed like nature's perfect politician. The product of an Irish household in Carteret, New Jersey, he earned a quick succession of degrees at Columbia, Georgetown, and Harvard. He became

Governor James McGreevey, wife Dina by his side, announces: "I am a gay American" on August 12, 2004. (*The Trentonian* / David P. Cardaciotto)

an assistant prosecutor, state assemblyman, state senator, and mayor of Woodbridge Township. Every step in his career was intended to put him closer to his dream of occupying the White House. To motivate himself, he repeated his Marine father's motto: "Plan your work and work your plan."

But if McGreevey was born to be a public servant, he also felt born to another lifestyle, one his Catholic faith made him feel hideously ashamed of. Starting in high school, he began to have sexual liaisons with men—"*scores* of men," he later wrote in his tell-all autobiography. At rest stops on the Garden State Parkway, he would have anonymous liaisons with strangers young and old. Once, he was beaten up by a pickup at a Times Square porno theater.

All of this being unacceptable behavior to much of the electorate, McGreevey determined to act like a red-blooded heterosexual in public. "I knew I would have to lie for the rest of my life," McGreevey would later admit. His first marriage broke up when wife Kari accused him of using their baby daughter as a political prop. He then married a beautiful public relations professional, Dina Matos, who did not suspect where his true sexual orientations lay. The marriage was a "contrivance," he said.

McGreevey first ran for governor in 1997, the year he turned forty. He lost—but by just a single percentage point against a strong incumbent, Christie Whitman. His next run, in 2001, was the ultimate in overachieving. He campaigned on promises to freeze taxes and clean up Trenton's culture of corruption, and won in a landslide. Of course, McGreevey's promises to the voters were not kept—many of them, such as spending more on education while reining in the budget, were self-contradictory. But he did fulfill the expectations of his key supporters.

One of these men was his chief campaign contributor. Charles Kushner, who founded a $1 billion real estate business on high-rises and garden apartments, donated a total of $1.5 million to McGreevey's campaign or political committees allied to him. After McGreevey took office in January 2002, he nominated Kushner to a seat on the Port Authority of New York and New Jersey.

Another of McGreevey's initial appointments was more puzzling. In a February interview, the new governor let slip that he was hiring a homeland security adviser to help protect New Jersey in the wake of 9/11. This aide came from the Israeli Defense Forces—"probably the best in the world" at preventing terrorism, McGreevey said. Reporters did a little digging and found out he was talking about a man named Golan Cipel, a one-time campaign worker.

Cipel was paid $110,000 a year but had no apparent qualifications. As a non-U.S. citizen, he could not even hold a security clearance to be briefed by federal authorities. Narcissistic and insolent, he infuriated McGreevey's aides by meddling in their work and bragging of his direct access to the governor. There were reports of McGreevey and Cipel traveling together to scout "terrorism targets," such as the George Washington Bridge. "People say you have a homosexual relationship," one reporter told McGreevey. "Absurd," he said.

But it was true. McGreevey had met Cipel in 2000 on a trip to Israel funded by one of Kushner's Jewish charities. The boyish-looking Israeli navy veteran came to the United States on a work visa sponsored by Kushner. As McGreevey later told it, he had sex with Cipel for the first time right after the election. It took place at the governor-elect's condo, while a State Police detail was parked outside—and with his wife, Dina, in the hospital recovering from a difficult childbirth.

McGreevey later told of the encounter in romance novel terms. "We undressed and he kissed me. It was the first time in my life that a kiss meant what it was supposed to mean—it sent me through the roof. I was like a man emerging from forty-four years in a cave to taste pure air for the first time, feel direct sunlight on pallid skin, warmth where there had only ever been a bone-chilling numbness."

It is important to note that Cipel never remembered it that way. As he later told it, he was hired by McGreevey solely for his policy expertise, then subjected to sexual harassment and forced to perform oral sex. But after Cipel's resignation in August 2002, he used McGreevey's connections to get a job with a public relations agency—seemingly not the act of an abuse victim.

In the summer of 2004, McGreevey's knack for choosing bad friends
came back to haunt him. That July, one of his top fund-raisers, David
D'Amiano, was indicted on bribery charges. It emerged that a Piscataway,
New Jersey, farmer was upset at being offered too little money for his
land as part of an eminent domain proceeding. He turned to D'Amiano
for help, and the money man promised to sweeten the deal in exchange
for $10,000. The farmer would supposedly know the deal was on if a cer-
tain state official used the code word "Machiavelli"—and McGreevey
was afterward overheard using that very word in conversation with the
farmer, who wore a wire. The governor insisted his use of the word was
a coincidence.

Later that month, McGreevey's main financial backer, Kushner, im-
ploded. For years, Kushner's business partner—also his brother-in-law—
had accused him of looting company accounts. Kushner responded by
hiring a prostitute to lure the in-law to a motel room. A video camera
was secretly there recording them. Kushner mailed a copy of the sex tape
to his own sister so she could see her husband's extracurricular activities.
Rather than ensure the brother-in-law stayed silent, however, Kushner's
stunt resulted in a two-year prison sentence for himself.

Then came Cipel. In late July, a lawyer approached McGreevey's
aides saying the former adviser was preparing a sexual harassment lawsuit against the governor. All it would take to prevent this act of political destruction was a $50 million settlement. For all the corruption
that surrounded him, the governor didn't have that kind of money.
For days, he anguished over the shame of exposure. Finally, he decided
to take the initiative. The stage was set for his out-of-the-closet press
conference.

In permanent retirement from politics, McGreevey penned his memoir, *The Confession*, in 2006. By peeling away a lifetime of lies, the author
insisted, "I become more authentic and integrated one day at a time."
The often-salacious details of his promiscuity brought him less sympathy than he may have wanted, especially as readers wondered what his
wife must have thought about the book. It did not take long to find out.
In less than a year, she had published her own tell-all.

✧ BAD MEDICINE ✧

THE UNIVERSITY OF MEDICINE AND
DENTISTRY OF NEW JERSEY

BY ANY RECKONING, it is the largest health university system in America. The University of Medicine and Dentistry of New Jersey consists of five regional campuses and eight schools, with more than five thousand students and thirteen thousand faculty and staff members. It operates a cancer research center, genetic laboratories, programs for curbing violence, and a major hospital in Newark.

But if the history of New Jersey government has a lesson, it is that anything can be corrupted—even medical schools. Beginning in 2005, a series of scandals rocked the state university, revealing it as a pit of patronage, influence peddling, nepotism, and thievery. The potential loss to taxpayers through waste, fraud, and overspending was placed at a staggering $243 million.

In an institution as large as the one that went by the acronym UMDNJ, politics will inevitably play a part. And since the university's inception in 1970, it largely earned goodwill. It pleased the politicians by creating jobs—in the struggling cities of Newark and Camden, as well as Stratford, New Brunswick, and Scotch Plains. It provided dental care to the poor and won praise for its innovative inner-city clinics.

At the same time, UMDNJ sprawled so greatly across the state that its various components were competing against each other for state funding. There was no rational growth plan, and decisions on what health centers to build were based on which city's turn it was. As one administrator later admitted: "The attitude has been, 'If some legislators can get us money for it, let's do it.'"

In 1994, Governor Christie Whitman eliminated the state Department of Higher Education along with its chancellor and board, as a cost-cutting measure. Afterward, there was no central authority to check the university's spending on a budget that swelled to $1.6 billion a year.

What was UMDNJ doing with all that money? For the most part, it was spent honestly—paying the checks of hardworking hospital staff, doing lab work, engaging in test trials of new drugs. But in March 2005, Newark's *Star-Ledger* began reporting on spending patterns that had a curious smell to them.

Over the previous six years, the paper revealed, the university had handed out $718 million in no-bid contracts. The contractors receiving this largesse were well connected politically and did little work. A health center operated by the Newark Democratic power broker Stephen Adubato Sr. was awarded $300,000. A Republican consultant, Chip Stapleton, had been paid a total of $1 million "to enhance the state recognition and reputation of the university." He never submitted a report detailing his work, yet his contract was renewed six times.

Cash outflow was the least of the university's woes. As early as 1999, internal memos warned that University Hospital in Newark was billing the federal Medicare and Medicaid programs for every procedure, including routine ones, at "acute care" prices—essentially ripping off millions of dollars. In 2002, the hospital's chief compliance officer, Karen Silliter, made the same discovery. When she reported it to the vice president, she was fired.

Just days after the *Star-Ledger* exposé, U.S. Attorney Christopher Christie opened a wide-ranging investigation into UMDNJ. The university agreed to pay $1.4 million in a civil settlement to satisfy the Medicare/Medicaid fraud, but this was not all that Christie was interested in. He subpoenaed all records of no-bid contracts, and scrutinized the perks given to highly paid administrators. As he worked, records began vanishing: burglarized from the central administration building in Newark and shredded at the School of Osteopathic Medicine in Stratford.

On December 20, 2005, Christie showed up at the university board's monthly meeting with an ultimatum. "This place is a public embarrassment," he told them, and there was only one solution. Submit to a federal monitor of all university finances, he said, or face prosecution as a criminal enterprise. The trustees readily agreed.

UMDNJ's federal monitor turned out to be Herbert Stern, the former prosecutor and judge famed for busting mob-tainted politicians in the 1970s. He started with a clean slate. Half the members of the board—most of them implicated in conflicts of interests because they worked for agencies doing university business—resigned. Also gone were six top administrators, among them the president.

Throughout 2006, Stern issued a series of reports on UMDNJ that made for bad cases of heartburn for the elected officials linked to the university's rampant cronyism. There was Wayne Bryant, deputy Democratic leader of the state Senate, whom the university paid $38,000 a year as a consultant. There was Warren Wallace, who served simultaneously as Gloucester County freeholder, commissioner for the Delaware River and Bay Authority, and a university dean of student affairs. Wallace, it was alleged, devoted "significant" amounts of university time to his political jobs, steered contracts to his friends, and tried to get his daughter into the osteopathic school—even though she didn't take the required tests.

And still more officials got tangled up in the investigation. Donald Bradley, the Newark City Council president, helped a campaign contributor get a dollar-a-year sublease on a clinic building that UMDNJ rented for $144,000. He was responsible for numerous patronage hires and pressured the university to allow his goddaughter to draw a salary even after she was fired. Michael Gallagher, dean of the osteopathic school, allegedly transferred funds to his money-losing clinical practice to garner $15,000 a year. He also had a penchant for $50-a-glass wines and Scotches that were billed to taxpayers. In March 2007, both he and Senator Bryant were indicted on fraud charges.

In July 2006, Stern placed UMDNJ's total losses—from overbilling, waste, and undocumented spending—at $243 million. In November, he issued a report stating that "the illegal activity persists to this day." Few were surprised.

Enemy Action
TERRORISTS, RADICALS, SPIES, AND INVADERS

✦ I KILLED A KING ✦

GAETANO BRESCI, ASSASSIN
1869–1901

IT WAS BECOMING AN occupational hazard of royalty. A Russian czar blown up, an Austrian empress stabbed to death, the Spanish king's prime minister gunned down—all assassinated by seething idealists calling themselves heralds of the coming revolution. The crowned heads of Europe fretted over their future. But King Umberto I of Italy betrayed no fear. Veteran of wars, survivor of two assassination attempts, he never hesitated to walk freely among his people.

Gaetano Bresci of Paterson, New Jersey, carried out the first great assassination of the twentieth century.

On the night of July 29, 1900, the fifty-five-year-old monarch visited an arena in the Milan suburb of Monza to watch gymnastic teams compete. As he awarded prizes to the winners, bands played the royal march and the spectators broke into applause. Umberto's enormous white mustaches curved into a smile. Just thirty feet away, cheering as loudly as anyone in the grandstand, was a dapper, slightly built young man who had traveled all the way from Paterson, New Jersey, for this occasion.

His name was Gaetano Bresci, age thirty. Born in Tuscany, he was apprenticed to a textile mill at age eleven. The long hours and harsh conditions made him despise a system that employed wage slavery to prop up an imperialistic monarchy. Anarchism, the belief in a world without any government at all, fired his passions.

By day, Bresci weaved; by night he attended meetings of anarchists. He was arrested for his radical beliefs and, after a stay in jail, found himself barred from a job. In January 1898, he immigrated to the United States to work in the silk city of Paterson.

Bresci seemed modest and hardworking in the mold of the immigrant cliché. He earned a good $15 a week at the Hamil and Booth Mill, saved prudently, and learned passable English. Soon after his arrival, he married an all-American native named Sophie Knieland, and they had a daughter. Sophie later eulogized him as a loving husband with a "timid, retiring disposition."

Bresci may have been silent, but he was hardly timid. Like hundreds of fellow Italians in crowded, polyglot Paterson, he was a dues-paying member of an anarchist club. His group, the Society for the Right of Existence, envisioned a world without kings or governments. Members debated among themselves whether to bring about this utopia by peaceful change, communist revolution, or the killing of heads of state. When Bresci took the side of the assassins, it seemed to his comrades he was only speaking theoretically.

In fact, Bresci resolved to commit a shocking act of violence himself—in revolutionary jargon, "propaganda of the deed." His mind was made up after reading how a general indiscriminately fired into a crowd of bread rioters in Milan. Afterward, King Umberto I awarded the general a medal for "brave defense of the royal house." For that outrage, Bresci decided, the king should die.

Bresci bought a 9mm pistol and practiced firing it during family picnics while his wife and daughter picked wildflowers. In May 1900, he quit his job and booked passage to Europe, telling his wife he was going home to collect an inheritance.

A leisurely two-month journey took Bresci to northern Italy, where he sat waiting patiently for his opportunity to draw a bead on Umberto I. This monarch so hated by leftists had his last conversation with a socialist politician that late July night. "You fit in better than me," Umberto joshed before leaving the arena. "I am too old. Bless those young men down there, I am jealous of them."

It was 10:35 P.M. when the king stepped into his horse-drawn carriage. He paused to wave at the cheering crowd gathered at the edge of the grandstand. Now, Bresci thought. Three shots rang out from his pistol. One pierced the king's neck and another buried itself in his chest. "It is nothing," he said before falling dead.

Bresci tried to flee, but was immediately pounced on by one of the gymnasts and the king's bodyguards. A furious mob threatened to kill him. "You killed Umberto!" one citizen shouted. "I didn't kill Umberto," the gunman spat back. "I killed a king."

Umberto's widowed queen called it "the greatest crime of the century," perhaps prematurely since this was the year 1900. The shock echoed across the Atlantic when it was realized that for the first time in history a crime of regicide had been planned on U.S. soil.

There were wild stories that Paterson was the center of a vast conspiracy set on wiping out the leaders of the world. New York papers printed stories about a desperate band that had drawn lots to determine which of its members went off to assassinate the king. The White House received an anonymous tip that the same Italian cabal behind the Umberto killing was sending an assassin to kill President William McKinley.

But at his murder trial, which took place over the course of a single day on August 29, 1900, Bresci insisted he acted alone. "Sentence me," he told the court. "I am indifferent. I await the next revolution." Italy had no death penalty, so the assassin was sent off to spend life in prison. He was found hanged in his cell the following May, and it was ruled a suicide.

Authorities in the United States ended up dismissing as fanciful the notion of an anarchist plot to kill the president. And so, on September 6, 1901, President McKinley was virtually unprotected when an assassin named Leon Czolgosz stepped up to him at a world's fair in Buffalo and shot him to death. Czolgosz was Polish, not Italian, and had never been in Paterson. But in his pocket was a newspaper clipping that he had been reading and rereading for more than a year. It was all about the assassination of the king of Italy.

✸ GROUND ZERO ✸

THE BLACK TOM SABOTEURS

WORLD WAR I has its unknown soldier in Arlington, and its unknown battlefield in New Jersey.

On July 30, 1916, at a peninsula known as Black Tom jutting out from Jersey City into New York Harbor, German saboteurs carried out a breathtaking act of war—blowing up a mountain of explosives destined for shipment to the European battlefields. The blast shattered windows throughout greater New York, shook the earth for hundreds of miles, and killed seven people. Like Pearl Harbor, it was a sneak attack that caught America unaware. But it was so successful that America stayed unaware of any treachery for years after the fact—assuming incorrectly that it was all just a big accident.

The Germans had done their work well. In March 1915, only seven months after the outbreak of hostilities, a German naval officer named Franz von Rintelen sailed into New York Harbor with a forged passport and a secret mission. He was to disrupt the outflow of American munitions to the Kaiser's enemies. It would be better not to hurt anyone or cause property damage on American soil—the United States was, after all, a neutral nation at this time—but in his own mind von Rintelen justified extreme measures. American industrial might, he said, was "a spectre, an intangible phantom, against which strategy, tactics and all the courage of the German soldier were helpless."

Just as enterprising robbers hold up banks because that's where the money is, von Rintelen zeroed in on New Jersey because that's where the munitions were. Factories there manufactured TNT, gunpowder, artillery shells, and cartridges. Fearsome weapons trains rolled to the Jersey docks, where the cargo was taken by barge to anchored ships. The largest of the dockside arms depots was the mile-long Black Tom. As von Rintelen scouted the waterfront for targets, this literal powder keg caught his eye. "What an ideal pier to destroy," he recalled saying to himself.

Rintelen was instructed to meet a certain Dr. Walter Scheele, an agricultural chemist in Hoboken who sidelined as a German spy. Scheele was the proud inventor of a tube-shaped incendiary device the size of a cigar. The chemical fuse could be set for as long as fifteen days. Just hide a few bombs in the cargo hold of a ship, and they would burst into flame somewhere in the Atlantic. Like a proud new papa, von Rintelen began handing out bundles of the "cigars" to Irish and German dockworkers with instructions to set Britain-bound ships on fire. Soon, mysterious blazes were flaring up in the middle of the vessels' trans-Atlantic voyages.

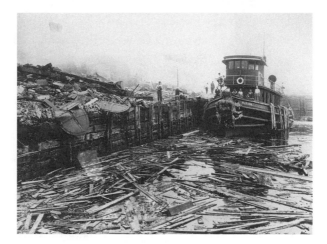

A fireboat makes its way past what remains of the Black Tom arms depot in July 1916.

For all his Prussian obedience, von Rintelen himself was no James Bond. A little too loudly, he styled himself "the Dark Invader" and wooed ladies by boasting of his feats of espionage. By late 1915 he had blabbed his way into jail. But the rest of the German spy network continued to have access to Scheele's cigars, as well as detailed intelligence on Black Tom.

Greater New York went to bed the night of July 29, 1916, secure in its belief that World War I was an ocean away. On Black Tom, railroad guards went about their paces, their way lit by the torch of the nearby Statue of Liberty and smudge pots that kept away mosquitoes. One guard thought he saw a small rowboat with two men paddling slowly from the piers toward New York. But curiosity-seekers had been skulking around Black Tom for weeks. It had to be nothing.

Shortly after midnight on July 30, the first flames were seen licking a row of railroad cars that awaited unloading at Pier 7. Inside were small-caliber shrapnel shells, which went off one by one, like a string of firecrackers. Soon, other fires were spotted on docked barges. Firefighters from Jersey City rushed down the dock connecting Black Tom to the mainland, only to collide with watchmen fleeing in the other direction.

At 2:08 A.M., Black Tom exploded. The blast wave had the force of battleship guns and shook the earth with a magnitude of up to 5.5 on the Richter scale. The roar could be heard for a hundred miles in all directions and echoed as far away as Philadelphia. The flash of 3 million pounds of high explosive turned night into day and tricked roosters into crowing a false dawn.

On the streets of lower Manhattan, Brooklyn, and the Jersey riverfront towns, tens of thousands of windows shattered. Shards of metal flew into Jersey City's Journal Square, stopping the hands on the clock tower. The Brooklyn Bridge swayed. In some New York neighborhoods, the rumor got started that a German warship was firing its guns off Sandy Hook, and excited crowds climbed hills to watch.

After a few minutes, a second roar was heard as Black Tom's barges exploded. In Jersey City, a fireman standing at his station's shattered window told of being sucked through the frame by backdraft. Families started out of their beds and ran out onto glass-littered sidewalks. A cry rang out: "It's the end of the world!"

The scene was far more hellish in the harbor itself. Shrapnel ripped holes in the Statue of Liberty's robes and rained down upon Ellis Island. Immigrants who had fled their own war-torn lands were evacuated by ferry to the Battery as sizzling bits of metal fell around them. Barges broke free from their moorings, drifted down the harbor, and bombarded the river islands with their still-exploding cargo.

It took more than a day for the fires of Black Tom to be extinguished, revealing the ruins of thirteen leveled warehouses and a ten-foot-deep crater. The official death toll was put at seven. The victims, all in Jersey City, included a policeman, the chief of the railroad police, and a ten-week-old baby tossed from his crib.

All evidence of the fires' origin had vaporized in the first milliseconds of the blasts. The Lehigh Railroad, which owned most of the property, wrote it off to "spontaneous combustion." Jersey City's commissioner of public safety, Frank Hague, said it was the railroad's fault for stacking explosives so carelessly.

The Black Tom explosion shook the earth, but it failed to alter the course of history. U.S. industry kept right on supplying the Allied armies with the merchandise of death they eventually used to beat Germany. President Woodrow Wilson eventually led his nation into war, not because of the sabotage campaign—which he barely knew about—but to avenge submarine attacks on American shipping and "make the world safe for democracy."

Not until 1930, twelve years after World War I's conclusion, did U.S. investigators learn the truth of what happened that night in Jersey City. In Havana, a German ex-agent admitted he was part of a vast network of sabotage run by Franz von Papen, the Kaiser's military attaché in Washington. This exile, Lothar Witzke, told of being one of the men in the rowboat that the guards spotted. Hiding in the shadows of the rail cars, Witzke and another saboteur planted "cigar" bombs at various points, then rowed away to watch New York Harbor explode.

The Black Tom disaster, as it happened, was not to be the gravest act of harm carried out by Franz von Papen. By 1932, this old veteran had acquired great influence in the ministries of Berlin and had the power to hand-pick Germany's next chancellor. The man he chose was Adolf Hitler.

❯ BURNING CROSS ❮

ALMA BRIDWELL WHITE,
KU KLUX KLAN ADVOCATE
1862–1946

PILLAR OF FIRE WAS WHAT Alma White called her church, and fire was what she preached. Her eyes blazing, her contralto voice booming, she shouted from her pulpit in Zarephath, New Jersey, about the horrors of eternal damnation. Hell was where the world of the 1920s was headed, its path paved by flappers, jazz, dancing, card playing, moving pictures, speakeasies, the theory of evolution, and all-around saucy wickedness. To save humanity from Satan's lures, you had to fight fire with fire. And so, White exhorted her followers to join "the greatest moral and political movement of our generation"—the Ku Klux Klan.

Alma White proclaimed herself
the first female bishop in history.
From church headquarters in Zarephath,
New Jersey, she became the
Ku Klux Klan's leading spokeswoman.
(Franklin Township Public Library)

Under different circumstances, she might have been a feminist icon. Alma White campaigned for women's equality and, as founder of the Pillar of Fire sect, was widely known as the first woman bishop in history. Yet this seeming progressive was one of America's leading propagandists of hate. She wrote tract after tract denouncing Jews and Catholics, exalting white supremacy, and blessing the Klan as modern-day Christian knights.

Her name—describing her favorite skin color—might have been predestined, but she was born Mollie Alma Bridwell, one of eleven children in rural Kentucky. She set off for the wild frontier to teach school in the Montana Territory and ended up marrying a Methodist preacher named Kent White. She accompanied him on his circuit throughout the West and helped to spread the Gospel at open-air revival meetings by taking to the pulpit herself.

A woman preaching was a remarkable enough sight. Alma White, a stout five-foot-eight and radiating a terrible intensity behind her glasses, blew her audiences away. Her shouting of the lord's praises—"heavenly dynamite," she called it—could move worshipers to tears or make them dance with ecstasy.

Shocked by these displays of enthusiasm, the Methodist Church barred her from the pulpit. She responded in 1901 by founding her own congregation. Its name, Pillar of Fire, came from God's signal lighting the way for the Israelites to flee Egypt. Hundreds joined White's vigorous new sect, and one follower donated a farm near Bound Brook, New Jersey, as the church's new headquarters. She named the settlement Zarephath, after the biblical town where a widow miraculously fed Elijah.

The stern hand of Alma White guided Zarephath to self-sufficiency. Members of the sect studied at its bible college, raised crops on its fields, and went to nearby Newark and New York City to serve as missionaries. Kent White's influence on these activities was nil. He chafed at being called "Alma's husband," and vented steam by quarreling with her on the correct interpretations of Scripture. Alma let him walk out on their marriage rather than accept his domination. The two never divorced but remained separated for the rest of their lives.

Alma White was unchallenged for leadership of her church thereafter. In 1918, at age fifty-six, she was consecrated bishop. Shortly afterward, she learned to drive and became convinced there was nothing a man could do that a woman couldn't. She spoke out for woman suffrage, equal pay for equal work, and an equal rights amendment to the Constitution. What, besides simple male prejudice, could be holding up female progress? Her surprising answer was modernism. Modern thinking, she decided, was permitting drunkenness to contaminate hearth and home, immigrant races to prey upon virtuous Anglo-Saxon womanhood, and Roman Catholicism to weigh down America with the chains of ignorance.

As it happened, post-World War I America was giving rise to another organization that saw modernism as a threat. The Ku Klux Klan was busily organizing chapters, or "klaverns," across America to promote its blend of "100 percent Americanism," Protestant values, and the exclusion of blacks and foreigners. These cross-burning racists were not just yahoos in bedsheets, but lawyers, doctors, pastors, and other professionals. Nor were they limited to the South; New Jersey had more Klansmen than did Alabama, Tennessee, or Louisiana.

Alma White said her first encounter with the Klan came while preaching to a Pillar of Fire branch in 1922. After the service, two men in white robes and hoods approached her and gave her $50. Soon this gray-haired grandmother was inviting Klansmen to recruit members at Zarephath and touring the country, from Denver to St. Louis to Spotswood, New Jersey, giving speeches at Klan "Klonvocations." The Klan was, she said, an "instrument in God's hands to preserve our American ideals and institutions."

White denied being a Klan member, but her advocacy was worth an untold number of recruits. To promote Ku Kluxdom, White published a series of tracts with titles such as *Heroes of the Fiery Cross* and *Klansmen: Guardians of Liberty*. She pointed out that the patriots who took part in the Boston Tea Party were in a secret society—just like the Klan! A primordial Klan had even been around in biblical times, fighting for morality. One of her tracts printed a cartoon showing Jesus feeding the loaves and fishes to a multitude in full KKK regalia.

"Who are the enemies of the Klan?" White wrote. "They are the boot-leggers, law-breakers, corrupt politicians, weak-kneed Protestant church members, white slavers, toe-kissers, wafer-worshippers, and every spine-less character who takes the path of least resistance." Blacks had no reason to fear the Klan—so long as they shunned "their ambition to mix their blood with that of the white race." As for the Jews, they were a chosen people she respected. Except, that is, for "the great Hebrew syndicates that have acquired a monopoly of the motion-picture industry. These conscienceless, money-mad producers have no worthy ideals, either of dramatic art or virtue."

White reserved her most fiery wrath for the Catholic Church—that "scarlet mother," "foe of liberty," and center of "idolatrous shrines." In 1928, her printed screeds played a part in defeating Al Smith's bid to become the first Catholic president—a candidacy, White warned, that would give the pope a foothold in the White House.

Within a few years, the Klan was all but extinct, a victim of its own criminality and fractiousness, and of a public that decided the Great Depression was more worrying than race-mixing. By the 1930s, White was no longer heard to praise her hooded heroes.

White continued to preach the old-time religion into her eighties, and the revivals at Zarephath grew into ever-more popular events. When she died in 1946, all the obituaries made note of her historic role as founder of her own religious sect. Her Klan connections were not mentioned.

⇒ MASTER RACE ⇐

THE NEW JERSEY NAZIS

"HEIL! HEIL! HEIL!" The parade ground filled with zealots in brown shirts, armbands, and Sam Browne belts erupted in a throaty roar on the sunny afternoon of June 9, 1940. From the podium, in front of a swastika banner, came exhortations to fight for the German fatherland and crush its enemies. "Our day is coming," said one speaker. "We know who you all are—all Jews—and we'll get rid of you." Bellowed another:

"There are 30 million of us in this country—all Aryans. Don't pull your necks in, stick them out." And the next one: "Drive the Jew moneylenders out of the country!"

Nuremberg? No, New Jersey.

In the years leading up to World War II, America had its own version of the Nazi Party. Members of the German-American Bund heiled Hitler, goose-stepped, and looked toward *der tag*—"the day"—when fascism would reign supreme in the United States. And every summer starting in 1937, the Bund retreated to Camp Nordland, a wooded pleasure ground in Sussex County, New Jersey.

The property near the town of Andover (population 479) offered two hundred acres of unspoiled land for parading, speech-making, lager-drinking, and the training of battalions of uniformed children. Campers as young as six wore Nazi-style uniforms and marched the dirt paths singing: "Führer, we belong to you." Their parents rented bungalows by the lake and kept up a busy daily schedule of sports, picnics, and indoctrination in *Mein Kampf*. Pictures of Adolf Hitler hung in the beer hall.

The Bundesleiter—Bund leader—was Fritz Kuhn, a strutting windbag in spit-shined jackboots with his chin always jutting out. From headquarters in the Yorkville section of Manhattan, he collected membership

The Bundists of Camp Nordland, New Jersey, wave the swastika and the Stars and Stripes on their opening day in 1937. A state senator was there to praise the Nazis. (*New York Daily News*)

dues from perhaps eighteen thousand Bundists across the nation (in his own imagination, it was "hundreds of thousands"). Most were fellow German immigrants who cheered Hitler's rise to power and blamed the Jews for all their misfortunes in Depression days. Kuhn thrived on this hatred. At torch-lit rallies, he excoriated "Franklin D. Rosenfeld" and his "Jew deal." "The Jews are controlling everything and the white man is out of his job," he screeched.

Around him, Kuhn gathered an inner circle of fellow haters and strong-arm men. His chief deputy and press agent was Gerhard Wilhelm Kunze, a native of Camden, New Jersey. Hollow-eyed and weasely, he wore a square mustache of exact Hitler dimensions and called the führer "the greatest talker and thinker that Europe has ever produced." Camp Nordland's manager was August Klapprott, a six-foot-three Aryan mountain of a man. He also served as gauleiter of the East Coast, and as Kuhn's chief bodyguard.

The Bund made a show of its "100 percent American" values. It was patriotic, so long as patriotism meant loyalty to a "white, gentile-ruled United States," free of "Jewish-Moscow-directed domination." At the July 18, 1937, opening of Camp Nordland, the public was invited to a ceremony in which the word "Nazi" was carefully never mentioned. State senator William A. Dolan even gave his blessing to the event, looking over the row of Bundists in their uniforms and telling them: "Sussex County welcomes you as it has many other good German people."

It was possible to see the Bund as a gang of harmless buffoons, just playing Nazi. But the more the public read of Kuhn's vitriolic speeches, of Bund campaigns to "buy Aryan," of the chilling Hitler Youth-style rallies at Nordland, bemusement turned to revulsion. Congressmen feared the creation of a Fifth Column loyal to Germany. It was pointed out that Camp Nordland was ominously close to the New York City water supply, a tempting target for sabotage.

New Jersey passed laws making it a crime to advocate hatred toward minorities and banned the wearing of "foreign" uniforms. Nordland was denied its liquor license, and the police took down license plate numbers of those who visited. Bund members were hauled before the House

Un-American Activities Committee and quizzed about the seemingly subversive activities at the summer camp. Klapprott helpfully explained that the swastikas were all-American symbols, because the Navajo Indians wore them.

In Nordland's beer hall, visitors reported seeing a banner bearing the slogan: *"Ein volk, ein reich, ein führer."* Was that true? "Yes," Klapprott said, "but that was last year, and it was for the Americans."

Bund rallies drew increasingly unfriendly crowds. Hecklers and rock-throwers disrupted Nazi gatherings throughout New York City and in Union City, Elizabeth, and Trenton. In Newark, Jewish gangster Abner "Longie" Zwillman organized a squad of "Minutemen" to rough up Bund bullies. For once, Nazis had to call on the police to protect them from Jews.

Kuhn organized the Bund's greatest rally in 1939, on Washington's birthday, an extravaganza at Madison Square Garden where swastika banners hung from the rafters alongside a giant portrait of George Washington. Just months later, he was in jail—no political prisoner, but a common thief. Kuhn had lavished thousands of dollars of his working-class members' dues on mistresses and nightclubbing. The district attorney uncovered the embezzlement with a little help from Nazis Kunze and Klapprott, who forwarded damning records to New York. The Bundesleiter's deputies had staged a *putsch.*

Kunze appointed himself the new führer of the Bund. But suddenly Hitler's tanks and storm troopers were blitzkrieging through Western Europe, and the Nazi cause in America was losing what appeal it ever had. Bund membership fell by half, then fell some more. In June 1940, vicious anti-Jewish rants at a Nordland rally were carefully jotted down by police informers. Kunze and Klapprott were both arrested under New Jersey's ban on hate, and their camp was seized. The Nazi duo beat the rap when the state Supreme Court ruled on December 5, 1941, that the ordinance violated their right to free speech. Two days later came Pearl Harbor.

Kunze had vague hopes of leading a Nazi underground in the United States under the guise of "singing societies" but found no takers. Instead, he crossed the border into Mexico with the intention of rendezvousing with a U-boat and sailing back to Germany. In July 1942, Mexican authorities arrested him as he loaded supplies into a motorboat. He served seven years in prison for espionage.

The federal government threw the book at Klapprott, who was imprisoned for sedition and draft evasion for the duration of the war. Eventually, though, he was able to overturn the charges and beat back an attempt to deport him to Germany. For the rest of his years—and he lived to be ninety-six—Klapprott portrayed himself as a martyr to his fascist beliefs. He became a favored speaker among anti-Semites who sought to rehabilitate Nazi Germany's image by denying the Holocaust ever happened.

At one such event in 1987, Klapprott claimed Roosevelt's jails were worse than the concentration camps, and spoke of being overrun by cockroaches. He "pushed them together in one spot and exterminated them—all six million!" Laughter and applause followed. Of course, the old Bundist had the right to say any hateful and hurtful thing he wanted, because the United States, and not the Nazis, had won the war.

⇘ Up Periscope ⇙

U-Boats off the Jersey Shore

AT CERTAIN MOMENTS IN THE first half of 1942, you could stand at the Jersey Shore and be a spectator to World War II. Ships at sea exploded into fireballs, lighting up the night sky and rattling windows miles away. Oil slicks from torpedoed tankers coated the beaches. Even bodies could be seen floating to shore.

The attackers who wrought this devastation were the U-boats of Nazi Germany. Swift and sleek, these submarines treated the East Coast as their own private hunting ground—sinking as many as six vessels a day without suffering a loss of their own. The United States was threatened with being completely cut off from its shipping routes with Great Britain—and, as a consequence, losing the war. It was, the government concluded, "as much a national disaster as if saboteurs had destroyed half a dozen of our biggest war plants."

Operation Drumbeat, the Germans called it: a strategic blow that would resound in America's home waters before we knew what had hit us. Adolf Hitler's U-boat fleet commander, Karl Doenitz, improvised the plan in December 1941, days after Pearl Harbor brought the United States into the war. A half-dozen submarines, just a fraction of the German fleet, steamed across the Atlantic on their secret mission.

Some were to take up position off North Carolina, others off Florida, or in the Caribbean. The U-boats dispatched to New Jersey carried tourist maps to guide them to New York Harbor. When the first enemy craft, U-123, reached this destination, captain and crew were delighted with what they found. There were no mines, no patrol boats. Submerging during the daytime, they surfaced at night to prowl for targets.

A watch officer on the U-123 later recalled his amazement upon seeing the Shore town of Wildwood: "It was a special experience for us to be that close to the American shore, to be able to see the cars driving on land, to see the lights on the streets, to smell the forests. We were that close."

On the night of January 25, a Norwegian oil tanker, the *Varanger*, was sailing twenty-eight miles east of Wildwood. Backlit by those beautiful shore lights, its silhouette was clearly visible to the German U-130. Five torpedoes blew holes in its side with a roar that could be heard as far away

The *Pennsylvania Sun* goes up in flames after being torpedoed by a U-boat in July 1942 in the Gulf of Mexico. German submarines moved south that summer after turning the waters off New Jersey into a killing ground. (U.S. Navy)

as Atlantic City. The mighty vessel crashed to the bottom of the ocean in minutes. All forty crewmen made it to their lifeboats and survived.

They were lucky. In February, four more tankers were sunk off the Jersey coast with combined deaths of sixty-five men. The demise of the *R. P. Resor* off Barnegat was especially spectacular. Crowds gathered on the beach to watch a two hundred-foot-high pyre shooting from between the ship's two sinking halves. Many of the crew survived the initial blasts only to freeze to death in lifeboats or choke to death on oil floating on the surface.

What made these ships such easy prey for the U-boats? Most glaringly, there was the refusal of the Shore towns to dim their lights—bad for the tourist trade, local business owners said. At sea, merchantmen kept up a constant stream of radio chatter, allowing enemy craft to pinpoint their location even in the dark. The bullheaded skippers traveled unarmed and unescorted—distrusting the convoy system, even after it had proven its worth in protecting British ships from attack.

The German marauders had a field day. Crews began calling their campaign the "Second Happy Time"—the first happy time having taken place against the British before they got wise and adopted convoys. Hitler himself boasted: "The United States kept up the tall talk and left her coast unguarded. Now I dare say that she is quite surprised."

America's unpreparedness still boggles the mind of military historians. The U.S. military had advance word of the coming U-boat onslaught from British intelligence, which had cracked the submariners' code. Yet Navy chief of operations Ernest King seemed to treat the dire threat as a mere nuisance, keeping his battleships at port or on North Atlantic convoys where they were not needed.

When the Atlantic fleet did finally send a destroyer to protect home waters, it became the pursued and not the pursuer. On the moonlit night of February 28, the USS *Jacob Jones* was patrolling within sight of Cape May when it was hit by two torpedoes. As the ship disappeared beneath the waves, explosive bursts and columns of water erupted on the surface. The *Jacob Jones's* depth charges—intended to kill submarines—were instead killing the ship's own men. More than 150 died.

Amid the killing spree, it was inevitable that false rumors would pop up attributing U-boat success to a treasonous Fifth Column within the United States. It was said that enemy observers lurked in the hotels of Asbury Park, signaling the submarines when a ship sailed past. It was said that overly gabby sailors were tipping spies off to their ships' departure times—giving rise to the slogan "loose lips sink ships." Of course, the U-boat crews only needed their own eyes to find a full range of tempting targets.

Happily for the Allied war effort, the U-boats' "happy time" did not last. Merchantmen learned to maintain radio silence and dodge pursuers by zigzagging. The Navy instituted a "bucket brigade" convoy system— escorting vessels in 120-mile segments up and down the coast. The head-strong Shore shopowners were persuaded to obey blackout rules. And like modern-day militia, bands of civilians came to the rescue. Civilian air patrols, fishing boats, and yachts all acted as spotters to bolster shore defense.

By June 1942, the tide had turned. Admiral Doenitz redeployed his U-boat flotilla to the Caribbean, and the East Coast was generally free of enemy attacks for the duration of the war. Victory had come at a heavy price, however. Off the Jersey Shore alone, the U-boat campaign in the first six months of 1942 left at least nineteen vessels damaged or sunk, and 360 dead.

Years after the war, the many tankers and freighters sent to their ocean graves by Axis submarines became popular diving spots for deep-sea adventurers. In 1991, a team of New Jersey divers found a previously un-known U-boat wrecked sixty miles off Brielle. Years of dangerous return trips and archival research proved it was the U-869, which had vanished in the last months of World War II, in February 1945, with all fifty-six men lost. Apparently it had fired an acoustic torpedo that failed to find its target, then turned around and struck the sub itself. Like the Third Reich, the U-boats ran out of luck.

☀ PEACE UNTO YOU ☀

THE MALCOLM X ASSASSINS

"As-salaam aleikum [PEACE BE UNTO YOU]," Malcolm X told his audience. *"Wa-aleikum salaam* [and unto you, peace]," the crowd of four hundred responded. As the thirty-nine-year-old activist in his crisp suit and tie stepped to the lectern at the Audubon Ballroom in New York City for his weekly sermon on February 21, 1965, he had special reason to desire peace.

Once he had been the shining star of the Black Muslim religion and its most charismatic preacher of black pride, black brotherhood, and black self-sufficiency. In the civil rights movement, he was militant tough guy to Martin Luther King's nonviolent good guy. The Nation of Islam's holy man, the Honorable Elijah Muhammad, regarded Malcolm almost as his son. But in 1964, Malcolm began questioning the Black Muslims' theology of anti-white hatred and talked of openness toward other races. Soon he was declared an apostate. Nation of Islam newspapers began hinting that he must die for his sins.

A week before Malcolm X's appearance at the Audubon, his house in Queens had been firebombed. Death threats were being phoned in every day. Still, Malcolm had dismissed his bodyguards' suggestions that the audience be searched for weapons. If he couldn't be safe among his own people, what was the point of going on?

Malcolm X makes a public appearance in 1964, a few months before his assassination at the hands of a Black Muslim squad from New Jersey. (*New York Post* / Arty Pomerantz)

Before his speech could begin, there was a shout from the back rows: "Get your hand out of my pocket!" Malcolm stepped to one side, hands raised. "Now, brothers, let's cool it," he said.

He was the perfect target. A black man in the front row pulled a sawed-off shotgun from his trench coat and fired. The blast tore a circle through Malcolm's chest and sent him flying backward. Once he hit the floor, another round of gun volleys opened up from below the rostrum.

There were two more assassins, one with a .45-caliber semi-automatic, the other with a Luger, and they fired into Malcolm's dying body again and again. The martyr's vision of his own doom—"I live like a man who's already dead," he had said weeks before—was fulfilled.

Backstage, Malcolm's pregnant wife, Betty Shabazz, dropped to shield their four young daughters. "They're killing my husband!" she screamed helplessly. Panic swept through the ballroom. Audience members hurdled over chairs toward the exits. The killing squad maximized the confusion by tossing a smoke bomb and firing shots behind them. In the swirl of shouts, shots, and smoke, they melted away.

All of them, that is, except the one with the .45. Late to break from the stage, he took a bullet in the thigh from one of the few bodyguards who kept his cool. A furious mob pinned and pummeled him before two policemen dragged him from the heap.

On his way to the hospital, he identified himself as Talmadge Hayer. The police were able to flesh out his background only slightly: black, twenty-two, of Paterson, New Jersey. Who were his confederates? Who had put him up to the job? Hayer wasn't talking. "A real robot," one frustrated cop said of the mute gunman.

It was no rash guess that Hayer was an operative for the Black Muslims. Investigators found a photo of him suited up for karate at Nation of Islam Mosque No. 25 in Newark, but no other members could be connected to the murder. Hoping to strengthen the case of a Black Muslim conspiracy, the New York police rounded up two other known enforcers for the Nation in Harlem. Their names were Norman 3X Butler and Thomas 15X Johnson. Each, like Malcolm X, had dropped their "slave" names for the letter X, the unknown.

A mountain of evidence linked Hayer to the assassination: .45 cartridges in his pocket, witnesses, and his thumbprint on the smoke bomb. The case against Butler and Johnson was far weaker, resting on a few witness identifications amid the hundreds of people present. Hayer took the witness stand and surprised everyone by admitting he shot Malcolm as part of a conspiracy. But he insisted the other two defendants were not part of the scheme. Who were the real assassins? "I won't say."

The confession had the opposite of its desired effect—convincing the jury that the gunman was taking the rap for his two cohorts. All three were found guilty of murder and sentenced to life in prison.

But eleven years later, in 1977, Hayer swore out an affidavit repeating his insistence that Butler and Johnson were innocent of the murder—and naming the names of the guilty. There were five assassins, Hayer included, and all came from the Newark mosque.

Hayer had indeed joined the Nation, in 1962. He was a high school dropout who worked low-paying jobs in Paterson's silk mills and ran with gangs. But with the Black Muslims, he suddenly found discipline, spirituality, and a sense of purpose. He ate up the religion's beliefs in a black master race lately oppressed by white devils who would soon be liberated when UFOs brought about an Armageddon.

One day in the spring of 1964, Hayer was tooling about a street corner in Paterson when a car pulled up to him. Inside were some fellow members of Mosque No. 25. By indirection—"like a seed planting," he said—they suggested he help them kill Malcolm, the villainous rebel against the revered Elijah Muhammad. For a year, plans were hashed out in meetings at each other's houses. They cased Malcolm's house and his rallies in Harlem. They noted how porous his security was and decided to strike at him in public.

On the appointed day, they drove from Paterson to New York and made sure to arrive at the Audubon Ballroom early. They planted themselves in the audience and carried out their assigned roles. A brother named Wilbur McKinley was the one who shouted "Get your hand out of my pocket!" and threw the smoke bomb, Hayer said. Carrying the shotgun was someone he knew only as Willie X; the Luger was fired by

Leon Davis. The chief plotter was Benjamin Thomas, who carried no weapon but ran interference for the escape.

Some black activists seized on Hayer's story, adding theories of their own that the FBI or CIA had pulled the strings of the assassins. The Man wanted Malcolm dead, supposedly, because he spoke truth to power. This was not entirely far-fetched—the government had indeed been wiretapping and spying on Malcolm—but was unsupported by evidence.

But for the most part, Talmadge Hayer's confession was met by apathy. The Manhattan district attorney's office had no wish to admit error. All three men convicted of the assassination were free on parole by the late 1990s, and the prosecutors never pursued the men named by Hayer as the real assassins. One wonders what Malcolm X, denouncer of the white power structure, would have said about the whole thing.

✤ RUNAWAY ✤

JoAnne Chesimard, Black Revolutionary 1947–

THE BLACK PANTHERS' glory years were behind them, their revolutionary brotherhood weakened by police infiltration and factional squabbles. Gone were the openly toted rifles, the black berets, the public calls to off the pigs. New York City's Panthers had gone underground in small cells calling themselves the Black Liberation Army. They ambushed police cars by gun and grenade, and robbed banks to fund their war against white America. By 1973, this campaign had taken the lives of four patrolmen. "Wanted" posters bearing the pictures of the presumed killers were going up everywhere. "Armed and dangerous," they said.

Most striking of the images was that of the only woman, a twenty-five-year-old, one-time college student activist, with angular jaw and towering Afro. Her name was JoAnne Chesimard. Some in law enforcement considered her the out-and-out leader of the BLA; others thought of her as the movement's guiding "soul." She was sought for questioning in two cop murders and the bombing of a police car.

Chesimard, who gave herself the African name Assata Shakur, never admitted or disowned her participation. But she cheered every action that killed a "fascist." "As many Black people as the New York Police Department murdered every year, someone was finally paying them back," she later said.

While going about New York, Chesimard concealed herself with a wig and various aliases. But as the heat on her intensified, her brothers-in-arms decided to shift her to a Philadelphia safe house. Chesimard and two comrades set out in a white Pontiac bearing Vermont plates, and carrying a manual on urban guerrilla warfare. Nowhere in the guide did it warn black militants to avoid the New Jersey Turnpike.

It was just after midnight on May 2, 1973, near Turnpike headquarters in East Brunswick, when Trooper James Harper pulled over the Pontiac for a malfunctioning taillight. "Two black males, one female," he said as he radioed for backup. The Pontiac's driver was the BLA's "deputy

A wanted poster from 2005 shows the many faces of JoAnne Chesimard. After being convicted of the murder of a New Jersey trooper, she escaped from prison and fled to Cuba. (New Jersey State Police Museum)

minister for information," Clark Squire. He exchanged glances with Chesimard, sitting beside him in the front, and a third BLA militant, James Costan, in the back. They all had phony identification papers to avoid arrest, but were armed for battle.

Trooper Harper walked up to the driver's side window and asked Squire to step out. The backup trooper, Werner Foerster, came forward to conduct a search. Standing at the rear of the Pontiac, Foerster went through Squire's pockets and pulled out an ammunition clip. "Jim, look what I found," he shouted.

In a split second, gunshots exploded the night stillness. Who fired first will remain forever in dispute. The toll was heavy. One of the militants shot Trooper Harper in the shoulder. Two bullets from Harper's gun pierced Chesimard's arms and shoulders. The rear passenger fell dying. Trooper Foerster was hit in the arm and abdomen. Squire, the driver, then wrested the wounded cop's service pistol away and fired two shots into his skull. The officer, a Vietnam veteran and new father, died on the shoulder of the Turnpike. He was thirty-four.

Trooper Harper, bleeding and out of bullets, ran to the Turnpike building for help. The BLA squad piled back into the Pontiac and peeled off. They made it no more than eight miles south before Squire pulled over to tend to their wounded. He broke and ran when he heard sirens. Troopers found Costan's corpse in the car and a woozy Chesimard at the side of the road. "We ought to finish her off," she heard one of the lawmen mutter. But her life was spared.

Chesimard lost the shootout, but her war was not over. From jail, she mounted a publicity campaign that included a tape recording in which she preached revolution. "I have declared war on all forces that have raped our women, castrated our men, and kept our babies empty-bellied," she said. "I am a black revolutionary, and as such, I am a victim of all the wrath, hatred and slander that America is capable of. Like all other black revolutionaries, America is trying to lynch me."

At her trial, Chesimard maintained she had been targeted for execution by trigger-happy cops. Trooper Harper cast doubts on police credibility by telling two different versions of what happened. In his initial testimony, he claimed Chesimard pulled a pistol out of her purse and fired the first shot; later, he said he hadn't seen who shot him. Chesimard could offer a strong case that she never even carried a gun. There was no gunpowder residue on her fingers, and the direction of her wounds indicated she'd been shot while her hands were above her head. The police dismissed her charge of a setup. It was two troopers against three Panthers, they pointed out; if the police had wanted the militants dead, they would have called in an army.

Under New Jersey's felony murder statute, it didn't matter whether Chesimard pulled the trigger on Foerster. All that mattered was whether she aided and abetted the murder—an easy case to make before an all-white jury. In 1977, she was convicted of murder and sentenced to life in prison. It was "an empty charade" of a trial, growled her lawyer, the radical William Kunstler. "This beautiful young black woman never had a chance."

In fact, Chesimard's outlook was not so dire. While awaiting trial, she had already enjoyed jailhouse liaisons with a fellow Panther and had become pregnant. Security was just as lax after her conviction. A highly litigious prisoner, Chesimard charged racism when she couldn't get visitors. To stem her lawsuits, the New Jersey Correctional Institution for Women in Clinton let just about anyone in to see her without being frisked. On November 2, 1979, three black radicals posing as visitors pulled guns, took two prison guards hostage, and spirited Chesimard out in a car. There were no fences, so they simply drove to a parking lot, switched cars, and took off on the interstate.

Vanishing into the underground proved easier the second time around. Not until 1987 did Chesimard publicly appear—in Cuba, beyond the reach of extradition. Here in Fidel Castro's dictatorship she won asylum and a place of honor. She wrote an autobiography, gave interviews to visiting journalists, and emerged as a worldwide icon of the anti-American left. To admirers, she was Assata Shakur, "escaped twentieth-century slave." To the head of the troopers union, she was still JoAnne Chesimard, "a gutless coward engaged in a criminal enterprise, the same as any gangster or thug."

In 2005, the U.S. government offered a $1 million bounty for her capture—the largest in history for a female fugitive. Once Castro came to his inevitable end, it was hoped, his political prisoners would go free, while Chesimard would herself be extradited and become a prisoner in America. "It will be devastating for people worldwide who believe in justice," she said. For others, it would be simple justice.

❧ ONE-MAN ARMY ☙

YU KIKUMURA,
JAPANESE RED ARMY TERRORIST
1952–

AS THE PRIME REST STOP on the New Jersey Turnpike, the Vince Lombardi Service Area attracts millions of drivers a year who stretch their limbs, empty their bladders, and, occasionally, score some drugs. At 7 A.M. on April 12, 1988, state trooper Robert Cieplensky thought he spotted someone fitting that last category: a scruffy, bearded Japanese man, pacing by himself. Nervously, he kept circling his parked Mazda and shooting glances back at the trooper. A little too quickly, the fellow drove off. He made it a few hundred feet before being pulled over.

There were no drugs. But Trooper Cieplensky's suspicion was well placed. On the back seat of the Mazda was a cardboard box labeled

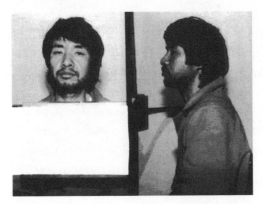

Japanese Red Army terrorist Yu Kikumura was stopped on the New Jersey Turnpike in 1988, two days before he could carry out a suspected bombing plot on behalf of the Libyan government. (Bergen County Sheriff's Office)

"Hercules Gunpowder." Further searching yielded three red fire extinguishers with their tops sawed off. "Souvenirs," said the driver, thirty-five-year-old Yu Kikumura. But they were not souvenirs, and he was no tourist. He was an international terrorist on a mission to bomb Americans.

The plan had its origins two years earlier and five thousand miles away, in the green ruggedness of Lebanon's Bekaa Valley. Gathered here were Arab militants training to strike the West by AK-47 or car bomb. Generally they adhered to a fanatical strain of Islam, yet infidels were also welcome if they shared the goal of harming Western governments. Into the terror camps settled South American narco-terrorists, Germans of the Baader-Meinhof gang, the Italian Red Brigades, and the Japanese Red Army.

Dedicating their lives to worldwide revolution, the soldiers of the Japanese Red Army merged left-wing anarchy with kamikaze fanaticism. Their leader was a feminist pioneer of sorts—a former go-go dancer named Shigenobu Fusako, who boasted of being "the germ of the plague" of terrorism. Around the world the Japanese terrorists traveled in the 1970s, one headline-grabbing atrocity after another: *Japan Air Lines jet blown up in Libya. French embassy staff taken hostage in the Netherlands. Tel Aviv airport shot up, twenty-six dead.*

By the mid-1980s, the Red Army was being decimated by arrests, and terrorism experts had written it off as a factor in the terrorism world. America was far more keenly focused on the threat posed by Libya's unbalanced strongman, Muammar Gadhafi. On April 14, 1986, U.S. Navy jets bombed Libya in retaliation for his support of terrorism. One of the sites blasted into rubble was Gadhafi's own home. He vowed revenge. Like a mob boss using outsiders to carry out a contract, the dictator contacted the Japanese Red Army with a request: bomb American interests.

Here Yu Kikumura enters the picture. A five-foot-three, 130-pounder from a rural Japanese village, he made an unlikely terrorist. But his revolutionary consciousness was awakened in college, and he became steeped in anti-Americanism and anti-capitalism. In the 1970s he operated a Japanese bookstore in Athens, and developed contacts with Red Army cells in Europe. They sent him to Lebanon to learn bomb engineering, and he acquired an Arab nom de guerre: Abu Shams.

Kikumura and his Red Army worked out a plan to strike at U.S. targets. Two sites, both associated with the U.S. Navy, which had bombed Tripoli, would be hit: one in Europe, one in the United States. Their D-Day was April 14, 1988, the second anniversary of the Libya airstrikes.

Kikumura flew from Paris to New York on March 8, 1988. He then bought a used 1980 Mazda and took off. Over a month, he went on a seven thousand-mile loop that took him west to Chicago, south to Tennessee, then back northeast toward New York.

By day, he would purchase some seemingly innocuous item at a small-town hardware store—wires, an on-off switch, fire extinguishers. By night, he assembled the parts into a whole. Each extinguisher became a bomb casing. Three pounds of gunpowder filled the centers. Lead shrapnel was packed into the edges. Once set off, the device would have enough force to blow apart a house.

Of course, Kikumura never did get to set off his ingenious devices, thanks to the alert eye of Trooper Cieplensky. On April 12, he was stopped at the rest stop in Ridgefield, New Jersey, and arrested for possession of explosives.

But by maintaining a stony silence, Kikumura enabled his Red Army confederates in Europe to go ahead with their end of the scheme. On April 14, a car bomb destroyed a bar in Naples, Italy, that was frequented by U.S. sailors. Five people were killed, including an American servicewoman. (That December, Gadhafi's agents leveled an even more vicious blow at the United States by bombing Pan Am flight 103 over Lockerbie, Scotland.)

What had Kikumura intended to do with his diabolical cargo? He never cooperated with interrogators, so the federal authorities could only speculate. One clue was a road map in which Kikumura used red ink to mark a spot at West Twenty-Fourth Street in Manhattan. At that address was a Navy recruiting office.

There are tantalizing hints that Kikumura had terrorist contacts within the United States. When he bought his Mazda at a Bronx dealership, he was with a seven-year-old boy; Kikumura was single, so whose child was this?

Kikumura was found guilty in Newark federal court and sentenced to twenty-one years in prison. "The people of the United States will rest more easily tonight," U.S. Attorney Samuel Alito, the future Supreme Court justice, said. But terrorists would be coming back for New York, again and again.

❧ BLIND HATRED ❧

SHEIK OMAR ABDEL RAHMAN, BOMBING CONSPIRATOR 1938–

THE DUMP OF AN APARTMENT in Cliffside Park, New Jersey, offered a bevy of clues that foreign terrorism had come to America. Inside were a thousand AK-47 cartridges and a stack of bomb-making manuals. In a notebook was a scribbled message in broken English. It called for the "breaking and destruction of the enemies of Allah. And this is by means of destroying exploding, the structure of their civilized pillars such as the touristic infrastructure which they are proud of and their high world buildings which they are proud of. . . ."

From his mosque in Jersey City, Sheik Omar Abdel Rahman denied being a terrorist. In private prayer sessions, he exhorted followers to violence—and to blow up "high world buildings." (*New York Post* / David Rentas)

But the detectives poking through this clutter on November 5, 1990, weren't looking for conspiracies and didn't want to find any. They had already determined that the man living here, an Egyptian immigrant named El Sayyid Nosair, was a lone gunman. Earlier that night in Manhattan he had assassinated the radical Zionist activist Rabbi Meir Kahane. The New York Police Department's chief of detectives was asked about the Cliffside Park evidence. "There was nothing there to stir your imagination," he said.

But there was a conspiracy.

The notebook manifesto was in Nosair's handwriting, but the violent language was copied from a revered mentor. His name was Omar Ahmad Abdel Rahman—the "blind sheik." From a mosque in Jersey City, he preached to a devout circle mesmerized by his calls to jihad. The shooting of Kahane was the first in a series of murderous schemes, organized by the sheik's faithful and given his personal blessing. In 1993, he would guide the plot to bomb some "high buildings"—the World Trade Center.

Sheik Abdel Rahman was blind from infancy, a victim of diabetes amid the rural poverty of his native Egypt. He studied the Koran in Braille and memorized it by age eleven. His studies convinced him that Egypt's secular government, in failing to rule by Islamic law, was an abomination. In 1981, he fell in with a group of terrorists who despised President Anwar Sadat. Asked by them what fate a ruler deserved for failing to respect God, Abdel Rahman responded: "Death." Sadat's assassination shortly afterward made him persona non grata in Egypt. Next stop was Afghanistan, where he provided spiritual guidance to mujahedeen fighting the Soviet army. It was here, terrorism experts later speculated, that Abdel Rahman obtained funding from a fellow jihadi, Osama bin Laden.

For safe haven, Abdel Rahman chose the one country other than Israel he despised the most: the United States. In 1990, U.S. consular officials in Sudan issued him a visa despite his presence on a watch list for undesirables. This puzzling fact has caused speculation that the CIA rewarded Abdel Rahman for his Afghan service. However, bureaucratic incompetence could also explain this mistake.

Abdel Rahman settled in Jersey City, rented a $500-a-month apartment, and took up residence with one of his three wives. His mosque, al-Salaam—"peace" in Arabic—was a fourth-story walkup that drew young worshipers alienated by the materialistic culture that surrounded them. Abdel Rahman was painfully human, with dead eyes, a shaggy gray beard, and a sagging body that he fattened—against all medical advice—with Snickers bars. But at prayer sessions an otherworldly spirit seemed to well up within him.

Sermons were calls to battle, not pious reflection. "Jihad is fighting the enemies," Abdel Rahman thundered, not spiritual battle but war with "guns, tanks and airplanes." For the fainthearted he had no apologies. "We welcome being terrorists," he said. "And the Koran makes it, terrorism, among the means to perform jihad."

Abdel Rahman had escaped imprisonment for Sadat's assassination because his incitements to violence were always couched in Koranic language. The members of his mosque came to him for general guidance but gave him deniability by never discussing the details of their terrorist plans. In this way he signaled his approval for Nosair's assassination of Kahane in 1990.

By this time, Abdel Rahman was well known to law enforcement. After the Kahane murder, New York police took note that Nosair was a member of Abdel Rahman's mosque. Separately, the FBI had videotaped other worshipers from Jersey City firing automatic rifles at weekly target practices. But neither agency shared the information with the other; the dots were never connected.

In August 1992, the sheik placed a call to a telephone number in Pakistan linked to a veteran of the Afghan campaign, an expert bomb maker named Ramzi Yousef. Weeks later Yousef and a partner flew into New York. At the immigration desk, the partner was caught with a fake passport and a bomb-making guide. Yousef walked free by claiming political asylum. The guide was not correctly translated until years later. Only then was its title understood as "the base"—in Arabic, al Qaeda.

With his easy passage, it was no wonder Yousef had such contempt for the democratic society he sought to bring to its knees. His dream was to kill 250,000 Americans in a single blow. From his apartment in Jersey City he eyed his target every day: the Twin Towers of the World Trade Center. They were the tallest landmarks on the New York skyline, the most arrogant "edifices of capitalism" that the sheik scorned. And they were virtually undefended. Yousef found he could drive in and out of the underground parking garage without being stopped.

The plan was diabolical. Plant a powerful car bomb at the base of one tower's wall, Yousef reasoned, and the blast would send the building, all 110 stories of it, toppling onto its twin. Four co-conspirators helped him gather the chemicals to build the 1,200-pound bomb and rent the Ryder moving van in which to stash it. In Yousef's apartment they mixed urea and ammonia into an explosive paste, enduring fumes so powerful they turned the walls blue.

On February 26, 1993, Yousef drove the truck and its hellish cargo into the B2 level of the World Trade Center garage. He set the gunpowder fuse to seven minutes. A getaway driver picked him up and headed up the exit ramp. They found themselves blocked by a car that wouldn't move. Two minutes ticked by. Yousef never panicked. Finally, the obstructing driver pulled out and the bombers made their escape.

The explosion was the most devastating, up to its time, in the history of American crime. The toll included six dead, a thousand injured, and half a billion dollars in property destruction. From Jersey City, Yousef saw smoke pouring from the Twin Towers but no collapse. Disappointed, he flew back to Pakistan that night.

Digging in the three-story-deep crater under the World Trade Center, police recovered an intact piece of the van marked with its vehicle identification number. Moving quickly, they traced it to a rental agency in Jersey City. It happened that the conspirator who rented the van, Mohammed Salameh, went back to claim his vehicle had been stolen and demand that his $400 deposit be refunded. He found the FBI waiting for him.

It became a nationwide joke—terrorists so stupid that they blew their cover to get back $400! Yet the plan was more sophisticated than anyone realized. Yousef made a clean getaway. All the suspects were small fry, foot soldiers in the sheik's holy army. Most maddeningly, the blind sheik himself was beyond reach. He had complete deniability.

But Abdel Rahman was brought down. An Egyptian member of the mosque worked his way into the sheik's inner circle, offering to serve as procurer of explosives for the next big strike. No one knew this aide actually despised everything militant Islamism stood for. He was an FBI informer. Wearing a wire, he asked the sheik whether blowing up the United Nations building would be legal, Koranically speaking.

"It is not illicit," Abdel Rahman replied. "However, it will be bad for Muslims. Find a plan to inflict damage on the American Army itself."

As evidence of terrorism, it was good enough. Abdel Rahman was rounded up that summer along with nine other jihadists and charged in a plot that would have dwarfed the Twin Towers bombing. They sought to blow up the United Nations, the main federal building in New York, the George Washington Bridge, and the Lincoln and Holland tunnels. All were found guilty, and Abdel Rahman was sentenced to life without parole. "God is great!" his co-defendants shouted.

Yousef was tracked down in Pakistan and arrested in 1995. On the helicopter to jail in New York, a federal agent ordered his captive to look out the windows and behold the Twin Towers. "They're still standing," the lawman told him. "They wouldn't be if I had enough money and explosives," Yousef said.

⤞ SENDER UNKNOWN ⤝

THEODORE KACZYNSKI, UNABOMBER
1942–

THOMAS MOSSER WAS SENTENCED to death for a crime he didn't commit. In 1993, the newsletter of an environmental group called Earth First! accused the New York public relations firm Burson Marsteller of responsibility for one of the great ecological calamities in recent years, the *Exxon Valdez* oil spill in Alaska. The company had helped restore Exxon's good-citizen image in the wake of the disaster, Earth First!

charged. This was not true. But one reader, the man the FBI called the Unabomber, did not bother to fact-check. With angry resolve, he looked up the name and address of Burson Marsteller's chief operating officer, Thomas Mosser. This man had to pay.

On Saturday, December 10, 1994, Mosser, fifty, had just returned from a business trip to his spacious house on a neat cul-de-sac in North Caldwell, New Jersey. He promised his wife, Susan, and his children, Kim, thirteen, and Kelly, fifteen months, to buy a Christmas tree that afternoon. But first, he went through the stack of mail that had piled up since he'd been gone.

One package, the size of a videotape, was tough to open. Still wearing his bathrobe, Thomas walked into the kitchen to get a knife. From the living room, Susan heard his last words: "I don't recognize the return address." As he cut open the seal, a wire snapped, setting off an electrical trigger attached to a blasting cap. There was a powerful explosion and a flash of white light.

Susan Mosser ran to the kitchen to see a mist of powder. When it cleared, her husband was lying amid charred wreckage. His stomach was sliced open, his face shredded by shards of nails and razor blades packed

Theodore Kaczynski in his mug shot in 1996, when he was finally arrested as the Unabomber. (Lewis and Clark County, Montana, Sheriff's Office)

into the bomb. She held his left hand—the only one still intact—and said, "I love you, Tom." At first she was encouraged to feel a pulse. Then she realized it was only her own heart beating furiously. Thomas's heart had stopped.

Well before the bombing in North Caldwell, the Unabomber ranked as the most elusive terrorist in the FBI's files. He began hitting his targets by mail bomb and booby trap in 1978. Each weapon was designed with ingenuity; the components were made from scratch and impossible to trace.

The FBI used the acronym UNABOM to code-name the case because the bomber's wrath seemed solely directed at universities (UN) and airlines (A). Soon it became apparent his grudge was with all of modern technology. In 1985, he recorded his first kill—a computer store owner in Sacramento, California.

The Unabomber had accounted for fifteen attacks and twenty-three injuries before the murder of Mosser in 1994. It was the most powerful of the blasts, both in explosive force and the shock it gave FBI investigators.

This time the victim, an advertising executive, had seemingly nothing to do with science. More worryingly, the Unabomber had dispensed with pipe bombs and was using a lighter and deadlier device: a hand-crafted, hand-molded explosive wrapped around a detonator. In April 1995, the Unabomber used another package of this sort to kill his third victim: a lobbyist for the lumber industry in Sacramento.

What did the Unabomber want? The answer came days after the Sacramento bombing in a letter to the *New York Times.* "This is a message from the terrorist group FC. We blew up Thomas Mosser last December because he was a Burston-Marsteller [*sic*] executive. Burston-Marsteller helped Exxon clean up its public image after the Exxon Valdez incident. But we attacked Burston-Marsteller less for its specific misdeeds than on general principles . . . its business is the development of techniques for manipulating people's attitudes."

In subsequent missives to the media, he went on to elaborate an anarchist philosophy opposed to everything that served to control human behavior. The Unabomber would "break down all society into very small, completely autonomous units" by breaking his victims into pieces. Delighted by the publicity he was receiving, he offered this bargain: Publish a thirty-seven thousand-word essay he had written, and the attacks would forever cease. In September 1995, this manifesto was published as a supplement in the *Washington Post.*

One of the manifesto's readers, a social worker in Schenectady, New York, named David Kaczynski, got a sick feeling as he read the opening pages. "It is obvious that modern leftist philosophers are not simply cool-headed logicians," the Unabomber had written. David's brother Theodore had used this phrase, "cool-headed logicians," over and over again since they were growing up in Chicago. Once a brilliant Harvard student and a Berkeley professor of mathematics, Ted had angrily broken off all contact with his family to lead a hermit's existence in the woods of Montana. Could Ted Kaczynski be the Unabomber?

David Kaczynski agonized for months over whether to turn his brother over to the government, weighing his responsibility as a citizen against loyalty to his own flesh and blood. Good citizenship won out.

On April 3, 1996, FBI agents descended on Kaczynski's home. The unwashed, wild-haired and bearded mountain man rarely left his remote cabin and had to be lured outside on a ruse before he could be arrested. Agents combing the ten-by-twelve-foot interior found bomb ingredients, the manual typewriter used to type the Unabomber's manifesto, and a fully functional mail bomb lacking only an envelope. Apparently his promise to desist from terrorism once he became a published author was not made on good faith.

A detailed diary recorded his plan for murder as it developed over the years. Each bombing was recorded as an experiment—the Mosser murder was "Experiment 244," with "a totally satisfactory result." "I emphasize that my motivation is personal revenge," he wrote. "I don't pretend to any kind of philosophical or moralistic justification. The concept of morality is simply one of the psychological tools by which society controls people's behavior."

Kaczynski insisted on defying his lawyers, who wanted to present a defense based on mental illness. The Unabomber believed he was fully sane, and would base his defense on an appeal to anarchist principles. But when a judge refused to let him make this argument, Kaczynski agreed to plead guilty and avoid the death penalty.

On May 4, 1998, the Unabomber was sentenced to four life sentences without parole. He exchanged his solitary life for solitary confinement in the federal "supermax" penitentiary in Colorado. This fulfilled the wish of Susan Mosser, the wife of the New Jerseyan Kaczynski had murdered. "Please keep this creature out of society forever," she told the sentencing judge. "Bury him so far down he'll be closer to hell, because that's where the devil belongs."

⇛ LET'S ROLL ⇚
UNITED FLIGHT 93

A LONG LINE OF PLANES sat on the tarmac ahead of United Airlines Flight 93, and that meant there was no way it could take off at the scheduled 8:01 A.M. Delays were common at Newark International Airport, and passengers were used to them. They stowed their carry-on bags, flipped open their laptops, and ate their breakfast muffins in preparation for the flight to San Francisco. Some of them on that exceptionally bright morning of September 11, 2001, took in the clear view of the New York skyline dominated by the World Trade Center.

Cranbury businessman Todd Beamer was one of the Flight 93 passengers who foiled al Qaeda's plot at the cost of their lives. Its most likely target was the U.S. Capitol building.

Forty-one minutes of delay. It would prove the most crucial factor explaining why Flight 93 did not play out the fate intended for it by al Qaeda. On a day when passengers aboard three other doomed airliners followed the old rules of engagement with hijackers—give them what they want, and above all, don't fight back—those aboard Flight 93 understood that the rules had suddenly changed. They could not save their own lives. But they did save the nation's capital.

Flight 93 took off at 8:42 A.M. with thirty-seven passengers—just 20 percent of the Boeing 757's capacity—and seven crew members. Seventeen of those aboard were New Jerseyans, and they were a microcosm of the Garden State. LeRoy Homer of Marlton, an African American, was co-pilot. Hilda Marcin of Mount Olive was a seventy-nine-year-old retiree planning to move in with her daughter in California. Todd Beamer of Cranbury was a go-getting software salesman on a business trip. Jeremy Glick of West Milford was a one-time college judo champion who had just become a father.

Among those in the first-class cabin were four men on one-way tickets. They had chosen their seats strategically, to be close to the cockpit. One of them barely made it this far. A week before, he had been pulled over in Maryland by a trooper who had no idea the driver was on a federal terrorist watch list. The officer let him go with a speeding ticket.

He was Ziad Jarrah, twenty-six, a citizen of Lebanon and leader of the four-man al Qaeda hijacking team. Well educated, handsome, and a

Ziad Jarrah's voice can be heard on flight recorders saying: "Shall we finish it off?" Seconds later, the plane crashed. (Federal Bureau of Investigation)

frequenter of discos and strip clubs, Jarrah is often cited as the unlike-
liest of the 9/11 terrorists. He had been converted to militant Islam by
attending a radical mosque in Hamburg, Germany, where he was a student. The night before he planned to die, he read in his Newark motel
room a set of instructions prepared by lead hijacker Mohamed Atta.
Cleanse your body, shave your body hair and sharpen your knives, the
message said. "Completely forget about something called 'this life.' The
time for play is over and the serious time is upon us. . . . This is the day,
God willing, you spend with the women of paradise."

The first forty-six minutes of Flight 93 proceeded normally. At 9:23
A.M. came an electronic message on the pilots' control panel: "Beware
cockpit intrusion." Two planes had already been slammed into the Twin
Towers, and another was on its way to the Pentagon, but these details
were not relayed.

Within minutes the hijackers made their move. All four wrapped
red bandannas around their foreheads, as if to signify blood martyrdom.
Jarrah and a cohort produced knives and held them to the necks of flight
attendants. This ruse apparently got them into the cockpit. At 9:28 A.M.,
air-traffic controllers in Cleveland heard a shout—"Get out of here!"—
and muffled screams. Cockpit recordings later yielded a female voice saying "I don't want to die" and a gurgling, as if the speaker were having her
throat cut.

Flight 93 was now in the hands of al Qaeda. Jarrah, the only one of the
four to have taken flight training, was pilot. A second operative, Saeed
al-Ghamdi, shared the cockpit with him. His two cohorts—Saudis like
al-Ghamdi, veterans of Osama bin Laden's Afghanistan terror camps—
served as the muscle, intimidating the passengers into staying in their
seats. One of them tied a box to his chest and claimed it was a bomb.
Jarrah made an announcement to the cabin: "Here's the captain. I would
like to tell you all to remain seated. We have a bomb aboard, and we are
going back to the airport, and we have our demands. So, please remain
seated."

Awkwardly, the 757 banked left in a hairpin turn that changed its
heading to the southeast. The plane was now setting a direct course for

Washington, D.C. Airplanes in the area were alerted to be on the look-out for the runaway flight. Air National Guard jets were scrambled over Washington. From the White House, Vice President Dick Cheney gave an order that would have seemed incomprehensible just two hours earlier—to shoot down any civilian plane approaching the capital.

By now, the passengers aboard Flight 93 understood the predicament they were in. One after the other, they called their loved ones on cell phones. From these conversations they learned of the day's deadly events in New York and Arlington, Virginia. No one could say where Flight 93 was headed, and no one may ever know. The most likely scenario puts the target as the White House or the Capitol building.

There were sobs, exclamations of "I can't believe it," last goodbyes. But many voices from Flight 93 evinced calm and calculation. Glick phoned his wife Lyzbeth to say "I love you" and pump for information. Was the plane heading for the World Trade Center? he asked. No, she said, the Twin Towers were already burning. What should they do? he pondered.

The solution was a democratic one—take a vote. The passengers agreed their only chance was to retake the plane. The terrorists did not appear numerous or well armed; their "bomb" was an obvious fake. It would be a tough assault, charging single-file down the center aisle. But if they were to die anyway, they might as well die fighting.

A 220-pound rugby player, Tom Burnett, helped lead the charge. Beamer, the salesman from Cranbury, managed to contact a telephone operator. He asked her to recite with him the Lord's Prayer. Then he told her the passengers were going for the cockpit. What did she think?

"I stand behind you," the operator said.

Beamer put the phone down but left the line open. "Are you ready, guys?" he was overheard saying. "Let's roll."

A group of strangers now assembled into an impromptu army. Some used coffee pots filled with boiling water as weapons and quickly overpowered the knife-wielding muscle men. The insurgent passengers then battered their way against the barred cockpit door. Each crash shook the hinges and rattled the hijackers' nerves. If the passengers could just get inside, they even had a shot at landing the airliner safely. One of them was a qualified small-plane pilot.

Jarrah, still at the controls, tried to throw his attackers off balance by violently rocking the wings back and forth. "Shall we finish it off?" he asked his fellow terrorist, al-Ghamdi. "When they all come, we finish it off."

Jarrah's voice is the last sound heard on the cockpit recorder, muttering "Allah is the greatest" nine times. A passenger can be heard crying out, "No." At 10 A.M., Flight 93 went into a nose dive, turned upside-down, and buried itself into a hillside in Shanksville, Pennsylvania. It was twenty minutes short of Washington.

✺ POISON PEN LETTERS ✺
THE ANTHRAX TERRORIST

When will they hit us again? The question in the immediate aftermath of September 11, 2001, was not *if* but *when.* Smoke was still rising from the crater in lower Manhattan as the TV talking heads went over all the nightmares that terrorists might unleash upon us: more hijackings, radioactive bombs, smallpox. One possible weapon, all the more terrifying for being so tiny, was anthrax. Inhale an amount one-fiftieth the size of an ant's eye and you could die. *What would it be? When?*

One of the anthrax envelopes that shut down Congress. It originated from Princeton and bore a fictitious return address in New Jersey. (Federal Bureau of Investigation)

Six days later, someone dropped a stack of envelopes into a mailbox across the street from Princeton's storied Nassau Hall and everyone's worst fears of biological terrorism came true.

There were five letters in the first wave. Each was postmarked "Trenton, NJ" on September 18. Each was addressed to a media organization: NBC, CBS, ABC, and the *New York Post*, all in New York City, and American Media, Inc., the publisher of the *National Enquirer* and other supermarket tabloids, in Boca Raton, Florida. Inside were a few grams of a coarse, brown substance that looked like Purina Dog Chow. It was a carefully prepared mixture of *B. anthracis.*

Accompanying the first delivery of the germ were photocopies of a letter, written in a hand at once childish and exact:

09-11-01

THIS IS NEXT

TAKE PENACILIN NOW

DEATH TO AMERICA

DEATH TO ISRAEL

ALLAH IS GREAT

On October 2, a photo editor at American Media, sixty-three-year-old Robert Stevens, was admitted to a hospital with an agonizing, paralyzing fever. Three days later he died. His lungs and lymph nodes seemed to have exploded. The doctors had a hard time believing what they were seeing: anthrax.

Inhalation anthrax had not caused a fatality anywhere in the United States since 1976, and now suddenly it had popped up in a time of increased fear of terrorism. Secretary of Health and Human Services Tommy Thompson, in a disastrously nonreassuring speech, told the American public that Stevens's death was an isolated incident—perhaps caused by taking a drink from a stream while on a nature hike. But this was medically impossible.

In the next few days, a second worker at American Media was diagnosed with inhalation anthrax. Swabs were taken in the office building, and it turned out to be a biohazardous waste site. Then, more cases of anthrax turned up in New York. Two aides to NBC News anchor Tom Brokaw. A CBS News assistant. A seven-month-old baby brought by his mother to work at ABC. Three employees at the *Post*.

In a way, these victims were all fortunate. The anthrax they developed was of the cutaneous form: the bacteria penetrated skin and created open, festering wounds, but did not kill. However, there was a troubling aspect to the letter mailed to the *Post*: it had never even been opened. The spores simply wafted through the pores of the envelope and onto the skin of people who touched it.

On October 9, two more letters went through the mail with the Trenton postmark. This time the target was Washington, D.C.

The bioterrorist was ratcheting up the fear factor. Each letter was addressed to a top Democrat in the Senate hierarchy: Majority Leader Tom Daschle and Judiciary Committee Chairman Patrick Leahy. The identical messages read:

```
09-11-01

YOU CAN NOT STOP US.

WE HAVE THIS ANTHRAX.

YOU DIE NOW.

ARE YOU AFRAID?

DEATH TO AMERICA.

DEATH TO ISRAEL.

ALLAH IS GREAT.
```

Only the letter to Daschle found its target, contaminating his office in a puff of spores. The business of Congress stopped in its tracks. Hundreds of Senate aides lined up for doses of Cipro, the antibiotic prescribed to ward off anthrax infection. Across the nation, people started to fear their mailbox or at least throw away letters from unknown return addresses.

Public health authorities assumed the only danger the anthrax letters posed was to the people who received them. They had not learned the lesson of the *New York Post*: the spores contaminated anyone in their very presence, whether envelopes were opened or not.

Soon, mail sorters and carriers who worked at the Postal Service's facility in the Trenton suburb of Hamilton began noticing skin lesions. Eventually, five employees in New Jersey became sick from anthrax; two nearly died. Against the advice of the Centers for Disease Control and Prevention, the state Health Department distributed Cipro to all twelve hundred postal workers in the Trenton area. The decision saved lives. In Washington, two employees who were told their workplace was safe ended up dying from anthrax.

And still the outbreak continued, the deadly germs carried throughout the New York metropolitan area by baffling means. A bookkeeper in Hamilton was diagnosed with an infected pimple—apparently caused by anthrax spores that seeped out of one of the letters to the Senate, found their way onto her mail, and spread to her skin. A sixty-one-year-old woman in New York City, who didn't work at any of the targeted media centers, died from anthrax by a route that couldn't be traced. On November 21 came the fifth and last fatality: a ninety-four-year-old widow in Oxford, Connecticut, who had apparently opened cross-contaminated mail.

A high concentration of anthrax spores were eventually found in the mailbox in Princeton, leading to the conclusion that the letters were dropped there. The killer seemed familiar with New Jersey geography. The return addresses on the Washington letters were "4th Grade, Greendale School, Franklin Park NJ 08852." No Greendale School existed, but there is a Franklin Park in New Jersey. The envelopes bore embossed postmarks, and were of the type sold at any post office.

The sender of the anthrax letters twice wrote "Allah is great" and "Death to Israel," familiar phrases in the world of Islamic extremism. But maybe this was a hammy ruse. An Arab writing in English would most likely translate "Allah" as "God" and simply write, "God is great." And why would the terrorist give the warning to take penicillin? Were his letters intended not to kill but to frighten?

Originally it was reported that the deadly strain appeared to contain sophisticated additives—it was "weaponized," in germ warfare jargon—allowing the spores to disperse more easily. This led to the theory that only a scientist from the U.S. government's bioweapons laboratory at Fort Detrick, in Frederick, Maryland, could have carried out the attack. It was a false belief. Whoever turned the bacteria cultures into dry powder was a professional, to be sure, but he or she could have come from anywhere in the United States—or the world.

FBI investigators drew up a profile of a domestic terrorist: a middle-aged, American-born man. He was most likely a microbiologist. Perhaps he had been motivated by 9/11 to create a bioterror scare that would be good for his profession. But by this theory, the FBI was casting suspicion on the very experts who might solve the case. One former government biologist, Steven Hatfill, sued the government when he was publicly labeled a "person of interest."

After 2001, the anthrax mailer never struck again. Did he decide his goals were achieved? Was he killed by his own germs? Or, perhaps, is he back in the lab, preparing to unloose a deadlier wave of terror?

❧ MISTAKEN IDENTITY ❧

THE COPTIC FAMILY MURDERS

FOR THREE DAYS, no one in the Armanious family went to work or to school. No one responded to knocks on a door or taps on the windows that still twinkled with Christmas lights. No one picked up the phone as loved ones called to ask about the daughter's upcoming Sweet Sixteen party. Finally, the Jersey City police broke down their front door in the wee hours of January 14, 2005. They found a house filled with corpses.

Lying in the main bedroom was the father, Hossam Armanious, forty-seven. In the other rooms were the bodies of his wife, Amal Garas, thirty-seven, and their daughters, Monica, eight, and Sylvia, fifteen. All had been tied up and gagged with duct tape, and all had their throats stabbed and slashed.

The clues pointed to simple if senseless robbery. Drawers and closets had been ransacked, no cash could be found in the mother's purse, and the father's automated teller machine card had been lifted from his wallet. But until the killer was actually in custody, no one could be sure of this. And the friends of the slain family suggested another motive for the crime: terrorism.

The Armanious family was Coptic Christian, members of an often-persecuted religious minority who had emigrated from Egypt a decade before. One compelling reason to get out was the threat of Islamic extremism. In Jersey City, they had been active in their church, and Hossam was known as an outspoken defender of Christianity. One of his favorite pastimes was chatting online. Using the screen name "I Love Jesus," he served as moderator of a room that engaged in a back-and-forth with Muslims. Once, a fellow chat room user insisted, someone had typed back a message to Hossam: "We are going to track you down like a chicken and kill you."

The Armanious family, in a photo displayed at their funeral in 2005. Jersey City's Coptic Christian population was convinced they were the victims of terrorists.

Could the Armanious killing be revenge by Muslims? In a post-9/11 world, it seemed, any atrocity was possible. Jersey City had been home to the blind sheik, Omar Abdel Rahman, and the first World Trade Center bombers. Now it was rumored that a relative of Armanious was assisting prosecutors in their case against Abdel Rahman's lawyer, Lynne Stewart, who was on trial for helping the sheik smuggle messages from prison to terrorists in Egypt. It was rumored that the assassins posed as Christian converts to gain access to the Armanious house. It was rumored that they had sliced a tattoo of a cross off teenaged Sylvia's wrist.

None of these rumors was true. But they stuck in people's minds. Arab Christians and Arab Muslims who had once peacefully coexisted in Jersey City stopped speaking to each other. At the funeral, relatives of the murdered family had to ask mourners to put away protest signs bearing anti-Islamic slogans. Scuffles broke out. When a sheik arrived at the Coptic church to pay his respects, a man screamed at him: "Muslim is the killer!"

The police refused to classify the murder as a hate crime, but also refused to speculate on the real motive. This only deepened the sense they were sitting on some sinister discovery. "This was a terrorist attack," said a longtime friend of Hossam Armanious. "It was to make an example of Egyptian Christians, to silence them." In Washington, D.C., the president of the U.S. Copts Association flatly called the killers "Muslim extremists" and the victims "modern-day martyrs in Islamic fundamentalists' war on Christianity." A London newspaper headlined the story "Critic of Islam murdered" and strongly implied a terrorist motive.

In fact, it was a robbery, just as the police first suspected. On March 4, two paroled drug dealers were arrested for the murders. They were Edward McDonald, twenty-five, and Hamilton Sanchez, thirty. McDonald was a former upstairs tenant at the Armanious house, where he lived with a girlfriend and two children. He couldn't have cared less if his landlord were Muslim, Christian, or Zoroastrian. "Greed was the cause of these murders," said Hudson County Prosecutor Edward DeFazio.

This was the chilling tale that DeFazio related. Somehow McDonald got the idea that Hossam Armanious—a catering manager at the Westin Princeton hotel whose wife worked at the post office—was actually a rich man. On the evening of January 11, McDonald wore a ski mask and carried a pistol; Sanchez went unmasked. They knocked on the door downstairs. At home were Amal Garas and her daughters. When she opened the door, the invaders barged in and tied everyone up.

Three and a half hours passed before Hossam came home from work. He too was tied up, then ordered to hand over his ATM card and personal identification number. The robbers rummaged through the house for more. As they did so, eight-year-old Monica managed to wriggle free of her ropes and make a break for the door. She saw McDonald's face, and he saw hers.

The two robbers now decided the girl could not be allowed to stay alive to be a witness. McDonald took a knife from the kitchen, led Monica to the bathroom, and slashed her throat. Sanchez used another knife to execute the remaining family members.

Over the next few weeks, the two suspects used Hossam's stolen ATM card to withdraw $3,000 from his accounts, DeFazio said. Videotapes had captured McDonald using the card, but it had taken seven weeks to make the identification.

With the arrests, a numb relief swept over Jersey City. "As a Christian, I'm ready to apologize to anybody," said one Coptic leader. The sheik who was jeered at the funeral said he too had overcome his hurt feelings: "Most Christians, they are good." But if religious fury had abated, the loss of security did not. "Evil knows no limits," one Coptic priest told mourners. "The hearts that are pure, the hearts that are closest to God, you will find that those are the hearts that are attacked by the evil one."

➤ IN THE MONEY ◄

THE "SUPERNOTE" SMUGGLERS

IN THE HISTORY OF COUNTERFEITING, no expert had seen anything this good: fake $100 bills, perfect in every detail. The so-called supernotes, first spotted in the Philippines in 1989, were printed by an expensive intaglio press, of a type no small-time criminal could afford. The color-shifting ink was nearly identical to the type used by the U.S. Treasury. And the paper was woven from the same mix of cotton and linen used in genuine bills.

It was as if the counterfeiters had use of a government printing plant—and the U.S. Secret Service came to believe this was exactly the case. Suspect No. 1 was the America-hating, hermit-like, communist government of North Korea. But the federal government could not prove it—not until some FBI agents in Atlantic City began going after what seemed like an entirely different species of criminal.

Operation Royal Charm was the code name of the FBI sting when it began in 1999. A group of undercovers pretended to be Mafia wiseguys interested in smuggling untaxed cigarettes into the United States. Through their sources, they learned of a Chinese husband and wife in their sixties living in Maryland. Chiang Shan Liu and May Liu were allegedly brokers for an Asian organized-crime ring called the Hsu enterprise. They had contacts in China who could manufacture real cigarettes— then slap any brand name on them, from Marlboro to duMaurier.

The Lius had made a good income smuggling these cigarettes through Long Beach, California, but lately Customs officials had become more efficient at intercepting the contraband. Could the mob help move them through a different port? Certainly, the FBI agents said. The undercover men took bribes and agreed to open up Port Newark to the smugglers. Beginning in December 2001, and for nearly every other month afterward, shipping containers arrived at Newark under false bills of lading claiming that bamboo furniture was inside. Each container was filled with 8 million to 12 million counterfeit cigarettes.

The success of this enterprise led the FBI undercovers to make new friends within the Hsu enterprise, and a sister outfit known as the Tang enterprise. Among them were a United Nations of ecstasy dealers, gun smugglers, and sellers of counterfeit Viagra—coming from Italy, Israel, China, and Chicago. One of the most tantalizing business propositions came from a man named Jimmy Horng, based in Phuket, Thailand. Through an agent, Horng told the undercovers that he had a ready supply of "green paper"—supernotes.

In June 2004, the undercover agents flew to Thailand to talk business with Horng—bringing along their "girlfriends," who were actually female agents providing backup. Horng agreed to send $330,000 worth of counterfeit $100 bills. All of it came from printing plants in North Korea, he said. He claimed his contact, a North Korean general, was also able to supply methamphetamine, marijuana, counterfeit postage stamps, and rocket launchers.

On October 2, 2004, a container ship sailing from Yantai, China, docked at Newark bearing the promised cache of fake bills hidden beneath cardboard boxes of toys. On December 17, a second shipment arrived—$3 million in supernotes. These were the first known appearances of supernotes on American soil. But FBI and Secret Service agents were at Newark to make sure the forgeries never got into the money supply.

By early 2005, the FBI was ready to close down Operation Royal Charm and roll up the dragnet. But how to catch everyone at once? An agent who played one of the mob girlfriends had the answer. Announce her wedding to her "boyfriend." The targets of the sting would walk right into the trap.

Invitations were duly mailed out announcing the nuptials, and RSVPs came back from around the world. Guests arrived at various hotel-casinos in Atlantic City. On August 21, 2005, they would be escorted by limousine to a yacht docked off Cape May. The name of the yacht—which never existed—was given as *Royal Charm*, the same name as the sting.

Ten suspects, including the Lius, Jimmy Horng, and their middlemen, walked into the trap. None suspected a thing; some even brought expensive gifts, such as Rolexes. The limousines never went to Cape May.

Instead, they pulled into the FBI building outside Atlantic City, where the wedding guests had cuffs slapped on them. Locked away in cells, wearing tuxedos and gowns, some of the suspects continued to ask when the wedding would take place.

Operation Royal Charm resulted in the indictments of eighty-seven people. By late 2006, most of the leading defendants had agreed to guilty pleas. The sting may also have brought about a further worsening of U.S.-North Korean relations. Afterward, the Treasury Department accused a Macao bank of laundering counterfeit money on behalf of North Korea. Dictator Kim Jong Il responded by refusing to engage in nuclear weapons talks unless the U.S. shut up about counterfeiting.

North Korean defectors have long told of a Pyongyang bureau called Office 39 that specializes in manufacturing counterfeit money, counterfeit consumer items, and drugs for foreign export. Supposedly, the office earns $1 billion a year, the equivalent of North Korea's legitimate export. For Kim, it constitutes a slush fund helping him to buy luxury cars and cognac while his people starve.

Whether or not Kim's illicit activities constitute an economic threat to America, a poignant irony is involved. Said one former State Department official: "If North Korea only produced conventional goods for export to the degree of quality and precision that they produce counterfeit United States currency, they would be a powerhouse . . . not an industrial basket case."

Causes Celebres

CONTROVERSIES
AND WHODUNITS

❧ OLD SMOKEY ❧

JERSEY'S FIRST ELECTRIC CHAIR

THE FIRST MAN TO BE EXECUTED in New Jersey's electric chair was an Italian named Saverio DiGiovanni, who in 1907 killed a fellow immigrant in a dispute over a debt. Just eleven weeks elapsed between crime and punishment. Had the same crime happened in 2007 instead of 1907, DiGiovanni almost certainly would have escaped the death penalty and might even have served a relatively short prison sentence. However, early twentieth-century America was far harsher in its justice.

New Jersey was just the fourth state to institute execution by the electric chair, a measure the Legislature passed in 1906; it followed New York (1890), Massachusetts (1896), and Ohio (1898).

Under the old code of justice, every county had its hangman, every county jail its gallows. But the method was a grim, hands-on business. Dying men fell through a trapdoor, then slowly thrashed about, choking, wetting and fouling themselves. Electrocution, by contrast, promised to be clean, progressive, and humane. The wonder technology of electricity could now provide efficiency in death as well as life.

However, when the execution site was designated in 1907 to be New Jersey State Prison in Trenton, thousands of people from that city sent petitions in protest. They were not opposed to the death penalty in principle, but they objected to having more murderers in their midst. "The people do not want the scum of other counties brought here and put out of existence in the state prison in old historic Trenton," a local editorialist thundered.

In the fall of 1907, the prison built its original death row, an annex with six cells at one end and the machinery of execution at the other. Wires ran from outside the prison walls to an instrument panel blinking with a fearsome display of lights. With a spin of a rheostat dial—not a "pull of the switch"—an executioner could deliver a fatal jolt of twenty-four hundred volts to whoever sat in the chair. Like Florida's "Old Sparky" and Louisiana's "Gruesome Gertie," it even acquired its own morbid nickname: "Old Smokey."

All that was left was to actually execute a criminal. He turned out to be DiGiovanni, thirty-four, described in newspapers as a "labor agitator." His home was the borough of Raritan, a tiny melting pot in the center of New Jersey's rural heartland. The Raritan Woolen Mills dominated the town's economy, employing Italian immigrants like DiGiovanni, along with Poles, Slovaks, and Hungarians.

On September 22, DiGiovanni was at a tobacconist on Raritan's Main Street. He approached Joseph Sansome, a barber who owed him money, and loudly demanded it back. Sansome, who was surrounded by friends, threw DiGiovanni out into the street.

DiGiovanni went berserk. With his bare hands, he smashed the tobacco store's windows. When Sansome and friends gave chase, DiGiovanni pulled a revolver and sent his pursuers scurrying. He fired a shot that hit Sansome in the back, then bent over his dying body in the gutter and fired twice more.

After a two-day trial, the jury took fifteen minutes to pronounce DiGiovanni guilty of first-degree murder, with no recommendation for mercy. The judge then sentenced him to be shocked until dead. When the fatal decree was read to the defendant through an interpreter, he shouted in protest and had to be subdued.

In prison, DiGiovanni, a five-foot-five, bullnecked man with gashes all over his body from a life of fighting, went through mood changes. One moment, he was boasting that the chair couldn't kill him. The next, he was bemoaning his fate and weeping for his wife and baby left behind in Italy.

DiGiovanni spent all of one month on death row. On December 11, he was led out of his cell barefoot. Two priests walked ahead, one holding a crucifix aloft. A pair of prison assistants showed him into his seat and put the helmet and straps in place. Quietly sobbing and praying, DiGiovanni offered no resistance as a hood was draped over his eyes.

Twenty-four hundred volts surged through DiGiovanni's body for a full minute, throwing it forward against the restraints. A wreath of smoke appeared above his head. After a few seconds passed, a second dose of electricity was delivered. Then came a third and final shock.

"It was the unanimous verdict of the witnesses, many of whom had attended hangings in the past, that the new method was a decided improvement over the old," one newspaper reported. It was "less gruesome to witness, and to outward appearances, at least, less terrifying to the condemned man."

With the smoothness and efficiency of the electric chair thus demonstrated, the people of Trenton raised no more objection to the apparatus of death in their midst. A total of 159 other men—and no women—would go on to die in the Trenton electric chair in its fifty-six years of operation.

The last execution took place in 1963. By the time a new capital punishment law was enacted a generation later, in 1982, electrocution, the one-time scientific wonder that promised a humane death, seemed like the relic of a barbarous age. New Jersey lawmakers replaced it with lethal injection.

But the will to enact a death penalty law was far stronger than the will to carry it out. Even as the new death row at Trenton filled up with dozens of murderers, a lengthy appeals process took root—ensuring that a prisoner could put off his execution for twenty years or longer. Finally, in January 2007, a legislative commission determined that the death penalty law was useless. New Jersey should abolish it and impose life in prison without parole as the maximum sentence, the panelists said. On the one hundredth anniversary year of the first use of the electric chair, it looked like execution was a thing of the past.

❧ DANGEROUS LIAISON ❦
THE HALL-MILLS MURDER MYSTERY

THE MAN AND WOMAN lay side by side in the tall grass under a crab apple tree. His arm lightly touched her shoulder, and her hand rested upon his knee. They were crisply dressed, she in a print frock, he in a suit and Panama hat tilted over his face. Scattered around them were pieces of paper—their love letters. From afar, it might have been a strangely serene tableau, as if the amorous couple had just taken a nap at this remote lover's lane outside New Brunswick, New Jersey. But a closer look told a different story: they were dead.

Another couple made the ghastly discovery the morning of September 16, 1922, and ran in terror for the police. Detectives surveyed a gruesome scene. Both victims had been shot in the head. A single blast went through the man's skull, fired from a .32-caliber pistol. Three bullets had gone through her, and her throat was slashed from ear to ear.

The Reverend Edward Hall in full vestments. The discovery of his body along with his dead mistress set off the most sensational murder trial of the 1920s. (Franklin Township Public Library)

Out of consideration or mockery, the killer had placed the man's business card upright at the heel of his shoe. It identified him as the Reverend Edward Wheeler Hall, rector of Saint John the Evangelist Episcopal Church in New Brunswick. He was forty-one and married— but not to the woman lying beside him. The dead woman was Eleanor Mills, thirty-four, a soprano in his congregation's choir.

Mills had a spouse, too, but the shredded notes surrounding her corpse indicated where her true passions lay. "I am holding my sweet babykins' face in my hand and looking deep into his heart," she had written to Reverend Hall. "Oh, honey, I am fiery today. Burning, flaming love. It seems ages since I saw my babykins' body and kissed every bit of you." And from another letter: "I know there are girls with more shapely bodies, but I do not care what they have. I have the greatest of all blessings, a noble man, deep, true and eternal love."

From the first day, the Hall-Mills case was marked by official incompetence. Gawkers and ghouls swarmed the murder scene, given free rein by hapless police. The officer who picked up Hall's business card handed it to a newspaper reporter, who handed it to other onlookers, who handed it back to the police—when the authorities later claimed to have found a suspect's fingerprint on the card, it was of dubious value.

Eleanor Mills was found dead side by side with Hall. "It seems ages since I saw my babykins' body and kissed every bit of you," she wrote him in one of several letters found shredded at the death scene. (Franklin Township Public Library)

Souvenir-hunters carted away clumps of grass and hacked off pieces of the crab apple tree. Within a week, nothing was left of the tree.

The obvious murder suspects were the victims' spouses. Eleanor's husband, James Mills, lamely claimed to have no idea he was being cuckolded. He told police he last saw his wife the night of September 14, when she left home to meet the minister; he assumed it was to discuss church business matters. Mills had an alibi for the time of the murder, which was placed at thirty-six hours before the bodies' discovery. Investigators assumed he was too stupid and guileless to have committed cold-blooded murder.

A better suspect seemed to be the minister's wife, Frances Stevens Hall. An heiress to the Johnson & Johnson fortune, she was seven years older than her husband and hid her resentment of his affairs behind an icy disdain. When Mrs. Mills called her home to arrange her last liaison with the minister, Mrs. Hall answered the phone. Witnesses saw the lights burning in her house all night afterward.

In the period during which both their spouses went missing, James Mills had suggested to Frances Hall that they had eloped. "I think they are dead," Mrs. Hall replied alarmingly. Mills's sixteen-year-old daughter, Charlotte, told reporters that the wealthy widow always loathed the girl's family. "Mrs. Hall does not like flappers," she told reporters, "and I'm a flapper."

By the end of 1922, the case had gone cold. But the newspapers, especially William Randolph Hearst's new tabloid, the *New York Daily Mirror*, showed greater persistence than the police. One editor, convinced that James Mills was the guilty party, tried to drag him to a séance where reporters hiding in the closet would pretend to be the spirits of the dead and scare a confession out of him. When this plan went awry, the *Mirror* labored long and hard to dig up dirt on Frances Hall. In July 1926, nearly four years after the murder, they got their scoop.

The story came in the form of a suit for a marriage annulment, filed by the husband of Frances Hall's former maid. He claimed that his wife accompanied Mrs. Hall and her brother, Willie Stevens, as they drove off the night of September 14, 1922, to stop the reverend and the choir singer from eloping. Once at the lover's lane, Willie Stevens shot the two lovers dead.

The story pressured New Jersey governor A. Harry Moore into appointing a special prosecutor. A grand jury handed up indictments against Mrs. Hall. Virtually every male member of her family was charged with murder as well. There was Willie Stevens, a bushy-haired man-child who loved to chase fire engines. Another devoted brother, Henry Stevens, was indicted largely because he was an expert marksman. A wealthy stockbroker cousin, Henry de la Bruyere Carpender, was indicted, too, but the case against him was so weak he was never brought to trial.

The Hall-Mills murder trial began November 3, 1926, at the Somerset County Courthouse in Somerville. The streets took on a carnival aspect, with vendors hawking peanuts and soft drinks to spectators. Sixty news wires were required to handle the incredible output of news stories.

But the most intensively followed murder trial of the Twenties turned out to be a mismatch. Mrs. Hall's well-paid team of lawyers discredited the prosecution's claim that Willie Stevens's fingerprint was on Reverend Hall's card. The widow, dressed in black every day, was unshakeable in testifying that she still loved her dead husband. Even Willie Stevens made for a good, believable witness as he insisted he was at home the night of the murders.

The most riveting testimony came from the only person claiming to be an eyewitness to the shootings. She was Jane Gibson, the owner of a pig farm overlooking the lover's lane. The night of September 14, she claimed, she rode on her mule to chase away corn thieves and came across four people arguing under the crab apple tree. "Explain these letters!" one of them said. A shot rang out. One woman moaned, "Oh, Henry," and a younger woman shouted, "Oh, my, oh my, oh my." Then came three more shots and Gibson fled. The older woman was Mrs. Hall, she said, and the men were her two brothers.

By the time of the trial, Gibson—dubbed "the pig woman" by the tabloids—was dying of cancer. She was driven to the courthouse in an ambulance, past excited children cheering: "Go on, pig woman! Do your squealing!" She testified from a witness bed instead of a witness stand, flanked by a nurse and a doctor. In a weak but dramatic voice, she recounted the violent sights she saw. But the pig woman was undone by her known past as a teller of tall tales. Her own mother sat in the spectator gallery, muttering: "She's a liar."

On December 2, the jury delivered its verdict. The three defendants were not guilty on all counts. "I cannot tell you how happy I am," Mrs. Hall said in a rare show of emotion. "Money can buy anything," scoffed Charlotte Mills, the choir singer's flapper daughter.

For the rest of the twentieth century, armchair detectives tried constructing new theories to solve the Hall-Mills murder. Perhaps the pig woman, far from being an innocent witness, was the real culprit. Or maybe James Mills was a less trusting husband than he seemed. Or maybe the prosecution was right and Mrs. Hall was guilty as sin. The truth remains as elusive today as it did on the crisp fall morning when a horrible discovery was made underneath a crab apple tree.

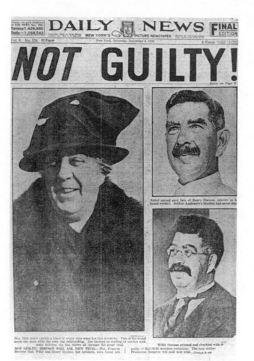

Page One of the *Daily News* in 1926 sums up the outcome, and the happy faces of defendants Frances Hall, Henry Stevens (top right), and Willie Stevens. (Franklin Township Public Library)

✖ CRIME OF THE CENTURY ✖

BRUNO RICHARD HAUPTMANN, LINDBERGH BABY KIDNAPPER 1899–1936

THE HOLLOW-EYED MAN peering out from the bars of Trenton state prison's death row wouldn't confess. Not when a newspaper offered his soon-to-be widow $90,000 for his story. Not when the governor of New Jersey promised to commute his sentence to life imprisonment. I didn't do it, Bruno Richard Hauptmann said. I was not the kidnapper of the Lindbergh baby. He kept saying it right up to the night of April 3, 1936, when he was led to the electric chair.

The public greeted the execution with grim satisfaction. Hauptmann, an illegal immigrant from Germany, inspired little sympathy. His crime, the abduction and murder of a baby, was shocking enough it its own right. But twenty-month-old Charles Augustus Lindbergh Jr. was the namesake son of America's greatest hero—the Lone Eagle, Lucky Lindy, the aviator who had amazed the world by flying nonstop from New York to Paris. Stealing his defenseless child was an offense against America itself.

However, in the years that followed this Crime of the Century, history took an intriguing turn. Hauptmann's wife and lawyers managed to convince a number of researchers that he was indeed innocent. Books and movies portrayed Hauptmann as a victim of circumstance, railroaded by overzealous prosecutors and a lynch mob atmosphere. Were they right? Was Hauptmann really innocent?

The facts of the case are well known to crime buffs. On March 1, 1932, the Lindberghs were staying at their new home, a fieldstone house outside Hopewell, New Jersey. The publicity-shy Lindbergh had selected this retreat in the Sourland Mountains for its remoteness; it was surrounded by thick woods and accessible only by a twisting dirt road. It was a cold, windy night, and Charles Jr. had a cold. His nursemaid, Betty Gow, tucked him into a crib in his second-story room. At about 9 P.M., Lindbergh heard a noise, but he dismissed it as nothing.

An hour later, Gow went upstairs to check on the baby. The bed was empty.

Gravely but calmly, Lindbergh examined his property. Outside was a homemade ladder in three pieces that had been placed against the side of the house and just reached the nursery's window. On the windowsill was an envelope. Inside it was a ransom note, written in broken English.

"Dear Sir!" it began. It ordered Lindbergh to have "50,000$ redy" as a ransom, and went on: "After 2–4 days we will inform you were to deliver the mony We warn you for making anyding public or for notify the police The child is in gut care."

Of course, the kidnapping was an instant sensation. Pictures of the toddler, whose blond hair and dimpled chin gave him such a close resemblance to his famous father, filled the front pages of every newspaper. Every day, hundreds of possible Lindbergh babies were sighted at train stations and bus depots. Most tips were from helpful citizens who were

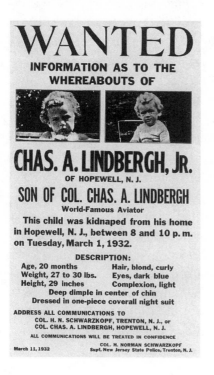

The wanted poster for Charles Lindbergh Jr. was issued after the baby had already been killed. (New Jersey State Police Museum)

nonetheless mistaken. A more sinister element came to the forefront as well: hoaxers, con men, and cranks, all offering their useless services.

In the Bronx, a retired school principal named John "Jafsie" Condon wrote a letter, printed in his local newspaper on March 8, offering to act as a go-between to exchange money for the baby. Much to his amazement, he got a response the next day. The letter from the kidnapper contained a symbol—two overlapping circles and three holes—identical to those on the genuine ransom note. Encouraged, Lindbergh authorized Condon to make a ransom drop on the kidnapper's terms.

It was a case marked by police bungling, and State Police Superintendent H. Norman Schwarzkopf made the biggest blunder by failing to rein in Lindbergh Sr. The aviator insisted that the cops make no effort to arrest or even follow whoever collected the ransom. Schwarzkopf was horrified by this idea, but so starstruck in Lindbergh's presence that he agreed.

Condon had several meetings with the kidnapper on park benches and in cemeteries in the Bronx. The stranger tried to disguise his face, but Condon was able to take in his appearance—about five-foot-ten, 160 pounds, with a pointy chin and a "triangle-shaped face." He was in his thirties, spoke with a thick Germanic accent, and called himself "John." And at one point, the stranger asked: "Would I burn if the baby is dead?"

It was a worrying sign that the kidnapper would never offer up his hostage, but Lindbergh was undiscouraged. On April 2, he accompanied

Bruno Richard Hauptmann went to the electric chair denying the crime. "You think you are a big shot, don't you?" a prosecutor asked him at the trial. (New Jersey State Police Museum)

Condon to the ransom drop, at a Bronx cemetery. "Hey, doctor!" they heard "John" cry from the shadows. Condon turned over a box containing $50,000 in $5, $10, and $20 notes, all of whose serial numbers had been carefully recorded beforehand. The kidnapper turned over a written slip saying the baby was on a boat off Cape Cod. No such boat was ever found.

On May 12, a truck driver pulled to the side of a road four miles from the Lindbergh estate. As he stepped into the woods to relieve himself, he stumbled over a mound of earth and leaves. Underneath was a small, skeletal body. It was Charles Lindbergh Jr.

The time of death was put at March 1, the day of the kidnapping. The baby's skull was fractured. Police theorized that the kidnapper had deliberately bashed his head in, or accidentally dropped him while climbing down the ladder. (A forensic expert who studied the autopsy report in the 1980s concluded the baby had actually been smothered.)

The only hope now left to the police was that the kidnapper would spend his ransom money, and cashiers would spot him. The banknotes did turn up all over New York City, centered on the Bronx. Finally, on September 18, 1934, a $20 bill from the Lindbergh stash was successfully traced. A gas station clerk, suspicious that the money was counterfeit, jotted down the license plate number of the man who passed it. It was a car owned by Bruno Richard Hauptmann, thirty-four, of the Bronx.

The police arrested him a day later. Hauptmann was the right age, and of the same "triangle-faced" appearance as Cemetery John. He was German, and his home was just blocks from the ransom drop. When he was hauled in, a $20 Lindbergh bill was in his pocket. Asked if he had more cash from the ransom at home, Hauptmann said no. A search of his garage proved otherwise. There were $14,590 in bills hidden under floorboards and in other secret places.

Hauptmann had quit his job as a carpenter at almost precisely the time of the kidnapping. In the worst year of the Great Depression, unemployed and with no explained source of income, he stayed well off. He plunged into the stock market, and bought expensive furniture for the house he shared with wife Anna and their newborn baby. A government auditor calculated that Hauptmann had spent $35,000 since 1932. When this amount was added to the ransom cash in his garage, it came to $50,000: the same as the Lindbergh ransom.

The ransom money was not the only physical evidence tying Hauptmann to the crime scene. Asked to write certain words, the suspect produced handwriting that closely matched the ransom letters—and idiosyncratic misspellings that were the same as the kidnapper's. Most damning of all was an open space in the wooden beams of Hauptmann's attic. One of the planks used in the ladder had nail holes in it. When this piece of wood was positioned in the gap, the exposed nails fit the holes perfectly.

Hauptmann stuck grimly to his claims of innocence. The money, he said, was left behind by his friend, a fur dealer named Isidor Fisch, who had gone back to Germany a year before. Hauptmann found the ransom money left behind and simply kept it for himself. Fisch had since died and was unable to contradict this story. But the fact he was buried in a pauper's grave belied any ill-gotten wealth.

There were gaps in the case against Hauptmann, and his lawyers and family seized on them. None of his fingerprints was found at the crime scene. No one could explain how he so deftly got in and out of the Lindbergh estate. Some of the evidence had been handled haphazardly; perhaps some rogue detective had tampered with the ladder rail.

Hauptmann's trial began in Flemington, New Jersey, in January 1935. H. L. Mencken was only half-joking when he called it "the greatest story since the Resurrection." Crowds of ten thousand people mobbed the Hunterdon County courthouse on especially dramatic days of testimony. Vendors sold them miniature kidnap ladders and phony locks of the Lindbergh baby's hair. But for all the hoopla, the case against the defendant was sealed when Lindbergh testified that the voice he heard on the night of the ransom drop was Hauptmann's.

Hauptmann testified to his innocence, but he came across as chilly and defiant. Under a withering cross-examination by the flamboyant prosecutor, David Wilentz, he admitted lying about the ransom money in his garage. At one point, a smirk creased his lips.

"You are having a lot of fun with me, aren't you?" an angry Wilentz asked him.

"No, that is not true," Hauptmann said calmly.

"You think you are a big shot, don't you?"

"No. Should I cry?"

On February 13, 1935, the jury spent most of a day deliberating before finding Hauptmann guilty of first-degree murder. It took a year for all his appeals to run out, and his death sentence was duly executed.

Anna Hauptmann spent the rest of her years—she died in 1994 at age ninety-five—trying to rewrite history. To some extent, she succeeded: several best-selling books were written supporting her claim of Bruno's innocence. But although she made a sympathetic widow, Anna stretched the truth.

Her husband, she told everyone, was always a law-abiding man, his only crime being stealing bread back in their native Germany to feed his family. In fact, back in the town of Kamenz, Hauptmann's criminal offenses were not trivial. He had robbed, at gunpoint, two women wheeling baby carriages. And he had burglarized the local mayor's house—by climbing a ladder to his second story.

Hauptmann's defenders have some strong arguments. It is widely accepted that the trial was flawed, and Lindbergh's claim to have recognized the kidnapper's voice is dubious. In the end, though, the weight of evidence leads to the conclusion that the man who died in Trenton's electric chair in 1936 really was the killer of the Lindbergh baby.

❖ OH, THE HUMANITY ❖

THE *HINDENBURG*

THE MOMENT REMAINS as ghastly today in black-and-white newsreels as when it happened the rainy dusk of May 6, 1937. The magnificent *Hindenburg*, coming in for a landing at Lakehurst, New Jersey, explodes into a fireball. At first, the zeppelin's nose rises into the air, spouting flame like a blowtorch. Then the entire craft crashes to the ground as survivors, some horribly burned, run for their lives. The radio announcer cries: "Oh, the humanity!"

Everyone has seen the images. But no one knows what really caused the death of the *Hindenburg*. Was the German craft ignited, as government investigators concluded, by a spark of electricity that combined with a leak of hydrogen gas? Was lightning the culprit? Or is there truth to the favorite explanation of conspiracy theorists—that a saboteur sneaked a bomb on board?

Like the *Titanic*, it was a giant. It remains the largest aircraft that has ever flown—804 feet long, more than three Boeing 747s stacked end to end. Seven million cubic feet of lighter-than-air hydrogen kept it aloft. Four diesel engines propelled it forward at a stately 84 miles per hour. Passengers felt nary a bump as they relaxed in their cabins, sipped Rhine wines in the dining salon, and listened to the music of an aluminum piano in the lounge.

At a time when regular airplane travel across the Atlantic was only dreamed of, the *Hindenburg* made seventeen such round-trip flights in 1936, its first year of service. Above small towns or the New York City skyline, it was an awe-inspiring sight. The craft floated so close to the top of the Empire State Building that tourists in the observation deck could make eye contact with the passengers. But one bit of ugliness took away from its sleek and silvery beauty—the swastikas on the tail fins.

The *Hindenburg* explodes and crashes at Lakehurst on May 6, 1937, as the Navy landing crew runs in terror. Was it sabotage? (U.S. Navy)

Adolf Hitler liked to showcase the *Hindenburg* as an example of supe-
rior Aryan technology. Soon it became a target for bomb threats. The
German Zeppelin Company, which operated the craft, tightened security.
Passengers and their luggage became subjected to unheard-of searches.
No one was allowed aboard with cigarette lighters or flashbulbs.

To the company's president, Hugo Eckener, the chief danger of zeppelin travel was always the highly combustible hydrogen gas. He had designed the *Hindenburg* for safer, nonflammable helium, but this gas was
impossible for the Third Reich to obtain. In any case, he was assured by
veteran fliers that no passenger had ever been lost on hydrogen-filled
zeppelins.

The *Hindenburg* lifted off from Frankfurt on May 2, 1937, for its first
transatlantic crossing of the year. On board was a crew of sixty-one,
along with thirty-six passengers. Rain squalls and lightning followed it
down the East Coast the afternoon of May 6. As it approached Lakehurst Naval Air Station—the only site in the United States capable of
docking zeppelins—Captain Max Pruss decided to ride out the storm
before landing. There was no impatience on board. On this scenic voyage, time was not of the essence.

The leviathan sailed down and up the Jersey Shore before coming
back into view of Lakehurst and its docking tower. A few hundred spectators cheered; passengers in the dining area waved back through open
windows. Within the zeppelin's vast belly, crewmen threw mooring ropes
to the ground crew of sailors and marines. The rain picked up. Someone saw a rippling in the airship's fabric, toward the stern. It was 7:23 P.M.

One of the watchers on the ground was Herbert Morrison, a radio
announcer. "Here it comes, ladies and gentlemen," he said into his microphone. "And what a sight it is, a thrilling one, a marvelous sight. . . . The
back motors of the ship are just holding it, er, just enough to keep it
from—"

"It's burst into flames! It's burst into flames and it's falling, it's crashing. . . . Get out of the way, get out of the way! . . . This is the, one of
the worst catastrophes in the world! Oh, my Jesus! . . . Oh, four to five
hundred feet into the sky. It's a terrific crash, ladies and gentlemen, it's

smoke and it's flames, now, and the frame is crashing to the ground, not quite to the mooring mast. Oh, the humanity!"

The fireball grew into a bright mushroom cloud larger than the *Hindenburg* itself. One after another, the sixteen giant gas bags keeping the airship aloft exploded. As the ship tilted, passengers were thrown on top of one another. Some leaped out the open windows too soon and were killed on impact. Others rode the flaming wreckage to the ground and were able to run away without a scratch.

Eleven of the twelve crewmen in the tail slid into the hell below them and were killed. One passenger, Matilda Doehner, threw her daughter and two sons out a window, crying out: "Be brave, children!" Mother and sons lived; the daughter did not.

It took thirty-four seconds for the fire to completely peel away the airship's skin, revealing a glowing metal skeleton. The last man to run from the smoldering pile, his clothes on fire, was Captain Pruss. He survived, as did most of those aboard the *Hindenburg*. The death toll of thirty-six included twenty-two crew members, thirteen passengers, and one member of the ground crew.

The era of giant dirigibles died with the *Hindenburg*. The company's president, Eckener, at first muttered that the tragedy had to have been caused by sabotage. But two governments—American and German—concluded it was an accident.

Most likely, the investigators said, a bracing wire snapped within the airship, puncturing a gas bag and causing the flutter that witnesses saw before the explosion. This would not have proven fatal had the hydrogen not ignited. But the *Hindenburg* had flown through humidity and rain and its skin had acquired a heavy static charge. When the mooring cables were tossed to the ground, they caused a spark to jump from the skin to the metal framework.

This is not the only possible explanation. Some claim lightning lit up the airship. In 1997, a former NASA scientist suggested that the metal coating on the *Hindenburg*'s skin—not the gas bags within—was set afire by a static spark. The skin's fabric had been treated with iron oxide and an aluminum powder, which are components of rocket fuel. However, even solid rocket fuel would have burned at a rate a thousand times slower than the rapid inferno that incinerated the *Hindenburg.*

The most intriguing theory remains sabotage, and there is even a candidate for saboteur. Eric Spehl, twenty-seven, was a rigger aboard the ship. His job was to maintain the gas bag nearest to where the explosion occurred. Those who believe he was guilty claim he had a communist girlfriend, and a motive to destroy Hitler's proudest airship. Two authors published books calling him the man who blew up the *Hindenburg.*

However, there is no evidence—only rumor and supposition—to blame Spehl. No historian has been able to interview or even locate his revolutionary lover. Hitler's Gestapo found he had no anti-Nazi connections. And the poor man never was able to defend himself. Like thirty-five others, he died in the fireball over Lakehurst.

❧ SHOTS IN THE DARK ❧
THE DUCK ISLAND LOVER'S LANE KILLINGS

THEY DROVE TO DUCK ISLAND to make love on a back seat, warm in each other's embrace even as a cold, heavy rain pounded the road into mud. Meeting like this in their Trenton neighborhood would have been trouble. His name was Vincenzo Tonzillo, twenty, married with a

The first of the Duck Island lover's lane victims lies dead beside his car in 1938. Five others died in four separate attacks. (Hamilton Township Police)

child on the way. She was Mary Myatovich, fifteen, a neighbor's daughter. Somehow she had sneaked away from her suspicious father the night of November 8, 1938, for this tryst.

Geographically, it's not an island at all. Duck Island is a marshy finger of land extending into the Delaware River, joined to the mainland by landfill. From Trenton, it was a few minutes' drive. The lonely setting amid scrub brush and tall reeds made for a perfect rendezvous point. Tonzillo and Myatovich thought they were alone in the rain. They were not.

Out of the gloom walked a man, and in his hands was a twelve-gauge shotgun. He pulled open the car door and aimed his weapon at the partially undressed couple. "This is a stickup," he said.

Tonzillo, frozen with fear, could barely move. The gunman shot him dead, letting the body drop out of the vehicle and into a puddle. Myatovich was ordered out of the car. She tried to run, and the attacker fired a blast square in her buttocks. Then he raped her.

An hour later, the headlights of a passing car lit up the teenaged girl, gasping for help. For thirty-six hours, she lingered in a Trenton hospital. Who did this? she was asked. "A colored man," she said—short and stocky. It was the only description she could offer before dying.

The newspapers called him the "lover's lane killer" and the "spooner slayer," and he terrorized 1930s Trenton as badly as the Son of Sam did 1970s New York City. The police of Hamilton Township, where Duck

Private Clarence Hill was beaten by military police and threatened with a lynching until he finally said, "I did those murders." (Hamilton Township Police)

Island is located, were baffled. A group of black men who camped in shanties in the marshland were all questioned and let go. Evidence at the murder scene—shotgun shells, a handkerchief marked with an "H," and a palm print on Tonzillo's car—could not be matched with any suspect.

The county prosecutor became convinced that there was no "colored man," and that the killer was a jealous relative of the girl or the married man. Working at cross-purposes, the Hamilton Police hunted for sexual deviants. More than seventy-five people were questioned by year's end, but the prosecutor declared that the investigation had "run up against a brick wall."

On September 30, 1939, the Duck Island killer struck again. Frank Kasper, twenty-eight, and Katherine Werner, thirty-six, were in the heat of passion in a parked Ford when the gunman stuck his shotgun into the car. The man was shot in the face, the woman in her arm and chest.

Now there were four murders in less than a year. To protect jittery lovers, the Hamilton police set up nighttime patrols on the killer's hunting ground. The killer simply moved in other directions. On November 2, 1940, across the river in Bristol, Pennsylvania, he fired into a parked car at two teenaged lovers and wounded the man.

Two weeks later, on November 16, came a deadlier attack. This time the shotgun killer picked a secluded roadside in Hamilton a few miles from Duck Island, where no police were watching. The victims were Louis Kovacs, twenty-five, and Caroline Morconi, twenty-seven. Prosecutor Andrew Duch had to admit his "revenge" theory was wrong. "We are up against a lunatic, a man obsessed with sex mania, probably a religious fanatic," he said.

The lover's lane killer did not strike again until April 7, 1942, when Trenton was absorbed in World War II and not on alert for a serial killer. The attacker crept back to Pennsylvania, found a parked car with two lovers inside, and fired. The driver was a soldier on leave from his base. He had his arm blown off, but he escaped with his girlfriend. The couple described their attacker as a tall, thin black man, about fifty.

At the lover's lane, police found a piece of wood that had fallen from the shotgun. It bore a partial serial number, which was traced to a Trenton pawn shop. The owner of the shop told detectives the gun had been sold at auction and could not be traced. This was not an answer they wanted to hear. Instead, the police decided to disbelieve the owner and perform some dubious detective work to connect the gun with a pawn ticket that never was found.

The police found the gun's original owner, who told them he had gotten rid of his pawnshop ticket nine years before. He had given it away to a fellow laborer, but he couldn't remember his name. The police dug up payroll records and looked for black men whose names began with "H"—the initial on the handkerchief dropped at the first murder. A detective's finger settled on the name of Clarence Hill. Was this the man? he asked the gun owner. It could be, the man said.

A bespectacled Sunday school teacher who lived in Hamilton, Hill was thirty-four, short, and stocky. He vaguely fit the first description of the shotgun killer, but not the description given by the soldier and his girlfriend. By 1943, Hill was an Army private. The military arranged for him to be transferred to Fort Dix, where he was held for thirty days in conditions close to torture.

Hill was ordered to stand naked day and night under a light bulb. Periodically, an MP showed up to punch him in the head and ribs. All his suffering would go away, he was told, if he confessed to the Duck Island killings. If he did not, he would be turned loose to a lynch mob. Frightened and out of his wits, he gave up. "I did those murders," he sighed.

The prosecutor's office knew it had a weak case, and put him on trial for only one murder: the shooting of Mary Myatovich. No shotgun was ever found in Hill's possession. His fingerprints were not on any of the murder cars. His alibi for the night of her killing—that he was voting at a Hamilton polling place—was not shaken. But an all-white jury refused to discredit his confession, and in December 1944 they found him guilty of first-degree murder. The jurors recommended life imprisonment instead of the death penalty. Why would they do that in a cold-blooded case of murder? Almost certainly, they thought he might be innocent.

Hill wasted away in Trenton state prison for the next twenty years before the parole board allowed him to go free. By then, he was already dying of throat cancer. Could he have been guilty? It is true that no Duck Island murders occurred after Hill joined the Army. However, if the killer were someone else, that person could also have gone into uniform and forever eluded justice.

⇒ RIGHTS AND WRONGS ⇐

THE TRENTON SIX

SIX TIMES THE JUDGE REPEATED THE WORD: death. Each of the six black men standing before him had been convicted of a robbery in Trenton that left a white, elderly shop owner dead. Someone had caved his skull in with a Royal Crown soda bottle, and all Trenton was outraged. Now, on August 6, 1948, the defendants were sentenced to New Jersey's electric chair. Six lives for one. It was the penalty that both the prosecutor and the press demanded.

But in the months afterward, the case of what headline writers called the "Trenton Six" became less clear-cut and more fraught with worrisome questions. Should all six men, even the five who never touched the

Civil rights protesters picket the State House in 1949 on behalf of the Trenton Six, a group of black men sentenced to die for the murder of a white shopkeeper. (Photographer: Bert Salwen. Photo courtesy of Peter Salwen)

murder weapon, actually pay with their lives for what one of them had done? What if some of them had never taken part in the crime at all, but were set up by racist cops? What if *all* were innocent?

Before there was a Trenton Six case, there was confusion and panic. On January 27, 1948, police arrived at the secondhand store of William Horner to find the seventy-three-year-old owner dead in a back room, blood spattered all over. Up front, his common-law wife lay groaning, also clubbed in the head. She survived to tell the story. Three light-skinned black men had come in, saying they wanted to buy a mattress and stove. Then they attacked, two of them swinging bottles, before getting away with thirty-five dollars swiped from the till.

The pressure to solve the case was overwhelming. Trenton had been in the midst of a crime wave that winter, and the postwar influx of blacks from the South added to white unease. The *Trenton Evening Times* ran an editorial titled "The Idle Death Chair" bemoaning a lack of executions. The police set up a "motorized bandit squad" that randomly stopped men for questioning.

On February 6, the police arrested the first of the Trenton Six. His name was Collis English, twenty-three, and he was taken to a precinct house because he had been using his father's car without permission. Once in custody, he stayed for four days. His brother-in-law, McKinley Forrest, thirty-five, was sent to ask if he had been arrested. Forrest vanished as well.

After a long captivity without any warrant, the two men were arraigned on capital murder charges in the death of Horner. Four others were charged as accessories, all of them named in confessions signed by English and Forrest. They were Ralph Cooper, twenty-three; John McKenzie, twenty-four; James Thorpe, twenty-four; and Horace Wilson, thirty-seven. All but Wilson signed confessions, too.

But there was good reason to doubt the confessions. English immediately repudiated his statement, saying it was forced out of him by threats and days of sleep deprivation. Others in the Trenton Six told of agreeing with whatever the police told them, after being told it would save them from the electric chair.

The murder victim's wife was brought in to identify her attackers. She recognized none of the six arrested men. Later, she picked three of them from a photo lineup—from pictures of the suspects only. Two other witnesses who had seen the robbers leaving Horner's store denied that the Trenton Six were at the scene. They, like Horner's wife, had identified the robbers as "light-skinned." All the defendants except Wilson were dark.

There was much more that undermined the case against the Trenton Six. Work logs showed Wilson was working on a potato farm miles away on the day of the murder. Thorpe only had one arm—the other had been amputated just eight days before the crime—and no witness saw anything so memorable as a one-armed man. A witness saw the robbers getting away in a green Plymouth, but English was alleged to have driven a black Ford.

Still, Mercer County Prosecutor Mario Volpe delivered an impassioned plea for guilty verdicts, and got his wish. An all-white jury convicted all six men, and the judge immediately sent them to death row at Trenton prison. They might all have been electrocuted had it not been for English's sister, Bessie Mitchell.

Mitchell, a seamstress in New York City, turned to the Communist Party to help finance an appeal. Her friends were aghast, but she explained: "God knows we couldn't be no worse off than we are now."

The campaign to free the Trenton Six was loud and unrelenting. The party's legal arm, the Civil Rights Congress, printed a pamphlet on the case: "Lynching, Northern Style." Its cover featured a cartoon of a judge smiling as six black men hanged from the bar of justice. Left-wing newspapers from Paris to New Delhi portrayed the case as a repeat of the Scottsboro boys, a group of young black men in Alabama wrongly imprisoned for rape.

In 1949, the Trenton murder convictions were overturned by the New Jersey Supreme Court, which found that the trial judge had made a serious error. He had never ordered the jury to specify what degree of murder the Trenton Six were guilty of, but assumed it was the first degree and sentenced the men to die. For the second trial, which began in March

1951, the Civil Rights Congress bowed out of the case. The new defense team was led by George Pellettieri, a fiery Trenton labor lawyer, with support from a Princeton-based committee of civil libertarians.

The Trenton Six were now able to mount a vigorous argument that they were victims of a frame-up. A new judge threw out most of the confessions as worthless evidence. And there was a startling new revelation from the defense: the bottle produced by the prosecution as the murder weapon never left the Royal Crown bottling plant until 1950, two years after the murder.

The jury didn't believe the prosecution's evidence, but was unable to accept the case as a total fabrication. On June 14 it reached a compromise verdict. For English and Cooper, guilty, with a recommendation of mercy. For the remaining four, not guilty. Mitchell, English's sister, declared only partial victory. "If they were white, they would be free today," she said of the two convicted men.

The saga of the Trenton Six came to a muddy conclusion that failed to satisfy either prosecution or defense. While appealing his conviction, English died in prison—the victim, at age twenty-seven, of a rheumatic heart. Cooper, wearying of the legal maneuvering, pleaded no contest to murder and agreed to a sentence of time served. Before going free, he implicated all five of his co-defendants.

It remains a possibility that some of the Trenton Six were in fact guilty and got away with murder. Then again, no innocent prisoner was executed.

❖ ALL LIES ❖

EDGAR SMITH, DEATH ROW INMATE
1933–

IN HIS STINGINGLY ERUDITE WAY, the commentator William F. Buckley could always give a conservative lashing to the soft-on-crime crowd. Odd, then, that in the 1960s Buckley turned champion of a convicted murderer. Odder still that he made Edgar Herbert Smith Jr. of New

Jersey into the most famous death row inmate in America and helped set him free.

The state of New Jersey called Smith a sex-crazed sociopath who had bashed in a fifteen-year-old girl's brains. But Buckley wrote: "I am convinced of his innocence." He based his conclusion largely on letters from the convicted man, written from an eight-by-eight-foot cell at Trenton state prison. Here was a man too aware, too literate, too witty—in short, too much like Buckley himself—to be a murderer. It would take Smith himself to prove Buckley wrong.

The murder for which Smith was found guilty took place March 4, 1957, on a frigid night in the town of Mahwah, New Jersey. A pretty high school cheerleader named Victoria Zielinski stayed late at a friend's house for a few hours of gossip and homework. She was supposed to walk home, but never showed up.

William F. Buckley Jr. (left) interviews Edgar Smith in 1971 for *Firing Line* upon the death row inmate's release from prison. Five years later, Buckley had to admit he was wrong: Smith was far from innocent. (*Firing Line* Collection, Hoover Institution Archives)

Vickie's body was found the next day, face-down in a large sand pit at the dead end of a rural road. Her bra was pulled down to the waist. A bite mark was on her breast, but she was not raped. Her skull had been caved in by two heavy rocks. Bits of brain were all over.

More than twenty of Vickie's friends were questioned over the next few days before police settled on a suspect. Edgar Smith, twenty-three, lived in a trailer park with his wife and newborn baby a short distance from the Mahwah sand pit. An ex-Marine, he was good-looking, with firm jaw and tousled blond hair. But he was an incorrigible loafer, preferring to hang out in pool rooms rather than with his family. As a juvenile, he had been convicted of trying to molest a nine-year-old girl.

The night of the murder, Smith had borrowed a friend's Mercury convertible. It was returned with a spot of blood on the back seat. Under relentless interrogation, the suspect said he had driven the Mercury to pick up kerosene and had not seen Vickie the night she died. He claimed he had changed his pants because he got sick all over them. But the cops had retrieved the trousers near the murder scene. They were stained not with vomit, but with blood.

Smith was ready to crack. "What did the girl do to you, Eddie?" a detective asked, playing good cop. "She hit me!" he blurted out. Smith then admitted he picked up Vickie on her way home and drove her to the sand pit. According to his story, she had swung her fist at him, he swung back, and "things turned sort of red and black." He couldn't remember what happened next.

Smith was careful never to confess to killing Vickie. And at his trial that spring, he came up with a new version of events. This time, he insisted he left Vickie at the pit alive, and she stayed there with a friend of his named Donald Hommell. He had omitted this crucial detail to the police, he said, because he feared Hommell would harm his family.

The Bergen County prosecutor presented a simpler case. Smith had driven Vickie to the sand pit to seduce her, he argued before a jury. He flew into a rage when she fought him off, and he beat her to death. The jury delivered its verdict in two hours: guilty of murder in the first degree. The sentence was death.

Smith went to Trenton's death row and was placed in the cell once occupied by Lindbergh kidnapper Bruno Hauptmann. When he ran out of money to pay his appeals lawyers, he became his own jailhouse lawyer, filing brief after brief in longhand. A weekly newspaper wrote a feature story in 1962 about his efforts, and this article caught the eye of a staffer at William F. Buckley's *National Review* magazine. Smith, it turned out, was a fan of *National Review*. On a whim, the patrician editor wrote a letter to the convicted murderer. Their correspondence eventually grew to twenty-nine hundred pages.

Smith had time to read a great deal on death row. His letters to Buckley were sprinkled with Latin phrases, observations on world affairs, and intellectual arrogance. Once, when Buckley marveled at Smith's coolness in the face of pending death, Smith wrote back: "Perhaps my letters should be appropriately tear-stained."

Nevertheless, Buckley agreed that Smith was a wronged man and wrote column after column on the subject. Attention was called to discrepancies in the coroner's estimated time of death, and to the fact Smith was not advised of his right to counsel before the police questioned him. Smith wrote his own book, published with Buckley's help in 1968, painting the convict as a victim of bad police work. However, he never flat-out claimed innocence. "Did justice triumph? Is Edgar Smith guilty?" he wrote about himself. "If at this point the reader cannot respond with an emphatic 'yes,' then I shall consider this book a success."

By 1971, Smith had spent fourteen years on death row, longer than any condemned man at the time. But his nineteenth appeal was successful. A U.S. District Court judge ruled that his statement to police back in 1957 was illegally obtained and ordered a new trial.

Rather than proceed with such an old case, the prosecutor's office allowed Smith to cut a deal. He pleaded guilty to second-degree murder, was given a suspended sentence, and walked free the same day. A limousine from Buckley's television show, *Firing Line,* was waiting for him. In a two-hour special, Smith told Buckley his plea was a sham because he didn't consider himself guilty.

For a time, Smith commanded $1,000 per engagement as he gave talks about his experience as a wrongly convicted prisoner. But soon he was out of work again in his new home of La Jolla, California. On October 1, 1976, he abducted a thirty-three-year-old woman from a parking lot, drove her off in his car, and stabbed her. The blade missed her heart by a quarter of an inch, and she made a remarkable escape.

Smith did not try to deny his crime. Throwing himself on the mercy of the court, he admitted not only this attempted murder, but the killing of Victoria Zielinski as well. In both cases, his intention was rape. "For the first time in my life, I recognized that the devil I had been looking at in the mirror for forty-three years was me," he told the judge.

The judge was not impressed, and sentenced Smith to life in prison. "It would seem plain that Edgar Smith must never be released from custody," Buckley wrote. "This is truly tragic." But when a Bergen County prosecutor wrote him, asking if he would make a public apology, Buckley coolly said no. "There will be guilty people freed this year and every year," he concluded.

❧ SPLIT DECISION ❧

RUBIN "HURRICANE" CARTER, MURDER SUSPECT
1937–

LOOK MEAN AND COME OUT SWINGING. That was the boxing strategy of Rubin "Hurricane" Carter, whose scowl, shaved head, and goatee radiated pure intimidation. His trademark inside the ring was a flurry of punches that gave him his stormy nickname. By the early 1960s he was the No. 3 contender for the middleweight championship and the talk of Paterson, New Jersey. An ex-convict turned local celebrity, he bopped around black bars every night, dressing in flashy suits and loudly holding court among his admirers.

But by 1966, Hurricane Carter had won just seven of his last fifteen fights and his fame was fading. In Paterson that summer, the fight talk was not about boxing but the threat of race riots in the city's hardscrabble neighborhoods. The evening of June 16, a white man walked into a bar to confront the owner, who was black, about a business dispute—then shot him to death.

The victim happened to be the stepfather of one of Carter's friends. At the boxer's favorite hangout, the Nite Spot, there was talk of a "shaking"—general retaliation against whites. Some patrons overheard Carter talking about how to get some guns. His penchant for arms was well known. In 1963, *Sports Illustrated* had quoted him as saying: "I've done bad things. I used to shoot people. I mean at them."

Six hours after the white-on-black killing—about 2:30 A.M. on June 17—it was nearing closing time at the Lafayette Grill. Four people were inside, all white. Bartender James Oliver, fifty-one, was counting out the day's receipts as his customers nursed their last drinks. Suddenly the front door swung open and two black men burst in. One carried a twelve-gauge shotgun, the other a .32-caliber pistol. Oliver instinctively hurled a bottle at them and missed. The shotgun blew a hole in his midsection and killed him instantly.

Rubin "Hurricane" Carter does a prison interview in 1974, before he won a retrial on his triple-murder conviction. Hollywood made him innocent, but the evidence for his guilt remains strong. (*The Trentonian* / Jim Holt)

The man with the handgun then fired a fatal shot into the head of Fred Nauyoks, sixty. He shot Willie Marins, forty-two, in the forehead. Marins fell to the floor blinded in the left eye, but he survived. The third customer, Hazel Tanis, fifty-one, backed into a corner and pleaded: "I'm a mother. I'm a grandmother. Please don't shoot me." Four pistol shots banged into her. She lingered a month before dying, the third of the victims to perish.

The police interviewed two witnesses who saw the laughing killers leave and hop into a late-model white car with butterfly-shaped taillights. A Dodge matching this description was pulled over five blocks from the Lafayette Grill. Inside were Carter, twenty-nine, and John Artis, twenty, both black.

There were tantalizing clues that made Carter and Artis suspects. Ammunition found in their vehicle matched the caliber, but not the brand, of the murder bullets. Both had left the Nite Spot fifteen minutes before the Lafayette Grill massacre, and conceivably had enough time to carry out the triple murder. While in the hospital, Tanis gave a description of her shooter that matched Artis.

But Marins, the sole survivor, could not identify either of his assailants. And neither Carter nor Artis had any connection with the victims. They agreed to a grand jury appearance and were not indicted. Carter even left the country in August to fight his last professional match, a losing bout in Argentina.

But the Paterson police had one more angle to explore. Al Bello, a small-time crook, was one of the witnesses who claimed to have seen the white getaway car—but he failed to mention that at the time of the murders he was acting as lookout for a nearby robbery.

After the killings, he took ghoulish advantage of the confusion by swiping $25 from the bar's cash register. Confronted with this evidence, Bello agreed to tell "the truth" about what he'd seen—that both Carter and Artis were the gunmen he saw leaving the bar. Bello's accomplice told police he had seen Carter with the shotgun.

When Carter and Artis went on trial for murder in May 1967, their lawyers accused Bello of being a liar who cut a dirty deal with the police.

They claimed Carter and Artis were guilty of nothing more than driving while black. "That's all you have here—Negro, Negro, Negro," said Carter's lawyer, Raymond Brown. "Apparently it means you are either suspect or more, guilty." But an all-white jury found the defendants guilty, and they each received three life sentences.

Carter, tough guy that he was, never lacked for charm. In prison, he launched a furious fight to rehabilitate his reputation—counting on his skill as a storyteller. In 1974, he published an autobiography, *The Sixteenth Round*, portraying himself as an innocent man railroaded by a racist criminal justice system.

It was a dramatic tale, but replete with lies and self-glorification. Carter claimed to have been thrown into a juvenile jail simply for protecting himself from a child molester. In fact, he was a repeat offender, as thief, mugger, and purse snatcher. He told false stories of marching for civil rights in the 1960s. The white authorities were always picking on him, he said, "just because I had happened to stumble upon their plan of black mass murder."

But if Carter's life story was improbable, his argument about an unfair trial seemed to hold more merit. Just as his book was rolling off the presses in 1974, murder witness Al Bello dramatically recanted. His identification of Carter and Artis was a lie, he said, to satisfy the police. The story became a national sensation. Bob Dylan recorded a protest song, "Hurricane," with the opening lines: "Here comes the story of the Hurricane / The man the authorities came to blame / For somethin' that he never done. . . ."

Carter won a second trial on the strength of the new evidence. But on the witness stand, Bello's story changed yet again. Now he recanted his recantation and said Carter and Artis were in fact the gunmen. He had lied about this, he said, because he expected to get a bribe from Carter's supporters.

More damning evidence came from Carter himself. Prosecutors produced letters he had written from jail coaching some of his friends to say he was with them at 2:30 A.M., the time of the murders. Four alibi witnesses who had testified for the boxer at the first trial now came forward to say they had lied on his behalf. On December 21, 1976, the racially mixed jury announced its verdict. For a second time, both he and Artis were found guilty.

In 1981, Artis was paroled after fifteen years in prison. Carter got no such break: prosecutors viewed him as the plotter of mass murder, with Artis mesmerized by the older man's celebrity. The boxer kept filing appeal after appeal until he hit pay dirt.

The man who finally struck down the guilty verdict against Hurricane Carter, Newark federal judge Lee Sarokin, never said he was innocent. He did not endorse the boxer's claims of a police conspiracy to frame him. But Judge Sarokin found grave fault with the prosecution's strategy of claiming "racial revenge" as the motive for the shootings. The convictions "were predicated upon an appeal to racism rather than reason, and concealment rather than disclosure," he wrote.

In November 1985, Carter walked out of Trenton prison a free man. Afterward, he made a living as an inspirational speaker and was the subject of a movie (*The Hurricane*, 1999) starring Denzel Washington as a sanitized and sanctified version of the real Carter. The state of New Jersey continued to argue that Carter was guilty as charged, and only ducked a third prosecution because an additional trial would have been too costly. But in the court of public opinion, and of pop culture, the Hurricane had won his sixteenth round.

⇥ LIFE OR DEATH ⇤

IN THE MATTER OF KAREN ANN QUINLAN

IT SEEMED TO Karen Ann Quinlan's parents as if the gray, boxy machine by her hospital bedside was more alive than she was. Every time the respirator known as an MA-1 registered that she was short of breath, it whirred into action and pumped pure oxygen through a tube into her throat. The twenty-one-year-old patient lying in a fetal position softly moaned but made no other response. When her eyes opened, they did not recognize her loved ones or even come into focus.

By the definition of medical science, she lived. "A persistent vegetative state," the doctors at St. Clare's Hospital in Denville, New Jersey, called it. But to Joseph and Julia Quinlan, this was no life at all—merely physical torture for their daughter and emotional anguish for them. In 1975, they sued to turn the respirator off. The courts would be forced to decide a new question in medical ethics: Would this be an act of homicide, or an exercise of the right to die?

The young woman at the center of this worldwide debate had been adopted as a baby into a middle-class household in Roxbury Township, New Jersey. Karen loved singing along to show tunes and playing rough-and-tumble sports with her brother and sister. Her high school yearbook portrait, later to be reproduced thousands of times over in the media, showed a petite teenager with long, straight hair, dimpled chin, and wide eyes.

After high school, Karen alternated between periods of cheer and moroseness. In an eerily prescient poem, she wrote: "I wish to curl myself into a Fetal rose / and rest in this eternal womb awhile." Deciding against college, she lived on her own with roommates and hung out with friends who liked to drink and get high. In Karen's last conversation with her mother, she talked of going on a swimsuit diet and moving to Florida.

All the public saw of Karen Ann Quinlan was her yearbook photograph, even as she lay in a "vegetative state" for ten years.

On April 15, 1975, Karen Ann Quinlan went to a friend's birthday party at a local bar. She swallowed some Valium pills, and drank three gin and tonics. The combination of depressants knocked her out. Her friends tried to give her mouth-to-mouth resuscitation and called an ambulance.

Whatever put her into the coma was never conclusively determined. Most likely, she had aspirated vomit into her windpipe, cutting off oxygen to her brain. Doctors at St. Clare's Hospital performed a tracheotomy, put her on the respirator, and inserted a feeding tube through her nostrils. With time, Karen's neurological functions might return to something close to normal. At one point, she was felt to squeeze her mother's hand. "God will bring back Karen," Joseph Quinlan said.

But that moment never came. With each passing day, Karen Ann became more of a shell of herself. Her hands and legs bent inward. When awake, her head shook back and forth with occasional moans and tears. Her eyes blinked open but betrayed no awareness of her surroundings. Physicians told the Quinlans that Karen's brain was capable of reflex but little else. Not even the most heroic measure could bring her back to the waking world.

"Karen wouldn't want this," Julia Quinlan kept saying. Finally she and her husband came to a heartbreaking conclusion—the respirator would have to be removed.

In 1976, parents Joseph and Julia won the historic right to turn off the respirator keeping their daughter alive. (*New York Post* / Michael Norcia)

Religious as always, they consulted their parish priest on whether this would be in keeping with church teachings. The reverend cited Vatican doctrine that while euthanasia was a sin, it was acceptable to deny a patient the "extraordinary means" to prolong her life when she could not recover.

The Quinlans made their solemn request to the hospital after Karen's third month in a coma. In many cases of this type, doctors would quietly agree to remove the respirator under a policy of "judicious neglect." But St. Clare's refused. The doctors clung to their policy of saving life in all cases but those where a patient had no brain activity whatsoever.

On September 12, 1975, Joseph Quinlan filed a lawsuit with the state Superior Court in Morris County seeking permission to let his daughter die. The case touched a chord for just about anyone with a badly ill loved one. Medical science, it seemed, had outpaced the ability of ethical standards to keep up with it.

Supporting the hospital's lifesaving measures were the New Jersey attorney general, the county prosecutor, and a guardian appointed by the court for Karen Quinlan. This advocate, Daniel Coburn, called the idea of death with dignity a "shell game" that concealed euthanasia. "Where there's hope, you can't just extinguish a human life because she's an eyesore," he said.

The Quinlans' lawyer, Paul Armstrong, contended that their religious beliefs and right to privacy enabled them to make the life-or-death decision. An anguished Joseph Quinlan was called to the stand, where he pleaded: "Take her from the machine and the tubes and let her pass into the hands of the Lord." His wife, Julia, then testified that Karen had seen friends die of cancer and said "don't ever let them keep me alive" if she were suffering like that.

Judge Robert Muir concluded that to disconnect the respirator would be an "act of homicide" and make him the first judicial officer ever to order an execution in a civil case. This he refused to do. The Quinlans appealed to the New Jersey Supreme Court.

On March 31, 1976, the state court issued its unanimous ruling. The Quinlans had every right to turn off the respirator. "No compelling

interest of the state," Chief Justice Richard Hughes wrote in his opinion, "could compel Karen to endure the unendurable, only to vegetate a
few measurable months with no realistic possibility of returning to any
semblance of cognitive or sapient state."

The Quinlans did not "pull the plug," to use an expression they hated.
Karen was weaned off the respirator over a period of days, in the hope
she might still recover from her coma, and finally removed from it in
May 1976. She was placed in a nursing home. Then, defying the doctors'
expectations, she remained alive.

Every day, her father would drop by Karen's room on his way to work.
Every week, her mother came to hold her hand and talk to her. A radio
always played Karen's favorite songs. A tube continued to feed her. None
of it improved Karen's quality of life: her eyes showed no awareness,
her body shriveled to seventy pounds. Karen Ann Quinlan lived another
ten years before dying on June 11, 1985. She was no victim of euthanasia.
But, her mother said, "She died with dignity."

❧ X THE UNKNOWN ☙

MARIO JASCALEVICH,
SUSPECTED "DR. X" KILLER
1927–1984

THE OPERATION WAS A SUCCESS, but the patient died. At Riverdell
Hospital in Oradell, New Jersey, the ironic adage could have served as a
motto.

From December 1965 to October 1966, as many as twenty-five patients
underwent routine surgeries, then died with a baffling suddenness. Causes
of death were listed as coronary failure or postoperative complications,
but these were feeble guesses in place of "unknown." Riverdell's doctors
wondered if they were cursed by a jinx—or an angel of death.

Nancy Savino, four, was admitted for removal of cysts on her small
intestine. She recovered nicely from the surgery, cried a little bit that night
out of homesickness, then died in the morning from unknown causes.

Margaret Henderson, twenty-six, was operated on for abdominal pain. She had a "fairly comfortable night" afterward, her chart showed, awakened in a "tense and apprehensive" state, and was dead within two hours. Eileen Shaw, thirty-six, gave birth to a healthy child by Caesarian section and appeared to be on the mend. The following morning, she too was gone.

One newly hired surgeon, Stanley Harris, was devastated. His patients, among them little Nancy and Mrs. Shaw, were dying at the incredible rate of two a month. Over time he put together the pieces of the mystery. The patients tended to die between 7 and 9 in the morning. Each had an intravenous line stuck into a vein, usually just before the vital signs failed.

One person seemed to connect all the deaths. Riverdell's chief surgeon, Mario Jascalevich, had paid visits to all of them. Sometimes he was the one who ordered the IV infusion. As Mrs. Shaw lay dying, Harris remembered Jascalevich hurrying down the hall, telling him he had better take care of her. Why was he leaving? There was another curious fact. "Dr. Jascalevich's patients never die," Harris observed to a colleague. "It's only the other doctors."

Dr. Mario Enrique Jascalevich, thirty-nine, was a surgeon of undoubted skill. An immigrant from Argentina, he had established a successful

Mario Jascalevich and wife on their way to Bergen County court in 1978. The so-called "Dr. X" was found not guilty of mass murder by the poison curare, then left the country. (*New York Post* / Vernon Shibla)

clinic for Spanish speakers in the nearby Jersey town of West New York. The doctor had polished manners and a charming smile. But his relations with Riverdell's staff were frosty at best.

In 1966, the year of the hospital's wave of mysterious deaths, he wrote a memo to the hospital board of directors complaining about the hiring of new surgeons. This would inevitably reduce his own income, he wrote, because more people would be dividing the same amount of work: "Restlessness, insecurity, and unhappiness in the general staff will inevitably follow."

On October 31, Harris and a fellow surgeon decided to open up Jascalevich's private locker to look for evidence of foul play. What they saw gave them a shudder of horror. Inside were syringes and eighteen mostly empty vials of curare. A poison originating in a South American vine, curare is used by tribesmen on the ends of their extremely lethal darts. Once injected into the bloodstream, curare paralyzes the lungs and can cause near-instant death. Hospital laboratories sometimes stocked the drug as a muscle relaxant. But there was no logical reason to keep it in a private locker.

The next day, the directors of Riverdell Hospital took the extraordinary step of contacting the Bergen County prosecutor. Medical charts on thirteen suspicious deaths were handed over; all of them, the hospital believed, were connected to Jascalevich.

Acting like a man with nothing to hide, Jascalevich insisted on giving a sworn deposition. The chief surgeon explained that he used his curare to experiment on dogs. But when asked where and when he performed these experiments, Jascalevich gave contradictory answers. Laboratory technicians at Seton Hall medical school could not recall him using their facilities except on November 2, after Jascalevich knew he was under suspicion and needed an alibi.

Nevertheless, the Bergen County prosecutor found insufficient evidence to present the case to a grand jury. The doctor offered to resign on the condition that the whole affair stay quiet. His wish was granted, and he continued to earn a good living at hospitals in Jersey City and New York.

A decade later, reporter Myron Farber of the *New York Times* received an anonymous letter about the deaths at Riverdell Hospital. His investigative work spurred the new Bergen prosecutor to reopen the investigation. On January 8, 1976, the *Times* published the first of its stories revealing that a hospital surgeon was under suspicion for murder. Because he had not been charged with a crime, the doctor was identified simply as "Dr. X."

Five bodies were exhumed, and in all five cases curare was found. New York City's medical examiner, Michael Baden, noted: "There was no cause that could compete with poisoning." Dr. Jascalevich was unmasked as "Dr. X" shortly before a grand jury indicted him on five counts of murder, among them the deaths of Nancy Savino and Margaret Henderson.

But when the trial began in March 1978, Jascalevich had the advantage. The prosecution could not articulate a clear reason for mass murder. Jascalevich's charismatic defense lawyer, Raymond Brown, presented an easier-to-follow argument. Other, less expert surgeons had caused the patients' deaths, he said, then framed Jascalevich to cover up their ineptitude.

As the highly technical and arcane medical testimony plodded on—it was, up to that time, the longest criminal trial in U.S. history—everyone in the courtroom grew restless and bored. Judge and jurors alike nodded off at times. The defense produced experts of their own to claim the curare could have been introduced into the corpses after embalming.

Jascalevich's lawyer pulled his most attention-getting maneuver outside the jury's presence when he subpoenaed the *Times* reporter, Farber. The defense tactic was ostensibly to obtain Farber's notes and to compel him to name his sources, thus proving a conspiracy between the *Times* and the prosecution. Farber refused and was jailed for forty days for contempt of court. Journalists across the country protested, to no avail.

The jury did not bother to review the trial exhibits. On October 24, it deliberated for two hours before finding Jascalevich not guilty. The courtroom, which had been packed with the doctor's clients, erupted in cheers.

The state of New Jersey forced Jascalevich to surrender his medical license—not for the curare murders, but for unrelated malpractice. Among his offenses was falsely diagnosing cancer in a woman, then performing unnecessary surgery. Hounded by lawsuits and debt, Jascalevich moved back to his native Argentina in 1981. He died three years later, in disgrace but with a clear criminal record. The only person ever jailed as a result of the "Dr. X" murders was the journalist who exposed them.

☀ RUMOR HAS IT ❧

THE SMEARING OF RAYMOND DONOVAN

FOR SIX YEARS THEY DRIPPED upon Raymond Donovan like a water torture—the leaks, the lies, the investigations, the innuendoes, all of them seeking to connect him with the New Jersey mob. Finally on May 26, 1987, came vindication, when a jury in the Bronx found Donovan, the former U.S. secretary of labor, not guilty of fraud. The cleared man told reporters he had one question for the prosecutor. "Which office do I go to to get my reputation back?"

His words continue to echo strongly. In retrospect it seems unreal that Donovan, with his record as an honest public servant, could go through such an ordeal on such flimsy evidence. But it did happen.

He was one of twelve children who grew up in an Irish Catholic household in Bayonne, New Jersey. For a time he thought of becoming a priest and attended seminary. But he came to work as an insurance salesman, supporting his younger siblings when both parents died. By the late 1950s he was so highly thought of by one of his clients, the small Schiavone Construction Company of nearby Secaucus, that they hired him.

Donovan invested his talent and savings in the organization, helping it grow into a $150 million-a-year giant. Its specialties were highway building and tunnel digging; Donovan's bailiwick, as executive vice president, was bonding and labor relations. He became a millionaire, moved to suburban Short Hills, and got heavily involved in both charitable work and Republican politics.

In 1980, Donovan was Ronald Reagan's choice to manage his presidential campaign in New Jersey. When Reagan won, he surprised the pundits by nominating Donovan to head the Department of Labor. As a man of blue-collar origins—he still held a union card from summers as a laborer—the burly, soft-spoken Donovan was seen as holding appeal for that new voter, the Reagan Democrat. He was expected to sail through his Senate confirmation hearings. Then in January 1981 came the first rumblings of trouble. An FBI informant claimed to have seen Donovan in the company of mobsters.

As a man who had to deal with construction unions, Donovan rubbed shoulders with unsavory characters. But in a friendly way? It seemed preposterous. Well remembered was an incident two years earlier when a Teamsters business agent stopped work at a job site over some arcane

Former Secretary of Labor Raymond Donovan is mobbed by the media after his indictment in 1984. The New Jerseyan is now regarded as the prototypical victim of smear by newspaper leaks. (*New York Post* / Don Halasy)

union rule. Donovan protested. "My friend, keep your headlights on high beam when you get in your doorway at home," the Teamster told him. "Get off this property, or I'll have you arrested for threatening my life," Donovan growled back.

The nominee proved equally feisty when it came to defending his ethics before the Senate Labor Committee. Why, he was asked, were there so many stories about Schiavone Construction and the mob? "The New Jersey syndrome," Donovan said. "If you're in the contracting business in New Jersey, you're indictable. If you're in the contracting business in New Jersey and you're Italian, you're convicted."

Donovan was confirmed, but at a heavy price. More FBI sources emerged to spread stories about his "mob links." Some told of him shaking down subcontractors for donations to Reagan's campaign. Others had him bribing the notorious Teamsters gangster "Tony Pro" Provenzano. Newspaper reporters faithfully reported each new allegation, each new story dragging Donovan further into disrepute.

"False and scurrilous," Donovan said of the stories. He was right. Most of the tale-tellers were mobsters looking to get in good graces with the FBI. One of them was facing a murder indictment after it emerged that he committed a contract killing while in federal pay. Another was a notorious liar who claimed to know where Jimmy Hoffa was buried.

A year into his job, Donovan became the subject of an investigation by a special prosecutor named Leon Silverman. The counsel went over every allegation of wrongdoing and found "insufficient credible evidence" for any of them. Reagan supported Donovan even as his aides urged he be cut loose. "The case is closed," the president said.

But it wasn't. In 1982, a witness who had been scheduled to testify for the special prosecutor was found murdered in the Bronx. The district attorney there could not connect the killing with Donovan or Schiavone, but developed information linking the slain man with an alleged contracting scam. On October 1, 1984, a month before Reagan's re-election, the D.A. announced indictments. Donovan and five fellow executives were all charged in connection with this scam. Also named were a New York state senator and a Genovese mob associate.

Before he joined the Reagan cabinet, Donovan's company Schiavone had been awarded a $186 million contract to dig a New York City subway tunnel. Contractors were supposed to satisfy a rule that 10 percent of their work go to minority-owned businesses. To do this, the prosecutor charged, Schiavone hired a subcontractor, Jopel Trucking, that acted as a front for a mobster named "Billy the Butcher" Masselli. Schiavone was alleged to have received $7.4 million in kickbacks from this company.

Donovan became the first sitting cabinet officer in U.S. history to be indicted. At first he vowed to stay in office, calling his prosecution a sham case brought by a Democratic district attorney for political reasons. But by the following year, he resigned to work full-time on defending himself.

The trial lasted from September 1986 to May 1987, every day of it filled with excruciating tedium. The $7.4 million in supposed plunder was actually the amount that Jopel had paid Schiavone for leasing equipment. Prosecutors went over the lease in mind-numbing detail, but failed to convince anyone that this amounted to an accounting irregularity, much less a crime. The subway tunnel came in $8 million under budget. Where was the theft?

The case was so weak that lawyers for Donovan and the other executives didn't even present a defense. The jury needed a single ballot to vote "not guilty" on each of the one hundred criminal counts. After delivering the verdict, the jury forewoman told reporters: "The indictment should never have been brought."

After the trial, Donovan rejoined his old construction company, rebuilt its shattered business, and rehired its laid-off workers. Over time, both Democrats and Republicans came to see him as unfairly tarnished, and his name became a byword for the victims of prosecutorial excess. Finally, he had his reputation back.

✳ WITCH HUNT ✦

HYSTERIA OVER THE WEE CARE NURSERY

WHEN THE POLICE CAME KNOCKING at Margaret Kelly Michaels's door with some questions about sexual abuse at the day care center where she once worked in Maplewood, New Jersey, she was eager to come help. The twenty-four-year-old aspiring actress had good memories of those fifty kids at the Wee Care Nursery School, and she wanted to protect them.

But when Michaels came to the Essex County prosecutor's office for her interview on May 6, 1985, she learned that *she* was the one accused of molesting the children. No matter, she thought. She would answer all their questions. It had to be a misunderstanding.

She was right about it being a misunderstanding, wrong that she would escape unharmed. Kelly Michaels ended up being convicted of multiple counts of abuse and sentenced to forty-seven years in prison. She was painted as a monster who committed appalling acts of sexual perversion. But with the distance of time, it is now possible to see her for what she really was—the victim of mass hysteria.

Wrongfully convicted day care worker Margaret Kelly Michaels after she won back her freedom in 1993 on sex abuse charges. Winning back her reputation was another matter. (*New York Post* / Robin Graubard)

The great day care sex outrages of the 1980s were the product of two converging trends. More working parents were leaving their vulnerable toddlers in the hands of strangers at day cares, and feeling guilt and anxiety about it. Simultaneously, the once-hidden secret of child sexual abuse was gaining national publicity. Most notorious was the McMartin preschool case in California, in which an innocent family went to prison on fictitious stories of Satan worship and ritualistic sex abuse.

Sometime in the early spring of 1985, a four-year-old boy at a Maplewood doctor's office was having his temperature taken with a rectal thermometer. "That's what my teacher does to me at nap time," he commented. What? "Her takes my temperature." The child showed no signs of being upset about this, but his mother was alarmed. She contacted police and social services professionals, and the word spread quickly through Maplewood: a child molester was in their midst.

The boy who had his temperature taken identified his teacher as "Kelly," so prosecutors quickly zeroed in on Kelly Michaels. It would be a difficult case to prove. Michaels had recently quit at Wee Care to take a better teaching job; her bosses and pupils alike were sad to see her go. During Michaels's stint, no parents had reported their child being hurt or upset about being in day care. None had physical signs of abuse.

But there had been unusual changes in the children's behavior. Some erupted in temper tantrums. Others wet their beds, experienced night terrors, and talked back at their parents. Never mind that this was not unusual in young kids. Peg Foster, the head of a child abuse treatment center in Newark, became convinced these were signs of hidden abuse.

Foster and other counselors hoped to glean details of Michaels's crimes by interviewing the children. But the kids liked Kelly and said she hadn't done anything bad to them. In the looking-glass world of Essex County justice, this became evidence against her: the kids had been so badly abused that they were in total denial!

Kids were bullied with threats ("You have to behave . . . police can punish bad people"), bribes ("Tell me what Kelly did to your hiney and then you can go"), and peer pressure ("Boy, I'd hate having to tell your friends that you didn't want to help them"). They were shown anatomically correct dolls and asked to show where Michaels had touched them. Fascinated by the genitalia on these dolls, the children naturally pointed there.

A typical session went:

"Do you think Kelly was not good when she was hurting you all?"

"Wasn't hurting me. I like her."

"I can't hear you. You got to look at me when you talk to me. Now, when Kelly was bothering kids in the music room—"

"I got socks off."

After a few more exchanges—after the interviewers made repeated references to "blood" and "poopy" and "pee-pee"—the children would begin to agree that, yes, they had been abused. In reality, they were supplying the answers that would end the painful sessions, and telling the authority figures what they wanted to hear. Investigators heard the echoes of their own fears and believed them. Child psychology now recognizes these "truth-finding" techniques as anything but. They instead implant suggestible children with false memories.

In December 1985, prosecutors indicted Kelly Michaels on 235 charges. They said she had forced all fifty kids in her class to strip naked and play leapfrog. She had made them urinate on top of her and drink and eat their own bodily wastes. She had inserted forks, knives, and Lego blocks into their orifices. Somehow she had done all this in Wee Care's cramped space within an Episcopal church, with no teachers or parents noticing a thing.

Michaels was shocked by the allegations and certain that the whole thing would eventually resolve itself as a bad mistake. Certainly she was a poor fit for the stereotypical pedophile. She had a sweet nature, a good education at a Catholic college, and pretty, delicate features. Never had she been hit with so much as a parking ticket.

But Kelly Michaels's very ordinariness made prosecutors more determined to build a case against her. They wanted to prove that sex criminals could be not just a leering middle-aged man, but the girl next door.

The trial was badly weighted against Michaels. The children, now five to seven years old, were not allowed to be examined by any experts for the defense. They testified not in court but by closed-circuit television from the judge's private chambers. The judge allowed boys to testify while sitting in his lap. He coaxed them to talk, whispered encouraging words into their ears, and complimented them on their bravery.

The trial lasted ten months and cost taxpayers more than $3 million. On April 15, 1988, a jury found Michaels guilty of 115 abuse counts. Ironically, she was acquitted of molesting the boy whose comment about a thermometer had started the whole thing. Michaels held back her instinct to scream at the jurors: "Can't you see my humanity staring right back at yours? Don't any of you have minds of your own?"

Michaels was sent to a women's prison, where she spent time in solitary because of the scorn and threats dished out by her fellow inmates. Her parents ran out of money for an appeal. Constitutional rights lawyers largely shied away from the case. They feared the taint from representing a convicted molester and the outrage from denying the slogan of the Maplewood parents: "Believe the children."

Her vindication was sparked by the work of an investigative journalist, Dorothy Rabinowitz, who wrote a piece arguing for Michaels's innocence. A new team of pro bono lawyers successfully argued in appellate court for overturning the Essex trial. In March 1993, she was finally freed from prison. The following year, the state Supreme Court upheld the ruling with a blast against "egregious prosecutorial abuses."

Kelly Michaels survived her ordeal with good humor and a strengthened Christian faith. She married, had five children, wrote an unpublished memoir, and attempted unsuccessfully to sue her prosecutors. "The prayer I have," she said, "is that someone will come to me . . . maybe a parent or a child all grown up, and say, 'We got sucked into this horrible madness, and looking back we see that it just didn't happen, and I was led by these experts to believe . . . and I'm really sorry.'"

But abuse experts say that false memories of abuse, once implanted into small children, are likely to become ever more real with time, forever scarring them emotionally. No matter that crimes were never committed at the Wee Care Nursery, the children were victims—and their abuser was the state of New Jersey.

⇻ TUG OF LOVE ⇺

BABY M

KING SOLOMON HAD IT EASY. When he reigned over the Israelites, there were no such things as artificial insemination or surrogate-mother contracts. All he needed to do in a custody ruling was offer to cut the baby in half—and the real mother would show herself to be worthy.

Three thousand years later, the state of New Jersey had no Solomon and no simple solutions. Baby M was the name the courts gave to the first child in legal history whose parentage was disputed between the surrogate mother who conceived her and the couple who paid for her. Who should win? The natural mother, who called her contract a form of slavery depriving her of her own flesh and blood? Or the sperm donor and his wife, who so desperately wanted a first child?

One thing the Baby M case made clear was that surrogate mothers would not likely come from the high end of the socioeconomic ladder. Mary Beth Whitehead was sixteen when she married a Vietnam veteran with a drinking problem. He drove a garbage truck; she stayed at home to raise two children, once earning extra cash as a go-go dancer.

In 1986, Mary Beth Whitehead gave birth to a baby under a surrogate contract and refused to give it up. The New Jersey Supreme Court would later rule the contract was unenforceable, but Whitehead lost custody anyway. (*New York Post* / David Rentas)

By the mid-1980s, they were living more comfortably in a house in Brick Township, but were always in need of more cash. That was when Mrs. Whitehead saw a newspaper advertisement asking for women willing to help infertile couples bear children.

The ad intrigued her, and not merely for the $10,000 promised on delivery of a healthy baby. Whitehead's sister was infertile, and she said that becoming a surrogate mother felt like an altruistic deed. When she met the couple who were hiring her, their relations were at first friendly.

William and Betsy Stern had picked their surrogate mother from a list of more than three hundred women brought to them by a for-profit brokerage known as the Infertility Center of New York. The Sterns, who were in their late thirties and lived in Tenafly, New Jersey, had put off a family as they pursued their careers: he as a biochemist, she as a pediatrician. Betsy Stern was not infertile. She had early stages of multiple sclerosis, and feared harm to both herself and her child were she to become pregnant.

Whitehead signed a contract agreeing to be artificially inseminated. The baby was to be conceived with William Stern's sperm and Whitehead's egg. Upon delivery, she would surrender all rights to her biological child and make no attempts to have contact with it.

William Stern was the birth father of "Baby M." His wife, Betsy, was afraid to carry a child because she suffered from multiple sclerosis. (*New York Post* / Arty Pomerantz)

On March 27, 1986, Whitehead, twenty-nine, gave birth to a healthy girl. It was a difficult labor, and she was flooded with emotion. Instantly she regretted her contract to give up the baby. "Oh, God, what have I done?" she told her husband, Rick. "I want my baby!" On the birth certificate, the child was Sara Elizabeth Whitehead, Mary Beth's choice of a name. The other couple named her Melissa Elizabeth Stern.

Other surrogate mothers before Whitehead had had the same reaction to pregnancy, refusing to give up the child. In every previous case, the couple who had hired the surrogate agreed to terminate the contract and not pay the fee. The Sterns chose to fight back. They obtained a court order declaring Bill Stern the father and granting him temporary custody. Sheriff's officers came to the Whiteheads' house on May 12 to seize the girl. Mary Beth foiled them by passing the baby out of a back window into the arms of her husband.

Dodging detectives and process-servers, the Whiteheads then went on the lam in Florida. Desperate to get Bill Stern off her trail, she placed a phone call to him. Unknown to her, he tape recorded the conversation.

"I want my daughter back," Stern said.

"And I want her, too," Whitehead said angrily. "So what do we do, cut her in half? . . . I've been breast-feeding her for four months. She's bonded to me, Bill."

A rare glimpse of Baby M during one of her visits to her birth mother. The trial turned surrogate motherhood into a national debate. (*New York Post* / David Rentas)

"You made an agreement. You signed an agreement."

"Forget it, Bill. I'll tell you right now I'd rather see me and her dead before you get her."

In July, the baby was finally found and seized by police. To get her back, Whitehead went to court, and then to various media outlets pleading her case. By the time the trial began the following January in Bergen County Family Court in Hackensack, it was a national story. Judge Harvey Sorkow was being asked to make two separate rulings. Was the surrogacy contract valid? And who should get custody?

The case of Baby M—the initial stood for Melissa—was both a soap opera and an ethics debate come to life. Many found their hearts tugged by the dilemma of the Sterns, who received a gift of life only to have it taken away. And they were clearly better able to provide for Baby M than were the Whiteheads.

But it was just that issue—one couple being able to essentially buy a baby from another—that troubled others. Future advances of reproductive technology could give rise to an exploited "breeder class" of women, they warned. "It will always be the wife of the sanitation worker who must bear the children for the pediatrician," said Whitehead's lawyer, Harold Cassidy.

However, most of the trial testimony was harmful to Whitehead. Her flight to Florida and her death threat were recounted for the court to show she was unstable and unfit. "Immature" and "narcissistic," said one psychological expert, Marshall Schecter. He had observed her playing patty-cake with Baby M on a supervised visit, and she said "Hooray!" when the child clapped her hands. This was, somehow, not an "appropriate response."

Judge Sorkow announced his decision on March 31, 1987. It was a complete victory for the Sterns. Not only was their contract declared legal, not only did they get custody of Baby M, but Whitehead was denied any contact with the child.

The defeated plaintiff took her case to the New Jersey Supreme Court. And on February 2, 1988, the state's highest court agreed with her. Essentially making new law, the judges declared that surrogate motherhood was only legal if the woman agreed to carry a child without pay or contract. "There are, in a civilized society, some things that money cannot buy," their opinion declared.

Unwilling to uproot the baby after more than a year, the court ruled that she must remain in the Sterns' custody. But Whitehead was granted generous visiting rights. In the end, a certain Solomonic judgment did prevail. The child who was at the center of the divisive battle grew up calling two women "mom," while both families zealously guarded her privacy, even as the two mothers co-existed in icy hostility. By the time the girl reached adulthood, she had chosen to call herself not Sara, not Melissa, but "Sassy." Baby M was her own woman.

❯ SPOILED ROTTEN ❮
THE GLEN RIDGE HIGH SCHOOL RAPISTS

IF FOOTBALL PLAYERS stand at the very pinnacle of high school society, strutting down hallways, earning cheers, and making local paper headlines, then retarded students are close to invisible. The seventeen-year-old girl who liked to shoot basketballs in the parks of picture perfect

CHRIS ARCHER   **KEVIN SCHERZER**   **KYLE SCHERZER**

Football players Christopher Archer and twins Kevin and Kyle Scherzer were the pride of Glen Ridge High School until their arrest for raping a retarded girl with an IQ of 64.

Glen Ridge, New Jersey, was just such an outsider. Although physically large and good at sports, she had the social skills and intelligence of an eight-year-old. All she wanted was to be liked. But almost no one at Glen Ridge High School wanted to be seen with her.

So it surprised her when Christopher Archer, a junior member of the football team, approached her on the asphalt hoops court on the afternoon of March 1, 1989. Come over to the Scherzer twins' home, he said, we're having a party. The girl was initially hesitant, remembering all the times Chris and his jock buddies had taunted her as "retard" and "special ed."

But she brightened up when he told her his older, more handsome brother, Paul, would be there. Paul was nice, she thought. Maybe they'd even get a chance to date. The walk over to the party, arm in arm with Chris Archer, felt "romantic," she later said. Her trusting nature and mental immaturity did not make her a good judge of character.

The basement of the Scherzers' was set up like a movie theater, with folding chairs arranged in rows in front of a couch, and the female guest was told to sit on the couch. Seven of the thirteen boys left when they saw what was about to take place. Their discomfort was not so strong, however, as to get them to call the police.

Take your shirt off, the girl was told, and she did. Finger yourself down there. Again, she complied, and heard cheers and hoots. One of the football kids, Bryant Grober, stepped forward, grabbed her by the back of the head, and made her perform oral sex on him.

Kyle and Kevin Scherzer, the eighteen-year-old co-captains of the football team, got into the act. Kyle handed his fraternal twin a broomstick, and Kevin raped the girl with it. Then he and Chris Archer violated her a second time, with the barrel end of a baseball bat. "Stop, you're hurting her," Kyle said. But his protests were drowned out by a chant: "Further! Further! Further!"

The "party" broke up with the jocks warning their victim not to tell any adult what had happened. She kept the secret, but the rapists didn't see anything shameful about what they had done. All week, they bragged to friends about the new sexual toy they had acquired. Only one boy among those in the know—he also happened to be the only nonwhite member of the football team—went to a teacher to report the troubling things he had heard. Three more weeks passed before the police were finally notified of the rape, on March 22.

Six Glen Ridge students were arrested for aggravated sexual assault, and two were hit with lesser charges. Rumors about the awful deed in the Scherzers' basement had been going around, but the commuter suburb was still stunned. Could it be a misunderstanding? parents asked. Would such handsome young men, with such bright futures ahead of them, do something so brutal?

But even for jocks, the Glen Ridge group had a long record of outrageous behavior toward the other sex. Kevin Scherzer, the boy who wielded the broomstick, was known to drop his pants and expose himself in class. And Chris Archer had once made obscene phone calls to the retarded girl's house. None of their misdeeds was punished by anything more severe than a few days of suspension. Boys will be boys.

A large part of the town assumed the victim had it coming. Exaggerated stories got around that the teen girl went up to boys offering to perform sexual favors. But even those who refused to play blame-the-victim tended to downplay the enormity of what happened. In a speech, Glen Ridge's mayor called for "deep and mature compassion for the victim of these alleged acts" as well as "the accused." It was as if all had suffered equally.

Three and a half years elapsed between crime and trial as the prosecution sought to sift the hardcore abusers from lesser offenders, who were offered plea deals. Chris Archer's brother, along with another boy in the rapists' cheering section, pleaded guilty to misdemeanors. Charges were dropped against two alleged participants. One of them, Richard Corcoran—the son of Glen Ridge's chief of detectives—later joined the Army and served in Afghanistan. Soon after his return, in 2005, he shot and wounded his estranged wife, then killed himself.

The trial of the remaining four Glen Ridge defendants began in October 1992 at the Essex County Courthouse in Newark. By then, the tragedy of the mentally disabled girl preyed upon by elite athletes had become a national story—as well as a flashpoint for feminist anger. Women had for too long been made to feel shame for being victims of rape, the activists said. And now, the defense strategy of the accused rapists was to say that the sex was consensual. A retarded teenager with an IQ of 64 was to be depicted as a wily seductress.

There was no physical evidence connecting the four defendants to the rape; the Scherzer boys had made sure it vanished. Only the girl, now twenty-one, could name her molesters. But calling her as a witness would have pitfalls. She might lose the train of questioning and get confused about the sequence of events. Most poignantly, she still craved popularity with the jockocracy of Glen Ridge.

The victim took the stand, clutching a doll. When she spoke, it was totally without affect. Casually using phrases like "blow job" and "dick," she described the degrading acts performed on her in the Scherzer basement. What happened after the oral sex? the prosecutor asked.

"Oh, then came the broomstick," she said.

What had Kevin Scherzer done with it?

"He stuck it in me."

How did that make you feel?

"OK, I guess."

The prosecutor winced. And it got even more frustrating when the lawyers for the accused rapists cross-examined her. She said Grober, who forced oral sex on her, was a "sweetheart." She called Kevin "handsome." Asked if she loved him, she said, "Uh-huh."

But there came a telling moment when Chris Archer's lawyer asked her: "As you think back, Chris never did anything to hurt you, did he?"

"Yes, he did," the young woman answered. "He did the bat."

Later she was asked if she didn't want to hurt the defendants. "Right," she said. "I care about them. I know they don't give a hoot about me, but I care about them."

The jurors understood her answers perfectly—she was no willing partner in sex, but a lonely figure who had come to accept abuse. On March 16, 1993, after eight days of deliberation, came a verdict. Chris Archer and the Scherzers were all guilty of the most serious counts of rape. Grober was not guilty of rape, but guilty of conspiracy.

Justice was neither harsh nor swift. Not until after a four-year-long appeals process did the rapists begin to serve their sentences. Grober escaped with probation and no prison; the others received twenty-two months behind bars. Their time was served in a minimum-security youth facility.

Judge Benjamin Cohen reasoned that as the offspring of successful, middle-class families, the convicts were "not without redeeming values."

Back at home, the victim's father asked himself about the decision to press rape charges: "Was it worth it?" After all the humiliation his daughter had suffered, it was hard to say yes.

✷ DRIVING WHILE BLACK ✦

THE TURNPIKE TROOPERS

TRUE, HE WAS BREAKING THE LAW. Keshon Moore was driving at sixty miles per hour on the New Jersey Turnpike, putting him over the fifty-five miles-per-hour speed limit—just like every other motorist whooshing past. But speeding was not the offense for which he got pulled over on April 23, 1998, he later claimed. All four men in his rental Dodge Caravan were racial minorities between ages twenty and twenty-three, and this made them guilty of driving while black.

Moore and his friends, fired up by dreams of athletic stardom, were on their way from the Bronx to a basketball clinic at North Carolina Central University. Two of them, Rayshawn Brown and Jermaine Grant, dozed off. Moore and one of his back seat passengers, Danny Reyes, listened to music on the van's radio. A few minutes before 11 P.M., and just north of Exit 7A in Washington Township, the red and blue lights of a State Police cruiser flashed in the driver's rearview mirror. Obediently, he pulled over.

Troopers John Hogan, twenty-eight, and James Kenna, twenty-nine, stepped onto the shoulder, still slick from recent rainfall, and approached the driver's side. It had been a light day for the two square-jawed lawmen from the Trenton suburbs. Like eighty-five percent of the State Police, they were white. Hogan, who loved weightlifting, protein drinks, and rap, was the more aggressive of the two. He dreamed of making "trooper of the year" and knew one way of achieving the honor was to rack up narcotics busts.

"Arresting people became my drug," Hogan later said. "It was something I was good at, and I was getting a lot of praise for it. I obviously didn't feel I was doing anything wrong."

Moore, fumbling with his gearshift, tried to put it in park but accidentally got stuck in reverse. Then he made the mistake of asking Reyes to switch places with him. Moore had a bad driving record and could not afford another violation.

As Moore tried to jump into the back seat, his foot hit the accelerator. The van lurched backward, hitting Hogan on the leg. On the other side of the vehicle, Kenna shattered the back seat window with his baton, pointed his revolver at Reyes, and fired. From a crouch, Hogan blazed away with his gun.

Slowly, the van continued rolling back, bumping the parked police cruiser. It kept going across two lanes of Turnpike traffic, shot after shot thumping into its rear. Finally it came to rest at the edge of the median.

Lawyer Gerald Arsenault (left) represents Turnpike Troopers James Kenna (standing, center) and John Hogan (seated) at their 2002 plea agreement. Each paid a $280 fine for the shooting that turned a national spotlight on racial profiling. (*The Trentonian* / Gregg Slaboda)

Eleven bullets were fired, and every one of them hit flesh. Three of the four passengers were wounded. Reyes got it the worst; three shots hit him, one missing his spine by an inch and remaining in his stomach for life. The troopers handcuffed the bleeding men and pushed them face-first into a ditch before ambulances could arrive. Another trooper told a reporter: "The bad guys got it this time."

But a search of the vehicle yielded no weapons, no drugs—only basket-ball clothes, a term paper about John Steinbeck, and a Bible. Hogan and Kenna gave noncredible accounts of the shooting. They claimed the van came roaring backward at them at a high speed, its tires squealing. However, a re-enactment of the shooting showed that the van moved at no faster than four miles per hour.

Soon, civil rights activists—led by the wounded men's lawyer, super-star Johnnie Cochran—came forward to accuse the troopers of reckless overreaction. What was more, the activists said, the victims had been pulled over simply for being black. The officers had, in the jargon of law enforcement, "profiled" the motorists as drug dealers based on race.

Within a few weeks, racial profiling was a national issue. Governor Christie Whitman's administration had for years denied that police discriminated when they chose how to make highway stops. But the unit to which Hogan and Kenna belonged pulled over black motorists in disproportionate numbers. As investigators pored over the records of their traffic stops, they found a pattern: the troopers were faking reports, saying they'd pulled over white drivers when they were really going after blacks.

In 1999 came the indictments of Hogan and Kenna on charges of attempted murder, assault, and falsifying reports. The investigation forced Whitman to concede for the first time that New Jersey troopers did in fact engage in racial profiling. The State Police accepted a court-appointed monitor to ensure racial fairness.

The biggest crisis of Whitman's administration got worse in the next year. First, State Police Superintendent Carl Williams gave a newspaper interview in which he discussed which minorities were most likely to deal in which drugs. The interview cost him his job. Then an old photo of the governor surfaced. She had gone on a ride-along with some troopers in Camden, and was invited to frisk a black teenager. The picture of Whitman grinning as she patted down the youth hit front pages all over New Jersey.

On January 14, 2002, John Hogan and James Kenna pleaded guilty to official misconduct. They were spared jail time and probation; the only penalty they suffered was to quit the State Police and pay a $280 fine each. Prosecutors agreed with the lenient sentence, saying that the troopers had been following the biased policy of their superiors. The shooting was committed out of genuine fear.

"I've been thinking about you ever since this happened," Kenna said in comments directed at the victims, who were not at the Trenton courthouse. "I'm sorry."

The four young men settled their personal injury suit against New Jersey for $12.9 million. But due to trauma and injuries, they said they'd never be able to do what they loved most—play basketball. Grant, one of the victims, had questions for the governor: "Why couldn't she acknowledge us . . . not as a political leader, but as a parent? Why didn't she come forward about what happened, and that racial profiling did exist all these years and was ignored?"

✺ ROUGH PLAY ✺

JAYSON WILLIAMS, BASKETBALL STAR, HOMICIDE DEFENDANT
1968–

WITHIN THE WIRY, six-foot-ten body born to play basketball, there were two Jayson Williamses. The one adored by fans of the New Jersey Nets in the late 1990s was an aggressive rebounder on the court and a philanthropist off it. He gave millions of dollars to charity, paid unannounced visits to children's hospitals, and lavished expensive gifts on friends. During a rough childhood spent in the projects of New York's Lower East Side, Williams had lost a sister to AIDS, and it seemed to deeply affect him. His coach at St. John's University, Lou Carnesecca, once said, "He has a heart as big as the Lincoln Tunnel."

But there was another Jayson Williams, too. With a few drinks in him, his good-natured jesting became bellicose cursing. He loved guns and could become reckless with them. Once he was charged with shooting out the tires of a security vehicle outside the Nets' Continental Arena. Another time, he allegedly pointed to his pet Rottweiler and bet that a teammate couldn't drag it out of the house. When the friend won the bet, Williams took out a shotgun and blew the dog's head off.

Through a modestly successful career—he made the NBA's All-Star team once, in 1998—the public mostly saw Williams's sunny side. Even when a broken leg ended his playing career the following year, it was no hard-luck story, for he remained locked into an $86 million contract. After retirement, he got work as a network analyst whose smile and easy-going nature reached a broad audience. Then came February 13, 2002, when the image of a kind and warm-hearted Jayson Williams was forever blown away.

Williams hired a limousine service that night to take him and some friends from his mansion in Alexandria Township, New Jersey, to a Harlem Globetrotters game in Pennsylvania. The players were invited to dine out afterward. It was a mix of black and white men, and the biracial Williams wanted them all to have a grand time. He even welcomed the limo driver, Costas "Gus" Christofi, to their table.

New Jersey Nets star Jayson Williams clowns around in 1999, his last season in the NBA. Three years later he accidentally shot and killed his chauffeur. (*New York Post* / Nury Hernandez)

Christofi, fifty-five, was a dedicated sports fan and starstruck in the presence of Williams. As chardonnay, cognac, and sambuca flowed, Williams grew boisterous. Apropos of nothing, he shouted "Get your shine box!" at Christofi, quoting a gangster's insult from the movie *Goodfellas.* The bill for the party of nine was $1,613.55. Williams paid.

Afterward, the thirty-three-year-old Williams led his entourage back home for a grand tour of his forty-room house. The guests were driven past his horse stables, petting zoo, and skeet-shooting range. The immense estate was named Who Knew?, because who knew he would attain such wealth?

Christofi and two of the Globetrotters were upstairs in one of the eight bedroom suites at about 2:40 A.M. when Williams opened his gun cabinet to show it off. Williams's friend Kent Culuko, a one-time European basketball pro, saw him hold a cracked-open shotgun, look down at it, and say: "Motherfucker." The barrels were pointed at Christofi, who rolled his eyes in dismay. Then Williams snapped the twelve-gauge up, closing the weapon.

Boom! A dozen pellets pierced Christofi's chest. He staggered backward, put his hand on a table, and fell to the ground. As the driver lay bleeding to death, Williams went down, too—collapsing on his knees, bellowing: "Oh, my God! Oh, my God! My life is over!"

If toying with the shotgun was reckless, what Williams did next was brainless. He used a towel to wipe his fingerprints off the shotgun. Then he took off his clothes, jumped into his indoor swimming pool to wash away the bloody evidence, and changed into a new suit. His friend Culuko asked everyone in the house to lie about what they had seen and heard, and to report Christofi's death as a suicide. "Just stick to the story," Williams said.

Of course, the cover-up was a failure. State troopers who examined the scene quickly determined Christofi could not have shot himself, whether on purpose or by accident. The victim's three-inch-wide wound indicated that the barrels were held two feet away from him.

It was not an intentional killing. But Hunterdon County Prosecutor Steven Lember believed Williams had committed the most serious homicide short of murder—aggravated manslaughter, punishable by up to thirty years in prison. To prove this crime, the state had to show Williams acted with "extreme indifference to human life."

This was the prosecution's argument: Williams was drunk. He was cursing, and recklessly waving a loaded gun. He had been taunting Christofi with the "shine box" comment earlier in the night. One of the Globetrotters—Williams's old Nets teammate Benoit Benjamin—came forward with the most damning testimony. Benjamin claimed he saw Williams putting his finger on the trigger before the gun went off. He also testified that Williams repeatedly cursed at Christofi in the minutes before the man's death.

But even before the trial began in January 2004, Williams's team of defense lawyers had some useful strategic cards to play. They moved the venue from nearly all-white Hunterdon to Somerset County, which enabled them to get a racially diverse jury pool. Blood-alcohol tests showing that Williams was drunk after the shooting were thrown out.

Perhaps most crucially, the defense lawyers were able to damage Benjamin's credibility by showing he resented Williams for not helping him get a job. There was also room to doubt if Williams put his finger on the trigger. Perhaps the shotgun's firing mechanism was defective and went off from the force of Williams's snapping the weapon shut.

On April 30, the jury reached a mixed verdict. Williams was guilty of four counts of covering up the crime. On the charge of aggravated manslaughter, he was not guilty. And on a less serious charge of simple manslaughter, the jury split eight to four for acquittal, resulting in a mistrial.

Even though the prosecution vowed to retry the case, chances were slim that the star would serve significant prison time. Without testifying in his own defense, the good Jayson Williams, not the bad, had shown up for the trial. "He didn't have the look of a cold-blooded killer," said one female juror. "I didn't see it in his eyes."

⇒ HOUSE OF HORRORS ⇐

THE STARVING CHILDREN OF
RAYMOND AND VANESSA JACKSON

"I'M HUNGRY," the small fellow whispered to the neighbor who found him rooting around in garbage cans at 2:30 in the morning. As the youth spoke, the bones in his face could be seen moving behind shriveled, gray skin. He stood four feet tall and weighed forty-five pounds. When the Good Samaritan handed him a package of Tastykakes, he couldn't muster the strength to open the plastic wrap.

The Collingswood, New Jersey, police officers who answered the neighbor's call on October 10, 2003, were visibly shaken. How old are you? they asked the kid, thinking he'd say seven at most. "Nineteen," he told them.

No one could believe it. But everything the starving young man, Bruce Jackson, said was true. And there was more. In his three-story home—two houses from where he'd been scavenging for food—lived three other boys whose skeletal bodies made them look half their ages. All, like Bruce, were foster children who had been legally adopted. They were Keith, fourteen; Tyrone, ten; and Michael, nine. None weighed more than forty pounds. Each stood at least a foot under the normal height for his age. Some had rotting teeth and lice.

Raymond and Vanessa Jackson with their well-fed biological children and adopted daughters—and malnourished adopted boys (front row, from left) Tyrone, Keith, and Michael. Adopted son Bruce, to the right of Vanessa, was nineteen and weighed less than fifty pounds when he was rescued from the home.

Meals consisted of pancake batter, breakfast cereal, and occasional servings of peanut butter and jelly. An alarm system on the refrigerator prevented the boys from eating much else. Bruce surreptitiously munched on kitty litter and wallboard, and there were tooth marks on the window-sills where he gnawed into the wood.

The agony these boys had suffered seemed all the more baffling when it turned out their parents were regarded as community role models. Raymond and Vanessa Jackson attended an evangelical church and volunteered for homeless charities. The husband, fifty, was a financial planner; the wife, forty-eight, was a stay-at-home mother. They had five biological children, boys and girls, who had all turned out well and were never abused.

The Jacksons' very willingness to become foster parents was taken as evidence of their generous nature. Two adopted girls were well fed and healthy; a third girl, a foster child awaiting adoption, was also in good shape.

As for the boys—all home-schooled and rarely seen by outsiders except at church functions—the parents explained to neighbors that they had stunted growth because of being crack babies or victims of fetal alcohol syndrome. The adopted boys did in fact come from abusive inner-city homes and were developmentally slow, but none had a medical condition that would prevent him from growing or gaining weight.

Within two weeks of the shocking discovery of Bruce Jackson, all the adopted children were removed from the house. Raymond and Vanessa were both charged with aggravated assault and child endangerment. The Camden County prosecutor, Vincent Sarubbi, presented the motive for their abuse as greed: they received $28,000 a year in government subsidies for being adoptive parents.

But was it that simple? The girls had been adopted, too, and not abused. Perhaps, experts said, the parents saw boys as more challenging, and used food as a tool to control their behavior. "They didn't do it on purpose," adopted girl Keziah later said of her parents. "I guess they thought they must have been doing the right thing. I don't think she was trying to kill them."

The state of New Jersey had failed these kids, too. An overworked, inexperienced caseworker visited the Jackson household regularly, but failed to notice the children's shriveled faces or the fact that none had seen a doctor in seven years. The state's child welfare agency, the Division of Youth and Family Services, tried to quell the furor by suspending eight employees and setting up a computerized tracking system for all foster children.

As this dysfunctional family became a national story, the Jacksons put up a spirited defense. Friends said their children had eating disorders and were never deliberately starved. Their fault was not deliberate neglect so much as being overwhelmed by parenting so many children in an overcrowded house while falling behind in rent. Bruce had a tendency to binge and purge, the parents said, and this explained why they had put an alarm on the refrigerator. "I believe it's a responsibility to mentor some kids," Raymond Jackson insisted to a reporter a year after his arrest. "And then all of a sudden, for the state to say that I would do harm to some kids?"

Raymond Jackson never got a chance to plead his case in a court of law. Two weeks after his interview saw print, he died of a stroke. Vanessa Jackson accepted a bargain with prosecutors by pleading guilty to a single count of child endangerment. Her sentence was seven years in prison—two years with good behavior.

"I never saw her do the bad or evil things that people are saying," Vanessa's biological daughter Vernee said at the sentencing hearing on February 10, 2006. But the last word went to the adopted boys. All were given the chance to speak at the sentencing, more than two years after being removed from their loveless prison. Each youth had made significant weight gains, even though they had suffered permanent physical damage.

Bruce Jackson, at age 21, had grown fifteen inches and gained ninety-five pounds. He lived in a group home and spoke like a child. But however halting his voice, he made clear that the Jacksons' attempt at media spin—that he starved himself—was cruelly false. "You didn't feed me, or my brothers," he told the mother that he referred to as "Ms. Jackson."

"You would make us eat pancake batter, dried-up grits and oatmeal, un-cooked Cream of Wheat, and raw potatoes instead of cooked food. . . .

"You yelled at us, you cursed at us, hit us with brooms, rulers, sticks, shoes and belt buckles. I still have the marks to prove it. . . . You were mean to me my whole life, so you deserve the same thing you did to me for the rest of your life. You took my childhood."

✳ BIBLIOGRAPHY ✦

SOURCES AND FURTHER READING

GENERAL SOURCES ON NEW JERSEY AND CRIME HISTORY

Baden, Michael M., and Judith A. Hennessee. *Unnatural Death: Confessions of a Medical Examiner.* New York: Ivy, 1992.

Barnes, Ed, and Alison McFarlane. "Mafia House Tour." *New Jersey Monthly,* April 1980, 58–63.

Beck, Henry Charlton. *The Roads of Home: Life and Legends of New Jersey.* New Brunswick, N.J.: Rutgers Univ. Press, 1956.

Broderick, James F. *Paging New Jersey: A Literary Guide to the Garden State.* New Brunswick, N.J.: Rutgers Univ. Press, 2003.

Camisa, Harry, and Jim Franklin. *Inside Out: Fifty Years Behind the Walls of New Jersey's Trenton State Prison.* Windsor, N.J.: Windsor Press, 2003.

Capeci, Jerry. *The Complete Idiot's Guide to the Mafia.* New York: Alpha, 2004.

————. *Gang Land.* New York: Alpha 2003.

Coakley, Leo J. *Jersey Troopers: A Fifty-Year History of the New Jersey State Police.* New Brunswick, N.J.: Rutgers Univ. Press, 1971.

Fleming, Thomas J. *New Jersey: A History.* New York: Norton, 1984.

Fried, Albert. *The Rise and Fall of the Jewish Gangster in America.* New York: Columbia Univ. Press, 1994.

Garraty, John A., and Mark C. Carnes, gen. eds. *American National Biography.* 24 vols. New York: Oxford Univ. Press, 1999.

Hearn, Daniel Allen. *Legal Executions in New Jersey: A Comprehensive Registry, 1691–1963.* Jefferson, N.C.: McFarland, 2005.

Hoffman, Paul. *Tiger in the Court.* Chicago: Playboy Press, 1973.

Karcher, Alan J. *New Jersey's Multiple Municipal Madness.* New Brunswick, N.J.: Rutgers Univ. Press, 1999.

Knappman, Edward W., ed. *American Trials of the 20th Century.* Detroit: New England Publishing Associates, 1995.

Kutler, Stanley I., ed. in chief. *Dictionary of American History.* New York: Scribner's, 2003.

Lane, Brian, and Wilfred Gregg. *The Encyclopedia of Mass Murder.* New York: Carroll and Graf, 2004.

Lavery, David, ed. *Investigating the Sopranos.* New York: Columbia Univ. Press, 2002.

Lurie, Maxine N., and Marc Mappen. *Encyclopedia of New Jersey.* New Brunswick, N.J.: Rutgers Univ. Press, 2004.

Maeder, Jay, ed. *Big Town Big Time.* New York: Daily News Books, 1999.

Mappen, Marc. *Jerseyana: The Underside of New Jersey History.* New Brunswick, N.J.: Rutgers Univ. Press, 1992.

Moran, Mark, and Mark Sceurman. *Weird N.J.: Your Travel Guide to New Jersey's Local Legends and Best Kept Secrets.* New York: Sterling, 2003.

————. *Weird N.J., Vol. 2.* New York: Sterling, 2006.

Nash, Jay Robert. *Bloodletters and Badmen: A Narrative Encyclopedia of American Criminals from the Pilgrims to the Present.* New York: M. Evans and Co., 1995.

New Jersey Commission of Investigation. *The Changing Face of Organized Crime in New Jersey.* Trenton: New Jersey Commission of Investigation, 2004.

New Jersey Historical Society. *Murder Did Pay: 19th Century New Jersey Murders.* Newark: New Jersey Historical Society, 1982.

Newton, Michael. *The Encyclopedia of Serial Killers.* New York: Facts on File, 2000.

Raab, Selwyn. *Five Families: The Rise, Decline, and Resurgence of America's Most Powerful Mafia Empires.* New York: Thomas Dunne, 2005.

Schwartzman, Paul, and Rob Polner. *New York Notorious.* New York: Crown, 1992.

Sifakis, Carl. *Encyclopedia of American Crime.* New York: Facts on File, 1982.

————. *The Mafia Encyclopedia.* New York: Facts on File, 2005.

Stapinski, Helene. *Five-Finger Discount: A Crooked Family History.* New York: Random House, 2001.

Stellhorn, Paul A., and Michael J. Birkner. *The Governors of New Jersey, 1664–1974: Biographical Essays.* Trenton: New Jersey Historical Commission, 1982.

Tomlinson, Gerald. *Murdered in Jersey.* New Brunswick, N.J.: Rutgers Univ. Press, 1997.

CHAPTER 1

Original Sin: Willem Kieft

Burrows, Edwin G., and Mike Wallace. *Gotham: A History of New York City to 1898.* New York: Oxford Univ. Press, 1999.

Shorto, Russell. *The Island at the Center of the World: The Epic Story of Dutch Manhattan and the Forgotten Colony That Shaped America.* New York: Doubleday, 2004.

Van der Zee, Henri A., and Barbara Van der Zee. *A Sweet and Alien Land: The Story of Dutch New York.* New York: Viking, 1978.

Blood Will Out: Thomas Lutherland

Blood Will Out, or an Example of Justice in the Tryal, Condemnation, Confession and Execution of Thomas Lutherland. Philadelphia: Will. Bradford, 1692.

Hearn. *Legal Executions.*

Dead Man's Chest: William Kidd

Bonner, William. *Pirate Laureate: Life and Legends of Captain Kidd.* New Brunswick, N.J.: Rutgers Univ. Press, 1947.

Broderick. *Paging New Jersey.*

Garraty and Carnes, gen. eds. *American National Biography.*

Hinrichs, Dunbar. *The Fateful Voyage of Captain Kidd.* New York: Bookman Associates, 1955.

Ritchie, Robert C. *Captain Kidd and the War against the Pirates.* Cambridge: Harvard Univ. Press, 1986.

Zacks, Richard. *The Pirate Hunter.* New York: Theia, 2002.

God Save the Queen: Lord Cornbury

Bonomi, Patricia. *The Lord Cornbury Scandal: The Politics of Reputation in British America.* Chapel Hill: Univ. of North Carolina Press, 1998.

deKaye, Ormonde, Jr. "His Most Detestable High Mightiness." *American Heritage,* April 1976, 60–61, 89.

Garraty and Carnes, gen. eds. *American National Biography.*

Mappen. *Jerseyana.*

New York Times, 1990.

On the Warpath: Tom Quick

Beck. *The Roads of Home.*

Crumb, Frederick W. *Tom Quick: Early American.* Narrowsburg, N.Y.: Delaware Valley Press, 1936.

Quinlan, James Eldridge. *Tom Quick the Indian Slayer.* Monticello, N.Y.: De Voe and Quinlan, 1851.

McGraw, Seamus. "Death, Be Quick." Crimelibrary.com.

Randall, Willard Sterne. *Forgotten Americans: Footnote Figures Who Changed American History.* Boston: Addison-Wesley, 1998.

Bad Seed: William Franklin

Garraty and Carnes, gen. eds. *American National Biography*.

Mappen. *Jerseyana*.

Randall, Willard Sterne. *A Little Revenge: Benjamin Franklin and His Son*. Boston: Little, Brown, 1984

Skemp, Sheila L. *William Franklin: Son of a Patriot, Servant of a King*. New York: Oxford, 1990.

Stellhorn and Birkner. *The Governors of New Jersey*.

Loyal to No One: Joseph Mulliner

Beck, Henry Charlton. "Legend of Revolutionary War Bandit Revived in South Jersey." *Sunday Star-Ledger*, February 24, 1957.

Hearn. *Legal Executions*.

Sifakis. *Encyclopedia of American Crime*.

New Jersey Gazette, 1781.

Big Shot: Aaron Burr

Burr, Samuel Engle. *The Burr-Hamilton Duel and Related Matters*. San Antonio: Naylor, 1971.

Fleming, Thomas. *Duel: Alexander Hamilton, Aaron Burr, and the Future of America*. New York: Basic Books, 1999.

Parton, James. *The Life and Times of Aaron Burr*. New York: Mason Brothers, 1858.

Rogow, Arnold. *A Fatal Friendship: Alexander Hamilton and Aaron Burr*. New York: Hill and Wang, 1998.

Syrett, Harold Coffin, and Jean G. Cooke. *Interview at Weehawken: The Burr-Hamilton Duel as Told in the Original Documents*. Middletown, Conn.: Wesleyan Univ. Press, 1960.

Vail, Philip. *The Great American Rascal: The Turbulent Life of Aaron Burr*. New York: Hawthorne Books, 1973.

Webb, James R. "The Fateful Encounter." *American Heritage*, August 1975, 45–52, 92–93.

New York Times, 2004.

In the Rough: Baltus Roll

Parks, Brad. "Years before the Golf Course, There Was Murder in the Countryside." *Star-Ledger*, August 7, 2005.

"Trial of Peter B. Davis for the Murder of Baltus Roll." Newark: Daily Journal Printing, 1883.

Hell for Leather: Antoine LeBlanc

Hearn, *Legal Executions*.

Moran and Sceurman. *Weird N.J.*

Report of the Trial and Conviction of Antoine LeBlanc for the Murder of the Sayre Family, at Morristown, N.J. New York: Lewis Nichols, 1833. Reprinted in New Jersey Historical Society, *Murder Did Pay.*

Sifakis. *The Encyclopedia of American Crime.*

Fool's Gold: Rodman Price

Clayton, W. Woodward. *History of Bergen and Passaic Counties, New Jersey.* Philadelphia: Everts and Peck, 1882.

Dewey, Squire P. *Rodman M. Price of New Jersey in Search of the Golden Fleece: History of a Million-Dollar Claim.* San Francisco: Self-published, 1880.

Gillette, William. *Jersey Blue: Civil War Politics in New Jersey, 1854–1865.* New Brunswick, N.J.: Rutgers Univ. Press, 1995.

Stellhorn and Birkner. *The Governors of New Jersey.*

New York Times, 1893–1894.

Newark Evening News, 1893–1894.

Domestic Disturbance: Bridget Dergan

Hearn. *Legal Executions.*

The Life and Confession of Bridget Dergan. Philadelphia: Barclay, 1867. Reprinted in New Jersey Historical Society, *Murder Did Pay.*

Death Alley: The Trunk Mystery

The Great "Trunk Mystery" of New York City; Murder of the Beautiful Miss Alice A. Bowlsby, of Paterson, N.J. Philadelphia: Barclay, 1872. Reprinted in New Jersey Historical Society, *Murder Did Pay.*

Lutzy, Rebecca. "The Evil of the Age." In *Providence: An Anthology of Creative Nonfiction,* spring 2002, at www.stg.brown.edu/projects/CreativeNonfiction/2001-2002/lutzy.html.

New York Times, 1871–1873.

Woodhill and Claflin's Weekly, 1871.

Newark Daily Advertiser, 1871.

Paterson Daily Monitor, 1871.

Crazy Love: Charles K. Landis

Landis, Charles K. *The Founder's Own Story of the Founding of Vineland, New Jersey.* Vineland, N.J.: Vineland Historical and Antiquarian Society, 1903.

Philadelphia Inquirer, 1875–1876.

Atlanta Constitution, 1886.

New York Times, 1900.

Washington Post, 1904.
Daily Journal (of Vineland), 1999.

Mob Rule: Lynching

Barrow, Janice Hittinger. "Lynching in the Mid-Atlantic, 1882–1940." *American Nineteenth Century History* 6, no. 3 (September 2005): 241–271.

Pike, Helen C., and Glenn D. Vogel. *Eatontown and Fort Monmouth: Images of America*. Dover, N.H.: Arcadia, 1995.

New York Times, 1886–1887.

Ripping Yarn: Jack the Ripper

Evans, Stewart P., and Keith Skinner. *The Ultimate Jack the Ripper Companion*. New York: Carroll and Graf, 2000.

Gordon, R. Michael. *The American Murders of Jack the Ripper*. Westport, Conn.: Prager, 2003.

Pearson, Edmund Lester. *More Studies in Murder*. New York: H. Smith and R. Haas, 1936.

Artful Dodger: Emanuel Ninger

Bloom, Murray Teigh. "The Money Maker." *American Heritage*, August/September 1984, 98–101.

————. *Money of Their Own: The Great Counterfeiters*. New York: Scribner's, 1957.

New York Times, 1896.

New York Herald, 1896.

CHAPTER 2

Sea of Sorrow: Ocey Snead

Tomlinson, Gerald. *Seven Jersey Murders*. Philadelphia: Xlibris, 2003.

Zierold, Norman. *Three Sisters in Black*. Boston: Little, Brown, 1968.

New York Times, 1909–1911, 1913.

New York World, 1909–1911.

Newark Evening News, 1909–1911.

Newark Evening Star, 1909–1911.

Ill Will: Frances Creighton

Hearn, Daniel Allen. *Legal Executions in New York State: A Comprehensive Reference, 1639–1963*. Jefferson, N.C.: McFarland, 1997.

Hoffmann, Richard H., and Jim Bishop. *The Girl in Poison Cottage*. New York: Fawcett, 1953.

Gado, Mark. "An Immoral Woman." Crimelibrary.com.

New York Daily News, 1923.

New York Times, 1923, 1935–1936.

Fallen Idol: George White Rogers

Burton, Hal. *The Morro Castle: Tragedy at Sea*. New York: Viking, 1973.

Gallagher, Thomas. *Fire at Sea: The Mysterious Tragedy of the Morro Castle*. New York: Rinehart, 1959.

Hicks, Brian. *When the Dancing Stopped: The Real Story of the Morro Castle Disaster and Its Deadly Wake*. New York: Free Press, 2006.

Mappen, Marc. "Jerseyana." *New York Times*, August 14, 1994, NJ11.

Thomas, Gordon. *Shipwreck: The Strange Fate of the Morro Castle*. New York: Stern and Day, 1972.

Tomlinson. *Murdered in Jersey.*

New York Times, 1934, 1938, 1953–1954, 1958, 1988.

New York Daily News, 1958.

Asbury Park Press, 1934, 1999.

Jersey Journal, 1953–1954.

With a Vengeance: Howard Unruh

Considine, Bob. "13 Kept Rendezvous." *International News Service* column, September 11, 1949.

Jeffers, H. Paul. *Who Killed Precious? How FBI Special Agents Combine High Technology and Psychology to Identify Violent Criminals*. New York: Pharos, 1991.

Ramsland, Katherine. "Rampage in Camden." Crimelibrary.com.

New York Times, 1949, 1982.

Newark Evening News, 1949.

Camden Courier, 1949.

Philadelphia Inquirer, 1949.

Times (of Trenton), 2003.

Badman: Ernest Ingenito

Nash. *Bloodletters and Badmen.*

New York Daily News, 1950–1951.

New York Post, 1950–1951.

Philadelphia Inquirer, 1950–1951.

New York Times, 1950.

Trentonian, 1993–1994.

Old Wounds: Robert Zarinsky

Gallo, Joseph. "Robert Zarinsky." Crimelibrary.com.
"The Murder of Officer Bernoskie." *60 Minutes II,* CBS, March 27, 2002.
Star-Ledger, 1999, 2001, 2003, 2006.
Newark Evening News, 1962–1963, 1970.
Asbury Park Press, 1999.
New York Post, 1999.
New York Daily News, 1983.
New York Times, 1975, 1999, 2003.

Seeing the Devil: Thomas Trantino

Camisa and Franklin. *Inside Out.*
Stout, Edgar. *Night of the Devil: The Untold Story of Thomas Trantino and the Angel Lounge.*
    Philadelphia: Camino Books, 2003.
Tomlinson. *Murdered in Jersey.*
Trantino, Thomas. *Lock the Lock.* New York: Knopf, 1974.
New York Times, 1963–1964, 1973, 1981, 1996, 2001–2002, 2004.
Bergen Record, 1963–1964, 2001–2002.
New York Post, 2000–2002.

Spellbinding: Carl Coppolino

Baden and Hennessee, *Unnatural Death.*
Bailey, F. Lee., with Harvey Aronson. *The Defense Never Rests.* New York: Stein and Day,
    1971.
Coppolino, Carl. *The Crime That Never Was.* Tampa, Fla.: Justice Press, 1980.
Holmes, Paul. *The Trials of Dr. Coppolino.* New York: New American Library, 1968.
Katz, Leonard. *The Coppolino Murder Trial.* New York: Bee-Line Books, 1967.
MacDonald, John D. *No Deadly Drug.* Garden City, N.Y.: Doubleday, 1968.
New York Times, 1966–1967, 1979.
New York Post, 1966–1967, 1979.
New York Daily News, 1966–1967, 1979.
Pittsburgh Post-Gazette, 2003.

Family Man: John List

Benford, Timothy B., and James P. Johnson. *Righteous Carnage: The List Murders.* New York:
    Scribner's, 1991.
Camisa and Franklin. *Inside Out.*
Ryzuk, Mary. *Thou Shalt Not Kill.* New York: Warner Books, 1990.

Sharkey, Joe. *Death Sentence: The Inside Story of the John List Murders.* New York: Signet, 1990.

New York Times, 1971–1972, 1989–1990, 1996

Star-Ledger, 1989–1990.

Mad World: Joseph Kallinger

Downs, Thomas. *The Door-to-Door Killer.* New York: Dell, 1984.

Ramsland, Katherine. "The Enigmatic Cobbler: Clever or Crazy?" Crimelibrary.com.

Schreiber, Flora Rheta. *The Shoemaker: The Anatomy of a Psychotic.* New York: Simon and Schuster, 1983.

Tomlinson. *Murdered in Jersey.*

New York Times, 1975–1976, 1996.

Bergen Record, 1975–1976, 1996.

Philadelphia Inquirer, 1984, 1996.

Model Prisoner: Richard Reldan

Camisa and Franklin. *Inside Out.*

McNamara, Joseph. "Stop Him Before He Kills Again." *Front Page Detective,* May 1977, 28–33, 64–68.

Zugibe, Frederick, and David L. Carroll. *Dissecting Death: Secrets of a Medical Examiner.* New York: Broadway, 2005.

Star-Ledger, 1975–1977, 1979, 1982–1986.

New York Times, 1963, 1975, 1977–1979, 1993.

New York Post, 1964, 1975, 1977–1979.

New York Daily News, 1963.

Bad Faith: Robert O. Marshall

Marshall, Robert O. *Tunnel Vision: Trial and Error.* New York: Algora, 2002.

McGinniss, Joe. *Blind Faith.* New York: Putnam, 1989.

McGraw, Seamus. "Justice Delayed: The Robert Marshall Story." Crimelibrary.com.

Tomlinson. *Murdered in Jersey.*

Asbury Park Press, 1984–1986, 1989, 2006.

New York Times, 1984–1986, 1989, 2006.

Bergen Record, 2006.

Star-Ledger, 2006.

Locked Box: Arthur and Jackie Seale

McGraw, Seamus. "Envy: The Kidnapping and Murder of Sidney Reso." Crimelibrary. com.

Tomlinson. *Murdered in Jersey.*

New York Times, 1992.
Star-Ledger, 1992.
New York Post, 1992.
New York Daily News, 1992.
Newsday, 1992.
Christian Science Monitor, 2003.

Monster Next Door: Jesse Timmendequas

Mickle. Paul. "Justice for Megan." *Trentonian,* November 28, 1999, 82–83.
Terry, Karen, and B. J. Cling. "Megan's Law: New Protections Against Sex Abuse." In
    Sexualized Violence Against Women and Children: A Psychology and Law Perspective, edited by
    B. J. Cling. New York: Guilford Press, 2004.
New York Times, 1994, 1996–1997.
Trentonian, 1994–1997.
Times (of Trenton), 1997.
Star-Ledger, 1997.

Thou Shalt Not: Fred Neulander

Francis, Eric. *Broken Vows.* New York: St. Martin's, 2002.
Magida, Arthur J. *The Rabbi and the Hit Man: A True Tale of Murder, Passion, and Shattered Faith.*
    New York: HarperCollins, 2003.
Mazo, Gary. *And the Flames Did Not Consume Us: A Rabbi's Journey Through Communal Crisis.*
    Bend, Ore.: Rising Star, 2000.
Courier-Post (Cherry Hill, N.J.), 1994, 1997, 1999–2003.
Philadelphia Inquirer, 1994, 1997, 1999–2003.
New York Times, 2000–2003.

Murder by Design: Andrew Cunanan

Indiana, Gary. *Three Month Fever: The Andrew Cunanan Story.* New York: Cliff Street Books,
    1999.
Orth, Maureen. *Vulgar Favors: Andrew Cunanan, Gianni Versace, and the Largest Failed Manhunt
    in U.S. History.* New York: Delacorte, 1999.
New York Times, 1997.
New York Daily News, 1997.
New York Post, 1997.

Steel Cage Match: Ambrose Harris and Mudman Simon

Marshall, Robert O. *Tunnel Vision: Trial and Error.* New York: Algora, 2002.
Trentonian, 1992–1993, 1998–1999.

Philadelphia Inquirer, 1995, 1997, 1999.
Star-Ledger, 1999–2001.
New York Times, 1999–2001.
Asbury Park Press, 2001.

No Angel: Charles Cullen

Linedecker, Clifford L., and Zach T. Martin. *Death Angel.* New York: Pinnacle, 2005.
Ramsland, Katherine. "Angels of Death: The Male Nurses." Crimelibrary.com.
———. "Charles Cullen: Serial Health Care Killer." Crimelibrary.com.
Star-Ledger, 2003–2006.
New York Times, 2003–2006.
New York Post, 2003.

CHAPTER 3

Thirst for Power: Waxey Gordon

Dewey, Thomas E. *Twenty Against the Underworld.* Garden City, N.Y.: Doubleday, 1974.
Fried. *The Rise and Fall of the Jewish Gangster in America.*
Katcher, Leo. *The Big Bankroll: The Life and Times of Arnold Rothstein.* New York: Harper,
    1959.
Thompson, Craig, and Allen Raymond. *Gang Rule in New York: The Story of a Lawless Era.*
    New York: Dial, 1940.
New York Times, 1914, 1917, 1926, 1931–1933, 1940, 1951–1952.
Newark Evening News, 1952.

Chop House: Dutch Schultz

Cohen, Richard. *Tough Jews: Fathers, Sons, and Gangster Dreams.* New York: Vintage, 1997.
Dewey, Thomas E. *Twenty Against the Underworld.* Garden City, N.Y.: Doubleday, 1974.
Mappen. *Jerseyana.*
May, Allan. "Dutch Schultz: Beer Baron of the Bronx." Crimelibrary.com.
Sann, Paul. *Kill the Dutchman! The Story of Dutch Schultz.* New Rochelle, N.Y.: Arlington
    House, 1971.
Thompson, Craig, and Allen Raymond. *Gang Rule in New York: The Story of a Lawless Era.*
    New York: Dial, 1940.
Turkus, Burton B., and Sid Feder. *Murder Inc.: The Story of "The Syndicate."* New York:
    Farrar, Straus, and Young, 1951.
New York Times, 1935, 1941.
Newark Evening News, 1935.

Last Laugh: Willie Moretti

Bonanno, Joseph, with Sergio Lalli. *A Man of Honor: The Autobiography of Joseph Bonanno.* New York: Simon and Schuster, 1983.

Kelley, Kitty. *His Way: The Unauthorized Biography of Frank Sinatra.* New York: Bantam, 1986.

Maas, Peter. *The Valachi Papers.* New York: G. P. Putnam's Sons, 1968.

Mortimer, Lee. "Frank Sinatra Confidential: Gangsters in the Night Clubs." *American Mercury,* August 1951, 29–36.

Sifakis. *The Mafia Encyclopedia.*

New York Daily News, 1950–1951.

New York Post, 1950–1951.

New York Journal-American, 1950–1951.

New York World-Telegram and Sun, 1950–1951.

New York Herald Tribune, 1950.

New York Times, 1943, 1950–1952.

Life, 1951.

Hasbrouck Heights Observer, 1947.

Herald-News of Paterson, 1950.

Kiss of Death: Vito Genovese

Cook, Fred J. *The Secret Rulers: Criminal Syndicates and How They Control the U.S. Underworld.* New York: Duell, Sloan, and Pearce, 1966.

Feder, Sid, and Joachim Joesten. *The Luciano Story.* New York: D. McKay, 1954.

Frasca, Dom. *King of Crime.* New York: Crown, 1959.

Gosch, Martin A., and Richard Hammer. *The Last Testament of Lucky Luciano.* Boston: Little, Brown, 1975.

Maas, Peter. *The Valachi Papers.* New York: G. P. Putnam's Sons, 1968.

Sifakis. *The Mafia Encyclopedia.*

Asbury Park Press, 1999.

New York Times, 1969.

If Looks Could Kill: Joe Adonis

"Ask Andy." This Week in Gang Land. Ganglandnews.com, December 15, 1997.

Camisa and Franklin, *Inside Out.*

Lacey, Robert. *Little Man: Meyer Lansky and the Gangster Life.* London: Century, 1991.

Sifakis. *The Mafia Encyclopedia.*

Newark Evening News, 1971.

New York Times, 1971.

Clipped: Albert Anastasia

Gosch, Martin A., and Richard Hammer. *The Last Testament of Lucky Luciano.* Boston: Little, Brown, 1975.

Kleinzahler, August. "Diary." *London Review of Books,* September 20, 2001, 35.

Maas, Peter. *The Valachi Papers.* New York: G. P. Putnam's Sons, 1968.

Sifakis. *The Mafia Encyclopedia.*

Turkus, Burton B., and Sid Feder. *Murder Inc.: The Story of "The Syndicate."* New York: Farrar, Straus, and Young, 1951.

New York Daily News, 1957.

New York Post, 1957.

New York Times, 1952, 1957.

Newark Evening News, 1952–1955, 1957.

Bergen Record, 1957.

Silent Partner: Abner Zwillman

Cook, Fred J. "The People v. the Mob; Or, Who Rules New Jersey?" *New York Times Magazine,* February 1, 1970, 9–11, 32–36.

Reid, Ed, and Ovid Demaris. *The Green Felt Jungle.* New York: Trident Press, 1963.

Samuels, David. "Last of the Bally Bingo Kings." *Civilization,* 1998, at www.rwatts.cdyn. com/download/LASTBINGO%20KINGS.TXT.

Sifakis. *The Mafia Encyclopedia.*

Stuart, Mark A. *Gangster #2: Longy Zwillman, the Man Who Invented Organized Crime.* Secaucus, N.J.: Lyle Stuart, 1985.

Velie, Lester. "The Man to See in New Jersey." *Collier's,* August 25, 1951, 16–17, 70–73; September 1, 1951, 28–29, 48–51.

New York Times, 1939, 1951, 1959.

Newark Evening News, 1959.

Burying Their Differences: Tony Pro Provenzano

Brandt, Charles. *"I Heard You Paint Houses": Frank "The Irishman" Sheeran and the Inside Story of the Mafia, the Teamsters, and the Last Ride of Jimmy Hoffa.* Hanover, N.H.: Steerforth Press, 2004.

Moldea, Dan E. *The Hoffa Wars: Teamsters, Rebels, Politicians, and the Mob.* New York: Paddington Press, 1978.

Sifakis. *The Mafia Encyclopedia.*

Sloane, Arthur A. *Hoffa.* Cambridge, Mass.: MIT Press, 1991.

New York Herald Tribune, 1963, 1965.

Bergen Record, 1966, 1975.

New York Daily News, 1961–1963, 1988.

New York Times, 1963, 1966, 1975, 1983, 1988.

New York Post, 1961–1963, 1966, 1975, 1988.

Secret Garden: Richie the Boot Boiardo

Cook, Fred J. "The People v. the Mob; Or, Who Rules New Jersey?" *New York Times Magazine*, February 1, 1970, 9–11, 32–36.

Demaris, Ovid. *The Boardwalk Jungle*. New York: Bantam, 1986.

Hoffman. *Tiger in the Court*.

Immerso, Michael. *Newark's Little Italy: The Vanished First Ward*. New Brunswick, N.J.: Rutgers Univ. Press and Newark Public Library, 1997.

Zeiger, Henry A. *The Jersey Mob*. New York: Signet, 1975.

Life, 1967.

New York Post, 1963, 1970, 1979–1980.

New York Daily News, 1969–1971.

New York Times, 1971, 1979–1980.

Thanks a Million: Newsboy Moriarty

English, T. J. *Paddy Whacked: The Untold Story of the Irish-American Gangster*. New York: Regan Books, 2005.

Jersey Journal, 1962, 1969, 1979.

Star-Ledger, 1979.

New York Times, 1962, 1979.

New York Post, 1962.

In His Own Words: Sam DeCavalcante

Federal Bureau of Investigation. *The FBI Transcripts on Exhibit in U.S.A. vs. DeCavalcante*. 13 vols. New York: Lemma Publishing, 1970.

Hoffman. *Tiger in the Court*.

Sifakis. *The Mafia Encyclopedia*.

Talese, Gay. *Honor Thy Father*. New York: World, 1971.

Zeiger, Henry A. *Sam the Plumber*. Signet Books, 1970.

New York Times, 1969–1971, 1973, 1997.

New York Post, 1969–1972.

New York Daily News, 1969.

Newsday, 1969.

Trentonian, 1997, 1998.

El Padrino: Jose Miguel Battle

New Jersey Commission of Investigation. *The Changing Face of Organized Crime in New Jersey.*

President's Commission on Organized Crime. *Organized Crime and Gambling: Record of Hearing VII: June 24–26, 1985.* Washington, D.C.: President's Commission on Organized Crime, 1985.

Star-Ledger, 1997, 1999.

Bergen Record, 2006.

Jersey Journal, 1997, 2006.

Miami Herald, 1998, 2004–2006.

Fort Lauderdale (Fla.) Sun Sentinel, 1998.

Cowboy Style: Nicodemo Scarfo

Anastasia, George. *Blood and Honor: Inside the Scarfo Mob—The Mafia's Most Violent Family.* New York: Morrow, 1991.

Demaris, Ovid. *The Boardwalk Jungle.* New York: Bantam, 1986.

New Jersey Commission of Investigation. *Report on the Incursion by Organized Crime into Certain Legitimate Businesses in Atlantic City.* Trenton: New Jersey Commission of Investigation, 1977.

Salerno, Joseph, and Stephen J. Rivele. *The Plumber: The True Story of How One Good Man Helped Destroy the Entire Philadelphia Mafia.* New York: Knightsbridge, 1990.

Philadelphia Inquirer, 1986–1989.

New York Times, 1973, 1980, 1982, 1984, 1986–1989, 1991, 1994.

Who's Sorry Now?: George Franconero

Adler, William M. *Mollie's Job: A Story of Life and Work on the Global Assembly Line.* New York: Scribner's, 2000.

Demaris, Ovid. *The Boardwalk Jungle.* New York: Bantam, 1986.

Francis, Connie. *Who's Sorry Now?* New York: St. Martin's, 1984.

Star-Ledger, 1977–1981, 1996.

Philadelphia Inquirer, 1977

New York Daily News, 1981.

New York Post, 1981.

New York Times, 1981.

Cold Blooded: Richard Kuklinski

Baden and Hennessee. *Unnatural Death.*

Bruno, Anthony. *The Iceman: The True Story of a Cold-Blooded Killer.* New York: Delacorte, 1993.

Carlo, Philip. *The Ice Man: Confessions of a Mafia Contract Killer.* New York: St. Martin's, 2006.

Ramsland, Katherine. "Richard Kuklinski: The Iceman." Crimelibrary.com.

Code of Silence: Anthony Accetturo

Bruno, Anthony. "The Lucchese Family." Crimelibrary.com.

———. "What're You Gonna Do Now, Tough Guy?" Crimelibrary.com.

Capeci. *The Complete Idiot's Guide to the Mafia.*

Raab. *Five Families.*

Rudolph, Robert. *The Boys from New Jersey: How the Mob Beat the Feds.* New Brunswick, N.J.: Rutgers Univ. Press, 1995.

New York Times, 1985–1988, 1991, 1993–1994.

Star-Ledger, 1985–1988.

Violent Episode: Vincent Palermo

Capeci, Jerry. "Respect—Real or Imagined." This Week in Gang Land. Ganglandnews.com, January 6, 2000.

———. "An Unspeakable Crime." This Week in Gang Land. Ganglandnews.com, June 14, 2001.

———. "New Jersey Family Is Second Class." This Week in Gang Land. Ganglandnews.com, June 12, 2003.

Smith, Greg B. *Made Men: The True Rise-and-Fall Story of a New Jersey Mob Family.* New York: Berkley, 2003.

New York Post, 2003.

New York Daily News, 2003.

Star-Ledger, 2002–2003.

CHAPTER 4

Yes, Boss: Frank Hague

Connors, Richard J. *A Cycle of Power: The Career of Jersey City Mayor Frank Hague.* Metuchen, N.J.: Scarecrow Press, 1971.

Fleming, Thomas. "I Am the Law." *American Heritage,* June 1969, 32–48.

Garraty and Carnes, gen. eds. *American National Biography.*

Leinwand, Gerald. *Mackerels in the Moonlight: Four Corrupt American Mayors.* Jefferson, N.C.: McFarland, 2004

McKean, Dayton David. *The Boss: The Hague Machine in Action.* Boston: Houghton Mifflin, 1940.

Smith, Thomas F. X. *The Powerticians.* Secaucus, N.J.: Lyle Stewart, 1982.

New York Post, 1938, 1940.
New York Times, 1938, 1956.

Living Large: Nucky Johnson

Alexander, Jack. "Boss on the Spot: The Case History of Nucky Johnson." *Saturday Evening Post*, August 26, 1939, 5–7, 49–52.
D'Amato, Grace Anselmo. *Chance of a Lifetime: Nucky Johnson, Skinny D'Amato, and How Atlantic City Became the Naughty Queen of Resorts.* Harvey Cedars, N.J.: Down the Shore Publishing, 2001.
Gosch, Martin A., and Richard Hammer. *The Last Testament of Lucky Luciano.* Boston: Little, Brown, 1975.
Irey, Elmer R., as told to William J. Slocum. *The Tax Dodgers: The Inside Story of the T-Men's War with America's Political and Underworld Hoodlums.* New York: Greenberg, 1948.
Mappen, Marc. "Jerseyana." *New York Times*, May 9, 1993, NJ13.
Van Meter, Jonathan. *The Last Good Time: Skinny D'Amato, the Notorious 500 Club, and the Rise and Fall of Atlantic City.* New York: Crown, 2003.
New York Post, 1939, 1941, 1946.
New York Times, 1941, 1968.
New York Evening Journal, 1931.
AP, 1959.
Philadelphia Inquirer, 1968.

Unearthly Glow: U.S. Radium

Clark, Claudia. *Radium Girls: Women and Industrial Health Reform, 1910–1935.* Chapel Hill: Univ. of North Carolina Press, 1997.
Kovarik, William. "The Radium Girls." In *Mass Media and Environmental Conflict: America's Green Crusades*, by Mark Neuzil and William Kovarik. Thousand Oaks, Calif.: Sage Publications, 1996.
Mappen, *Jerseyana.*
New York World, 1928.
New York Times, 1925, 1928–1929, 1933, 1949.

Without a Clue: Ellis Parker

Fisher, Jim. *The Lindbergh Case.* New Brunswick, N.J.: Rutgers Univ. Press, 1987.
Mappen, Marc. "Jerseyana." *New York Times*, March 14, 1993, NJ13.
Pratt, Fletcher. *The Cunning Mulatto and Other Cases of Ellis Parker, American Detective.* New York: H. Smith and R. Haas, 1935.
Reisinger, John. *Master Detective: The Life and Crimes of Ellis Parker, America's Sherlock Holmes.* New York: Citadel Press, 2006.

Wendel, Paul H. *The Lindbergh-Hauptmann Aftermath.* Brooklyn: Loft Publishing, 1940.
New York Times, 1936–1937, 1940.
New York Herald Tribune, 1940.

Child of Destiny: Harold Hoffman

Angelo, Lou. *I Socked Hoffman: The Why and Wherefore of the Second Battle of Trenton.* Trenton: Mrs. Anna Angelo, Publisher, 1940.
Hoffman, Harold. *Nor Long Remember.* New York: S. French, 1939.
Martin, Harold H. "The Mystery of Harold Hoffman." *Saturday Evening Post,* October 23, 1954, 17–18, 116–121.
New Jersey Department of Law and Public Safety. *Final Report on the Investigation of the New Jersey State Division of Employment Security, Department of Labor and Industry.* Trenton: New Jersey Department of Law and Public Safety, 1955.
Stellhorn and Birkner. *The Governors of New Jersey.*
Newark Evening News, 1934–1937, 1946, 1952, 1954.
New York Times, 1935–1936, 1952, 1954–1955.
Trentonian, 1954.

Red-Faced: J. Parnell Thomas

Bentley, Eric. *Are You Now or Have You Ever Been? The Investigation of Show Business by the Un-American Activities Committee, 1947–1958.* New York: Harper and Row, 1972.
Carr, Robert Kenneth. *The House Committee on Un-American Activities, 1945–1950.* Ithaca: Cornell Univ. Press, 1952.
Garraty and Carnes, gen. eds. *American National Biography.*
Goodman, Walter. *The Committee: The Extraordinary Career of the House Committee on Un-American Activities.* New York: Farrar, Straus, and Giroux, 1968.
Lardner, Ring, Jr. *I'd Hate Myself in the Morning: A Memoir.* New York: Thunder's Mouth Press/Nation Books, 2000.
Pearson, Drew. Washington Merry-Go-Round (syndicated column), August 4, 1948.
New York Times, 1936–1940, 1946–1950, 1970.
New York Post, 1947–1949, 1954.
New York Daily News, 1947–1948.
New York World-Telegram, 1949–1951.

Fired: Hugh Addonizio

Hayden, Thomas. *Rebellion in Newark: Official Violence and Ghetto Response.* New York: Random House, 1967.
Hoffman. *Tiger in the Court.*
Porambo, Ron. *No Cause for Indictment.* New York: Holt, Rinehart, and Winston, 1971.

Newark Evening News, 1967–1972.
New York Times, 1967–1972, 1977, 1981.
Star-Ledger, 1981.

Arabian Nights: Abscam

Berman, Jerry J. *The Lessons of Abscam.* Washington, D.C.: American Civil Liberties Union, 1982.
Greene, Robert W. *The Sting Man.* New York: Dutton, 1981.
Kutler, ed. in chief. *Dictionary of American History.*
New York Times, 1980–1982, 1989.
Star-Ledger, 1980–1981.
Trentonian, 1980–1981, 1999.
Time, 1980.

Snow Job: Johns-Manville

Brodeur, Paul. *Outrageous Misconduct: The Asbestos Industry on Trial.* New York: Pantheon, 1985.
Goodwin, William Richard. *The Johns-Manville Story.* New York: Newcomen Society, 1972.
Star-Ledger, 1969, 1979, 1982, 1999–2000.
New York Times, 1939, 1971–1972, 1982–1983, 1985–1987, 1990, 1995, 2001–2002.
Time, 1939, 1982.

Deep Cover: David Friedland

Star-Ledger, 1980–1981, 1984–1988.
Trentonian, 1999.
Jersey Journal, 1987–1988.
New York Times, 1985, 1987–1988.

Pushing His Luck: Nicholas Bissell

McGraw, Seamus. "Dancing for Gambler: The Nick Bissell Story." Crimelibrary.com.
New York Times, 1996.
Star-Ledger, 1996.
Trentonian, 1996.
Courier News (Bridgewater, N.J.), 1996.

Man's Man: Milton Milan

Anastasia, George. *The Last Gangster.* New York: Regan Books, 2004.
Courier-Post (Cherry Hill, N.J.), 1997, 1999–2002.
Philadelphia Inquirer, 1997, 1999–2002.

New York Times, 1999–2001.
Star-Ledger, 1999–2001.

The Fix Was In: Robert W. Lee
Newfield, Jack. "The Shame of Boxing." *The Nation,* November 12, 2001, 13–22.
New Jersey Commission of Investigation. *Organized Crime in Boxing.* Trenton: New Jersey Commission of Investigation, 1986.
New York Times, 1982, 1984, 1990, 1992; 1999–2001.
Star-Ledger, 1999–2001.
Bergen Record, 1999–2001.
The Ring, 2000.
Philadelphia Daily News, 2006.

Passing the Torch: Robert Torricelli
Levine, Art. "The Adventures of . . . Money Man!" *American Prospect,* April 24, 2000, 26–31.
New York Times, 1978, 1982, 1996, 1998, 2000–2002. Key investigative articles by Tim Golden and David Kocieniewski appeared on April 18, 2001, and May 9, 2001.
Star-Ledger, 1996–1997, 2000–2003.
Bergen Record, 1997, 2000–2002.
Trentonian, 1997.
Slate.com, 2001.

Some Friend You Are: Robert Janiszewski
Smith, Thomas F. X. *The Powerticians.* Secaucus, N.J.: Lyle Stewart, 1982.
Jersey Journal, 1999–2003.
Star-Ledger, 2001–2003.
New York Times, 1997, 2001–2003.

Out: James McGreevey
McGreevey, Dina Matos. *Silent Partner.* New York: Hyperion, 2007.
McGreevey, James E. *The Confession.* New York: Regan Books, 2006.
Star-Ledger, 1997, 2000–2006.
New York Times, 1997, 2000–2004, 2006.
New York Post, 2004.
Trentonian, 1997, 2001, 2004.

Bad Medicine: UMDNJ
Stern, Herbert J. Interim reports of April 24, June 5, September 18, and November 13, 2006. At www.umdnj.edu.

Star-Ledger, 2005–2006.
New York Times, 2005–2006.

CHAPTER 5

I Killed a King: Gaetano Bresci

Mappen. *Jerseyana.*
Pettaco, Arrigo. *L'anarchico che venne dall'America: Storia di Gaetano Bresci e del complotto per uccidere Umberto I.* Milan: A. Mondadori, 2000.
New York Times, 1900–1901.

Ground Zero: Black Tom

Balkhage, H.R., and A. A. Hahling. "The Black Tom Explosion." *American Legion*, August 1964, 14–15, 49–50.
Mappen. *Jerseyana.*
Millman, Chad. *The Detonators: The Secret Plot to Destroy America and an Epic Hunt for Justice.* New York: Little, Brown, 2006.
Witcover, Jules. *Sabotage at Black Tom: Imperial Germany's Secret War in America, 1914–1917.* Chapel Hill, N.C.: Algonquin, 1989
New York Times, 1916.
New York World, 1916.
New York Post, 1916.
Jersey Journal, 1916.

Burning Cross: Alma White

Blee, Kathleen. *Women of the Klan: Racism and Gender in the 1920s.* Berkeley: Univ. of California Press, 1991.
Garraty and Carnes, gen. eds. *American National Biography.*
Kandt, Kristin E. "In the Name of God: An American Story of Feminism, Racism, and Religious Intolerance." *Journal of Gender, Social Policy and the Law* 8, no. 3 (2000): 753–794.
Stanley, Susie Cunningham. *Feminist Pillar of Fire: The Life of Alma White.* Cleveland: Pilgrim Press, 1993.
White, Alma. *Heroes of the Fiery Cross.* Zarephath, N.J.: The Good Citizen, 1925.
———. *The Ku Klux Klan in Prophecy.* Zarephath, N.J.: The Good Citizen, 1925.
———. *The Story of My Life.* Zarephath, N.J.: The Good Citizen, 1919.
New York Times, 1907, 1925, 1946.
New York Herald Tribune, 1933, 1935–1937.
New York World, 1914.

New York Tribune, 1923.

Time, 1946.

Master Race: Nazis

Diamond, Sander A. *The Nazi Movement in the United States, 1924–1941.* Ithaca, N.Y.: Cornell Univ. Press, 1974.

Glaser, Martha. "The German-American Bund in New Jersey." *New Jersey History* 92 (spring 1974): 33–49.

Grover, Warren. *Nazis in Newark.* New Brunswick, N.J.: Transaction, 2003.

Lee, Martin A. *The Beast Reawakens: Fascism's Resurgence from Hitler's Spymasters to Today's Neo-Nazi Groups and Right-Wing Extremists.* New York: Routledge, 1997.

Miller, Marvin D. *Wunderlich's Salute.* Smithtown, N.Y.: Malamud-Rose, 1983.

Up Periscope: U-Boats

Gannon, Michael. *Operation Drumbeat: The Dramatic True Story of Germany's First U-Boat Attacks along the American Coast in World War II.* New York: Harper and Row, 1990.

Hickam, Homer H. *Torpedo Junction: U-Boat War off America's Coast, 1942.* Annapolis, Md.: Naval Institute Press, 1989.

Mappen, Marc. "Jerseyana." *New York Times,* January 9, 1994, NJ19.

Morison, Samuel Eliot. *History of United States Naval Operations in World War II.* 10 vols. Boston: Little, Brown, 1950.

White, David Fairbank. *Bitter Ocean: The Battle of the Atlantic, 1939–1945.* New York: Simon and Schuster, 2006.

New York Times, 1942.

Star-Ledger, 1998.

Newark Evening News, 1942, 1944–1945.

Asbury Park Press, 1942.

Peace unto You: Malcolm X

Breitman, George, Herman Porter, and Baxter Smith. *The Assassination of Malcolm X.* New York: Pathfinder, 1991.

DiEugenio, James, and Lisa Pease, eds. *The Assassinations: Probe Magazine on JFK, MLK, RFK and Malcolm X.* Los Angeles: Feral House, 2003.

Goldman, Peter. *The Death and Life of Malcolm X.* Urbana: Univ. of Illinois Press, 1979.

Jenkins, Robert L., ed. *The Malcolm X Encyclopedia.* Westport, Conn.: Greenwood Press, 2002.

Malcolm X, with Alex Haley. *The Autobiography of Malcolm X.* New York: Ballantine, 1992.

New York Times, 1965–1966.

New York Post, 1965–1966.

Runaway: JoAnne Chesimard

Daley, Robert. *Target Blue: An Insider's View of the NYPD.* New York: Delacorte, 1973.

Perkins, Margo V. *Autobiography as Activism: Three Black Women of the Sixties.* Jackson, Miss.: Univ. Press of Mississippi, 2000.

Shakur, Assata. *Assata: An Autobiography.* Westport, Conn.: Lawrence Hill, 1987.

Tomlinson. *Murdered in Jersey.*

Williams, Evelyn. *Inadmissible Evidence.* Chicago: Lawrence Hill, 1993.

Star-Ledger, 1973, 1979, 1998, 2004–2005.

New York Times, 1973–1977, 1979, 1987, 1998–1999.

New York Daily News, 1973, 2004.

Times (London), 1999.

One-Man Army: Yu Kikumura

Farrell, William R. *Blood and Rage: The Story of the Japanese Red Army.* Lexington, Mass.: Lexington Books, 1990.

U.S. Attorney Samuel Alito's sentencing opinion. *United States vs. Yu Kikumura,* criminal number 88-166. Newark: U.S. District Court, 1989. At www.tkb.org/documents/ Cases/USA_v_Yu_88-CR-166_(NJ)_Sentencing_Memorandum _001.pdf.

New York Times, 1988–1989.

Star-Ledger, 1988–1989.

Blind Hatred: Omar Abdel Rahman

Benjamin, Daniel, and Steven Simon. *The Age of Sacred Terror: Radical Islam's War Against America.* New York: Random House, 2002.

Dwyer, Jim, David Kocieniewski, Deidre Murphy, and Peg Tyre. *Two Seconds under the World.* New York: Crown Publishers, 1994.

Emerson, Steven. *American Jihad: The Terrorists Living Among Us.* New York: Free Press, 2002.

Friedman, Robert I. "The CIA and the Sheik." *Village Voice,* March 30, 1993, 20–27.

Lance, Peter. *1000 Years for Revenge: International Terrorism and the FBI—the Untold Story.* New York: Regan Books, 2003.

Precht, Robert E. *Defending Mohammed: Justice on Trial.* Ithaca, N.Y.: Cornell Univ. Press, 2003.

New York Times, 1993–1996, 1998, 2001.

Star-Ledger, 1990, 1993, 1998, 2004.

Time, 1993.

Sender Unknown: Theodore Kaczynski

Chase, Alston. *Harvard and the Unabomber.* New York: Norton, 2003.

Mello, Michael. *The United States of America versus Theodore John Kaczynski : Ethics, Power and the Invention of the Unabomber.* New York: Context Books, 1999.

New York Times, 1994–1998.
Star-Ledger, 1994, 1998.

Let's Roll: Flight 93

Beamer, Lisa, with Ken Abraham. *Let's Roll! Ordinary People, Extraordinary Courage.* Tyndale House, 2002.

Longman, Jere. *Among the Heroes: United Flight 93 and the Passengers and Crew Who Fought Back.* New York: HarperCollins, 2002.

National Commission on Terrorist Attacks Upon the United States. *The 9/11 Report.* New York: Norton, 2004.

Roddy, Dennis B., et al. "Flight 93: Forty Lives, One Destiny." *Pittsburgh Post-Gazette,* October 28, 2001, www.postgazette.com/headlines/20011028flt93mainstoryp7.asp.

Newsweek, 2001.

Poison Pen Letters: Anthrax

Beecher, Douglas J. "Forensic Application of Microbiological Culture Analysis to Identify Mail Intentionally Contaminated with *Bacillus anthracis* Spores." *Applied and Environmental Microbiology* (August 2006): 5304–5310.

Cole, Leonard A. *The Anthrax Letters: A Medical Detective Story.* Washington, D.C.: Joseph Henry Press, 2003.

Foster, Don. "The Message in the Anthrax." *Vanity Fair,* October 2003, 180–200.

Lake, Ed. Anthraxinvestigation.com.

Thompson, Marilyn W. *The Killer Strain: Anthrax and a Government Exposed.* New York: HarperCollins, 2003.

New York Post, 2001.
Trentonian, 2001.
New York Times, 2001–2002, 2006.
Christian Science Monitor, 2005.

Mistaken Identity: Copts

Jersey Journal, 2005.
Star-Ledger, 2005.
New York Post, 2005.
New York Daily News, 2005.
New York Times, 2005.

In the Money: North Korea

Martin, Bradley K. *Under the Loving Care of the Fatherly Leader.* New York: Thomas Dunn Books, 2004.

Mihm, Stephen. "No Ordinary Counterfeit." *New York Times Magazine*, July 23, 2006, 36–41.

The Press of Atlantic City, 2005–2006.

Philadelphia Inquirer, 2005.

New York Times, 2005.

Los Angeles Times, 2005.

CHAPTER 6

Old Smokey: DiGiovanni

Blackwell, Jon. "A Comfortable Chair to Die In." *Trentonian*, September 20, 1998, 22–23.

Hearn. *Legal Executions.*

Newark News, 1907.

Dangerous Liaison: Hall-Mills

Boswell, Charles, and Lewis Thompson. *The Girl in Lover's Lane*. New York: Fawcett, 1953.

Kunstler, William M. *The Minister and the Choir Singer: The Hall-Mills Murder Case*. New York: Morrow, 1964.

Mappen. *Jerseyana.*

Ramsland, Katherine. "The Hall-Mills Murders." Crimelibrary.com.

Sifakis. *Encyclopedia of American Crime.*

Tomlinson, Gerald. *Fatal Tryst: Who Killed the Minister and the Choir Singer?* Lake Hopatcong, N.J.: Home Run Press, 1999.

New York Times, 1922, 1926.

Star-Ledger, 1997, 2003.

Crime of the Century: Bruno Hauptmann

Berg, A. Scott. *Lindbergh*. New York: G. P. Putnam's Sons, 1998.

Fisher, Jim. *The Ghosts of Hopewell: Setting the Record Straight in the Lindbergh Case*. Carbondale, Ill.: Southern Illinois Univ. Press, 1999.

———. *The Lindbergh Case*. New Brunswick, N.J.: Rutgers Univ. Press, 1987.

Gardner, Lloyd. *The Case That Never Dies: The Lindbergh Kidnapping*. New Brunswick, N.J.: Rutgers Univ. Press, 2004

Kennedy, Ludovic. *The Airman and the Carpenter: The Lindbergh Kidnapping and the Framing of Richard Hauptmann*. New York: Viking, 1985.

Scaduto, Anthony. *Scapegoat: The Lonesome Death of Bruno Richard Hauptmann*. New York: G. P. Putnam's Sons, 1976.

Waller, George. *Kidnap: The Story of the Lindbergh Case*. New York: Dial Press, 1961.

Oh, the Humanity: The Hindenburg

Bain, Addison. *The Freedom Element: Living with Hydrogen.* Cocoa Beach, Fla.: Blue Note, 2004.
Dessler, A. J., D. E. Overs, and W. H. Appleby. "The *Hindenburg* Fire: Hydrogen or Incendiary Paint?" *Buoyant Flight,* January/February 2005 and March/April 2005, available at http://spot.colorado.edu/~dziadeck/zf/LZ129fire2005jan12.pdf.
Hoehling, Adolph A. *Who Destroyed the Hindenburg?* Boston: Little, Brown, 1962.
Mappen. *Jerseyana.*
Mooney, Michael Macdonald. *The Hindenburg.* New York: Dodd, Mead, 1972.
New York Times, 1937.
New York Daily News, 1937.
New York Post, 1937.
New York Herald Tribune, 1937.

Shots in the Dark: Duck Island Killings

Cameron, John. "Did Injustice Triumph?" *Inside Detective,* May 1960, 38–39, 72–76.
Coakley. *Jersey Troopers.*
Queen, Robert. *Jersey Justice in the "Duck Island" Murders.* Trenton: Clarence Hill Defense Committee, 1945.
Trentonian, 1999.
Trenton Times, 1938–1940, 1942, 1944–1945.
Newark Evening News, 1964.

Rights and Wrongs: The Trenton Six

Blackwell, Jon. "A Fight for Justice." *Trentonian,* June 7, 1999, 16–17.
Horne, Gerald. *Communist Front? The Civil Rights Congress, 1946–1956.* Rutherford, N.J.: Fairleigh Dickinson Univ. Press, 1988.
Tomlinson. *Murdered in Jersey.*
Daily Worker, 1951.
Masses and Mainstream, 1951.
The Nation, 1951.
New York Times, 1948–1951, 1955.
Trentonian, 1948–1951.

All Lies: Edgar Smith

Buckley, William F., Jr. *Right Reason: A Collection.* Garden City, N.Y.: Doubleday, 1985.
Manning, Lona, "The Great Prevaricator." Crimemagazine.com.
Smith, Edgar. *Brief Against Death.* New York: Knopf, 1968.
———. *Getting Out.* New York: Coward, McCann, and Geoghegan, 1972.
New York Daily News, 1957–1959, 1968, 1970–1972, 1976–1977.

Star-Ledger, 1992.
New York Times, 1968, 1970–1972, 1975–1977, 1979.
New York Post, 1957–1959, 1970–1972, 1976–1977.
Journal-American, 1964.
New York Herald Tribune, 1957.
Buckley, William F., Jr. Various columns, 1965, 1971, 1976, 1977.

Split Decision: Hurricane Carter

Carter, Rubin. *The Sixteenth Round: From Number 1 Contender to #45472.* New York: Viking, 1974.
Chaiton, Sam, and Terry Swinton. *Lazarus and the Hurricane: The Freeing of Rubin "Hurricane" Carter.* New York: St. Martin's, 2000.
Hirsch, James. *Hurricane: The Miraculous Journey of Rubin Carter.* Boston: Houghton Mifflin, 2000.
Manning, Lona. "The Hurricane Hoax." Crimemagazine.com.
Wice, Paul B. *Rubin "Hurricane" Carter and the American Justice System.* New Brunswick, N.J.: Rutgers Univ. Press, 2000.

Life or Death: Karen Ann Quinlan

Colen, B. D. *Karen Ann Quinlan.* New York: Nash, 1976.
Quinlan, Joseph, and Julia Quinlan, with Phyllis Battelle. *Karen Ann: The Quinlans Tell Their Story.* Garden City, N.Y.: Doubleday, 1977.
New York Times, 1975–1977, 1985.
Star-Ledger, 1975–1977, 2005.
Time, 1985.
AP, 1996, 2005.

X the Unknown: Mario Jascalevich

Baden and Hennessee. *Unnatural Death.*
Lifflander, Matthew L. *Final Treatment: The File on Dr. X.* New York: Norton, 1979.
Farber, Myron. *"Somebody Is Lying": The Story of Dr. X.* New York: Doubleday, 1982.
New York Times, 1976–1978, 1985.
Bergen Record, 1978.

Rumor Has It: Raymond Donovan

Star-Ledger, 1980–1981, 1984, 1987, 1998.
Bergen Record, 1987.
New York Times, 1980–1987.
Time, 1982, 1987.

Witch Hunt: Kelly Michaels

Manning, Lona. "Nightmare at the Day Care: The Wee Care Case." Crimemagazine. com.

Manshel, Lisa. *Nap Time.* New York: Morrow, 1990.

Michaels, Margaret Kelly. "Eight Years in Kafkaland." *National Review,* September 6, 1993, 36–37.

Rabinowitz, Dorothy. *No Crueler Tyrannies: Accusation, False Witness, and Other Terrors of Our Times.* New York: Free Press, 2003.

New York Times, 1993, 1998.

Tug of Love: Baby M

Chesler, Phyllis. *The Sacred Bond: The Legacy of Baby M.* New York: Times Books, 1988.

Whitehead, Mary Beth, with Loretta Schwartz-Nobel. *A Mother's Story: The Truth About the Baby M Case.* New York: St. Martin's, 1989.

New York Times, 1986–1989.

Bergen Record, 1986–1988, 1999, 2002.

Time, 1987.

Star-Ledger, 1987–1988.

Spoiled Rotten: Glen Ridge Rape

Laufer, Peter. *A Question of Consent: Innocence and Complicity in the Glen Ridge Rape Case.* San Francisco: Mercury House, 1994.

Lefkowitz, Bernard. *Our Guys: The Glen Ridge Rape and the Secret Life of the Perfect Suburb.* Berkeley: Univ. of California Press, 1997.

Star-Ledger, 1989, 1992–1993, 1997.

New York Times, 1989, 1992–1993.

New York Post, 1989, 1992–1993.

New York Daily News, 1989, 1992–1993.

Driving While Black: Troopers John Hogan and James Kenna

Hogan, John I. *Turnpike Trooper: Racial Profiling and the New Jersey State Police.* Philadelphia: Xlibris, 2005 (available at trooperhogan.com).

New York Times, 1998–2002.

Star-Ledger, 1998–2002.

Trentonian, 1998–2002.

Rough Play: Jayson Williams

Williams, Jayson, with Steve Friedman. *Loose Balls: Easy Money, Hard Fouls, Cheap Laughs and True Love in the NBA.* New York: Doubleday, 2000.

New York Post, 2002–2005.

New York Times, 2004.

Star-Ledger, 2002, 2004.

House of Horrors: Raymond and Vanessa Jackson

France, David. "Hell House Revisited." *New York,* November 22, 2004, 40–45, 125.

Courier-Post (Cherry Hill, N.J.), 2003, 2004–2006.

Philadelphia Inquirer, 2003, 2004–2006.

New York Post, 2003, 2006.

New York Times, 2003, 2006.

✷ INDEX ✦

✤ ABOUT THE AUTHOR ✤

Jon Blackwell, a copy editor at the *New York Post* since 2000, has been researching, reporting on, and writing about New Jersey crime for years. Before his job at the *Post*, he worked in New Jersey newspapers, first as a reporter covering city government and crime at *The Trentonian* and then as a copy editor at the *Asbury Park Press*. He won awards for news reporting in 1992 and 1998. Blackwell also contributed more than a dozen entries to *The Encyclopedia of New Jersey* (Rutgers Univ. Press, 2004). He is a 1992 graduate of Hamilton College.